CU01288439

THE DELUGE

'Sir Kennedy Trevaskis had an outlook on Africa and the Middle East that differed radically from that of many of his contemporaries... His unvarnished autobiography gives insight into the complex and dangerous problems of the British Empire, especially in the Middle East from the 1940s to the mid-1960s.'

WM. ROGER LOUIS,
Kerr Chair in English History and Culture and Distinguished Teaching Professor at the University of Texas, Austin, USA

'Kennedy Trevaskis was a big man in every sense. Physically imposing, he strode the South Arabian stage with confidence. His colourful memoir is refreshingly direct, showing him to be a keen advocate for a new Federation, supporting his government's policy of maintaining a military base in Aden. His shrewd and lively descriptions of the "Sultans of Aden", on whose loyalty Britain depends, are a stark contrast to the Whitehall politicians. But despite Trevaskis's deliberate steps, the reader knows that the sands are shifting underfoot. He fails to sense that the light touch that had kept the old up-country tribes onside is no match for the increasingly violent urban radicals in Aden town. In this searingly honest account, even he realises that he is out of his time and facing a new world order.'

JONATHAN WALKER,
author of *Churchill's Third World War* (2017)

'*The Deluge* is an illuminating account of British Decolonization from the front line of the British Empire. Trevaskis's memoirs provide a unique insight into the ethos of colonial administration in the Middle East and the personal experience of the retreat of Empire.'

WARREN DOCKTER,
Lecturer in International Politics at Aberystwyth University, Wales, author of *Churchill and the Islamic World* (2015)

THE DELUGE

*A Personal View of the
End of Empire in the Middle East*

SIR KENNEDY TREVASKIS, KCMG, OBE

Edited with an Introduction by
WM. ROGER LOUIS

With a Foreword by
THE RIGHT HON JULIAN AMERY, PC, MP

I.B. TAURIS
LONDON · NEW YORK

Published in 2019 by
I.B.Tauris & Co. Ltd
London • New York
www.ibtauris.com

Copyright © 2019 Kate Sloane

The right of Kennedy Trevaskis to be identified as the author of this work has been asserted by the author in accordance with the Copyright, Designs and Patents Act 1988.

Cover design by danileighdesign.com

Cover images: [top] Sir (Gerald) Kennedy Nicholas Trevaskis by Walter Bird, 10 July 1963 (Courtesy of the author's family); [bottom] Yemeni fighters at the Anglo-Yemeni border in Aden (© AFP / Stringer / Getty Images).

All rights reserved. Except for brief quotations in a review, this book, or any part thereof, may not be reproduced, stored in or introduced into a retrieval system, or transmitted, in any form or by any means, electronic, mechanical, photocopying, recording or otherwise, without the prior written permission of the publisher.

Every attempt has been made to gain permission for the use of the images in this book. Any omissions will be rectified in future editions.

References to websites were correct at the time of writing.

ISBN (HB):   978 1 78453 827 9
eISBN: 978 1 78672 578 3
ePDF: 978 1 78673 578 2

A full CIP record for this book is available from the British Library
A full CIP record is available from the Library of Congress

Library of Congress Catalog Card Number: available

Typeset by Tetragon, London
Printed and bound in Great Britain

Yet did we wish to change those wilder ways,
The pride that soared with kite and lammergeyer
In knife-edged days,
When young men sought to etch an honoured name
Upon recited epics of the tribe?
We tried on anarchy to force a form,
To press amorphous dust into a mould,
Half hoping that the pattern would not hold.

Though one apart, I also loved this land
With passion just as potent as your own,
Wept for dead friends, your heirs,
And was consoled by brothers of your tribe.
Now what remains? Some fading photographs,
Curled sepia memories of past beliefs,
Whose truths are tangled into fairy tales
And turn to myths as recollection fails.

FROM 'ADEN' BY JAMES NASH
DISTRICT OFFICER—WESTERN PROTECTORATE

Contents

List of Illustrations	ix
Map of Eritrea Administrative Divisions	x
Map of the Federation of South Arabia	xi
Introduction by Wm. Roger Louis	xiii
Foreword by Julian Amery	xxvii

I	PRELUDE	1
1	A Little 'Sahib' at the Turn of the Tide in India	3
2	Life with an Imperialist Father	8

II	CENTRAL AFRICA (ZAMBIA): 1938–39: DON QUIXOTE IN THE NORTHERN RHODESIAN (ZAMBIAN) JUNGLE	19

III	EMPIRES AT WAR IN EAST AFRICA: 1939–41	31
1	Defeat	33
2	Imprisonment and Victory	43

IV	THE OCCUPATION AND DISPOSAL OF ITALIAN ERITREA	47
1	The Spoils of War	49
2	Taking Over Without Tears	54
3	The Abyssinian People and Church Militant	60
4	Encounter with a Prophet	67
5	Moslems in Trouble	72

6	Peace, Progress and a Little Prosperity	81
7	A Whiff of Ethiopian Imperialism in the Air	88
8	Ethiopian Mischief	93
9	The Christian Abyssinians and Ethiopia's Claims to Eritrea	100
10	As the War Ends, the Allies Turn Their Attention to the Italian Colonies	110
11	The Moslem Awakening	115
12	The Emancipation of the Moslem Tribal Serfs and the Birth of an Anti-Ethiopian Moslem League	124
13	A Divided Eritrea Awaits a Decision	133
14	The Four Powers Agree to Disagree	142
15	Struggle and Strife	150
16	The United Nations Brings the Curtain Down on Eritrea	160
17	Eritrean Postscript	165
V	NORTHERN RHODESIA (ZAMBIA) REVISITED	167
VI	THE END OF ADEN AND THE RAJ	175
1	A Chip off the Old British Indian Block	177
2	Marking Time	185
3	Forward with the Forward Policy	194
4	Drafting a Blueprint for the Future	204
5	A Hideous Self-inflicted Wound	215
6	A Surrogate War with the Yemen	218
7	A Coup that Failed	232
8	The Lahej Conspiracy	244
9	The Arab Emirates of the South Take the Floor	260
10	Our Enemies Confounded	268
11	Aden and the Federation Unite in the Nick of Time	278
12	Civil War in the Yemen Tempers the Nasserite Threats	290
13	Finis	296
14	South Arabian Postscript	310
Index		313

List of Illustrations

1. Sir Kennedy Trevaskis
2. Trevaskis in uniform as a member of the Northern Rhodesian Regiment, 1939–41
3. POWs, c. 1940. Trevaskis is in the top row, left.
4. Sudanese Beja tribesman
5. Feudal dignitary
6. Trevaskis on home leave with family, 1944–45
7. Trevaskis with friends and family
8. Trevaskis with Sir Douglas Newbold in Sudan
9. Local government in Eritrea
10. Trevaskis as political secretary in Eritrea, 1949–50
11. Trevaskis as chief secretary
12. Tribal gathering, Radfan, Yemen
13. Trevaskis with Sultan Fadhel bin Ali, Minister of Defence
14. Northern Yemenis
15. Trevaskis with British Army commander

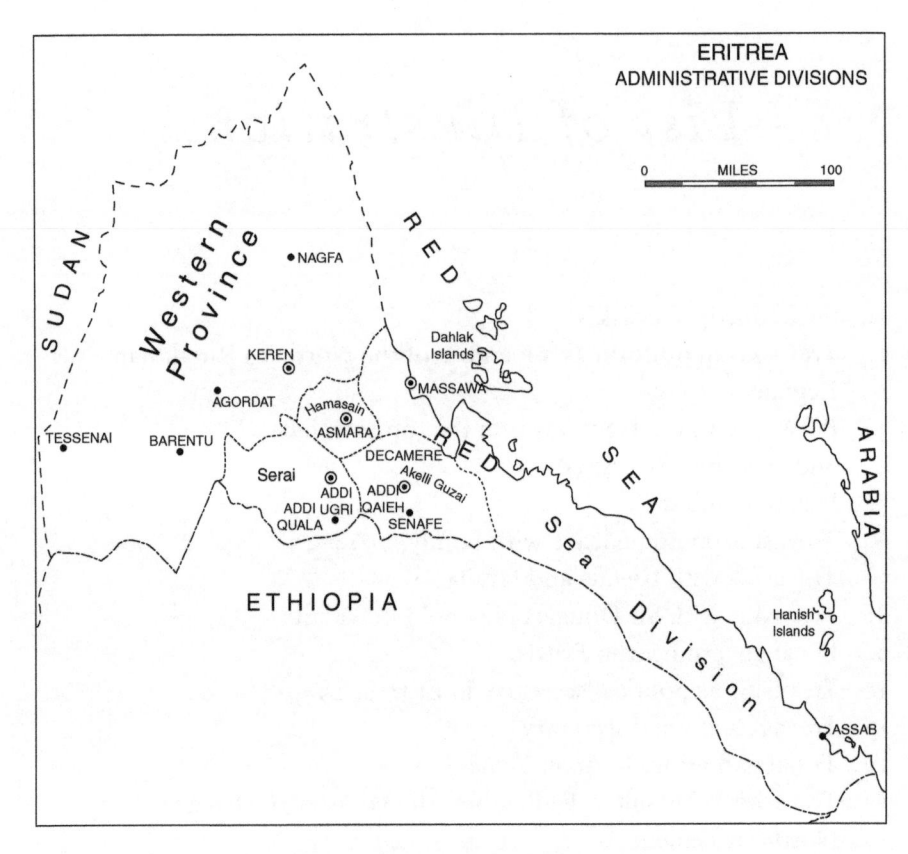

Eritrea Administrative Divisions

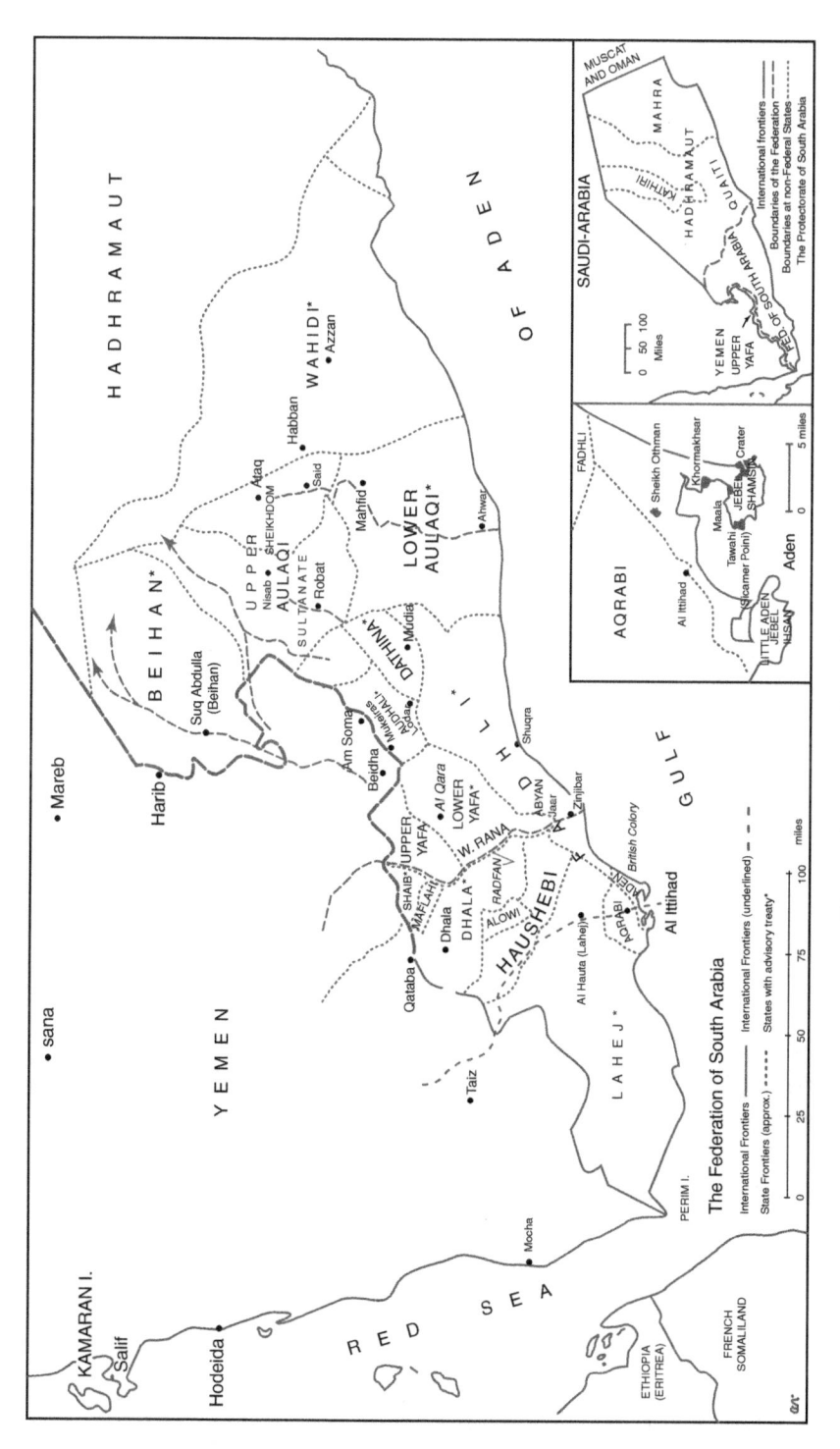

The Federation of South Arabia

Introduction

WM. ROGER LOUIS

SIR KENNEDY TREVASKIS had an outlook on Africa and the Middle East that differed radically from that of many of his contemporaries. Though sometimes condescending, he looked on the peoples in the British Empire as possessing distinct identities and cultures to be respected. He had the instincts of an anthropologist. He seldom missed the mark when criticising his fellow officers in the Colonial Service as blimpish or lacking in curiosity about native languages and traditions or the people themselves. Possessing a keen intellect, he was fair-minded and intellectually honest, though he had his own vanities and disliked certain types of officials, especially, as he described them, of Foreign Office ilk. He possessed a firm set of ethical principles. His unvarnished autobiography gives insight into the complex and dangerous problems of the British Empire, especially in the Middle East from the 1940s to the mid-1960s.

Trevaskis was born in 1915 and lived until 1990. He joined the Colonial Service in Northern Rhodesia in 1938. During World War II, he fought in Eritrea and later returned there, learning Arabic as well as Italian. He played a significant part in defending Eritrea from Ethiopian claims before the merger of Eritrea and Ethiopia in 1950. From 1952 until his dismissal in 1964, he served in Aden, rising to the rank of High Commissioner (the highest position in the Aden Protectorate). As will be seen, he was wounded in an assassination attempt. He survived after a grenade was thrown at him at the Aden airport in protest against his plans to unite the Colony of Aden with the Protectorate in the hinterland. Trevaskis came to symbolise the lost cause of the South Arabian Federation.

Introduction

A few biographical details about his early life, regarded by Trevaskis himself as noteworthy or at least slightly bizarre, will help situate him as a man of his time in the British Empire. His father was a District Commissioner in the Punjab, where Trevaskis in 1919 had his earliest memories of General Reginald Dyer 'shooting his way into the history books at Amritsar'. He later referred to Dyer as 'thick-headed'. As a child, Trevaskis spoke Punjabi as fluently as he did English. His mother he described affectionately as a bobbed-hair 'flapper' and his father as 'The Government', as indeed his father referred to himself in his district in the Punjab. His parents occasionally relaxed in the evening over a glass of port listening to Gilbert and Sullivan on a phonograph with a horn the size of an open umbrella. His father, disillusioned with concessions made to Gandhi 'and his power-hungry friends', retired early to become a newly ordained rector in a country parish. He continued to have robust views about India, hoping in the early 1930s that Churchill might be the saviour. He was once invited to tea with Churchill, discovering that his tipple was not tea but brandy. He later blamed Churchill for the disaster of Indian independence: 'It was his drinking brandy at teatime that had lost us India.'

At Marlborough School, Trevaskis experienced a 'suffocating' time. He shocked his tutors with reactionary views towards India that he had picked up from his father. He was introduced to the League of Nations' principle of self-determination at about the same time that he experienced a revelation: throughout the world there now existed a revolt 'against our imperial paramountcy'. After Marlborough, Trevaskis felt 'the intoxicating free air' of Cambridge. He did not take his studies seriously. In his own phrase, he spent his Cambridge days in 'idleness and dissipation'. It came as no surprise to him, but it was a disappointment to his father, when he failed in his examination to enter the Indian Civil Service. But in 1938 he succeeded in gaining an appointment in the Colonial Service, where strength of character and all-around ability took priority.

His first posting was to Northern Rhodesia. He found himself in a remote village, Mpika (in the far north of the colony, about halfway between Elizabethville in the Congo and Lake Nyasa). His superior was a District Commissioner named T. Fox-Pitt, who had previously served as an officer in the Royal Navy. Trevaskis referred to him, perhaps for

Introduction

good reason, as 'Captain Hornblower' and 'a raving crackpot'. Inspired by the notion of colonial trusteeship and leading Africans 'out of darkness into the light', Fox-Pitt's job in practice consisted of protecting them, in his view, from wild elephants, rhinoceroses and lions. Shooting 'real game' was his principal occupation, but quite improbably he also had a stable of horses, a kennel of hounds, and a groom who wore a formal English hunt coat. A neighbouring English settler, 'monocled and patrician', presided over his estate in a mock Italian castle. Trevaskis was assigned to a village in the north, near the Belgian Congo. He arrived to find it deserted. The Africans feared capture by what they believed to be a 'cannibal tribe' from the Congo that would press them into service in the neighbouring copper mines. When Trevaskis returned to Mpika on a visit for supplies, he was greeted by Captain Hornblower with the words 'we are at war'. It was September 1939.

After joining the Northern Rhodesia Regiment, Trevaskis served in Italian Eritrea and then Somaliland, where he was captured by the Italians and briefly became a prisoner of war. These events are easily followed in the autobiography, but there are two points that deserve comment. After the defeat of the Italians in eastern Africa, Trevaskis and others in his unit made a 900-mile slog across the Horn of Africa through former Italian Somaliland and Ethiopia to Eritrea. The striking feature of this part of the account is the admiration for the achievements of the Italians under Mussolini: modern buildings, factories and workshops, 'superb asphalted highways' through hundreds of miles of plains and mountains, not least the neo-modern architecture in Eritrea. In his words, 'The Italians have far more to show than we had after nearly fifty years in our East African Colonies.'

The other curious feature of this part of his account is the modest contribution that Trevaskis made to the social history of World War II. After an Indian officer joined the British unit, the South African troops jeered that they would never recognise his rank or authority—to which a British District Officer spoke 'in ponderous regal terms' that the Indian officer held the King's Commission. There was no more protest from the South Africans.

Trevaskis records the language of British officers as it was actually spoken. His Company Commander, Major Frederic Clegg-Hill, of aristocratic lineage, used imaginatively obscene language:

In addition to the usual four-letter words, he made constant use of the words 'piss' and 'fart'. A soldier was a 'piss-cat', a car a 'fart-box', a rifle 'a piss-rod' and a pair of trousers 'fart bags'. Senior officers he invariably described as being in the 'farting forties' [...] 'I don't care a fornicating fart how pissed you get,' he would say, 'as long as you get on to parade on time in the morning.'

If necessary, Clegg-Hill would change the time of morning parade to make sure he arrived on time. The explanation given by this linguistically imaginative son of a peer of the realm was 'You can't have responsibility without privilege.' Trevaskis would probably have put it a little differently, without denying the virtue of colourful language. Responsibility was the principal duty of a District Officer.

After his release from the British Army, Trevaskis served in the British administration of Eritrea until the summer of 1950. He became familiar with virtually all its districts and was closely involved with two international commissions of inquiry about the future of the territory.

ERITREA

With an area of 50,000 square miles, Eritrea is about the size of England. In the 1940s, most of the country was an uninhabited scrubland of desert and gravel, with only 5 per cent cultivable terrain. It had a population of some 2 million, a little less than Saudi Arabia's. Trevaskis described it as a triangular wedge with a long base on the Red Sea and the two sides at its tip facing the Sudan in the north and west, and the Ethiopian highlands in the south. Eritrea's lowlands were inhabited by semi-nomads, mainly Muslims, who made up 85 per cent of the population. The rest lived in towns, for example, Asmara, which eventually became the capital, and the Red Sea port of Massawa. Asmara in the 1940s had an estimated population of 250,000. Most town residents followed Coptic Christianity, in other words, the religion of Ethiopia. They spoke Tigrinya, a Semitic language of the area near Ethiopia with the same name. The other language of the territory was Arabic. Eritrea in the 1940s could be summed up, in the words used by Trevaskis, as a mosaic of peoples and communities. They had little in common other than Italian conquest and rule until 1941.

Introduction

The Italian Empire at its peak had a short duration of five years, from the time of the Italian invasion of Ethiopia to the second year of World War II. Yet the Italians had possessed a foothold in Eritrea since the late nineteenth century. They always viewed Eritrea as a logistic step towards Ethiopia, and the Italian population of Eritrea increased from 40,000 in the early 1930s to more than 50,000 by the end of the decade.

The British, including Trevaskis, had a condescending attitude towards the Italians, but he, for one, changed his mind after seeing the territory's network of roads and Asmara's boulevards, office buildings, cathedral, opera house, restaurants, and, he noted, brothels. The Italians left no doubt about white supremacy, but they cultivated both the Arabs and Christians of Eritrea with gifts, consumer goods and food imports. Yet the tax rate was negligible. Trevaskis discovered that the reason for Italian extravagance—virtually unimaginable in a British protectorate or colony—could be found in Fascist Italy's prioritising of empire. Eritrea was subsidised by the Italian government. As a result of Italian beneficence, the Eritreans on the whole were 'docile and obedient', though Trevaskis noted an undertow of 'Italophobia'. But it was a fragile prosperity, snapped by Mussolini's decision to declare war on Britain and France in June 1940.

For reasons not directly concerned with Eritrea but rather with the tide of the war and the defeat of Italian forces in eastern Africa, British troops occupied the territory in April 1941. Trevaskis records in his memoir that the British civil authority in his district consisted of six British officers and eight Sudanese to take over the administration. The British found themselves reliant on the Italian police force. Here the collaborative nature of British rule could be seen at all levels: the British needed the assistance of the Italian police and administrative officers in the districts, who in turn relied on tribal chiefs, who had a lingering loyalty to the Italians and regarded the British with suspicion and even dislike. The British depended on the Italian market farmers to provide fruit and vegetables to the towns. Trevaskis identified one crucial personality: Count Antonelli, a retired cavalry general whose principal interest was horses. He was willing to regard the Italian loss of Eritrea as an unfortunate incident and, like most other Italians in the region, could not sustain a hostile attitude towards the British—in the view of Trevaskis, an Italian characteristic of buoyant life regardless of setbacks.

Trevaskis viewed friendly relations with the Italians as essential, but it was not the military view. The British civilian authority, the equivalent of a colonial administration in British colonies, held that it was important to foster goodwill among all inhabitants, including the Coptic Christians and Arabs as well as the Italians. The military command held that the Italians should not be 'mollycoddled' and that the British should regard Eritrea as being under military occupation. This was a valid point; a Hague convention from an earlier era held that there could be no changes in administration until after a peace settlement. Trevaskis and others in the civilian authority nevertheless worked to bring the Eritreans the benefit of British colonial rule.

Trevaskis often thought about the Italian colonial tradition, which he believed to be virtually the opposite of the British. Since the 1930s Eritrea had thrived because of Italian subsidies. Colonial possessions played a prominent part in Fascist ideology. Eritrea was always regarded as a stepping stone towards Ethiopia, but nevertheless it attracted Italian engineers, mechanics, bankers and, especially, architects, who made the buildings and green boulevards of Asmara an architectural showpiece that held its own with any colonial city in any part of the world. The colonial system by British standards was corrupt, but from the Italian point of view it served the purpose of keeping the chiefs content and docile with financial and other gifts—in Trevaskis's view, bribes—which worked well in keeping the native population subdued—until Italian defeat in 1942. When the subsidies ceased, latent anti-Italian sentiment grew into ferocious discontent, resulting in one incident described by Trevaskis as the butchering of a market farmer's family in cold blood. The British needed the Italians as collaborators, but by the end of the war they had become a liability.

Trevaskis served as a District Officer in several places, but the key assignment was the town of Keren, situated in the plateau leading to the mountainous region of Ethiopia in the south. He believed that there were distinct inequities in the tribal society. In one incident that burned itself into his soul, he attempted to redistribute some of the tribal resources to benefit peasants, or 'serfs', at the bottom of the system. He incurred the wrath of the acting government, Brigadier S. H. Longrigg, whom

Introduction

Trevaskis described as 'cold of eye and sharp of tongue'. Did Trevaskis not realise that the British were fighting a war? There would be no changes in the 'feudal' system. Trevaskis thus learned a lesson that went to the heart of the British system of indirect rule. Tribal society was to retain its own traditions, with as little interference as possible from the British.

Longrigg was a major influence on Trevaskis. Previously in the British administration in Iraq, he had joined the Iraq Petroleum Company and played a critical part in the building of the pipeline to the Mediterranean. The author of a major book on Iraq under the Ottoman Empire, *Four Centuries of Modern Iraq* (1925), he was fluent in Arabic. During World War II, he held the rank of brigadier and served as Chief Administrator (military governor) of Eritrea from 1942 to 1944. He was one of two figures who had an unquestionable influence on Travaskis at this stage in his career.

Trevaskis believed Longrigg to be cold and severely demanding yet exceptionally able. In the history of Eritrea, he was an innovative figure. He left no doubt about British purpose. As elsewhere in the colonial empire, the British would bring order and accountability to tribal authority and would make public health facilities available for the first time. Above all, he promoted educational opportunity, both at basic and more advanced levels. Longrigg recognised that greater literacy would lead to demands by the 'half-educated' for more control over their own affairs and, with it, a resistance to British control. Trevaskis witnessed the development of greater political consciousness largely or ironically brought about by the Longrigg administration.

The other figure was Douglas Newbold, the head of the Sudan Political Service. While making a short excursion from Eritrea across the border and down the Nile to Khartoum, Trevaskis was astonished to find an invitation from Newbold to dine. Through the Sudan intelligence service, Newbold had learned of his arrival and responded to the opportunity to learn of the state of play in Eritrea, especially its future after the war.

Both Longrigg and Newbold believed that Eritrea should be partitioned. The Muslim part would be integrated into the eastern section. The ethnic, linguistic and cultural similarities seemed a natural fit. Trevaskis, along with his two superiors, opposed the claim to Eritrea by 'Mother Ethiopia', in other words, the view that Eritrea was a lost province, regardless of the Muslim part of the population.

Introduction

Trevaskis worked wholeheartedly towards partition. But the problem was not merely one of Ethiopian irredentism. There was a lack of Muslim initiative. When the danger of Coptic expansion became increasingly manifest, Trevaskis despaired. The fractured nature of Muslim Eritrea prevented a unified response. Yet by the end of the war, a Muslim or Arab political movement had begun to take shape. The question was, would it make any difference to the Allied powers determining Eritrea's fate?

A unified Ethiopia including Eritrea had attracted the attention of the United States. Though ranking towards the bottom in the list of postwar priorities, Ethiopia now seemed to have stability. The restoration of Haile Selassie and his willingness to negotiate base rights had captured American public attention. Since the time of the toppling of the Italians and his return as emperor, he had a pro-American outlook and seemed to offer the possibility of an indirect American ally in the Middle East and Indian Ocean, an anchor of postwar American security.

The other powers directly concerned were Britain, as the administering authority, and Italy, as the former colonial power. The hope of the Italians that their former colony might be returned was short-lived, though not entirely extinguished: hope lived in the possibility that the United States and the Soviet Union could not agree on the general future of the former Italian colonies. The British acquiesced in the proposal to let the United Nations decide. Trevaskis listened with disbelief to the debate among Norwegians, Guatemalans and Burmese who had no knowledge of the country or its peoples. He became friends with the principal British member of the commission, even though his new friend followed the Foreign Office line that the best solution would be union with Ethiopia—but with Eritrea as a self-governing province.

Trevaskis always regarded Ethiopia as a mediaeval colonial power and not, as seemed to be the view of the Americans, as a liberated and possibly enlightened member of the world community. Trevaskis left Eritrea for a new assignment before Eritrea became part of Ethiopia in 1952. But his suspicion about Ethiopian aims proved to be accurate. Ethiopia dismantled the guarantees of a self-governing province and absorbed it in 1954. A three-decade fight for Eritrean independence, 1961–91, followed soon thereafter.

Introduction

ADEN

When Trevaskis arrived in Aden in November 1951, he began a part of his career that lasted until the end of his official life in late 1964. He rose in rank from Political Agent (the equivalent of District Officer in most British colonies) to that of High Commissioner, the highest position in the Aden Protectorate. For administrative purposes, the territory was divided into two protectorates, Western and Eastern, but Trevaskis usually referred to them simply as the Protectorate.

There was a substantial difference—Trevaskis called it 'gigantic'—between the Aden Protectorate and Aden Colony. Aden Colony was sovereign British territory, essentially the port on the tip of the Arabian Peninsula often referred to as Steamer Point. It was occupied by the Royal Marines in 1839, mainly to prevent pirate attacks on British ships on the way to and from India. It soon became an important coaling station, but it was the opening of the Suez Canal in 1869 that transformed it into a strategic and commercial port that became one of the busiest in the world—in the 1950s, second only to New York. It was the only major British port between Cyprus and Singapore, and the key to the British defence system in the Indian Ocean and the Persian Gulf. It was only 75 square miles—yet large in comparison with another strategic colony, Gibraltar, with only 2.6 square miles.

Until 1937, Aden was governed as part of British India. Thereafter it fell under the jurisdiction of the Colonial Office, but in 1952 Trevaskis was struck by the way in which it continued to have an Indian ambience, as if it were still part of the old India before independence. In a steep rock slope overlooking the port stood an unmistakably English church and, near it, a statue of Queen Victoria. There were red pillar boxes for the Royal Mail. 'Aden Town', another way of referring to the port, was situated in the large crater of a dormant volcano. It was dominated by the oil refinery build by the Anglo-Iranian Oil Company after its expulsion from Iran in 1951. The Royal Air Force had a base at Khormaksar, a major staging post between Britain and Singapore. In an earlier era, the RAF's aerial bombardment of the villages in the Protectorate had proved effective in keeping the tribes subdued as British clients. In the post-1945 era, bombing as a way of exerting control caused problems in the United Nations. (Although the strafing of tribes' livestock herds, known as the 'goat technique', usually had the desired effect.) Trevaskis was sometimes frustrated that the RAF now saw its assignment in Aden as protecting it from external attack, little else.

The Aden Protectorate evolved in the hinterland of the port. Its size constituted an area half that of northern Italy, a comparison frequently made because of mountainous regions and historic problems of unification. According to calculations made by Trevaskis, there were twenty-six major tribes or sheikdoms in the hinterland, with a population estimated at slightly over 1 million (as compared with Saudi Arabia at mid-twentieth century, with a population of well over 3 million). For over a hundred years, the basic purpose of the British presence was mainly to prevent any incursion from the Protectorate into the port. The goal was to keep things as quiet as possible. Here was an example of the British philosophy of indirect rule: let the tribes develop entirely along their own lines with as little British interference as possible. It was not until the 1950s that the institutions of British colonial rule became significant enough for Trevaskis to boast of courts of justice, tax collection, schools and health clinics.

Of the twenty-six tribes, each had a structure that most British observers referred to as feudal or mediaeval. Trevaskis was an exception. As in Eritrea, he recognised a sophisticated system in which the chiefs had no direct authority—what Trevaskis called no 'executive authority'—but acted on the consensus within the tribe. He perceived a basic identity. The tribes saw themselves as Arabs with a common language. There was, in his phrase, 'a vague sense of Arab nationalism'.

Over time the British had been able gradually to win tribal allegiance by modest amounts of financial support and by the gifts of rifles to chiefs and others who would in turn prove to be favourably disposed to the British presence. By 1952, Trevaskis could remark that each tribesman had a rifle slung over his soldier. Yet the basic change was the import of arms and ammunition from the Yemen—and transistor radios carrying the Voice of the Arabs broadcast from Cairo. These changing circumstances of the 1950s did not necessarily pose serious risks for the British, but did mean that there was an increase in the number of 'well-armed tribesmen', mainly along the border with the Yemen. Among them on the Aden side were a significant number of 'discontents' and 'rebels'.

Trevaskis had the misfortune of arriving in Aden in the same year as the new Governor, Sir Tom Hickinbotham, who was a martinet. He insisted on a strict application of all regulations. Having a background in the Indian Army, he had served previously in various capacities in Aden and possessed a thorough knowledge of the country, even though he had a highly condescending view of its inhabitants. 'He was a strange, unlovable man,' Trevaskis reflected. In one of his more charitable moments, Trevaskis described him as irritable and tough-minded. The two were not only temperamentally mismatched but also at odds on the purpose of British rule, especially in the Protectorate and on the question of the tribes. Hickinbotham made it clear that he regarded the chiefs and their peoples as little more than children. They needed firm advice and, if necessary, discipline. The tension between the two did not lessen during the five years of Hickinbotham's tenure.

Hickinbotham clashed immediately with Trevaskis's superior officer in the Protectorate, Basil Seager (who distinguished himself on the frontier by wearing a loincloth and sporting a monocle). They disagreed on the question of Aden's neighbour to the east, the Yemen. In 1952, the kingdom was ruled by a king who was also the Imam, the spiritual leader of the Yemen's dominant Shia branch of Muslims. By contrast, the tribes in British Aden were mainly Sunni. Seager believed the Imam to be the cause of unrest in the eastern part of Aden. He went so far as to say that in 'trying to pick off our people in rotation', the Imam resembled Hitler. The governor disagreed. The Imam would mind his own business if Seager would stop treating the chiefs in the Protectorate as if they were on the North-West Frontier of India. In a querulous tone, he meant that Seager seemed to be encouraging the chiefs not merely to defend themselves but also to extend their influence beyond the borders of the Protectorate. By acting defensively, the Imam was not a danger to Aden. For that matter, Hickinbotham regarded Egyptian propaganda and the stirrings of Arab nationalism as merely a minor annoyance.

There was one significant point on which Hickinbotham agreed with Trevaskis and urged him to take the initiative. The goal in the Protectorate would be a federation. Trevaskis thus penned his first proposal for a political plan that would bring the tribes together. They would cooperate and unite in self-interest. When he submitted the proposal to the governor, he was astonished to see that he not only welcomed it but also declared that he would send it on to the Colonial Office for approval. It came back in several months later, but in a form that chagrined Trevaskis. It now proposed that the tribes and their leaders would submit to British initiative in forging the links of cooperation. It was exactly the opposite of what Trevaskis had in mind. He believed that the chiefs and sultans should find their own way towards federation. When the governor submitted the proposal to them, they simply replied that it would require further consideration—which never occurred. It was a humiliating episode for Trevaskis, yet one that convinced him further that the political future of the region had to be forged by the tribal leaders themselves. But future plans had to wait until Hickinbotham's departure at the end of his tenure in 1956.

From mid-1956 onwards, one of the major problems facing Trevaskis and other colonial officers in Aden was Nasser's growing influence in the Yemen. Nasser made it clear that he aimed to extinguish British influence in Aden and the Gulf. Trevaskis was intensely aware of the Egyptian danger, but he did not think that Nasser possessed the qualities of a mastermind that were often attributed to him. With skill and organisation, the Adenis could defend themselves against Egyptian aggression.

The crisis continued to develop. In 1962, the Imam was overthrown by nationalists who proclaimed allegiance, even if not loyalty, to Nasser. The nationalists continued to confront royalist forces loyal to the Imam, but nonetheless succeeded in establishing a republican government. Yemen was now divided between a revolutionary regime and royalist forces aiming to restore the Imam. Nasser threw his weight around by ordering troops—eventually, one-third of the Egyptian army—to fight against the royalist forces. He supplied the revolutionaries with rifles and other supplies, including bazookas and grenades indirectly provided by the Soviet Union.

To Trevaskis, one major problem was the sheer number of weapons being smuggled from the Yemen to the 'discontents' and rebels in the Protectorate. Innovations in technology also caused him concern. Transistor radios gave Voice of the Arabs unprecedented direct influence. Arab nationalism, barely detectable at the beginning of the 1950s, was now a popular force, especially with rebels who could acquire weapons much more easily than before.

From the point of view of Trevaskis and others, protest against British authority could still be kept under control, if possible with the help of the Royal Air Force. In a retaliatory strike in 1964, the RAF bombed a Yemen fort called Harib on the Yemen side of the border. It was an effective hit, but internationally it raised basic issues of whether British security forces could operate beyond the Aden Protectorate into the Yemen. Trevaskis believed that every provocation had to be met immediately and decisively. The problem was that each counterattack now had to be approved in London. He began to rely on covert action. He helped coordinate and provide intelligence to a group of former intelligence officers and others—including mercenaries—coordinated in London by Julian Amery, the leading public spokesman for the British Empire in Parliament and in the government at the Colonial Office and then at the Air Ministry. Above all, Trevaskis worked closely with the Colonial Secretary in the early 1960s, Duncan Sandys.

Trevaskis continued to be robustly optimistic. He worked towards an independent, federated state that would continue to have close ties to the British, along the lines of one of the more successful federated post-colonial states, Malaya. In his more buoyant moments, he hoped for something similar to T. E. Lawrence's aspiration during World War I: a Middle Eastern state of 'brown brothers' becoming a member of the Commonwealth. His disillusion was similar to, and indeed greater than, Lawrence's.

Trevaskis became the High Commissioner in the Protectorate, the central figure in giving life to a system of colonial administration by district officers, many of whom had served in the Sudan Civil Service and spoke Arabic. Trevaskis was not an easy taskmaster, but he relished his work and his subordinates believed him to be fair-minded and dedicated. One of his more effective officers, Robin Young, referred to him as 'Uncle Ken'. At the critical planning stage of the federation, Trevaskis got on harmoniously with Sir William Luce, previously Governor General of the Sudan, whose tenure as Governor of Aden lasted until 1960. Luce had wide experience in the Sudan and later played a critical part in the Gulf. His chief significance in Aden is that he insisted that the Adenis themselves had to want the federation of their own volition. He believed, like Trevaskis, that federation could not be imposed on them. The chiefs and sultans would have to agree on it themselves.

At the height of his progress, Trevaskis faced a life-threatening incident in 1963. At the Khormaksar airport, he survived an assassination attempt. A grenade exploded near him, by luck injuring only one of his hands. One of his district officers was nearly killed—he died later—by throwing himself in front of Trevaskis to protect him from the blast. It was a revelation to Trevaskis that such a small grenade could cause such a large explosion, especially in view of the hundreds of grenades now in the hands of the rebels. Trevaskis declared a state of emergency.

He also faced severe problems within the British bureaucracy. With the winding down of the Colonial Office, Aden had been transferred to the Foreign Office, where officials increasingly questioned whether federation was a good plan. Trevaskis held a bolder vision of Aden's future than did his Foreign Office compatriots, who asked: might not the possibility of withdrawal be better? The Foreign Office was fortified especially by Labour Party politicians who believed that Trevaskis was too dominating a figure who, by force of personality, had presented a view of federation that was unrealistic. Trevaskis had critics who thought he was moving in the opposite direction from the necessary retrenchment of the mid-1960s.

The climax of the story as far as Trevaskis is concerned came from England, with the election in October 1964 and the triumph of Harold Wilson and the Labour Party. Trevaskis was sacked within the next month, abruptly and with no recognition of his long and dedicated service.

The Labour Government took immediate steps to liquidate a dangerous situation that had the potential, so it was believed at the time, to develop into a full-scale anti-British revolution. Plans were made for evacuation, which took place in late 1967 under fire and with combatants being lifted out by helicopter—as would occur shortly thereafter with the Americans in Vietnam. Trevaskis believed it was the low point in the history of the British Empire. He is remembered, if at all, as a figure who tried but failed to bring about a federated and independent Aden—perhaps in a larger sense he fought for the last chance in the twentieth century for Aden to emerge as a united and stable state. The book includes a foreword by Julian Amery, the foremost Conservative statesman who represented the ideals of the British Empire and believed that Aden, like Gibraltar, should be regarded as a permanent British fortress.

A NOTE ON THE TEXT

The text of this book reproduces, with only very minor changes, the unedited manuscript of Sir Kennedy's memoir of his time in Eritrea and Aden, which he regarded as parts of the greater Middle East. Inconsistencies of spelling, punctuation, and grammar have not been corrected.

Foreword

JULIAN AMERY

KENNEDY TREVASKIS was tall and broad. He had the dark countenance of the true Cornishman. His speech and movements were markedly deliberate. He smoked a pipe. Like many of his pro-Consular contemporaries he combined a strict attachment to British standards with a tolerance and understanding of the rather different values of other nations.

His father had been a distinguished member of the Indian Civil Service—the handful of elitist administrators who governed the 400 millions of the Indian subcontinent by skill more than by force. In those days, and indeed until the resignation of Winston Churchill in 1955 and our defeat at Suez, the maintenance and development of the British Empire was almost a national religion. Political leaders of all parties preached the civilising mission of Britain in what is now called the Third World. Our most eminent writers propagated their views. Statesmen and intellectuals were the prophets of the religion. The administrators in India, Sudan and the colonies were its priesthood. Ken's father was one of these. It was thus not surprising that, when he retired prematurely, on some issue of principle, he found an outlet for his missionary zeal by taking Holy Orders as a country vicar devoting himself to what he doubtless considered a secondary faith.

Ken was thought unqualified for the Indian Civil Service but opted instead for the Colonial Service. His first posting was to Northern Rhodesia. He found the combination of very primitive Bantu tribesmen and rather coarse white settlers uncongenial; but destiny soon intervened.

Foreword

Italy entered World War II and attacked British Somaliland. Ken, by then a volunteer officer in the Rhodesia regiment, was sent off to experience a short but in retrospect entertaining baptism of fire. He was captured by the Italians and was for a short time their prisoner. Then Wavell intervened. Ethiopia was liberated; and Ken was drafted into the military government administering Eritrea.

As the war turned in favour of the Alliance, Britain's authority east of Suez grew by the day. Trevaskis, embroiled in the rival claims of Ethiopians, Eritreans, Christians and Muslims, had come to the conclusion that the best solution would be to detach the northern—Muslim—part of Eritrea and link it up with the Sudan where Britain still reigned supreme. Had his recommendations on that score been accepted, the long civil war between Eritrea and Ethiopia might have had a different ending. The Labour Government at home, however, shrank from any further imperial expansion and after some curious adventures in Eritrea, Ken was posted back to Northern Rhodesia.

I had first met Trevaskis at our preparatory school when I was nine years old and he was a senior prefect of thirteen. Another boy was trying to bully me; Trevaskis gave him a cuff over the ear and sent him packing. I formed a good opinion of him then. We did not, however, meet again until 1951, when he was a District Commissioner in Northern Rhodesia and I was on a Parliamentary delegation. We found each other's company congenial from the first and sat up much of one night discussing our respective experiences in World War II.

Ken made no secret of his lack of enthusiasm for Colonial Service among the North Rhodesian Bantus. His ambition was to get back to the wilder but more sophisticated climates of the Horn of Africa and South Arabia.

Whether because of or in spite of my intervention, he was in fact posted to Aden, with responsibilities for the West Aden Protectorate.

The West Aden Protectorate consisted of a number of tribal communities with whom the Governor of Aden had rather vague agreements. They were ruled, more or less, by tribal chiefs, many of whom, as in renaissance Scotland, were individually cultured men, governing wild and unruly clansmen. The neighbouring kingdom of the Yemen was the mirror image of the West Aden Protectorate. In discharging his responsibilities Ken had to use persuasion and to a very limited extent British military force.

Foreword

By the time Ken arrived in Aden Britain had withdrawn from India and been seen off by Nasser in Egypt. The Iraqi monarchy had fallen. Aden, which until then had been a backwater of the Empire, became the vital strategic imperial base. It was from Aden, in the imperial sunset, that we exercised influence southwards down to Kenya and Tanganyika, northwards up the Gulf to Kuwait, protecting our oil interests in the Arabian Peninsula. The importance of these to European, American, Japanese and Third World societies was still only dimly understood. But it was clear enough to Trevaskis and his close colleagues.

The problem as they saw it was how to safeguard Aden from the seemingly ineluctable movement of decolonisation. Trevaskis came to the conclusion that the best way to keep the British base was by including what was then a Crown Colony into an independent state or federation of South Arabia. His views attracted the interest of Alan Lennox-Boyd, then Colonial Secretary, and later the enthusiastic support of Duncan Sandys, Secretary of State for the Commonwealth and the Colonies.

Ken accordingly put together a Federal Government consisting of his old friends, the principal tribal leaders, a Federal Army made up of their tribal levees, and built a new Federal Capital outside Aden for them.

This was first of all seen as an open challenge to the Egyptians, who had invaded Yemen with a sizeable army to support a republican regime against the Imam. Nasser's men made every effort to undermine and sabotage the South Arabian Federation. Ken himself had a narrow escape when a bomb blew up close to him at Aden airport, killing one of his entourage.

Could the South Arabian Federation have prospered? There is good reason to think that it might have done. In 1967 the Egyptians were vanquished by the Israelis in the Six-Day War and had to withdraw all their forces from the Yemen. The pressures on South Arabia were greatly reduced. But by then a Labour Government had come to power in Britain, with Mr Anthony Greenwood as Colonial Secretary. For reasons political not economic, as the Crossman Diaries made plain, the Labour Government decided to withdraw from east of Suez. Trevaskis took early retirement at the instance of the Colonial Secretary.

He then had to endure the frustrating experience of seeing another Cornishman, Humphrey Trevelyan, less stout in heart or body, undo what Ken regarded as his life's work. The leaders of the Federal Government

Foreword

were betrayed—the word is not too strong—and were lucky enough to escape with their lives. The Federal Army and Government were abandoned. Britain withdrew in what can only be called a 'scuttle' from the great naval and air base, handing over, though without much formality, to a Soviet-controlled guerrilla movement. This proclaimed Aden and the rest of the Federation to be the socialist republic of South Yemen. By 1972 a Conservative Government, deprived of its main base in Aden, withdrew the few remaining garrisons from Kuwait, Bahrein and Sharjah. The last chapter in imperial history had closed.

Ken spent the next twenty years in retirement, with some success in business in the Gulf, where he was always a welcome visitor. It was in this period that he wrote these memoirs, which I understand he never had time to revise. In a sense they are the better for that. They have the freshness of a diary and are studded with rough judgements on his superiors and colleagues which he might well have found it appropriate to modify.

Aden was the last stronghold of the old British Empire. Ken was the last constructive Governor or pro-Consul before the flag was lowered. His recollections of a strenuous life dedicated to the imperial cause form a fitting closing chapter to a noble chapter in British, as indeed, world history.

JULIAN AMERY
13 August 1991

I
PRELUDE

1

A LITTLE 'SAHIB' AT THE TURN OF THE TIDE IN INDIA

IF I WERE TO SAY that the Raj went into terminal decline on the day that an Indian policeman suddenly presented himself outside my nursery door, I would not be far wrong. 'I have come to look after you, Sahib,' he said with a grin on his face and a rifle in his hand. Look after me? I did not understand. I was only four years old and my small head was crammed with far too many unanswered questions to try and answer this one. A few days before, my father had galloped off with a posse of baggy-trousered retainers and had not been seen since. My pretty young 'flapper' of a mother, usually so full of smiling fun, had become a restless stranger, saying nothing and smoking cigarettes with an intemperate lack of restraint. What was all this about? God willing, all would be well, Raymath my nurse mumbled, giving me a quivering, red-eyed look. This was April 1919 and we were in the Punjab where my father was in charge of the Gurgaon district. Not far from where a little-known Brigadier General Dyer was shooting his way into the history books at Amritsar.

The Punjab was being ravaged by rebellion at the time. Post-War inflation, the Government's thoughtless introduction of Draconian measures known as the Rowlatt Acts and Moslem fury over the demise of the Caliphate with the end of the Ottomans had spawned seething discontent throughout the province. Gandhi, who had just returned from South

Africa as the rapturously acclaimed champion of Indian rights, had done the rest. Everywhere mobs were on the rampage, baying for British blood and nowhere had they got so thoroughly out of hand as in Amritsar. It was the simple, thick-headed Dyer's luck to be sent to put things right. He did so in his own simple, thick-headed way. Where two or, perhaps, three salvoes of rifle fire would have done the trick, his troops carried on firing until their ammunition ran out. In the process they killed four hundred and wounded three times as many. It was a massacre.

A massacre, maybe, but for the British Sahibs and Memsahibs who had been living on their nerves for the past ten days it was salvation. Within an hour of the shooting, Amritsar was as dead as a morgue. Within the week the Punjab was as tranquil as Sussex by the Sea. Everywhere—in their Clubs, Messes and high ceilinged residences—the British were toasting 'good old Dyer'. For us at Gurgaon it was Christmas all over again. Splendidly attired Indian gentry arrived in scores to pay their loyal respects. Bemedalled old soldiers, not to be outdone, stood outside our house saluting with much stamping of feet. In the bazaar it was all smiles and salaams. And my father? Normally reserved and austere, he had, by his standards, let himself go. He spent the first evening after his return with a drink in his hand listening to excerpts from Gilbert and Sullivan played on a gramophone with a horn the size of an open umbrella. That was something he did only on special occasions and this was a very special occasion indeed.

The crisis ended, it was back to normal: which in his case meant doing what District Officers normally did. Once, on being asked what this was, he replied, 'I rule.' And so he did. Within his district he was 'The Government'. Whether it was a matter of tackling an outbreak of plague or fixing the site of a new school, the responsibility was his. He was a Pooh Bah who had to do everything. District Officer Rule was personal rule and that was why they spent at least half their time on the hoof, touring around their districts. Not surprisingly, then, my own memories of those days are largely of packing and unpacking with servants tearing wooden cases open or hammering them shut and of my father towering over the whole chaotic scene booming displeasure. Off and on we were continually on the move and we moved in the old-fashioned way. Early each morning after striking camp my father would ride off into the haze attended by a prancing cavalcade of grandees to visit and inspect whatever needed visiting and inspecting along our route. My mother and I would follow on ponies or sometimes in bullock carts with the baggage train under a persistent cloud of dust. Since my father was king in his district, we would be treated like Royalty: which is to say that we would have to spend hours in the company of people with whom we had nothing in common and hours, too, in eating meals we did not want. I have felt sorry for Royalty ever since.

The handicap of being 'Royal' apart, we did not have too enviable a life. Oh yes, we had platoons of salaaming servants and deferential hands were always available to attend to our needs but that was about all that could be said for it. Our bane was isolation. We did not live in the British India of film and fiction where 'Sahibs' played polo and knocked back whisky in their Clubs. Where we were there were no Clubs and very seldom any other Sahibs. And so I hardly ever saw another English child and, though I spoke Punjabi as well as I spoke English, I was seldom able to make friends with the sons of the local Indian gentry: not by reason of racial prejudice but because they invariably gave me presents coupled with requests to ask my father to give their fathers favours of some kind. Because of this, I could only look to our servants and their families for companionship, but even that small comfort was eventually denied me. It was denied by a young English girl called Miss Cockins who arrived to take charge of me as my governess. I left a lot to be desired, she said, after looking me over. My manners, habits and appearance were not those of a 'little gentleman' and, for a start, there was to be no more 'hobnobbing' with 'Natives'. Natives, she explained, were different. They were dirty and diseased: which was why they had those dirty, brown skins. I had never thought of Indians as being different before.

Though self-evidently an Indiaphobe, Miss Cockins was young, human and in the solitude of the Indian backwoods yearning for companionship. And so, when a very presentable young Indian magistrate on my father's staff invited her to play tennis with him, she cast away her prejudices and agreed. Games of tennis led to rides along the canal bank and, then, to the inevitable: to the besotted young man putting an amorous arm round her waist. Every prejudice in her narrow little person promptly came to the alert. 'Take your dirty black hands off me!' she shrieked, giving him a sharp slap in the face. The incident greatly upset my father: not because Miss Cockins' honour had been assailed but because the Indian magistrate, whose services he valued, demanded an immediate transfer.

That, however, was not the end of the matter. Some months later, my father and mother did something they rarely did: they drank a glass of port after their dinner. Miss Cockins, who regularly did so, was by chance not there that particular evening. Within minutes of sipping the stuff both my parents were convulsed in agonies. The port had been poisoned and, had an Indian doctor not hurried to the scene with a stomach pump at the ready, my sisters and I would have been orphans within the hour. The Police bustled about investigating and arresting but got nowhere. Eventually the case was dropped. It was only later that the truth came travelling down the grapevine of Indian gossip. It was in fact the doctor himself who had arranged for the poison to be slipped into the port! He was not after my parents: he was after Miss Cockins for humiliating the magistrate. The magistrate was his cousin!

Fortunately for Miss Cockins, my time in India and so hers, too, came to an end soon afterwards. On my reaching the age of eight, my mother put on a brave smile and said, 'Next birthday you will be back home at school, darling!' What did she mean? This was 'home'. 'No, no, no!' she laughed. England was home. This was India and it was home for the Indians. Then why were we here? My mother smiled through a thin veil of perplexity and explained that, since Indians did not know how to look after themselves, Daddy had to tell them what to do. It had never entered her pretty, 'bobbed' little head that Daddy's right to tell them what to do might be coming to an end.

She had probably never heard of Edwin Montagu, the Secretary of State for India, still less of his declaration in 1917 that our aim was 'the progressive realization of responsible government in India as an integral part of the British Empire'. Nor was she likely to have known very much about the Government of India Act which followed in 1919 to put India firmly on the road to self-government.[1] Alas for those dreams of peace, progress and Anglo-Indian partnership which Montagu and his fellow Liberals had hoped to realise by this act of unprecedented generosity and good faith. Nothing came of them. That moderate majority of Congress members whose good will and support had seemed so assured suddenly went alarmingly sour. There could be no cooperation with what Gandhi called a 'Satanic Government'. It was Dyer who had brought this about:

not so much Dyer as the British Sahibs and Memsahibs who had acclaimed him as a hero for massacring Indians. That was the last thing my mother would have suspected.

My last months in India were none too promising for the Raj and, though I knew very little about what was going on, I knew enough to grasp that there was trouble of some kind in the wind. One of the Hindu garden boys told me with a sly little laugh that Gandhi was going to drive the British out of India. Gandhi? Hadn't I heard of him? He was a saint who could cure the sick and feed the hungry. The young Moslem Pathan who looked after my pony said that was nonsense. He was a rascal and, God willing, would come to an early end. I would have thought no more of the matter had I not been given a quite unexpected shock. While seated on the shoulders of one of my father's orderlies, watching a wrestling match at a country fair, a clod of earth came sailing out of the crowd and hit me on the side of the head. Silence fell as if the sound had been switched off and then, some way off, a mocking cry of 'Hind Zindabad'—'Victory for India'—went up. Nothing like that had ever happened to me before.

NOTES

[1] The Government of India Act 1919 introduced a system of what was known as dyarchy. At provincial level responsibility for what were described as 'nation building' subjects such as Education, Health and Agriculture was transferred to Indian Ministers, leaving finance, security and general administration in British hands.

2

LIFE WITH AN IMPERIALIST FATHER

At about the time when I was singing the 'Nunc Dimittis' for the last time in the little Victorian chapel of my preparatory school, Summer Fields, my parents were disembarking at Tilbury. They would not be returning to India, my father told me. Serving a Government who fawned on our enemies and betrayed our friends was more than he could endure and so he had retired prematurely. India was finished and he was finished with India. He never wanted to hear another word about the place. Having said as much a few dozen times in the first few dozen hours after his arrival, he never stopped talking about it. His obsession was understandable. India had been his life and he had lost it.

His India was the India he had known as a young man in the golden days of Empire when Curzon the Magnificent had sat on the Viceregal throne: when everything British had been best and when the British had been proud of it. At that time the Indian Civil Service had attracted the elite of the Oxbridge elite and as the elite of all elites they were known with jocular respect as 'the Heaven born'. Olympians they certainly were and it was as Olympians that they looked on the Empire. They were not imperialists of the vulgar, flag-wagging kind; nor were they imperialists of the land and wealth grabbing sort. Imperialism to them was a quasi-divine mission to bestow the inestimable blessings of British rule on backward peoples less fortunate than ourselves. What India needed, so the Heaven Born believed, was the uniquely good government which only they could provide. To protect the peasantry against rapacious landlords and money lenders; to improve and increase their herds, flocks and crops; to Sweeten their lives with Health, Education and other facilities; and, above all, to administer the Law without fear or favour: that was what they meant by good government. They knew that was what mattered most to an habitually penurious and simple-minded people and that was what they had painstakingly provided without ostentation or fuss over the past decades.

But now? My father would heave a sigh of infinite exasperation at the thought of what had happened. The Heaven Born, who had been left to run India in their own superlative fashion for so long, had been relegated to the sidelines while jumped-up clerks like Montagu, who knew nothing of Indian village life, decided what was best for India. And what did they think was best for India? More technical training colleges? More pump irrigation schemes? More restrictions on money lending? No! Not a single one of a hundred and one projects which could have added something to Indian health and happiness ever occurred to them. Their only thought was to appease Gandhi and his power-hungry friends. That was the sombre theme of my father's unending lament. Good government was out. Self-government was in. My father's India was no more.

Fortunately, he slipped easily into a new and satisfying life which, as the newly ordained Rector of a country parish in Sussex, left him ample opportunity to fulminate the days away damning H[is] Majesty's deplorable Government for their mishandling of India.

He had a lot to fulminate about for, though a Commission headed by Sir John Simon was still at work in 1929 considering what should be done to improve on the Government of India Act of 1919 Irwin, the soulful and Suratlike Viceroy, suddenly announced that our objective for India was Dominion status. My father erupted at once on hearing of this unbelievable 'act of betrayal'. Who was this bone-headed peer to give India away, he wanted to know. Tell Gandhi and his crooked crowd that we were out to give them Dominion status and you could bet your boots on their demanding complete independence without even the most tenuous link with the British Crown. And, of course, that was precisely what they did. He travelled rapidly from moods of voluble rage to weary despair or then, occasionally to quivering hope. The continuing news of commotions and disorders in India and the gloomy accounts of the progressive collapse of 'good government' from Heaven Born friends on leave convinced him that the day would come when even a Labour Government would see that they had gone too far and that the only way of preventing total collapse was to revert to old fashioned Heaven Born rule.

That, he firmly believed, was the wish of all Indians excluding, of course, the corrupt and slippery followers of the Congress Party. He was consequently puzzled to find that his Indian visitors were not always of the same mind. The first of these came strutting into the house booming delight with a voice like a trombone. He was a convert to Christianity called Sorabji who had recently been ordained an Anglican priest and was happy to say that he and my father were 'brothers in Christ'. My father's surprise at being so addressed was quickly surpassed by his even greater surprise on being told that our victor had come on a special mission to save English souls. Yes he [Sorabji] said with a smile that strove to be a benediction, he had a duty to God and, dare he say it, a duty to England for all the good she had done in the past. And what about the present, my father asked. Weren't we still doing any good? Sorabji's smile widened as did his eyes. Politics were not for him, he said. As a good Christian he rendered Caesar his due. If Caesar was an Englishman, he would render it to him. If he was an Indian, well… he gestured what he would do. This 'brother in Christ stuff' and coming here to save English souls did not appeal to my father at all. Nor did his evasive talk about English and Indian Caesars. And you could take it from him, he grumbled, after Sorabji had ambled off, that before Montagu and his friends had poisoned the atmosphere in India that fellow would have been a straightforward, decent chap.

Even my father's very favourite Indian whom he always held up as the paragon of all loyalists did not quite come up to scratch. He was a splendidly turbanned Sikh of princely appearance called Naunihal Singh Mann. And what would he like to do, my father asked on the first day of his visit. A trip to Arundel Castle or Brighton, perhaps? No, thank you very much, he would prefer to have a look at the 'Natives'. My father blinked. The Natives? Yes, the Natives in the village. He duly saw them, to their giggling delight, for few of them had ever seen an Indian before. How contented they all seemed, our visitor remarked. He wished he could say the same of the people in the Punjab but, alas, since we had handed so much over to those gangsters and thieves we had made Ministers, they had been shamelessly neglected. The Ministers and politicians were interested only in feathering their own nests and buying support. They did not spare a thought for the peasant in the village. Surely this could not be allowed to go on? Surely the British Government would intervene before it was too late?

This was pure Gilbert and Sullivan to my father's ears. What this splendid fellow was saying was almost word for word what he himself had been saying for so long. He wanted us to dismantle the democratic farce we had laid on for the benefit of Gandhi and his friends and revert to benevolent Heaven Born rule. But that was not quite what our friend had in mind. The solution to India's problem, he believed, was to get rid of the politicians, replace the British with good honest loyalists like himself and then give India Dominion status. This was all very puzzling, my father mused after he had left. He could only imagine that it was the strain of living in the shambles which was now India that had given poor old Naunihal these funny ideas.

The most distinguished of my father's Indian visitors was a venerable little man called Lord Sinha. Formerly Under Secretary of State at the India Office and a provincial governor, he was, as India's only ever peer, British India's Top Indian. Having, as he mentioned with becoming modesty, had a hand in framing Montagu's Reforms, Sinha took a protective, avuncular view of them and, equally, he took the poorest view of Gandhi for boycotting them. Any fool knew that the only feasible way ahead for India was stage by stage constitutional advance, he said, and our 'good Mr Gandhi' was no fool. So what was 'Mr Gandhi' playing at? And why, for that matter, was he deliberately stirring up Hindu nationalist passions? Surely he would know that this could only alarm and alienate the Moslems and end up in splitting India? The British Raj had done India many good turns but, of them all, he believed its achievement of Indian unity was the greatest. If 'Mr Gandhi' should destroy it by his reckless irresponsibility, he would have done India irreparable harm. It was all very well Sinha making such a fuss about Gandhi, my father grumbled, but if it had not been for wooly-minded idiots like him and Montagu, Gandhi would never have been the nuisance he was.

Like most other members of the comfortable classes at this time, my father was heavily infected with Bolshevist phobia; and so, when a Colonel Grogan on a visit from Kenya happened to remark that our policy in

India was all part of a Communist plot to destroy the Empire, he was easily persuaded that the Colonel was right. Grogan had made a name for himself as a young man by walking from Cape Town to Cairo to win the hand of his future wife. Later, he had become one of Kenya's more eccentric gentleman-cowboys and had played a prominent part in White Settler agitation against 'namby pamby pro-Native Colonial Office rule'. Always contemptuous of the Colonial Office Administration, he once personally flogged two African servants of his after a 'damned do-gooding' magistrate had acquitted them both of stealing his cash. Believing, like most Settlers, that the Colonial Office would eventually give in and let the Settlers take East Africa over as they had Southern Rhodesia, he was appalled when Lord Passfield, the Colonial Secretary, as good as declared that White Settler rule for East Africa was not on the cards. We held East Africa in trust for its African inhabitants, he announced, and we were duty bound to treat their interests as 'paramount'. How was that for imperial sabotage? Grogan would ask. Here was the Colonial Secretary saying that our colonies were not ours. That was Red stuff, just as the Government's give-away in India had been.

Though hardly a reliable judge of the political scene, this wild statement of Grogan's could not be dismissed with complete derision. The fact of the matter was that Passfield was none other than the well-known Left Wing intellectual and gushing admirer of the Soviet Union, Sidney Webb. So how was it that Ramsay MacDonald, the Labour Prime Minister, had put a man such as this in charge of our Colonial Empire? That was what Grogan wanted to know and that, of course, was what my father wanted to know. There was only one possible explanation, Grogan said, and that was that 'Red Ramsay' was in cahoots with Moscow. My father had no urge to disagree but he was not unduly dismayed, for the Labour Government were on the rocks and the chances of a sound, Empire-loving Conservative Government taking over seemed as good as certain. So one may well imagine his feelings soon afterwards on hearing that Baldwin, the leader of the Conservative Opposition, had pledged full support for MacDonald's policy over India. That 'Red Ramsay' and Passfield should lend themselves to a Red Plot he could understand. But Baldwin?

It was at this critical point in the Indian saga that the most English of what my father called 'brown Englishmen' paid us a call. Straight backed, immaculately suited and with an Old Wellingtonian tie round his neck, Seyid Waris Amir Ali dropped in for a chat. Like my father, he was a former member of the Heaven Born and a firm believer in Heaven Born rule. My father was enchanted with this delightful man, his 'sensible views' and friendly 'my good fellow's'. What enchanted him most was his insistence that all was not lost. Baldwin might be leader of the Conservative Party, he said, but would the Conservative Party follow him? That, the Seyid believed, was far from certain. In any event, the Indian Empire Society, to which he belonged, had persuaded Winston Churchill to lead a revolt against the Conservative leadership over India. They needed all the support they could get. My father signed up there and then.

At Marlborough, when I was there at school, interest in India was minimal. Most young Marlburians were inclined to dismiss the subcontinent as nothing more than a playground for curry-eating Colonels who said 'Gad, sir!' whenever they opened their mouths. Nevertheless, some began to take a more responsible look at it after Irwin had persuaded Gandhi and Congress to attend a Round Table Conference at the end of 1931. One of the stouter advocates of Government policy amongst us was a studious member of my form called Jock Butler, son of Sir Montagu Butler, Governor of the Central Provinces, and brother of 'Rab' who had become Parliamentary Private Secretary to Sir Samuel Hoare, the Secretary of State for India. Here, I had thought, was a fellow soul who would see India as my father had taught me to see it. Not a bit of it! This earnest youth thought the Government was right. To talk about dealing with Gandhi by 'firm action' was unrealistic, he argued. In the long run, repression would fail and, when it did, we would lose India and all hope of having a friendly one. Far better to give India Dominion status as soon as it was feasible. That was our only hope of its being a friendly partner. My father was not surprised to hear that 'young Butler' was talking nonsense of this kind. His father, 'Monty' Butler, had abandoned all principles to cooperate with the Government in their deplorable plans solely to advance his career. He would not accept the possibility of Sir Montagu merely doing what a dutiful civil servant was expected to do. By my father's criteria he had let the side down.

As a loyal son, I would echo my father's views and arguments at Marlborough to the visible distress of the thin-lipped liberal, Mr Wylie, who taught me History. Blenching at what I said, he would tell me that, instead of tossing off thoughtless provocative remarks, I should try to get India in perspective. What was happening there was not unique. We were also having trouble of the same kind in Egypt, Palestine, Iraq, Persia, Cyprus and, for that matter, Southern Ireland. Did I know why? 'Well, um, er...' 'Dear me!' Wylie said, with a little sigh of disbelief. It was obvious enough. The formation of the League of Nations, President Wilson's call for self-determination, the libertarian message of the Russian Revolution and the development of Asiatic Japan as a major power, had all made people question our right to tell them what to do. So what we were now faced with was not just a troublesome situation in India, as I apparently thought, but a spreading revolt against our imperial paramountcy. And that, Wylie said, with a sniff of distaste, was something no number of General Dyers would ever halt.

Another purveyor of anti-imperialist thought was my study companion, Peter Medawar, the future Nobel Prize winner. He was at that time in full revolutionary bloom and his deft, agile tongue was waging continuous war against everything conventional or sacrosanct. Of all that he spoke of with iced contempt the Empire probably topped his list. Even if the Indians had been cannibals who spent all their time eating each other, he could see no conceivable justification for our taking them over. If they wanted to eat each other, so be it. That was their business, not ours. Every people had a human or inhuman right to do as they pleased. Nothing riled him more than imperialist talk about our civilising mission. It was pure humbug! The truth of the matter was that the Empire meant status and jobs for the sons of the bourgeoisie and that was why our bourgeois governments tried so desperately to hang onto it. And did I really imagine that the British Public would go on throwing money and lives away to hold down the Empire for the benefit of a few thousand ex-Public School oafs?

I found Wylie, Medawar and others disturbing but I would comfort myself with the thought that, since they had never been to India, they did not really know what they were talking about. In any event, thanks to that charming Seyid Warus Amir Ali, my father was now booming with optimism. During the latter part of 1932 and throughout 1933 Churchill's campaign to arouse the Conservative rank and file to revolt against their treasonable leadership went full steam ahead under the auspices of an organisation called the India Defence League. No one could have given it more zealous support than my father, always excepting the splendidly eccentric 'grande dame' of our neighbourhood, Lady de la Rue, whom he had the good sense to enlist as his aide. When my father was not firing off letters to promote the League's interests, he and Lady de la Rue were haunting and harassing Lord Winterton, the Irish peer who was our our pro-Baldwin MP. They heckled and argued with him at public meetings and, on one occasion, my father gave him a fiery piece of his mind at a meet of the Crawley and Horsham foxhounds. No wonder the poor man was once heard to say, 'Good God! Trevaskis again! Who, oh who, will rid me of this turbulent priest?'

Though the League eventually failed in its purpose, my father at least had the satisfaction of contributing to its one glittering success. This was when the Horsham and Worthing Conservative Association shouted Winterton down at its Annual General Meeting in 1933 and rejected the Government's Indian policy by 161 votes to 17. My liveliest memory of that great occasion was of Lady de la Rue waving her umbrella at Winterton and of his quavering demand that she should sit down. For Winterton, who had been our MP for twenty years, it was a humiliating defeat and, with the news in the headlines, Churchill came hurrying down to offer his congratulations. Following a reception for him, my father and a few others were invited to take tea with the great man. Tea, however, was not his tipple. Brandy was. Brandy at tea time! How could you trust a 'boozy tight' like that? my father wished to know. When the League eventually failed in its purpose and a new Government of India Act appeared on the statute book in 1935, my father blamed Churchill. It was his drinking brandy at teatime that had lost us India.

Though deeply wounded and dismayed by the outcome of the 'battle for India', my father was no defeatist. And so, where others saw the Government's proposals to set up an Indian Federation of provincial and princely states which would become a British Dominion as being unstoppable, he persuaded himself that all was not lost. It was one thing to draft proposals and get them approved by the 'politically halt, lame and blind in Parliament', he would say, quite another to implement them and, of all 'packages of impractical nonsense', these proposals for an Indian Federation 'took the biscuit'. Who supported them? No one. Congress, Moslems, Princes: everybody was against them. An old friend of his, Sir Evan Jenkins, who was then Governor of the Punjab, did not go so far as to say that he was right but he did admit that it would not be an easy ride to Federation. Communal fighting between Moslems and Hindus, with the Sikhs as Jokers in the pack, was all too inescapable and, as for the princes with their private armies, who could say what they would get up to? There was little doubt about it: if India was to survive the threat of massive and multiple disorders, a British presence would be needed for a very long time. Even members of Congress admitted as much in private.

This did not surprise my father but it greatly comforted him for he had always taken it for granted that I would follow him into the Indian Civil Service and the doubts I sometimes mumbled about the wisdom of embarking on a career in an India which would soon be independent, had left him vexed though without any adequate answer. But now, he pointed out, I had all that I needed to banish my doubts and from the Governor of the Punjab himself. For my father this was splendid news. For myself, I had to admit it was not. The truth of the matter was that, on coming to the intoxicating free air of Cambridge after monastic imprisonment at Marlborough, I had led so idle and dissipated a life that I had as little chance of passing the Indian Civil Service entrance exam as a cripple of winning a marathon.

Entrance was by first past the post competitive exam and no matter that question marks hovered over India's future, candidates were still mostly holders of First Class Honours at Oxbridge. I was a nonstarter long before I came under Starter's Orders. Even so, I had the luck to escape the total ignominy I so patently deserved. This was because one third of the winnable marks for the exam were ear-marked for an oral inquisition, because the time for my own appearance before the interviewing body was three o'clock in the afternoon and because it was to take place at Burlington Gardens which lay within easy guffawing distance of the young buck's favourite luncheon place, the Berkely Buttery in Bond Street. And so it was with a good luncheon and the best part of a bottle of champagne inside me that I wished my inquisitors a very good afternoon. We got on famously and at the end of a stimulating chat I was awarded a hundred out of a hundred marks for my performance. It was not enough to compensate for the poor quality of my written work but it got me a pat on the back for a near miss. I had failed but failed with honour.

It was, nevertheless, hard to believe that India was no longer to be a part of my life. I had spent my childhood there and I had subsequently lived with my father who was the personification of the old Raj. And so now, having always assumed that I was India-bound for the whole of my short life, it was good bye to India. It was the end of a long affair. It was also a step into the unknown for I had, fortunately, had sufficient sense to insure against failure by applying for the Colonial Service. Since that admirable organisation selected its recruits by interview alone, I had been accepted into it as a recruit for Northern Rhodesia, or Zambia as we now call it. It meant nothing to me. I had been in love with India for far too long.

II

CENTRAL AFRICA
(ZAMBIA): 1938–39

*Don Quixote in the Northern
Rhodesian (Zambian) Jungle*

So I was going to Northern Rhodesia, the man with windswept hair and a smile on his face remarked, looking out at the watery wastes of the Atlantic. We were both passengers on the *Dunregan Castle* bound for Cape Town and he was Geoffrey Dawson, Editor of *The Times*. Northern Rhodesia was a bit of an enigma, wasn't it, Dawson laughed. I was not quite sure what he meant. Well, put it this way, he suggested. Since it had been founded by Cecil Rhodes' British South African Company as an extension of White-ruled Southern Rhodesia, you would think that it would either end up by uniting with Southern Rhodesia or going the same way and getting White self-government on its own. That was certainly what its Whites thought and yet, because Rhodes' Company had been unwilling to go on carrying the cost of running it, it was now under the Colonial Office. And what, Dawson asked, did that mean? It meant colonial trusteeship and that meant no White rule.

A look at the map revealed a curiously divided country. To link up with the copper mines near the Belgian Congo border Rhodes' Company had pushed a railway line from the South and small White communities had sprouted up along it and in the mining towns. In the vast spaces east and west up the railway line there was barely a White to be seen. So I could guess how things stood, Dawson smiled. Along the railway line the ambience was unmistakably Southern Rhodesian: colour bar, all-White municipalities and so on. In the wide open spaces away from it there was Colonial Office rule, as you would expect. So where did he think Northern Rhodesia would end up? That was not for him to say, Dawson replied. We would have to wait and see what Bledisloe had to propose.

On arriving at Northern Rhodesia's one-street capital, Lusaka, I was told to make my way to a dot on the map called Mpika. It lay two hundred miles or so to the East of the railway line and it took me two days

The Deluge

in an asthmatic truck to reach it from a mining camp called Broken Hill. It was not quite what I had expected. There was no town, no bustling bazaar. There was not even a village. Mpika was nothing more than a clearing in the jungle around which there were scattered a few buildings to accommodate the District Commissioner and his staff. I had arrived in limbo-land.

Fox-Pitt, the District Commissioner, my master, was a large battleship of a man with the clearest of clear blue eyes and, as became a former Naval Commander, he was strong and silent. He greeted me impassively, introduced me to a smiling young wife and said that they had had rather a busy day. They had been burying 'old Ross', a visiting Game Warden. An elephant, he explained, had 'wrapped' him around a tree. He spoke rather as a gardener might of slugs and greenfly which had damaged his roses. Later at dinner he asked if I shot. Oh yes, a little, I replied. Pheasant, rabbits and so on. 'I see,' he said a little severely. 'Scatter gun stuff!' I would not get very much of that out here. Here I would have to learn how to shoot real game by which I understood him to mean animals which could wrap me around trees. And was there much game here, I asked a little apprehensively. Yes, the district had a wealth of it, he replied, and then proceeded to list the intimidating variety of fauna roaming about it. And did any wild game ever come into Mpika itself? Oh yes, indeed it did! Why, a lion had bitten off the door handle of his bathroom only the week before. I slept fitfully that night.

Nor did I feel very much more at ease the next morning when Fox-Pitt tut-tutted and said that the sooner I got used to handling a rifle the better. To shoot man-eating lions, crop-raiding elephants and buffalos and generally to protect Africans from marauding beasts was, he asked me to understand, all part of my job. He himself had been at it for a good dozen years and, by this time, he had shot almost every kind of obnoxious beast in the neighbourhood, including a rhinoceros which had had the impertinence to charge him one morning as he sat breakfasting outside his tent. For someone so glutted with the thrills of the chase, I found it odd that, during his spells in Mpika, he should want to relax by hunting 'a l'anglais'. Incredibly, here in the African wilds, he had a stable-load of horses, a kennel-full of beagles and an African groom, called Mungololo, colourfully attired in a Blackmore Vale Hunt coat. Early each morning Fox-Pitt, Marjorie, his wife, and I would spend a couple of hours cantering around after the beagles with Mungololo whipping in. It was good fun but hardly what I had expected to find in one of the darker corners of Darkest Africa.

Did I find it absurd that he should hunt beagles out here? Fox-Pitt asked me one day. Well, perhaps a little unexpected, I replied, reaching for a diplomatic answer. If he were to ask any of our colleagues, he said, they would tell me that he was mad. Mad! He let out a laugh that was a growl. If only the fools knew it, they were the ones the Africans thought mad. Hunting, even with beagles, was something that Africans could understand and accept; but could I imagine what they thought when they saw grown men hitting balls about on golf courses and tennis courts in almost every District Head Quarters, including Mpika? He gazed sternly into the distance and muttered, 'It's these bourgeois values that are the curse of this country!'

'Bourgeois values' was a recurring theme of his conversation and as I sat listening to him grumbling away about them I came to realise that, for all his empire-building appearance and Squire-like ways, this was no Conservative die-hard. Behind this Captain Hornblower there lurked as starry-eyed an idealist as had ever read *The Manchester Guardian*. Having embarked on what was to have been a regular Naval career during the First World War, he had had second thoughts after it had ended. He was by instinct a crusader and, since the Navy had no crusade to offer in peacetime, he looked elsewhere and his eye fell on something that Lugard had written about 'colonial trusteeship'. To lead Africans out of darkness into the light! Here was just the kind of crusade to excite the young Fox-Pitt. He was out of the Navy and into the Colonial Service as fast as his passage from one to the other could be arranged. And so, expecting to find himself as part of a mission manned by a team of secular Livingstones, he felt cheated on discovering that few, if any, of his colleagues shared his missionary zeal. The 'whole damned lot' were bourgeois, he sighed: bourgeois with ghastly bourgeois values. They had come for cheap servants and status. Petty positions and paltry packets of power were all that mattered to them.

For a young man like myself, Fox-Pitt's idealism was stirring stuff but there were times when I could have done with rather less of it. One occurred soon after my arrival. Finding that all I had by way of a bath in my little box of a house was a diminutive tin tub, imagine my delight when two king-size porcelain baths arrived one day on a lorry from Broken Hill with the compliments of the Public Works Department. As I was having them unloaded, Fox-Pitt hove to with a grim look on his face. 'What are those things?!' he barked, as if baths were unmentionables. I explained. 'Put the bloody things back on the truck!' he thundered and then sailed majestically away. And so back the baths went to Broken Hill. A letter to the Chief Secretary from Fox-Pitt followed. At a time when the Government was denying Africans what was essential for their welfare on the grounds that it was short of funds, he protested, it was monstrous that it should indulge its officials with unnecessary luxuries. That was Fox-Pitt for you.

Ever anxious to sweeten African life, Fox-Pitt was continually asking those uncaring bourgeois officials in Lusaka for funds to finance the schemes for African betterment he spent so much of his time churning out. Almost invariably, their answer was 'no'. By chance, however, he got a 'yes' soon after my arrival and with it £150 to hack out a road from Mpika to some chief's village nearby. Calculating that, if he did this, that and the other, he could stretch the cash to cover the cost also of an experimental rice growing scheme which Lusaka had flatly turned down, he stepped happily off on the road to official disaster. Predictably, he spent all the money without completing the road or the experimental rice project. Undaunted, he then rifled our budgetary allocation for the maintenance of the main trunk road running through the district and so, by breaking the rules, eventually got the two schemes completed. He had hardly done so, however, when messages came homing in to say that a spate of flood water had washed a large slice of the trunk road away. So there was Fox-Pitt with the trunk road out of action and the funds he should have been using to repair it exhausted. It was Lusaka's fault, he grunted. If they had given him money for his rice growing scheme in the first place, this would never have happened.

His disdain for the bourgeois bureaucrats in Lusaka and all their tiresome disciplines and procedures bred in him an almost obsessive contempt for office work. Our job was to help Africans, he would say, and how the Devil could we help them sitting in an office answering fatuous letters on fatuous subjects to boost the self-importance of those useless clerks in Lusaka? To show how he felt, he would usually ignore letters he thought 'irrelevant': by which he meant unrelated to African welfare. To show his contempt, too, for the conventions of office practice, he adopted a novel filing system and trained our two quaintly named African clerks, Nelson and Napoleon, to use it. To spare the Government wasting good money on buying filing cabinets which could be better spent on African welfare, he hammered a number of nails into the wall behind his desk. These were his files and to the relevant nails he affixed the various contents of his weekly mail bag. One file extended in fact to half a dozen nails or more. That was the 'Balls File' on which most of his letters from Lusaka and Province Head Quarters were placed.

For an ardent St George like Fox-Pitt who yearned to rescue Africans from the pains and perils of their primitive lives, Mpika was disappointingly inadequate. On the map the district looked impressive enough, covering as it did a vast chunk of territory stretching from the malarial swamps of Lake Bangwelu in the North to the steaming valley of the Luangwa river in the South. As a zoological asylum it had some claim to interest: elephants, hippopotami, lions, rhinoceri, zebra, leopards, hyenas, wart hogs, crocodiles, gazelle of umpteen different kinds and serpents in a number of unpleasant varieties roamed and lurked in its jungles and waters. The district was spacious and teeming with fauna. What it lacked was people. In the district's entire 20,000 square miles there were only 15–20,000 human beings. There was not a single town and even the very largest villages could only claim a few hundred inhabitants. That was the depressing and dreary background against which Fox-Pitt tilted at windmills.

For him, however, it was everything and telling me that, until I had got the feel of it, I would be of no use to him, he packed me off within days of my arrival to have a look at it. And so, complete with an escort of rural police or 'District Messengers' and a crocodile of porters, off I went, Dr Livingstone–style, with Napoleon as my minder. After tramping for half a day through jungle and swamp, we eventually reached our first objective—a cluster of huts euphemistically called a village. It was empty but a couple of smouldering fires told us that someone had been there only shortly before. We trekked on to the next village. That, too, was empty. And so was every other village along our route until at last, approaching one we came upon two Africans who had failed to get away in time. Grey with fear they told us all. The Mining Companies had apparently been recruiting labour from a reputedly cannibal tribe in the Belgian Congo and the word had got about that the Government was rounding up Africans to provide them with rations. Hence the exodus. 'These are very silly people,' Napoleon said. 'They should have known that the Government was their father and mother.'

Had these poor wretches had access to the Government's archives and been able to read and understand what was in them, they would have seen plenty of evidence of paternal concern for them: mostly in the system of Indirect Rule with chiefs, Native Courts, Native Authorities and Native Treasuries on the classic Lugard model. To read the Government's reports you would have imagined that, at Local Government level, the Africans were already running their own show. You could not have asked for a more encouraging picture of African progress in the spirit of 'Colonial trusteeship'. Unhappily, the picture was unreal. It was not the Africans but the District Commissioners who were running the show. That is not to say that the chiefs and other authorities did not exist. They were all there but they were little more than puppets in the District Commissioners' hands. Without the District Commissioners nothing could have been done. A couple of days with the Bisa Native Authority told me all.

The district's inhabitants mostly belonged to the Bisa tribe and came under the jurisdiction of a dozen Bisa chiefs who had recently been constituted into a Bisa Native Authority. When Fox-Pitt informed them of their new status, they listened with the same dead pan impassivity as they had shortly before when he had been urging them to get villagers to dig latrines. They came to life, however, quickly enough when he said that they would all be Councillors in future. Would they get paid for it? they asked.

The first item on the newly formed Bisa Council's Agenda was to approve a budget and I was entrusted with the task of piloting them through the exercise. The Council assembled for the occasion at the village of Chief Kopa, the senior chief, and sitting within easy reach of huge gourds of African beer they had managed to drink themselves into an amicable stupor by the time of my arrival. This was unpromising. Nevertheless, I pressed ahead with my business, knowing that the budget which we had drafted for them was of the simplest and most intelligible kind. A Government grant accounted for almost all the revenue and the salaries of the chiefs, their various retainers and a handful of employees accounted for all but £5 of the expenditure. I explained what their revenue was and, item by item, how it should be spent, only to find myself up against looks of vacuous incomprehension. There was a reason for this, quite apart from their libations. They could not count beyond the number of their fingers and thumbs. This was a difficulty I had not anticipated but recalling how Miss Cockins had first introduced me to arithmetic, I collected a quantity of pebbles equivalent in number to the pounds which they would receive as revenue and then went slowly ahead, removing the appropriate number for each item of expenditure. To my relief, they began to understand what I was up to and, after having gone through the budget in this laborious fashion a couple of times more, I was rewarded with a unanimous grunt of approval. There remained, however, the surplus of £5 to be spent. How did they want to spend it? After a short whispered conference, Chief Kopa presented me with a sly grin. The Chiefs, he declared, wished it to be used to give each of them a new wife. On that bizarre note, the meeting closed.

You could hardly say that an absurdity such as this Native Authority did anything for African political development or that any Africans—excepting, of course, the Bisa chiefs and their bottle washers—got anything out of it. So what good were we doing? What benefits were we bestowing on our colonial wards? Education? There was one mission school subsidised by Government. Health? The nearest doctor was nearly a hundred miles away at Province HQ and we had to share him with four other districts. Otherwise, all we could offer were five itinerant dressers. Not many Africans could even have known of these meagre services, let alone enjoyed them. So what, I would wonder, did we mean to the Africans? How did they see us?

Not, I had to conclude, as the caring, paternalistic custodians of their welfare that we would have wished. It was not for our lack of trying. Month in, month out, either Fox-Pitt or I would be tramping through the jungle to make sure that every village in the district was visited in the course of the year. At each we would ask if they had anything to say or if there was anything we could do for them. Apart from routine complaints about elephants or monkeys raiding their crops, they seldom had anything to say and even when they had there was precious little we could do for them. So, since we could offer them virtually nothing and since our main function on these expeditions was to collect a poll-tax and arrest defaulters, the Africans could only have seen us with the

The Deluge

same despondent sense of helplessness as they saw monkeys, elephants and locusts. To these Africans we were, above all, tax gatherers and tax gatherers are seldom loved.

Any mention of the polltax would have Fox-Pitt glowering and growling about bureaucrats and bourgeois values. If we had acted in the Lugard spirit, he would say, we would have made the Africans pay taxes as they always had before our time—in grain and services. But no, we had insisted on their paying in cash and did I know why? It was to keep the Mining companies supplied with labour. There was barely a pennyworth of cash to be earned in the country districts. To get it, the Africans had to turn to the Mines for work. And so, to please the Mining companies, the Government sabotaged the rural economy. How was that for a Government which pretended to practice what Lugard and Passfield preached?

Travelling around I began to see what he meant. Young men were a rarity and all too often I found myself confronted by pot-bellied children, women with breasts that were empty flaps and collections of creaking bones that were old men. This, I had to remind myself, was our doing. When we took over Bisa, they had not been like this. They had been tough, warlike and, it followed, well fed. Admittedly they had been doing themselves well by capturing and selling slaves to Arab traders from Zanzibar but, even so, they had, by all accounts, been able to live reasonably well. Though handicapped by the tsetse fly which made it impossible to keep domestic animals in many parts of their country, they had been able to keep themselves supplied with proteins and meat by hunting. Agriculturally, they had been more than self-sufficient Then, they had young men and the young muscles needed for hunting and clearing land for cultivation and scuffling it up with the labour-costly little hoes they still used. It was because our poll tax had driven so many young men away to the Mines that village after village was now beginning to show signs of galloping malnutrition. In Mpika it was visibly wrecking the rural economy.

The thundercloud which habitually hovered over poor, frustrated Fox-Pitt lifted one day. He had splendid news, he announced. Gore-Browne had just assumed the new appointment of Representative for Native Affairs on the Colony's Legislative Council. Colonel (later Sir Stewart) Gore-Browne was Northern Rhodesia's most affluent and, certainly, most presentable settler and lived sixty miles away on the fringes of the district by the side of a lake in a mock Italian castle at the centre of a flourishing citrus plantation. Though monocled and patrician in manner, the Colonel was an Afrophil who would tell you with pride that the Africans on his estate had nicknamed him Bwana Rhinoceros by reason of his large nose. His popularity with them was unquestionable. Nor was it surprising. He had housed them in neat little model villages, comprised of neat little model huts, and at the centre of the estate he had constructed a neat little model church where he read the Lesson each Sunday in the vernacular. With this decent fellow, who was our friend and neighbour, Representative for Native Affairs we would have a powerful friend at Court. With him on their backs, those unhelpful bourgeois bureaucrats would find it less easy to veto his projects. So poor Fox-Pitt thought.

Alas, it was not a friend at Court but a powerful rival that Fox-Pitt had acquired. Ever anxious to gild his Afrophil image, Gore-Browne now began to trot out little schemes of his own for Government support in order to make his plantation more of a show place than ever. Being the Very Important Person he was, his schemes were invariably approved but, since they were all chalked up to the Mpika district, Fox-Pitt's schemes had even less chance of approval than before. One disappointment led to another and then the day came when Fox-Pitt wanted to open a Bisa Native Authority School he had spent months setting up. He needed, of course, a school master. He would have to wait, the Education Department said. The only one available had been sent to Gore-Browne for the splendid new school he had built on his plantation. This however was not the end but only the beginning of quite an intriguing little story.

Educationally, Gore-Browne's new teacher may have been first class but he was a townee who lacked the Old World social graces of tribal society. And so, arriving to have a look at his new acquisition, the Colonel was outraged to be greeted with a bright 'Good morning, sir!' To someone used to Africans greeting him by getting down on their hunkers, as well-brought up Africans customarily did in the presence of their superiors, this was intolerable impudence and to no-one's surprise, except the teacher's, the Colonel gave the bumptious Smart Alec a taste of his stick. The teacher thereupon pedalled swiftly off to lodge a complaint with Fox-Pitt. Twenty-four hours later the Government's 'Representative for African Affairs' received a summons for assaulting an

African. Twenty-four hours later still, Fox-Pitt was ordered by Lusaka to withdraw it.

Fox-Pitt was understandably put out and rocketed off into one of his customary philippics about bureaucrats, humbugs and colonial trusteeship. He had reason to be upset but he was, I thought, getting a little paranoid. He was beginning to see this little dunghill of Mpika as something more than it was. No sooner had I thought it than I wondered why he had not by this time become a raving crackpot. How could anyone expect to be normal after the twelve years Fox-Pitt had spent in a succession of Mpikas? It was a hermit's life one had to lead in them and a life without any of the amenities or, in many cases, normal necessities. It was a life of solitude and discomfort, appealing no doubt to a Trappist monk but repellent to anyone with a normal complement of human instincts. It could be endurable only if one had the satisfaction of knowing that one was doing something really worthwhile. But what was poor Fox-Pitt doing? Nothing, except belly-aching against the system. Looking at him scribbling away at some fresh scheme which would never see the light of day, I thought, 'Good God! This could be me in twelve years' time!' The prospect was unthinkable.

It was September 3rd, 1939, and I had sat myself down to devour the batch of month-old *Times* which had just arrived when Fox-Pitt presented himself on the verandah of my house. 'We are at war!' he announced. He had heard the news by wireless from Lusaka together with a hotchpotch of absurdly irrelevant instructions. A few days later he left for Simonstown to rejoin the Navy. A few weeks later still, being a member of its Officer Reserve, I left for Lusaka to enlist with the Northern Rhodesian Regiment. It was goodbye to Mpika and, as far as I was concerned, not a day too soon.

III

EMPIRES AT WAR
IN EAST AFRICA: 1939–41

1

DEFEAT

WOULD FASCIST ITALY join Hitler and declare war against us? That was the question everyone in Lusaka was asking. If she did we would be at war with the Italian East African Empire which Mussolini had cobbled together out of the Italian colonies of Eritrea and Somalia and recently conquered Abyssinia. Opinion in the Gymkhana Club was that 'Musso' would sit on the fence until he saw which way things were going; in the Grand Hotel bar, no one believed that 'the bloody Wops' had the guts to fight; the officers' and sergeants' messes down at the Northern Rhodesia Regimental Depot wanted to know what we were waiting for. Why didn't we just go in and take over Italian East Africa? Nowhere did you hear anyone saying that the Italians in East Africa could put 225,000 men into the field, backed by any number of tanks, armoured cars and guns, while we had barely 5,000 men to put against them with little more than their rifles and a sprinkling of First World War Lewis guns. Like the King's African Rifles, the Northern Rhodesia Regiment was an African unit under seconded British officers who were being strengthened, as a war-time measure, by local Europeans and the Officer Reserve. To strengthen the Regiment still further, local Europeans were also being enlisted as Sergeants who were to be sandwiched in between the Officers and African NCOs. Finding that there were no Officer vacancies left in the First Battalion, which was the only one in being, I willingly forfeited my right to a Commission as a holder of OTS Certificates I had gained at Marlborough and Cambridge and accepted a Sergeant's stripes. A fortnight later, the Battalion was instructed to move North but before leaving it turned out for a farewell parade before Sir John Maybin, the Governor. He had been on the Board I appeared before to join the Colonial Service and I remembered that we had had a little discussion about the merits of Charles Dickens. Standing at the back of my platoon as he came slowly down the ranks, I wondered whether he would remember me. He did. Halting in front of me, he gave me a wink. 'I don't suppose you will have much time for Dickens,' he said, 'but if you do, this may prove useful.' With that, he gave me a pocket edition of *Pickwick Papers*. It was a kindness which left me with a large lump in the throat.

We moved North by easy stages and, since Mussolini showed no disposition to declare war, we led a reasonably easy life. Its tempo and tone were set by our Commanding Officer, Colonel Lynne-Allen—or 'Bubbly' to his friends. His sole interest in life was shooting birds on the wing. For him, the Army was little more than a source of shooting facilities: something which could provide beaters, gun bearers and transport; and which could periodically enlarge his sporting horizons by moving him from one shooting ground to another. My Company Commander, Freddie Clegg-Hill, had more to offer but it was not military zeal. He was the son of a Shropshire peer and, with his loud, swashbuckling manner and obscene expletives, he could have been the cherry-picking Cardigan come to life. In addition to the usual four-letter words, he made constant use of the words 'piss' and 'fart'. A soldier was a 'piss-cat', a car a 'fart-box', a rifle 'a piss-rod' and a pair of trousers 'fart bags'. Senior officers he invariably described as being in the 'farting forties'. He drank copiously and expected his officers to do the same, his particular delight being to challenge anyone nearby to a 'steeplechase'. This was a form of drinking race in which the bottles lined up behind the bar would be taken as hurdles. Beginning with the first, you would both drink your way drink for drink along the line of bottles until one or the other of you collapsed or, as Freddie would say, 'fell at the fence'. 'I don't care a fornicating fart how pissed you get,' he would say, 'as long as you get on to parade on time in the morning.' He made a particular virtue of never being late himself. If necessary, he would change the time of a parade to ensure that he was punctual. 'You can't have responsibility without privilege' was his bland explanation.

Ours was a shamelessly easy going life but suddenly the merry-go-round came to a halt. It was April 1940. The Germans had occupied Norway and, for the first time, Mussolini began making bellicose speeches as though he meant what he said. It looked as if things might begin to happen. Orders began to fly around for stores to be checked, spare parts obtained and equipment inspected. In the middle of the confusion the officers, of whom I was by this time one, received a summons to appear before Lynne-Allen. We found him in a sunny mood. 'Well, we're off!' he said. 'Here are our movement orders,' pointing to a wad of foolscap before him. Our destination was British Somaliland. It was a hot, dirty and unpleasant place, Lynne-Allen told us, but there were compensations. Picking up a book on birds, he cast an eye at the page at which it stood open. 'It's not Kenya,' he admitted, 'but there are bags of sand grouse and guineafowl and for turkey bustard it is one of the finest places in the world. Not too bad, really.' On that cheering note, we left to prepare ourselves for departure.

As we were sailing towards Berbera, British Somaliland's capital, Clegg-Hill looked sourly at the drab khaki of the coastline dancing in the heat. 'Christ!' he exploded, wiping the sweat trickling down his face. 'Those farting fools in Cairo must be off their heads to want us to defend this sodding place!' Somaliland was certainly no jewel in the crown. It produced nothing except skins and hides and was run at a loss which the British Treasury had to make good. Since the French had developed their base at Djibuti as a counterpart to Aden, it had lost whatever questionable strategic value it may once have had. It offered us nothing and it was not even as if the Somalis were loyal friends whom we were reluctant to let down. Some or other of them had been in rebellion against us from the day we first took over their country. Why on earth were we committing troops to their defence when we were still so thin on the ground? It did not make sense. Ah, but it did, our Intelligence Officer explained. In itself, Somaliland was nothing to us. Djibuti next door with its powerfully armed division of French troops, however, was everything. It was the only fighting force on our side which could give the Italians a bloody nose and the French had asked us to reinforce Somaliland to give their left flank greater protection. Clegg-Hill let out an impatient snort. 'Trust those farting Frogs to kick up a fuss about nothing!' he snarled.

After a prolonged and frizzling disembarkation at Berbera, we trundled inland by truck up the main road towards Italian East Africa across a stretch of coastal desert and then up into some gentle hills. It was past midnight by the time we reached our destination and it was there that our defence plan was disclosed by the Commanding Officer of the Somali Camel Corps under whose command, we now learned, we had been placed. He was a leathery little Royal Marine called Colonel Chater and his plan was as simple as himself. We were to sit astride the road at the point where it entered the so-called 'Tug Argan Pass'. The pass was, in fact, an eight mile wide gap in a low range of high ground dispersed across which were four isolated hills of which one—a massive Gibraltar—stood right over the road. Each of these hills was to be held by one of our companies with our Head Quarters Company perched on a fifth to their rear. The privilege of holding Gibraltar, the key position, was allotted to Clegg-Hill who lost no time in saying what he thought of Chater and his plan. 'Only a bloody Marine could have thought up such a piss-awful nonsense,' he grumbled. 'He seems to think that those farting hills are battleships and that all he has to do is to put us on board and shove his bloody Camel Corps out in front as if they were a screen of fornicating destroyers and Bob's your Uncle! Well, it's not and I'll tell you why. Battleships have got guns and all we've got are peashooters. How the blazes does he think we will be able to support each other? Every bloody hill is out of range of the others!' He had put his finger on the fatal flaw of the plan. The hills were so widely dispersed that they could be knocked out one by one.

Even while we were sweating and cursing, trying to make Gibraltar liveable and defensible, dramatic events were taking place on the other side of the world. During the first week of June, Dunkirk had become History. Within days, Italy had come into the war and France had capitulated. Where did this leave Djibuti on which the whole of our strategy hinged? After some days of uncertainty, we heard that Legentillehomme, Djibuti's Commander-in-Chief, had defied the Civil Governor and the defeatists in Paris and intended to stand by us. All was well, but now we knew that we would have to fight, Clegg-Hill began to complain that he had been given an impossible job to do. 'Why can't those short-sighted bastards see that this isn't a bloody molehill? Anyone with a glass eye could see it's a fornicating mountain and that we haven't got enough to defend it!'

Defeat

Surprisingly, his protests bore fruit in the form of a machine gun platoon from the Camel Corps in the charge of a Marlburian acquaintance of mine called Eric Wilson. Within an hour of his arrival, however, Wilson was at loggerheads with Clegg-Hill and, after an hour more, Wilson's Somalis and our Africans were exchanging insults. How it all began, heaven knows. I myself arrived on the scene at the point where Clegg-Hill was denouncing Colonel Chater as a 'useless mariner' who didn't know 'his arse from his elbow' and Wilson was asking for these interesting views in writing so that he might convey them to his Commanding Officer. At the end of it all Wilson and his Somalis retired to their position at the furthest extremity of Gibraltar and thereafter remained totally incommunicado. To add to our problems we were now at war with each other.

The days passed without any sign of the Italians but we had news of them. A Franco-Italian armistice had been signed and an Italian Commission, accompanied by a representative of France's new Vichy Government, was sitting outside Djibuti demanding entry to enforce its terms. Inside Djibuti the French were all at sixes and sevens. The Civil Governor was insisting on obedience to Vichy, Legentillehomme on defying it. Messages from Legentillehomme suggested that his cause would be helped by a British build-up in Somaliland. As a result, a battalion of Kings African Rifles arrived and another of Punjabis joined us and though one was deployed nearly ten miles to our rear and the other as many miles away from our left flank, it was comforting to know that we were no longer alone. Unhappily, it did Legentillehomme little good for by the end of July he had lost the argument. Late at night on 3rd August he arrived as a refugee in Berbera. I was there at the time, drawing rations, and I shall not easily forget seeing his sad, red-eyed ADC, Captain L'Oiseau, as he came tottering into the Transit Camp where I was staying. 'We are finished,' he mumbled with tears rolling down his pallid cheeks.

The defection of Djibuti had changed everything. There was now no reason for us to remain in Somaliland and, given the massive force the Italians would almost certainly be sending against us, there was every reason, one would have thought, to get away while we still could. Nevertheless, the decision was to stay and fight. After Dunkirk and our scuttle from Norway, there was a reluctance at home to present the British public with news of yet another withdrawal.

The Deluge

The Italians lost no time in moving once Djibuti had caved in. Spotter planes fluttered over us photographing our positions. Cumbersome Caproni bombers followed to unload cascades of antipersonnel bombs on each of our hills in turn. There was nothing we could do but watch helplessly. We had no anti-aircraft guns and no air cover. We were sitting ducks. Our impotence was sickeningly revealed and we stood there alone. And there, poised to attack us, were (as we now know) twenty-three batteries of artillery, a squadron and a half of tanks, an assortment of armoured cars and five 'groups' of native irregulars with fifty-seven aircraft in support. And what had we to stop them? Nothing but ourselves—one African battalion—and a recently-arrived light battery of four small howitzers. You could say that we were a David opposing an Italian Goliath. But at least David had had a sling. As the inescapable catastrophe awaiting us drew nearer, I took stock of the morale of the Africans in my platoon. By this time I knew them well. Most of them had served for some years in the Regiment and living closely together we had our family jokes and our family personalities. There was Corporal Shila, the platoon wag, who came from a tribe claiming blood brotherhood with snakes. Having caught and removed the fangs from a cobra, on one occasion, he reduced the platoon to hysterics by putting it surreptitiously into my haversack. Then there was Pte Kenani, the platoon scapegrace, who was always improperly dressed, always short of equipment at kit inspections and who—even at Tug Argan—managed to get infected with VD. There was my Sergeant Kabanda (nicknamed 'Mfumu' or 'the Chief') who listened and watched by my side with the sharp eye of an umpire and made sure that no one over-stepped the mark. Almost every one of the thirty-odd African souls in my care had his own recognised place in our family circle. How did they all feel, I asked Kabanda, now that they knew we were going to be heavily outnumbered by the advancing Italians? He looked surprised. They were looking forward to the fight, he replied, because they knew that we would win... the British always won. How guilty I felt, knowing that his faith was so sadly misplaced.

Late in the evening of the 10th the Italians came into view. A distant purring had us all looking out onto the road leading to Hargeisa and there, snaking its way through the tumbling hills, we saw an endless procession of dancing lights. 'That shows what those buggers think of us,' Clegg-Hill murmured as he peered out at this chilling sight. 'The way they come with their lights blazing, you'd think they were fornicating around the Via Veneto!' The Italians did not appear to take any precautions and yet we did nothing about it. The Chater plan had left the job of harassing the advancing Italians to the Camel Corps but they had deserted en masse the day before. Why, then, Clegg-Hill wanted to know, had he to remain cooped up helplessly in Gibraltar when we could have been 'making macaroni out of the Wops'. What none of us knew was that, at that very moment, Chater was handing over his command to a Major General who had just arrived from Cairo.

The battle of Tug Argan began the next morning with an artillery bombardment of the hill to our immediate right. Barrage after barrage swept and combed it from one end to the other while a spotter plane circled slowly and impudently above. Our battery of small guns sited just between this hill and ours fired off a few barrages in reply but they were only wasting their ammunition. The Italian guns were well out of their reach and carried on pounding unhindered. It was a sickening sight but we were given no time to dwell on it for suddenly another Italian battery opened up on us. Within the first minutes of that shattering bombardment I realised how accurately that spotter plane had pin-pointed our every position. The whole of Gibraltar was criss-crossed with tell-tale paths which we had done nothing to camouflage. A child could have guessed where every platoon and section was sited. The Italian gunners did so almost to the yard. To lie huddled up, head down, with shells hammering down at the rate of one a minute was not so much terrifying as a paralysing experience. The noise, the choking and coughing from the asphyxiating stench of cordite and the scream of whirling showers of rock and stone ripping through the brittle air anaesthetised our thoughts. We were helpless and could do nothing but hope for the best. We had four hours of it that first unbelievable afternoon. When it was over, Kabanda came up to me, grey with dust. 'Why do we stay here to be killed?' he asked. 'Why don't we fight them from somewhere else?' He echoed the thoughts of us all.

It was madness to stay where we were. We were nothing more than fixed targets. Passionately-phrased messages from Clegg-Hill flew back to Head Quarters demanding artillery or permission to withdraw. Artillery was on its way, we were eventually assured, and would be sited on Gibraltar. Would we arrange to receive it? The job fell to me and imagine my surprise on seeing what the 'artillery' was. It was a small, two-inch saluting gun which had been prised off the deck of His Majesty's Australian Ship Hobart, then lying anchored off Berbera. With it came three sour-faced Australian sailors and why they were sour-faced was no secret. The gun could not be swivelled nor could it be elevated or depressed. It was, as Clegg-Hill observed, as much use as a pop-gun. In the event, it never fired a shot.

The next morning brought another shattering cannonade and then, after being pounded for several hours, we suddenly heard distant shouts and sounds of cheering. Looking out across the plain below us we could see hundreds of the Italians' native troops pouring across it. Our Africans were grey with fatigue but now that they had an enemy to hit, they were quickly on their feet and hitting back. The enemy advance gradually petered out and then, after an hour, they had gone. All was quiet and in that strange silence our eyes strayed to the corpses lying untidily in the sand and thornbush below us and then to the half a dozen or so unfortunates caught up in our perimeter wire. Inevitably we had casualties, too. A few direct hits had pulverised some of our men, flying rocks and stones had left others wounded. We were in a poor state and we only had to look at each other to know that we could hardly expect to survive another desperate day such as this. Head Quarters must surely know the score, we said to each other; and then a signal arrived telling us to prepare to withdraw. We had been reprieved. Oh, the blessed bliss of that moment… but it was no more than a moment. A few hours later another signal arrived telling us that we were to stay put.

The next day we knew what to expect and we got it. Incredibly, there was still enough fight left in our men to halt the advancing enemy but only when they had almost broken through our outer wire. We could not possibly be asked to survive another ordeal such as this, we told ourselves. What were the Black Watch doing? The Punjabis? None of those bastards had fired a shot. Why didn't they come up and relieve us? 'We're expendable,' said one of our European Sergeants, a vinous product of the Copper Mines called Sgt Quinn. 'We're bloody Africans.' Clegg-Hill was strangely silent and sat staring blank-faced out into the night. When a signaller eventually came running up with a message, he read it expressionless and without a word. Having done so, he tossed it over to those of us nearby. It was clear enough. British forces were

Defeat

withdrawing from Somaliland immediately and what was left of our mangled company was to sit tight on Gibraltar and cover the withdrawal. The message ended with the ludicrous valediction: 'Good hunting'. Only a buffoon like Lynne-Allen could have written it.

When morning came we were alone. The rest of the battalion, like the rest of 'Somali Force', were going as fast as their trucks and legs would carry them down the road to Berbera. We braced ourselves for the inevitable. Once more we endured the familiar bombardment and then gathered what was left of our wits to face the advancing infantry. They came pouring across the plain but our mortars, which had dealt so much punishment during previous attacks, fell silent, their ammunition exhausted. Wilson's machine guns chattered bravely on but the rifle fire from our platoon positions faltered, weakened and then faded away. The enemy were up to and almost over the wire when we heard an explosion of hoarse, jubilant voices shrieking and shouting to our rear. The enemy had broken in behind us and they were swarming all over Gibraltar.

It was by this time nearly dark. So long as we could remain unnoticed a little longer, we stood a fair chance of getting away. We waited. The evening light faded into darkness; all around us was silence. The time had come to move. My European Sergeant, d'Avray, peered out and there, to our horror, not ten yards away was the wildest looking savage you could ever have hoped to avoid. On seeing d'Avray he let out a shriek and we tumbled back into our dug-out with a hand grenade following in hot pursuit. Fortunately, it was one of those tinny Italian affairs which made more noise than they did damage and so, though shaken and peppered with fragments of tin, we were otherwise all right. Choking and coughing from the smoke we stumbled out with our hands in the air to face our assailant. He was by then in a highly excitable condition and, with his rifle pointing directly at us, anything might have happened had an angel disguised as an Italian Alpini officer not come running up. He shook us by the hand, offered us cigarettes and then, speaking in quite passable English, said 'I congratulate you. For you the war is over. You are safe. My life is still in danger.' And so, to quote the outspoken Sgt Quinn, that was the end of 'the great Somali cock-up'. It was the end of the only battle in history where we were defeated by the Italians.

The Italians, we now know, had 2,052 casualties. We had 260 of which 110 were suffered on Gibraltar. Wilson was awarded the VC and Clegg-Hill escaped to fight on until he lost his life at Arnhem. Winston Churchill was greatly put out by our defeat and let Wavell, our Commander-in-Chief, know that he found it shameful that we should have given up after suffering so few casualties. To this Wavell made his historic retort, that it was unacceptable to gauge military effort by the size of the butcher's bill.

This was a shameful defeat which should never have happened but, brooding over it in the days that followed, I found that what upset me most was that we had involved our Africans in it. The War meant nothing to them. It meant nothing, for that matter, to the Kings African Rifle battalion we had in Somaliland and probably not very much, if anything at all, to the three Punjabi battalions. Carrying on from there, I realised that it meant nothing either to the Native units who formed the bulk of the Italian force. And so, what was I to make of all that? The inescapable, if incongruous, fact of the matter was that a battle had just been fought largely by men who had little if any idea of what they were fighting about.

2

IMPRISONMENT AND VICTORY

'Join the army and see the World!' Wilson trotted out the old Army recruiting slogan and got a tired chuckle from the handful of us whom the Italians had picked up after the fighting. We did not see the world but we saw a good deal of what had been Abyssinia. Setting off from the low Somali hills, we climbed up into the lush province of Harar which had once so delighted Burton, the explorer, and then descended into the Ogaden plains, spending the next three months in the dusty settlement of Diredawa, the half-way halt on the railway linking Addis Ababa with Djibuti. From Diredawa we moved on up into the Abyssinian highlands to Addis Ababa and then, striking north, eventually came to rest in Italy's oldest colony, Eritrea, where the smiling little town of Adi Ugri became our home for the next few months. We had travelled nine hundred miles with Nature in all its infinite varieties displayed along our route. It had been a millionaire's tour which had cost us nothing.

It was also an eye-opener. Heavily infected as we all were with British disdain for 'those bloody hokey-pokey mongers', as Clegg-Hill described them, we were unprepared for what lay ahead of us. All along our route we were met with rivetting evidence of Italian achievement. Everywhere were signs of bustling progress, everywhere one could see the twentieth century flooding into a country that had stood still for hundreds of years. Modern, if not very beautiful, buildings; factories and workshops were going up; agricultural and other rural schemes were being introduced and, most spectacular of all, superb asphalted highways were being constructed to traverse hundreds of miles of mountain and plain. In barely four years, the Italians had far more to show here than we had after nearly fifty years in our East African colonies.

In addition to ourselves, the Italians had captured a couple of dozen South African airmen and why, Heaven knows, between us and them it was hate at first sight. They jeered at us, we sneered at them. It was all very trivial but once it flared up into something quite out of the ordinary. That was when the Italian Camp Commandant briefly announced that an Indian Officer, captured on the Sudan frontier, was on his way to join us. Indian! Every South African let out a gasp of incredulity. Over their dead bodies... it was a damned insult... they would draw up a formal protest... if the Italians went ahead with this they would refuse to cooperate... so they went clamouring on until, suddenly, a short, sharp, staccato shout shut them all up. It had been uttered by our only civilian prisoner, a District Commissioner from Somaliland called Gormley. Long years of dealing with turbulent Somalis had given him a formidable presence as well as a powerful voice. Speaking in ponderous regal tones, he informed the protesters that the Indian Officer held the King's Commission and that for them to try to exclude him would be an insult to His Majesty. If they went ahead and insulted the King, he would make sure that they paid for it once we were released. A rumble of dissent was quickly quelled by a look from his cold, imperious eye.

The newcomer—later to become a Pakistani—was no common or garden Army Captain. His father, Sir Sikander Hyatt Khan, was then Prime Minister of the Punjab and, as any Punjabi would have told you, he and this handsome young son of his, Shaukat, came from a family that was amongst the province's top ten. Like many other families of consequence in India, it owed its eminence to a British connection: in this case to the long association of Shaukat's great-grandfather, Mohammed, with that swashbuckling British frontiersman, John Nicholson, who did so much to put down the Indian Mutiny. Mortally wounded at Delhi, Nicholson's last act before dying was to write a note, using the blood from his wound for ink. In it he asked 'whom it concerned' to look after Mohammed Hyatt Khan, his faithful friend and loyal orderly. What he did became well known and was romanticised in a Punjabi ballad. The relevant part, translated Victorian style, reads as follows:

'And thus the dying hero wrote to Lawrence at Lahore
"Thou art the chief of Khalsa's land, my brother, chief of yore.
List to my prayer for Hyatt Khan, my brave Towana guide.
Make him a noble of the land with him by all is shared.

A gigantic column still stands on a ridge of hills near Rawal Pindi in memory of John Nicholson. It was erected by the Hyatt Khan family in tribute to their powerful friend.

Shaukat was far too big a man and too sure of himself to give a fig for the South Africans' ruderies and anyway within a few days he had totally disarmed them with his insouciance and charm. What he took less calmly was our lack of an escape plan. Surely we knew that it was our duty to attempt to escape? he glowered. We weren't lunatics, we assured him, and who but a lunatic would try to cross two hundred miles of unknown country inhabited by Eritrean tribes who were probably loyal to the Italians? If we chose to call him a madman we were welcome to do so, he replied, but no one was going to stop him from having a go at escaping. In the end, a fair number of us joined him in digging a tunnel. Thanks to the lackadaisical ways of our sentries, the tunneller's usual problem of earth disposal did not weigh too heavily on us. We just dumped the stuff in a corner of our exercise yard where we were ostensibly growing vegetables. All went well until the Camp Commandant appeared one day to announce that he was expecting a visit from the Viceroy, the Duke of Aosta. Saying that he would expect us to make our quarters presentable, his eyes fell on our tell-tale mounds of earth. What was all this? It would have to go before the Viceroy came... he stamped an indignant foot with vexation. An Italian fatigue party was whistled up to remove it.

By curious and, I suppose, happy coincidence we were released just after we had finished the tunnel and were still arguing about when to escape. We had known for some time that our troops were advancing into Italian East Africa from Kenya and the Sudan but we did not know how fast. And so, when the end came it came suddenly and unexpectedly as a shattering surprise. It was on April Fools' Day 1941 when one moment we were passing the time in our customary fashion and the next gazing intently through the barbed wire at a small column of armoured cars approaching us. Could they be British armoured cars? No sooner had we asked ourselves the question than a head popped out of the leading car wearing an unmistakably British steel helmet. A few minutes later we were shaking hands with our liberator, a young British Bimbashi of the Sudan Defence Force. What an April Fools Day that was!

Our captivity was at an end but, as the curtain came down, an unforgettable little scene took place. We were all shouting, shaking hands and thumping each other's backs when suddenly someone pointed to the flag staff which towered over the camp. Looking up, I saw Pte Kenani, the bad boy of my platoon, shinning up it. On reaching the top, he tore down the Italian tricolour and then replaced it with a diminutive home-made Union Jack. 'Long live Bwana King George!' he shouted. 'Long live British Empire!' Sgt Kabanda appeared at my side. 'We all knew that we would win,' he said. 'The British always do!'

IV

THE OCCUPATION AND DISPOSAL
OF ITALIAN ERITREA

1

THE SPOILS OF WAR

THE STAFF CAPTAIN dealing with released prisoners from Adi Ugri at our Head Quarters in Eritrea's capital, Asmara, peered at me with bloodshot eyes. 'Unit?' he croaked. 'Northern Rhodesia Regiment,' I replied. 'Christ!' he shuffled fussily through the papers on his desk and then sat back sharply to tell me that there was no such regiment. While he looked into the matter I would have to mess with the Odds and Sods at the Hamasien Hotel. 'I'll be in touch,' he said. I never heard from him again.

The 'Odds and Sods' were mostly on the senior side of Major and so they knew rather more than most about what was going on. For somebody who was suffering from severe news starvation like myself that meant a lot. Thanks to an early encounter in the hotel bar with a bibulous Major, I was soon being fed with news as fast as I could swallow it: the reason being that my informant was Oliver, the eccentric Socialist son of our former Prime Minister, Stanley Baldwin, and that, as someone in 'Intelligence' he was 'in the know'. What splendid news it all was! The Battle of Britain, the scotching of Germany's plans to invade Britain and Wavell's stupendous victories over the Italians in Libya! But what interested me most was what had been going on nearer home in East Africa. We had recovered British Somaliland, conquered Eritrea and Italian Somaliland and occupied the best part of Ethiopia.[1] Bar mopping up a few pockets of Italian resistance, the party was over. Mussolini's East African Empire was finished. And what would happen to these spoils of war? Ethiopia would, of course, be handed back to its

Emperor, Haile Selassie. But on what terms? That was the point, Baldwin grunted. If some bloody imperialists he could name got their way, he would only get it back as a puppet in an unofficial British protectorate. Baldwin spoke with a hot streak of whisky in his voice, face flushed and hand a-tremble. After the humiliations Haile Selassie had already suffered that, he thought, would be the last straw. Did I know that the poor little devil had been asking HMG for an Agreement to state where he stood for the last six months and HMG had done bugger all about it? And what were we doing about Eritrea and Italian Somaliland? What we would do and should do were two very different things, he said. What we should do was obvious. We should hand them over to the Emperor, partly as compensation for what the Italians had done to him and, partly, because the two territories were both part of 'Greater Ethiopia'. And what would we do? He sighed. We would hang on to them, he murmured. We still had the imperialist itch.

Apart from 'the maudlin Baldwin', as the Odds and Sods called him the officers in the Hamasien were in a very jolly mood of 'apres guerre', with everyone telling everyone else that the Italians were finished and serve the bastards right. That was what all those cheery, beery voices were saying and saying fortissimo. And then, even as the ice was still tinkling in their glasses, their laughter died away. Sobering news began to arrive. A German General called Rommel had landed in North Africa, seized Benghazi and sent Wavell's troops in full retreat towards Egypt. At the same time the Germans were marching into Yugoslavia and Greece and, with the pro-German Rashid Ali toppling our faithful ally, the King of Iraq, it looked as if they would very soon be marching into Baghdad as well. Everywhere we and our allies were in retreat. That was the size of the crisis. With the alarm bells clanging, our Fourth and Fifth Indian Divisions, which had just conquered Eritrea, were turned round swiftly and sent back to Egypt. The Hamasien Bar was less crowded after that and it was easier to hear oneself speak.

The news put instant smiles on Asmara's Italian faces. Everyone could see the Axis romping home to victory. 'We will win, "viva il Duce, viva Rommel"!' Insolent graffiti began to leer at us from every street corner. 'Unite against the Enemy. No collaboration!' appeared over the portico of the Hamasien Hotel, coincidentally with the disappearance of some of its Italian staff. 'Never underestimate the writing on the wall!' warned

The Spoils of War

Oliver Baldwin in a moment of rare sobriety. 'This spells sabotage and armed resistance.' It looked only too likely for the Italians held all the best cards. Thousands of their troops were still on the loose, arms and ammunition were to be had for the taking in dumps known only to the Italians and the greater part of the country was still in the hands of the Italian Police and Administration. And what did we have? A garrison that had been reduced to little more than a brigade of Sudanese troops, a handful of Political Officers hastily borrowed from the Sudan Political Service and half a dozen Sudanese police.

With Military Head Quarters flapping furiously, no one there was unduly concerned to restore me to the Northern Rhodesia Regiment. Killing time had become my sole occupation and while killing it one day I ran into a stern-faced man of impressive physique wearing a full Colonel's tabs. Who was I? What did I do? One question led to another and, on my revealing that in civilian life I had been a District Officer, I was rewarded with a widening smile. 'Well, well, well!' the Colonel exclaimed. 'If that's what you are, I've got a job for you!' My new acquaintance was Duncan (later Sir Duncan) Cumming who had been extracted from the Sudan Political Service to be Chief Secretary to a British Military Administration then being set up to run Eritrea and he was desperate for recruits. We were rather curiously placed, he explained. Though we had conquered it, in International Law Eritrea was still Italian and would continue to be so until or unless other arrangements were made for it by a Peace Treaty with Italy at the end of the War. So, we were caretakers with the job of holding the Eritrean baby on behalf of our allies. If I would agree to join the Military Administration he would have a job for me. I joined it the very same day.

Before War broke out, Cumming had been 'Eritrea watching' from Kassala just over the frontier in the Sudan and probably knew more about the country than any one else. Eritrea was an extraordinary little country, he said; how extraordinary few people were aware. To put it simply, neither Eritrea nor any piece of it had ever been a country before the Italians came along. Like its name, which was derived from the Romans' 'Mare Erythraeum', it was of exclusive Italian manufacture. Also, unbelievably, had the Italians scoured every beach, bay and mangrove swamp along the African coastline, they could never have hoped to find another 50,000 square mile patch as topographically diverse and with such a variety of people. What explained this was that the Italians happened to have grabbed a 'No Man's Land' where all kinds of people from Ethiopia, the Sudan, the Afar-Somali wastes and Arabia had mingled with and fought each other from time immemorial. Put it another way, the Italians had lopped off the extremities of their neighbours, cobbled them together and called the end product Eritrea. What they had got themselves by doing so was a chimera.

And a very costly one. Eritrea's economic potential was negligible. It could just about support half a million herdsmen and peasants at subsistence level but that was all. This did not, however, deter the Italians, for they had seen Eritrea as a stepping stone to mysterious, little-known Ethiopia and the fabulous riches it supposedly had. Their initial efforts to get their hands on them ended in defeat and humiliating disaster at Adowa;[2] and subsequently competition from the French in Djibuti and the hazards of trading in a country with flexible laws and capricious rulers had denied them anything in the way of significant success. And so it was not until Mussolini and his Fascists decided to invade Ethiopia in 1935 that Eritrea, at last, came into what the Italians had all along visualised as its own. It was transformed beyond imagination in the process. What had been one of Africa's sleepiest and most stagnant little colonies was converted into its most modern and go-ahead country outside Algeria, Egypt and the Union.

So, here we were with 70,000 Italians, butchers, bakers, candlestick makers, and a country equipped to give them a congenial life. To know how congenial, one had only to take a look at Asmara with its cathedral, opera house, cinemas, restaurants, bordellos and green boulevards. That was splendid but the provision and maintenance of Italian provincial towns in Africa did not come cheap. Nor did the maintenance of superb roads, a railway and modern ports, workshops, factories, depots and warehouses. The cost of running Eritrea was immense and since Eritrea itself could not pay so much as a paper lira, the account had had to be met out of metropolitan Italian public funds. All this was in aid of Ethiopian development and would, it was assumed, be fully repaid once Ethiopia's economy got on the move. But how? We had been left to meet the bills without the least prospect of getting anything out of Ethiopia towards them. As Cumming remarked, we had been saddled with a white elephant we didn't want.

The Spoils of War

Having been thoroughly alerted by Cumming to a sense of crisis, I was scarcely prepared for what awaited me when I reported, as instructed, the next day for duty to the Senior Political Officer[3] in charge of Asmara. I found him seated before a table littered with papers and files and surrounded by a dozen Italians all talking at once. 'You see what it is,' he said, running a tired hand through his hair. 'Twenty-four hours a day is just not enough.' Well, what could I do to help? He meditated for a moment and then said, 'Ah yes! You could go and inspect the Italian Officers' brothel. Will you be a good fellow and do that?'

The Italians may not have been much good at making war but when it came to making love they knew their stuff. The brothel could have been designed by Haroun al Rashid himself. It was all mirrors, bright lights and shady corners with fountains splashing seductively in the background. The girls were heavily made up, gowned in long, shiny dresses and loaded with beads and bangles. Their Madame, however, had 'haut monde' written all over her. Soberly clad in an elegant black suit with a single strand pearl necklace round her throat, she greeted me like a very gracious Grande Dame. Pouring me a cup of China tea, she said that the War was sad but she could not complain—it was good for business. I took myself off to Cumming the next day and told him Asmara was not for me. Twenty-four hours later I was on my way to Keren, the scene of the battle which won us Eritrea. It was a move that was to change my life.

NOTES

[1] 'Ethiopia' is the larger area of which 'Abyssinia' was the nucleus. The two terms tended to be used indiscriminately.

[2] Following disagreement between the Italians and the Emperor Menelik over the interpretation of the Treaty of Ucialli—which, according to the Italians' interpretation, as good as made Abyssinia, as Ethiopia was then known, an Italian protectorate, hostilities broke out. This ended in the humiliating defeat of the Italians at Adowa on 1 March 1896.

[3] Officers in charge of administrative districts who were usually known as 'District Officers' elsewhere were known in the Sudan as 'Political Officers'. Since the Eritrean Administration was set up by officers from the Sudan, the term was initially also used in Eritrea. This was changed to 'Divisional Officer' and, later, to Civil Affairs Officer. For the sake of simplicity the term 'Political Officer' has been used throughout.

2

TAKING OVER WITHOUT TEARS

KEREN WAS A JEWEL SET, like Salzburg, in a ring of wild mountains. Its white buildings, mosque, churches, bazaar and brilliant splashes of bougainvillea were the stuff of which picture postcards are made. Nothing could have looked more serene and yet it was here that the Italians had been defeated only a few weeks before. It was here, along the mountain wall shielding Keren, that they had made their last stand after withdrawing from the lowland plains rolling up from the Sudan. It took our troops eight back-breaking weeks and three thousand casualties to scale those forbidding heights and dislodge them. As modern battles go it was a modest affair but, as a victory, it ranks as one of our most spectacular.

I found Lea, the Senior Political Officer in charge of Keren, carrying out an inspection of the bazaar when I arrived. Small, leathery and terrier-like, he seemed to do everything at a near double. Darting here, darting there, flinging out an instruction in one direction and a rebuke in another, he was sweeping through the crowded market place like a little whirlwind, stopping only—and with evident reluctance—on seeing me. I would have to wait for him at the office, he said. When he had started a job nothing short of an Act of God would stop him from finishing it.

Like Cumming, Lea came from the Sudan Political Service. A former scholar of Eton and King's, he was not easily flummoxed, which was just as well for he had had no Italian officials or Police to turn to when he arrived to take over Keren. Every one of them had legged it for Asmara and, since their Eritrean subordinates, too, had all melted away, Lea had arrived to find Keren bereft of any sign of government. All he had to help him was the staff he had brought with him from the Sudan: two Sudanese clerks and a Sudanese Police Sergeant of villainous appearance called Mohammed Musa. It was with this handful that he had to take over a district with 150,000 inhabitants of which he knew nothing. It is hard to think of any more daunting task. Being Lea, he was undaunted.

He got down to business in dogged, pragmatic fashion. Sending Mohammad Musa off to recruit a gendarmerie, he got his clerks to find the fugitive Eritrean staff and bring them back to their desks. Within days he had a small police contingent at his disposal and an office that functioned. His first concern was to make sure that the rural Administration did not collapse for he knew only too well just how fragile it was likely to be and how quickly it could dissolve into chaos. The rural Administration was, in effect, the dozen or so chiefs appointed by the Italians to take charge of the district's tribes and regions. Since they were all Italian appointees, rivals to their positions and subjects with grievances against them were already beginning to raise rebellious heads in anticipation of our sacking them for being our enemy's men. In one or two cases, villages with claims to land held by their neighbours had already taken the law into their own hands. Decisive action was obviously needed to stop the rot and Lea took it. With little more than half a dozen of Mohammed Musa's newly-recruited thugs as an escort, he carried out a lightning tour of the district by mule and camel preaching the gospel of the sanctity of the 'status quo'. We backed the chiefs and we proposed to uphold past decisions. Anyone stepping out of line would get clobbered. That was the gist of his sermons and they did the trick.

Having made sure that the chiefly apparatus was intact and back to work, Lea turned his attention to the most pressing problem of the moment which was looting. Houses and other property which Italian civilians had abandoned were being rifled and so, more ominously, were the huge quantities of arms and ammunition lying scattered about the battle field. The job of putting an end to this Lea assigned to Mohammed Musa. He was a simple, uncomplicated character and he worked to two simple, inflexible rules. First, anyone caught with arms or loot on them was stripped and whipped on the spot. Secondly, suspects were never given the benefit of the doubt. Rough justice, no doubt, and perhaps some injustice, too, but it got results. Looting came to an end and we were able to trace and dispose of large quantities of explosives and weaponry. Given the limitations, I thought we had done rather well.

That, however, was not the view of General Selby, our military garrison's Commander. Big and bristly-moustached, he turned up one morning with a flurry of staff officers in tow. 'You in charge here?' he asked, lighting up a cigar. Since Lea was away at some conference in Asmara, I said that I was. 'Well, why the hell are you letting bloody Italians motor around the place as if they owned it?' he demanded to know. He was referring to two Italian farmers whom we had wanted to get back to work. 'Farmers!' the General snapped. 'I couldn't give a damn if they were nursemaids. They're the Enemy and it's about time you realised it!' What all this boiled down to was that, without reason or evidence of any kind, the General suspected the farmers of using their trucks to transport arms to some secret hiding place. 'Have you searched the Italian cemetery?' he asked. I hadn't. 'Nor the church?' I shook my head. The General rolled his eyeballs around in a gesture of despair. 'Christ-all-bloody-mighty!' he groaned. 'Well, see to it that every grave in the cemetery is dug up tonight! And tomorrow you will search the church, not forgetting to look under the altar! That's an order!' he barked, stamping off.

Fortunately, neither Lea nor I were under the preposterous Selby's orders. Our master wa[s] Brigadier Kennedy Cooke, the Military Administrator; and, as everyone knew, Kennedy Cooke was all too anxious to keep the Italians sweet. He had to. With truck loads of destitute Italian refugees from Ethiopia pouring across the frontier, the number of Italians in Asmara had passed the 80,000 mark and no one but a fathead like Selby would have risked upsetting them. These was, also, the problem of how to keep the wheels of government in Asmara and its satellites ticking over. Since we had as yet no Police Force of our own and only a mere handful of Political Officers, there was only one answer which was to let the old Italian apparatus carry on under our supervision. Having, in effect, turned to the Italian Civil Service for help, we were bound to humour them. To do a Selby and stamp on their toes could only have led to sabotage or worse.

As Keren returned to normal, its former Italian residents began drifting back and a very querulous and demanding lot they were. And so, when we were suddenly told that, to ease pressure in Asmara, 2,000 destitute refugees were being sent to us, Lea blenched but not half as much as he did after they had arrived. Imagining that the local Italians would open up their hearts and homes to their compatriots in distress, we had foreseen no difficulty in housing them. As it was, not a heart nor a home opened by so much as an inch. Did I seriously expect her to let these dirty, smelly people into her house, a lady with a well-powdered bourgeois face wished [to] know. Why didn't we put them into tents? I could get nowhere. Lea was not amused. 'Good God, man, we can't afford to frig about doing nothing!' he snapped. On that he stumped off to deal with the problem. Coming to Italian house number one, he sized up its cubic footage and then detailed so many refugees into it. On receiving a screech of protest from its owner, he gave him two minutes to decide whether to say 'Yes' or 'No', making it clear that in the event of the answer being 'No' he would be under arrest and on his way to internment as a political undesirable. That settled it. Every refugee had a roof over his head by nightfall.

With the arrival of the refugees, more water was consumed and, though we cut the water off for most of each day, it was still disappearing faster than we could afford. Lea was convinced that there was a leak or fault somewhere and suddenly hit on the thought that it was due to defective Italian plumbing. 'Pull the plug in any Italian lavatory,' he said, 'and the damned thing goes on dripping for ever!' So, would I check. I did so by asking a bemused Italian Town Engineer to carry out an inspection. He reported that the 'Gabinetti' were all in good order and I reported accordingly to Lea. Giving me a 'humph' of disbelief he asked if I had inspected every single lavatory myself. Well, no, the Italian Engineer had done so... Giving me a look like a searchlight, he jumped to his feet and took me off on a tour of every Italian house in the town. At each he knocked on the door and, to the open-eyed astonishment of its owner, asked for the lavatory. On being shown it he pulled the plug and then recorded his findings in his notebook. 'Just as I thought!' he said, consulting his notes at the end of the tour. 'The water ration of at least a hundred and fifty people is being lost by those useless lavatories.' That was my first but by no means last lesson in what Lea meant by being thorough. That is what father would have called 'good government'.

With three thousand articulate and often clamorous Italians on our hands, Lea became increasingly fretful. He had better things to do than play nursemaid to these 'importunate Latins', he complained. What he wanted was to put the whole tiresome, argumentative tribe under a chief. But who? There was no Italian in Keren with sufficient authority for the job. So he turned to Keren's ex-Commissario who had decamped to Asmara.

The ex-Commissario was a retired cavalry General called Count Antonelli and few names were better known in Italian colonial circles for his uncle was the Count Antonelli who had negotiated the ill-fated Treaty of Ucciali with the Emperor Menelik. The nephew of this legendary figure was a spare, elderly man with an absent-minded look which immediately brought Wodehouse's pig-loving Lord Emsworth to mind. Pigs, however, were not our Antonelli's weakness. His life was dedicated to horses and show jumping. Within minutes of our meeting he was giving me a jump by jump account of how he had won the King's Cup at Olympia in London and then telling me how it had been looted by our Cypriot Mule Corps after the Battle of Keren. 'C'est la guerre,' he smiled, with the gentlemanly air of the good loser. He was just what we wanted, Lea said. He would keep the Italians in order and let us get on with the job without interfering.

We could not have done better, said a suave Major of Levantine appearance in the Intelligence Corps called Max Harari. For the Italians to see a man with Antonelli's name happily collaborating with us was just what we needed to cool hot heads who were talking about armed revolution. Since we had not the force to cope with armed resistance, we had to fend it off as best we could. We had, that is to say, to get the Italians to realise that they were not doing too badly here.

What Harari was expounding was the Kennedy Cooke line. Though a Sudan Political, Kennedy Cooke had not the lean, camel-riding appearance of old Sudan hands like Lea and Cumming. He was a bit chubby and looked like a man who had just had a good lunch. He knew Italy well, liked Italians and delighted in the colour, charm and culture of Italian life. He had no time for the apostles of toughness, like Selby, who thought we should be rounding up every Italian in sight. That, he argued, would harden Italian opposition behind the Fascists and make the Italian officials working for us bloody-minded. No, what was required, he felt, was a more subtle approach. By behaving in a decent, civilised way towards the Italians, we could wean them away from the Fascist minority. Once that had been done, we should have no difficulty in rounding up the Fascists without provoking a furore. This was the voice of sophistication speaking.

It was not, of course, a voice with much appeal for General Selby. Nevertheless, though he and his staff had fretted and fumed about the way Kennedy Cooke and his officers spent their time mollycoddling Italians, they were unlikely to have taken issue with Kennedy Cooke had he not had the bright idea of encouraging his officers to get on drinking and eating terms with Italian upper crust. If Italians only saw you as a face across a desk between the hours of nine and five, how—he would ask—could you expect to win their hearts and minds? You had to show them that you were 'simpatico' and you could only do that if you met them over a drink or dinner or perhaps a game of tennis or bridge. This was not un-reasonable but Anglo-Italian get-togethers tended to get out of hand. Hospitable by nature and eager, no doubt, to cultivate potentially useful British friends, the Italian bourgeoisie entertained many of our officers in style and it was not long before corks were popping, Spumante flowing and love-starved officers getting themselves entangled with young signorinas to an extent that brought General Selby sharply to the boil. Fraternisation with the Enemy, he made it known, was an offence tantamount to treason and it was to cease at once. And that was an order! But could he give Kennedy Cooke orders? He thought he could. Kennedy Cooke thought he couldn't. Our military regime was split down the middle.

This farcical crisis arose from the fact that Kennedy Cooke was nominally an officer on Selby's staff. Technically, therefore, Selby was in the right but, however right, common sense said that you could not have a blundering blockhead of a soldier let loose on the treacherous seas of civil government and politics. And so, in the event, HQ Middle East resolved the dispute by ruling that Kennedy Cooke had exclusive responsibility for the civil government of the territory and Selby was to confine himself to military matters. Kennedy Cooke had won the argument but it was Selby who had the last word. Kennedy Cooke was removed.

Ironically, he left at the very time when he should have been getting a grateful Cairo's warmest thanks. By not being a Selby and by treating the Italians generously, he had lulled them into accepting us. That had got us through the dangerous months when with no police force of our own, we had had to depend on the Italian Police. After that it had all been plain sailing. In one splendid St Bartholomew's Night, 3,000 Fascist bad hats were rounded up. There was no more talk about Italian armed resistance after that.

3

THE ABYSSINIAN PEOPLE AND CHURCH MILITANT

ANTONELLI AND I were sitting on the terrace outside the Florentine-style palazzo where I was quartered admiring a fairyland sunset. This was a paradise, the old gentleman sighed. There was nowhere in Eritrea quite like it. Keren was certainly unique but never in a thousand Christmasses would Antonelli have guessed my reason for thinking so. It stood at the very heart of Eritrea, where life was likely to be at its most interesting.

To understand this one needs to take a look at what made up the chimera the Italians had turned into Eritrea. Geographically and politically it was a real hotch potch. Its central core consisted of a high plateau of near treeless moorland which was, in fact, the northernmost tip of Ethiopia's highland massif. In the southern part of this tip there were settled Christian Abyssinians who were one and the same people as their neighbours next door in the Ethiopian province of the Tigrai. Tapering away into a thinning range of mountains, the Plateau plunged into the sands of the Red Sea Coast in the East and, in the West, into the grit and gravel of lowland prairies which swept away into the Sudan. All three of these regions—Northern Highlands, Coastal Plain and Western Lowlands—were occupied by Moslems who, though they came from a variety of origins, nearly all spoke the same Tigrey dialect and almost all closely resembled in appearance the Beja tribes of the Eastern Sudan. That, plus a narrow ribbon of coastal desert to the South ending with the little port of Assab, was Eritrea. Essentially, the country was divided between the Christian Abyssinians and the Moslem tribes and it was because it stood at the very point where they met on the Plateau's Western flank that Keren was of such unique interest.

To the immediate north and west of where Antonelli and I were sitting, a solid expanse of Islamic territory stretched out to the shores of the Red Sea, the Mediterranean and the Atlantic. To our immediate south and east, the rainbow colours of the Abyssinian Church fluttered in every town and village between us and the heartlands of Ethiopia. Keren was the point where, after centuries of warfare, the changing frontiers between Islam and Abyssinian Christianity had eventually come to rest. Since he spoke Tigray and felt at home with Moslem tribesmen, Lea decided to take them under his wing, leaving me to deal with the Abyssinian minority. He was in his element. The same could hardly be said about me!

Nevertheless, my first excursion yielded a rather charming surprise. While marching along a dry river bed we came across an elderly citizen bobbing along on his donkey. Seeing us he stopped, dismounted and gave a respectful salute. 'Who is that?' he asked one of my escort. 'That,' he was told, 'is the British Government.' 'The British Government?' His mouth opened and shut in astonishment. Then, peering around, he asked, 'But where are his elephants?' Elephants? What on earth could the old idiot be talking about? And then I got it. His mind had travelled back seventy-five years to that vintage epic, the expedition of 1868 when Lord Napier had marched into Ethiopia with a baggage train of elephants to rescue an unfortunate British Consul whom the deranged Emperor Theodore had impounded. It was nice to think that that Victorian Hannibal was still remembered.

Seeing Abyssinians at close quarters for the first time, I was struck—as so many newcomers are—with a sense of surprise. This was Africa but could these Abyssinians really be Africans? They were not negroid, nor were they quite like the Somalis and other straight-nosed and straight-haired Hamites of Africa. They were a race apart. Put any of them in a crowd of Africans, Asians, Polynesians, Eskimos or whom you will and they would stand out at once. To understand why they are so distinctive one has to look back about two thousand years, to the time when their ancestors crossed the Red Sea from South Arabia and founded an African colony which was the nucleus of the future Ethiopia. Two thousand years is a long time and, since coming to Africa, the descendants of those early

The Deluge

South Arabian immigrants had mixed and intermarried with the indigenous Hamitic peoples whom they conquered. One might expect that by this time their ancient South Arabian selves would have been swallowed up by Africa. Surprisingly this did not happen. The Abyssinians of today still write in the quaint and clumsy script of ancient South Arabia and their dialects—Tigrey, Tigrinya and Amharic—are still as close to the dialects once spoken by the Sabaeans and Himyarites of ancient Yemen as, say, Spanish is to Italian. Why the civilisation of ancient Yemen, which has vanished from the Yemen itself, should have lived on in what was a Yemeni African colony remains an intriguing mystery.

Curiously though, it is not so much in South Arabia as in Israel that the Abyssinians see their roots. So much is apparent from the popular Abyssinian fable of Solomon and Bilqis, the Queen of the South Arabian state of Sheba: he, the wisest of men and she, the most comely of women. To see Bilqis was to desire her and on receiving her in Jerusalem, so the story goes, Solomon slyly proposed that they should get better acquainted in bed. Bilqis politely refused and, having dined, retired alone for the night. Solomon, however, had cunningly provided against this eventuality by doctoring her dinner with an overdose of salt; and, sure enough, half way through the night, a raging thirst had the poor girl up and about clamouring for water. Solomon was up and about too, and with a tempting jug of the stuff to hand. Fair was fair, the monarch said: she wanted water, he wanted something else. If he gave her water, she should give him that something. She did not argue. She gave it to him and on her return home was blessed with a son as a memento. His name was Menelik.

That is the beginning of the story but it is what follows that matters more. Some twenty years after his mother's visit to Solomon, young Menelik presented himself to his father and almost immediately Israel was in an uproar. The old King was so besotted by his son that he had eyes and ears for him and no other. Hot with envy, Israel's elders demanded that Menelik be sent home so that harmony could be restored. The King felt bound to agree but argued that, if he were forced to lose his son, it was only fair that each of Israel's twelve tribes should lose one too. That was agreed and one youth from each tribe was detailed to accompany Menelik home. On the eve of their departure, however, the young Levite among them got cold feet at the prospect of venturing into the unknown without the protection of the Ark of the Covenant. If he was to go he had to have it and, in the event, he did. He broke into the temple, stole the Ark and Moses' sacred tablets and, having replaced them with replicas, sailed off the next day with them in his baggage. And so Menelik returned to become Emperor of what had been his mother's African dominion of Ethiopia accompanied by his twelve Israelite companions and the Ark and Tablets. That, so credulous Abyssinians still believe, is how Ethiopia was founded.

I first heard this fairy tale from the chief of our Abyssinians, a moustachioed stalwart called Negassi. He was no dreamy-eyed bumpkin but as earthy an ex–Sergeant Major as ever stamped around a parade ground; and yet he believed every word of it. Having told me the story, he produced a wad of crumpled yellowing papers and then read out the names of his family tree, all the way back to the son of Judah who had supposedly accompanied Menelik on his voyage. It was the same everywhere. I had only to ask some grey-beard about his family and within seconds I would find myself listening to an ancestral roll call. 'Andinkiel, the son of Hailu, the son of Ghergis, the son of Taklemariam…' on and on through the centuries to one of those sons of Israel. To see the look on these village ancients' faces as they reached their genealogical journeys' ends was to know that they really believed they were God's elect.

This sometimes offensive Abyssinian hubris had been reared and faithfully sustained over the centuries by the Abyssinian branch of the Coptic church—surely the most bizarre in all Christendom. There is not much namby-pamby nonsense about loving your enemies and turning the other cheek in its teachings. There are no two ways about it: enemies are for thumping and thumping hard. They have a bible which includes some matter common to other Christian churches but also a good deal that is not, including innumerable miracles of which no one else has ever heard. Amongst their many saints there are some familiar to us all but many who are not, such as Balaam, with his ass. It is, however, the layout of the churches themselves that causes one to wonder whether, despite the crosses over them, the Abyssinian Church is a Christian institution at all. Their churches resemble, more than anything, the old Hebrew Temple at Jerusalem. At the centre of each is a Holy of Holies, for priests' eyes only, in which are stored replicas of the Ark and the Tablets which are, according to legend, now supposed to be at Axum. However weird and outlandish this Abyssinian Church may seem, it was the inspiration of

Abyssinian resistance to centuries of Islamic assault. Of necessity, it had to be an aggressively militant Church. To sustain morale it had to make the Abyssinians believe that they were God's own people.

The long-established place of the Church in Abyssinian life had made the Abyssinians priest-ridden 'par excellence'. How priest-ridden I discovered on visiting Chief Negassi at a time when his village was celebrating the sacred memory of St Teclehaimanoy, who was supposed to have converted the Devil to Christianity for a space of forty days. On my arrival the villagers congregated outside the church and parading before them was a platoon of turbanned priests banging drums and swaying to and fro in polka-like slow motion. Other priests, acolytes, novices and so on stood on one side chanting pieties and shaking silver-topped rattles. Most were garbed in purple cloaks: some carried umbrellas embroidered with silver and a number wore massive glittering crowns. Unmusical noises off were provided by an energetic troupe of fiddlers and horn blowers. There must have been at least fifty priests dancing and chanting to honour St Teclehaimanoy and of these, Negassi told me, about half were priests of the parish. A fifth of the village land was set aside to keep them fed and fit for duty.

That, however, was not the village's sole contribution to the custodians of their souls. Standing a little apart from the other celebrants on a piece of tattered carpet, and under an enormous umbrella, there was a tall, bearded man, black-gowned and with a black toque the size of a chimneypot on his head. This was the Abbot of the monastery of Zaadamba which was perched on the top of an impressive eminence 'to provide the angels with a convenient landing ground', His Beatitude explained. On another mountain top, also far up in the clouds, was the monastery of Debrasina which boasted hot springs that could purge sin and sickness from those who bathed in them. The two Abbots could not, of course, live on air. They had to keep up a dignified appearance; they had their monks to feed and clothe and they needed petty cash to make charitable gestures to the hordes of beggars and cripples whining and wailing outside their walls. Abbots such as these did not come cheap. The villagers enjoying their protection had to pay a high price to keep them.

To keep Abbots, priests and ourselves, their Government, happy, the Abyssinian peasants had to coax and squeeze what they could out of their land. It was hard going and never harder than when their grain stores and cash boxes were empty at the time for sowing. To sow they had to have seed. Where was it to come from? In many cases timely remittances from sons and nephews in employment solved the problem. In others there was no alternative to borrowing and that meant touching a merchant or shopkeeper for a loan. Borrowers and lenders are seldom the best of friends but here there could only be bare toothed enmity between them. Since no Christian would demean himself by indulging in trade, it was the exclusive province of a depressed class of Moslem known as the Jiberti. Add envy and fear to contempt and one has hatred. Hatred of Moslem merchants and a latent, congenital fear of the Moslem hordes just over the horizon were ingrained in these peculiarly insular people.

Italians would say that Christians and Moslems had buried the hatchet long ago. Italian rule had exorcised their unreasoning hatred of each other and now they were brothers. 'Brothers named Cain and Abel,' said the cynical Lea and, as a stormy little episode revealed, he was not far wrong. It began with the arrival of a Colonel Hugh Boustead and a battalion of Sudanese troops for a spell of training in Keren. Boustead, who hailed from the Sudan Political Service, was one of its more distinguished and colourful characters. His career had begun as a shore-based Midshipman in the First World War clamouring to go to sea and fight. Having appealed and protested to no purpose, he eventually deserted from the Navy, enlisted under a false name as a Private in the Army, got a commission, rose to Lieutenant Colonel, won an MM, MC and DSO in the process and finally got a King's Pardon for desertion. He was a man who could not live without a mission and who, having found one, pursued it with the blindest bulldoggish zeal. His particular mission at this time was the Sudan War effort, the war being seen by him now more as a Sudanese war against their old Abyssinian enemy than as one against the Italians. It followed, of course, that the Sudanese were angels, the Abyssinians fiends.

Alas, they were angels only in his imagination. In fact they were only too human and fallible and, having conquered, took the old-fashioned view that they had won the victor's right to loot and rape. And so they looted and raped merrily away, directing their attention, however, to Keren's Christian Abyssinians. Its Moslems they obligingly left alone. This quickly flooded my office with aggrieved Abyssinians and, since I myself had no jurisdiction over the turbulent soldiery, sent me hurrying off to

Boustead who had. As I paraded the sordid details of what his men had done before him, he sat as unmoved as a statue, his clear blue eyes gazing through and beyond me. When I had finished, he remained silent for a full minute and then, coming to life, said, 'That's a pretty bad show, old boy. We can't have these fellows doing that kind of thing. They deserve to be publicly birched.' Thinking that he was referring to his own scallywags, I agreed—but I was wrong. It was those 'bloody Habash'—that is to say the Abyssinians—whom he wished to see chastised. They were blatant liars, trying to blacken the reputation of his faithful Sudanese. When I politely demurred, his eyes fired salvoes of indignation. His men were incapable of doing what they had been accused of and if he did not know his own men he would like to know who did. Well, that was that. There was nothing more that I could do.

The Abyssinians, however, could. Like the Sudanese, they had old-fashioned views and the oldest of the lot was that, if you get a slap in the face, you slap back. This did not, however, mean that you necessarily retaliated against the particular person or persons who had hit you. You could, so their thinking went, hurt them equally well by hurting their friends and kinsmen. And so, having inferred from their immunity from Sudanese attention that their Moslem neighbours were in collusion with the Sudanese, they retaliated against them. For several days Keren was in a turmoil. Moslem shops were broken into and pillaged. Moslem ladies were outraged. Moslem dignitaries were insulted. Aggrieved Moslems paraded in protest outside my office. None of this would have happened, Boustead said, had I only listened to him in the first place. You had to take a tough line with these Habash. You couldn't afford to let them get away with it. Now, if I wanted his troops to teach them a lesson, he would give the necessary orders. I declined with thanks. Mercifully, the troubles abated soon afterwards.

This disturbing little episode was an eye-opener. The apparent sectarian harmony created by years of orderly government seemed to justify Italian claims that Moslem and Christian looked on each other as brothers and it was in any event easy enough to believe that religious sectarianism was a thing of the past in this increasingly secular present. Now I knew that sectarian harmony was a facade behind which old fears and passions still lived malevolently on.

4

ENCOUNTER WITH A PROPHET

ORDEAL BY WHAT old Middle Eastern hands called the 'Shuftiscope' was something to wish on your worst enemy. It was an assault on personal dignity which dysentery suspects had to endure and, having become one after a few months of Abyssinian hospitality, I was given the treatment. 'Positive!' the Army doctor announced on completing his inspection. 'Two weeks' treatment and then sick leave.' Lea was none too pleased, grumbling that he could see no reason for my taking leave after all those months of idleness I had enjoyed as a prisoner. I packed my bags and slunk off feeling like a common malingerer. I could never have guessed that I was on my way to see a prophet.

And that was only because I suddenly had the bright idea of using my leave to sail down the White Nile from Juba, on the Sudan's frontier with Uganda, to Khartoum. I was off my head, Lea said on hearing this. Did I realise that I was talking about a 3,000 mile round trip? And this was war time. Ironically, it was because it was war time that I was able to do what Lea so brusquely dismissed as impossible. Military transport of one kind or another was operating all along my proposed route and it was easy enough for a uniformed officer like myself to get travel warrants from one place to another. I met with only one hold-up and that was when the Transport Officer at Juba refused to give me a warrant. Without papers to show that I was travelling on duty, nothing doing, this Spanner in the Works said. So there I was, stuck fifteen hundred miles from base. When in difficulties, report to the District Commissioner, was the well-known maxim of colonial life. I did so and found myself looking at the familiar face of Jake Seamer who had given me my cricket colours at Marlborough! The Old School Tie had its uses! I got my warrant and was off to Khartoum by paddle steamer the next day.

Chugging down the White Nile in deck chaired ease with Nature at its rawest gliding by was a curious experience. A primaeval world of jungle and wild beasts stared up from the banks of that great sluggish river and now and again I found myself returning the compliment to Primitive Man. The Nuer, Dinka, Shilluk and Bongo seemed to be as innocent and untouched by the last three thousand years of human progress as Adam and Eve and, like Adam, the men displayed themselves in total nudity. The women wore tufts of grass or, in some cases, minute squares of cloth fore and aft. To see them as I was seeing them for a mere matter of days was entertaining but to see them and them alone for months on end, as the Sudan Politicals did, was hardly my idea of a full and satisfying life. Nevertheless, just as Fox-Pitt had found a contentment in Mpika which had eluded me, so here there were Sudan Politicals who wouldn't have been anywhere else. One of them climbed aboard at a place called Wau and talked like a typewriter about the joys of life with the Dinka in some district a hundred miles from it. He thought them the finest creatures on two feet and the only cloud in his sunny sky was the possibility that he might be transferred elsewhere. He needed two years more with them, he explained. He had just completed a dictionary of a dialect called Ndogo and was now planning to produce an Ndogo Grammar to go with it. I doubt if they make people like that any more.

When at last I arrived in the bustling sophistication of Khartoum I became a sight-seeing tourist no more. There was a note waiting for me at the Grand Hotel. It read, 'If you are free, drop in for a drink and supper at 8 this evening. Douglas Newbold.' Sir Douglas Newbold was head of the Sudan Administration and why he should send an invitation to a visiting nobody like myself I could not imagine. He was at home waiting for me when I called, a burly hulk of a man with the jolly avuncular manner of an Army padre. He greeted me with a big affable smile, saying that 'our chaps' in Juba had told him that I was coming. How did I enjoy the trip from Juba? Fine chaps, those Dinka, weren't they? Had I been to Khartoum before? He led me gently along with innocent small talk until he came to what our little chat was to be all about. Haile Selassie, it seemed, was beginning to kick up a fuss about Eritrea, saying that, since the Italians had taken it from Ethiopia, it should now be handed back. 'Oh yes,' Newbold said, and when it came to drafting the Peace Treaty the Allies would be all too likely to let him have it if only to ease their consciences for letting him down at the time of the Italian invasion. And did I see what that would mean for the Sudan? No, I couldn't say that I did. As someone based in Keren at the very point where Christians and Moslems met would I say that the Moslems would give three cheers on hearing that they had been taken over by the fiercely militant Ethiopian Christian regime which had fought Islam for centuries? Of course not. They would be appalled. But that would not be all, Newbold assured me. They would almost certainly rebel and, if they did, they would instantly appeal to their Moslem 'brothers' in the Sudan for help and you could be a hundred per cent sure that their Moslem 'brothers' would back them with cash and arms at the very least. And would Ethiopia take that lying down? No, the Ethiopians would retaliate by egging the non-Moslem Southern Sudanese to revolt against the Government in Khartoum. So, perhaps, I could now see why the prospect of Haile Selassie getting Eritrea was such a weight on his mind. Newbold looked out as if for comfort through the window at the light shimmering on the waters of the Nile outside. It could mean civil war for the Sudan, he said.

I found all this rather far fetched. Was it really conceivable that the Allies would be mad enough to hand neat, well-ordered Eritrea over to the mediaeval bear garden that was Ethiopia? Even if it was, what was all this about civil war in the Sudan? Newbold was talking as if the Sudan would be independent. And so he was—he was busy preparing it for early independence, he told me. But surely the Sudanese were not ready for independence, I said, thinking of those naked savages I had just seen in the southern reaches of the White Nile. 'If you will forgive the cliche,' Newbold replied, 'politics is the art of the possible and it will be impossible to carry on as we are for very much longer.' Did I realise how fast change was going to come once the War was over and how revolutionary it would be? Had I ever wondered how we had been able to run our empire on the cheap with nothing much more than a handful of District Commissioners and a few penny packets of Police? British genius? The excellence of our government? To some extent 'yes' but at bottom it had been because our colonies had been isolated and conveniently insulated against troublesome influences. Well that,

The Deluge

he said, was going to end. Education had already breached colonial isolation and, once the War was over, cheaper and better radios and greatly improved travel facilities, particularly by air, would finish it off. After that, whether we liked it or not, demands for independence would become impossible to resist. If we accepted that and were seen to be doing our best to bring independence about, we could expect to have good friends with the same ideas as ourselves in what had once been our colonies. The alternative was to fight for a hopeless cause and be left with nothing but enemies. This was strong wine for a young tyro of a mere twenty-seven!

If the Sudan were to get early independence, as Newbold seemed to think, and if Ethiopia did take over Eritrea, I could see that trouble of some kind would come from the Eritrean Moslems. Was there no way out? Newbold sucked his pipe for a bit in a thoughtful way and then said, 'Yes! There is!' His way out was to partition Eritrea, giving the Moslems of Western Eritrea to the Sudan and the mainly Christian and Abyssinian Eastern half of the country to Ethiopia. That, he said, was the only rational way of dealing with Eritrea but, however obvious, one could not count on the Allies seeing it. It would have to be put right under their noses and by the Moslems of the West themselves. If that were done, he felt pretty sure they would accept it. Would the Moslems' clamour for partition or would they just sit back and do nothing? What did I think? Having just seen Cain and Abel in action, I could not believe that the Moslems would meekly submit to what would be a Christian Abyssinian take-over. Given an escape route to the Sudan, I would have thought that they would tumble over themselves to use it. 'Fair enough,' Newbold said with a chuckle, 'that would be the reasonable thing for them to do but are they reasonable?' We would have to wait and see. I promised to keep him posted.

When I told Lea of my conversation with Newbold on my return to Keren, he dismissed it as 'froth'. Newbold was a good fellow, he said, one of the best but, like everyone else, he was human and influenced by his environment. As a provincial Governor in the real Sudan, where the hard facts of tribal life had to be faced, he had been excellent. But now, what did he see? Talkative young dreamers from Gordon College who would not know a hard fact of tribal life if they saw one. It was always the same. Take someone out of a district and stick him in Khartoum and within weeks he would be talking about Sudan and the Sudanese as if they were, say, Cornwall and the Cornish.

Being a graduate of Gordon College, Ahmed al Fiki, one of our two Sudanese clerks, took a rather different view of Newbold. He was one of the few British officers who really understood the Sudanese, he said. He was well respected but there were doubts about his sincerity over independence. But did he really believe that the Sudanese were fit for independence? Ahmed grinned. Of course not, he replied. If they got it the whole place would be awash with incompetence and corruption. 'But we must have it without further delay!' he laughed. What! Even though he admitted that everything would go wrong? Certainly. And why was that? Because British rule was so boring! They couldn't tolerate it for another minute! Year after year it was always the same: on January 1st the Governor General did this, on January 2nd he did that. Year in, year out, everyone knew precisely what was going to happen each day. Wasn't that intolerable? I had never thought of that before. I don't suppose there were many who had.

5

MOSLEMS IN TROUBLE

A FEW DAYS after my return Lea was recalled to the Sudan and, true to form, he left without formality or fuss. His successor, a fattish and fiftyish Major called Last, was all fuss if not formality. What he was fussed about was his prestige. He was a very senior member of the Colonial Service who had been administering Africans while I was still in the nursery, he wished me to know, and to expect him to look after a tin pot district like Keren was really not good enough. Having made his feelings clear, he retired to his house and refused to budge.

This was ridiculous. Since he would not answer the telephone I eventually pushed my way through his front door and into his sitting room. The Major was at home all right and so were two Abyssinian maidens—very much at home, I thought, seeing that one of them had her head on his lap and the other was playing 'ride a cock horse' on his disengaged knee. The Major goggled, the ladies screeched and scampered off. The Major eventually broke an awkward silence by saying that he had been having a language lesson. Hastening to offer me a drink, he helped himself and, gulping down beaker after beaker of powerful Cypriot brandy, was very soon gushing and gurgling in a most amiable fashion. He didn't like this stinking country, he confided. No class. Not like Zanzibar, his old stamping ground. Did I like it? Yes? Fair enough. I liked it, he didn't. OK, we could both be happy. I could get on with the day to day job of running the place. He would confine himself to policy. How would that suit me? Down to the ground!

Moslems in Trouble

Sorry though I was to say good bye to Lea, his departure meant that I would now be handling the Moslems and, in view of my talk with Newbold, that was all to the good. By chance, Lea had hardly slipped off when I had my first encounter with the World of Islam and a very startling one it was. Preceded by the Qadhi or Islamic Judge–cum–High Priest of Keren, a flotilla of Moslem dignitaries came sailing majestically into my office one morning, their flowing white robes billowing like sails around them. He and his friends had come, he said, to protest in the name of Islam. A Christian police constable had humiliated their revered and beloved leader, Seyid Bubakr al Mirghani. What had he done? The Qadhi found it impossible to tell me: it was too obscene, too shocking. A telephone call to the Police revealed that the Seyid had, in fact, been put on a charge for drunken driving. That made me sit up. It is not every day that the Moslem equivalent of an Archbishop is run in for hitting the bottle!

Seyid Bubakr was a member of the Mirghani family and, with the exception of the descendants of the Mahdi who had been knocked out at the Battle of Omdurman, the Mirghanis were top of the Islamic hierarchy south of the Egyptian border. Descendants of the Prophet and founders of an Islamic Order called the Khatmia, they were rulers of a spiritual kingdom which covered a large part of the Sudan and all of Moslem Eritrea. Seyid Bubakr was their Eritrean pro-Consul. He was a young man and anyone with eyes undimmed by faith could have seen at a glance that he had not acquired a body like a blancmange or that look of pop-eyed vacuity by saintly living. But what would the faithful think if he were put in the dock to answer a charge of drunken driving? Even though he had driven his car slap into a wall and vomited a quart of whisky all over a policeman, they would never believe it. They would only believe that the whole thing was the mischievous fabrication of a despicable Christian Police Constable. What was I to do? Let the Law take its course and unleash a Jihad or bend the rules in favour of a privileged debauchee? The answer was simple, the Qadhi said, taking me aside. To fine him publicly would provoke trouble; worse still, it could undermine respect for the Mirghanis and that could be disastrous. Moslem unity was of paramount importance in this sensitive region on the borders of Christian Abyssinia and it was loyalty to the Mirghanis that preserved it. His advice was to deal with the errant Seyid in private by removing his driving licence and fining him heavily. It made sense, and so I followed it.

Even though I was by this time no new boy to Eritrea, I still found the difference between the Christian Abyssinians and their immediate Moslem neighbours grotesque. One had but to step half a mile across the border between them to be in a different world. One moment you would be in Christian Abyssinia, the next in what would have been the Eastern Sudan. Between Eritrea's Moslem tribes and their Sudanese neighbours there was little difference. They had the same great shaggy manes which had earned their Sudanese neighbours Rudyard Kipling's nickname of 'Fuzzy Wuzzies'; they wore the same baggy pantaloons; they carried the same long crusader-like swords. They looked the same and they lived in the same lackadaisical fashion, cultivating an odd patch of ground here and there but otherwise roaming around with their herds and flocks and pitching their sprawling goathair tents wherever a patch of grazing was to be found. Most of them called themselves Arabs and had genealogies in their saddle bags to prove it. Whether one chose to believe, half believe or disbelieve them, it could safely be said that they shared most of the customs and prejudices common to millions of Moslems, Arab or otherwise. They would have been more at home with Kurdish or Afghan tribesmen thousands of miles away than they could ever be with their Abyssinian neighbours just round the corner. They and the Abyssinians were as different from each other as Gurkhas from Greeks.

There was, however, one characteristic which our Moslem tribes did not share with their Sudanese neighbours. They alone spoke an arcane Ethiopic language called Tigrey. How so antique a tongue had survived in a region so continually invaded and overrun and for so long is a mystery still to be explained. It is as if the Celtic used by Queen Boadicea was still in use in the England of today.

For my first exploratory journey to the Moslem tribes I decided to visit the largest and best known, a tribe called the Habab in the ragged highlands to the north of Keren. It was presided over by a tetchy little tyrant called Uthman Hadad who bore the Ethiopian title of Kantibai which a grateful Emperor had bestowed on an Abyssinian ancestor of his for occupying the region on his behalf. On my arrival at Nacfa, the Kantibai's seat, he greeted me with chilling courtesy and enquired what my plans were. I gave my proposed itinerary and said that I wanted to

Moslems in Trouble

get to know something about his tribe. His lips twitched with irritation. He could spare me the trouble, he said. If I wanted information about his tribe, he would be happy to oblige me. Well, that was one way of saying that he didn't want me nosing about his backyard. Should I pull my rank and carry on as if I had not understood him or should I bow to his wishes? I bowed to his wishes. To kick off by quarrelling with the doyen of the Moslem chiefs did not seem too good an idea.

Providence, however, was on my side. A few weeks later the Kantibai's eldest son, an elegant well-laundered young squireen called Hidad, strutted into my office to say that his father was having a little difficulty with some Bedouin over taxes and would like the loan of my police. Certainly he could have them, I said, and I would accompany them. His father would not hear of my inconveniencing myself, Sheikh Hidad purred with a silken smile. Had he purred like a prize Persian I was determined to go. He could have me AND the police or neither of us. After a few minutes of my saying it would in no way inconvenience me and the Sheikh saying yes it would, he got the message. The Kantibai later made a last ditch effort to deter me by saying that his Bedouin were ignorant savages and there was no knowing what they might do if they saw an infidel wandering about their country. I reminded him that I would have my police with me. He bared his gold teeth in a sick grin and shuffled off to his private quarters to have a good sulk.

After three days' hard slog up and down mountains and along canyons enclosed between them, Sheik Hidad brought me at last to our quarry. There were about fifty shaggy-headed men taking their ease in a valley and a few dozen women chattering to each other. Fussing around their tents was a rabble of urchins at play. Our arrival reduced them all to silence as two hundred pairs of eyes focussed suspiciously upon us. Sheik Hidad suggested that I should relax under an umbrella-like tree nearby while he disposed of his business. I wouldn't hear of it. My place was with him. He smiled his thanks with an effort and we got down to work. The tribesmen gathered round and their leader asked what he could do for us. On being told that he could pay the taxes they owed, he started up as if he had had a jab in the behind. What taxes? By God and on the heads of his numerous sons, he was ready to take a hundred oaths that the taxes had been paid. An explosion of expletives went up in his support from the assembled company. Yes, said Sheikh Hidad wearily, but what had been paid was not enough. This had the old gentleman offering to swear a hundred more oaths that what had been paid was what they had always paid. Sheik Hidad looked heavenwards with a sigh and pointed out that, since prices had gone up, taxes had been raised. Wasn't that reasonable? Of course it was. If they got more for their goats and sheep in the market, I said, they had to expect to pay more in taxes. As an afterthought I then asked how much they were now being asked to pay. It was about £200. I couldn't believe it—it was daylight robbery.

The system of taxation in force was the old Ottoman one which the Italians had taken over from their Egyptian predecessors. It was simplicity itself. Each tribe was assessed collectively and, so long as its chief stumped up the right amount on time, no questions were asked. That the chiefs and their underlings would pocket a bit for themselves was taken for granted but there are limits and, even by the standards of the Mafia, it was obvious that the Kantibai and his men had gone way beyond them. Consider the figures. The Habab, with 30,000 souls, were required to pay £3,000 and here were, say, 200 being asked to pay £200. At that rate the Kantibai would be trousering £30,000 of which a paltry £3,000 would be passed on to the Government. Taking Sheikh Hidad on one side, I gave him an earful of my feelings. 'It is our custom,' he said, as bland as you please. Maybe, I replied, but it was not ours and my police would not be available to enforce it. That ruffled his composure but he had no choice but to surrender. The Bet Ibrahim, as those wooly pates were called, were excused further payment and Sheikh Hidad and I returned to base without much in the way of light conversation to pass the time. The Kantibai was all pursed lips and peevishness on hearing what had happened. Now that I had let the Bet Ibrahim get away with it, he snapped, every half-naked Bedouin in the country would be getting ideas above his station. He grumbled on, prophesying revolt and ruin for a while and then left, bidding me an acid good bye. He was right: he knew what the consequences of the Bet Ibrahim affair would be very much better than a young greenhorn like myself. I was in for a surprise, not to say a shock. A few weeks later, one of the Kantibai's neighbours, Sheikh Ali, the chief of the Ad Takleis tribe, turned up in a state of breathless agitation. Part of his tribe was in revolt, he said. He needed help urgently. What were they revolting about? This reduced him to a fit of near incoherence which seemed to say, 'Well, that's pretty rich coming from you!' They were revolting, he replied, because they thought they were as good as he was. They were Bolshevists. I got the message. I had started a forest fire.

We found the rebels encamped by the side of a dry water course. There were about three hundred of them in all: looking, I was relieved to see, as peaceful as a party of choir boys. Sheikh Ali, who looked anything but peaceful, immediately began haranguing and threatening with his eye firmly fixed on a little gnome of a man. 'That,' he said, wagging a fierce finger at him, 'is the maker of this mischief!' This Wat Tyler's name was Mohammad Taiyeh and, unlike his companions, he was no Bedouin. He wore a turban which was the local equivalent of a white collar; and, as an instructor in the mysteries of the Holy Q'ran, he qualified as a man of letters. Was it true, I asked, that he had refused to obey his chief? No, he replied, it was not true. This gentleman was not his chief. Sheikh Ali immediately began reacting furiously and the assembled tribesmen to bay incomprehensibles at him. When both sides had grown tired, I carried on with my enquiry. A surprise awaited me.

What was at the bottom of this rumpus was the fact that these shock-headed tribesmen were serfs: the sort of serfs that there had been in Russia during the bad old Tsarist days. Serfs, that is to say, who had to part with so many goats, sheep and even camels when their masters celebrated births, circumcisions, marriages and deaths. The reason why they were serfs was that their own clan had been conquered in the distant past by Sheikh Ali's and had then been divided amongst them. It was against this feudal system that Mohammad Taiyeh was in revolt: not just against the payment of dues but also against the overlordship of Sheikh Ali and all his uncles, brothers, nephews, sons and cousins. When he refused to acknowledge Sheikh Ali as his chief, he was in effect issuing a unilateral declaration of his own clan's independence. He was trying to put the clock back to the 'status quo ante' before Sheikh Ali's ancestors carved it up. This was not the little storm in a teacup I had expected. It was a king-size hurricane.

This was because the same feudal system as that of the Ad Tekleis also prevailed among the Habab and every other tribe throughout Western Eritrea. Everywhere a patrician tenth of the population, decently robed and turbanned, lived in manicured and scented ease at the expense of the servile and sweaty rest. It didn't need a clairvoyant to [see] that, if

Mohammed Taiyeh got what he was after, other Mohammed Tayehs would be popping up all over the place. There were no two ways about it: whether he liked it or not, Mohammed Taiyeh's chief was Sheikh Ali and he would have to obey him. 'Never!' the little man shouted. I coaxed, wheedled and threatened but drew a blank. There was nothing for it but to resort to my ultimate deterrent—prison bars. 'Amen!' said Mohammed Taiyeh, dead pan and unblinking. 'Do as you please!' I gaoled him. His followers promptly caved in and that was that.

So I thought; but in fact it was what Churchill would have called the end of the beginning. Within a few weeks Sheikh Hidad arrived with a curt dispatch from the Kantibai who wanted the police again. He was having trouble with another lot of his 'Arabs'. A paragraph of 'I told you so's' followed. The 'Arabs' (according to Hidad) were refusing to pay their taxes which seemed odd because the Kantibai had only recently paid up the amount due from the Habab. Pressed, Sheikh Hidad explained that he was not talking about Government tax but about customary taxes, that was to say feudal dues. I was not concerned with customary taxes, I said, a little primly, nor were my police. His eyebrows signalled displeasure. Did I mean that I would let tribesmen defy their chief? Not if he were acting on behalf of the Government, I replied. He was in no mood for nit-picking. 'Either you support chiefs or you don't!' he said, giving my desk a thump. 'If you do not, the responsibility for the consequences is yours!' How could I let our police be used to bully the serfs into stocking the gentry's larders with mutton and goat? It was obviously not on. Even so, in my heart of hearts, I suspected that Sheikh Hidad was right and the coming months proved it. In some cases the noblesse managed to keep their serfs in hand, in others the serfs broke loose. When they did so, they defied their chiefs and then I had to step in. It was a tricky situation and I was at a loss to see where it would end.

My superiors in Asmara had, up to this point, shown only a token interest in our troubles. They had more pressing problems to tackle: not least that of humouring Kennedy Cooke's successor, Stephen Longrigg, the new Military Administrator. Cold of eye and sharp of tongue, Longrigg was not easily humoured. He was a scholar and Arabist of distinction but no dreamy academic. Having served for some years as chief negotiator to the Iraq Petroleum Company, he had rubbed shoulders with every Arab King, Prince and public nuisance in the Middle East and the experience had made him a shrewd, cynical and highly intolerant connoisseur of human frailty. Suffering fools at all, let alone gladly, was not his line and since, observed from his intellectual height, most of those around him had the appearance of fools, he always kept a sharp and suspicious weather eye open for follies and faults. A free-for-all amongst the Ad Takleis during which a couple of serfs bit the dust immediately caught his attention. Quiver loads of questions came homing in on me. In their wake came Longrigg himself.

On arrival he eyed me coldly. 'Where's Last?' he asked. 'He's the Senior Political Officer, isn't he?' Last had decided to go sick for the occasion. Longrigg received the news with a petulant sniff and then asked me to explain what had been happening. When I had finished he gave me a pulverising look. 'You are, I suppose, aware that we are fighting a war?' he asked, 'And you would, I imagine, agree that this is hardly the time to upset established institutions and so weaken authority?' His cold eye, long contemptuous nose and curling lip pronounced me guilty of unbelievable folly. The upshot of his visit was that there must be a stop to 'this nonsense'. The chiefs were to be given the fullest support and the serfs were to be kept in their customary places. There was to be no more tinkering about with the feudal system.

A few days later, Newbold appeared out of the blue looking a picture of avuncular bonhomie. He had taken a bit of leave to have a look round, he said. We talked for a while about his plans for partitioning Eritrea and where the partition line should run. After doodling about with a map for a while, Newbold suddenly gave me a sly look and asked how I was getting on with Longrigg. That, as you may imagine, set me off on a querulous rampage over the events which had ended with Longrigg's devastating visitation. I was full of youthful moral indignation. Newbold sucked pensively on his pipe and then, when I had run out of steam, said, 'Longrigg is a hundred per cent right.' Was this really Uncle Newbold speaking? It was indeed. There was, he argued, no possible way of disentangling the chiefs from their feudal system. If you tried to phase out feudalism, as I was doing, you would only undermine their authority and end up with anarchy. The alternatives were clear cut: either you kept the present system intact or you scrapped it and put something else in its place. To scrap it entailed risk and so, while the War was still being fought, that had to be ruled out. The time to scrap it was when the War was over. Now was the time to plan how and with what it should be replaced. That, he said, was what he was doing.

Yes, he was faced with much the same problem. The tribal system in the Eastern Sudan was not so very different from ours. In each there was a ruling patrician elite with similar customary rights and perks. Up to the present, Newbold explained, our policy had been one of upholding the system but not interfering with it. That was what we meant by 'indirect rule' and, for all its faults, 'indirect rule' had served us well. We could never have run a country as large as the Sudan without it. But, because it had served us well in the past, it did not mean that it would do so indefinitely in the future. We had to move with the times and once the upheavals which he could foresee took place after the War, he had no doubt that we would have to move very fast indeed. There would be no room for antique tribal systems in the Sudan of the future. 'So you had better put your thinking cap on!' Newbold said in conclusion. He left me with a lot to think about.

6

PEACE, PROGRESS AND A LITTLE PROSPERITY

Returning in late October 1942, saddle-sore and weary after a trip in the mountains sedating over-excitable serfs, I was met by our Sudanese Police Sergeant. Eyes dancing, hands waving and his throat gargling with delight, he told me that we had won the War. It couldn't be true! By God, it was! He had heard it on the BBC. Why, Zanos—the Greek with the little cafe just off the market square—had celebrated by punching a couple of Italians in the face and he would hardly have done that had he not known that we had won the War. My friend had not, in fact, got it quite right. What we had won was the Battle of El Alamein. We had, however, defeated the legendary Rommel and as good as won the War in Africa.

And what a blessed relief that was. With the sole exception of that one brief spell at the end of 1941 when Auchinleck had forced him to withdraw beyond Benghazi, Rommel had lurked menacingly in the background poised to overrun Egypt. He was a nightmare and yet ironically he, of all people, was Eritrea's Saviour. Because of his threat to Egypt, GHQ in Cairo decided to move some of their base installations to Eritrea with its superb infrastructure, silent workshops and highly skilled but idle work force. The effect of this had been to alert Eritrea's regiments of latent Italian entrepreneurs to the country's extraordinary industrial potential just as the Middle East's need for manufactured goods, previously imported from Europe, was beginning to make itself felt. Longrigg was the first to see that the Middle East's need was Eritrea's opportunity and he, more than anyone, made sure that Eritrea did not miss it. The light industrial revolution which followed transformed Eritrea. Within a month or two the bankrupt, desolate little country we had taken over was not only viable, it was flourishing.

Peace and what amounted to plenty brought an end to the siege atmosphere in which we had been living up to then; and so, where Longrigg's reaction to 'bright ideas' had been to knock them sharply on the head he now sometimes did their authors the courtesy of appraising them. The truth of the matter was that we Political Officers were getting restive. By this time we had sorted our districts out. Law and Order were being maintained, revenue was being collected and such public and social services as we had were working reasonably well. In other words, we were doing all that we could be expected to do as 'caretakers'. But was that enough? Should we be content to keep the Eritreans marking time indefinitely as the Italians had done? Since every one of us had been telling every Eritrean within earshot how, by contrast with the Italians, we were educating our colonial wards for self-government, the answer could only be 'no'.

Tackling Longrigg on the subject during a long, bumpy ride up the Coast to the Sudan frontier, I did not get too encouraging a reply. The Middle East where he had served for so long was a graveyard of strangled illusions and living cheek by jowl with the stark crudity of oriental life, had given him a hard, cold, unsentimental eye trained to see the worst and never the best in people. And so, on being told that the Eritreans would gush gratitude for being given a helping hand, he drily remarked that it would be more in character if they bit it. By his reckoning it was absurdly naive to imagine that a subject people like the Eritreans would ever be grateful or feel any affection for us. To talk about winning their hearts and minds was nonsense. They weren't on offer. The merest suggestion that Eritreans had hearts and minds or the least capacity for gratitude and affection immediately sent Longrigg off into a fit of the yawns. When he was not yawning, he was dozing.

Nevertheless, he swallowed his disdain for our fanciful notions and gave the 'go ahead' for District Advisory Councils and Native Courts to be set up on the conventional Colonial Office model. Here was a great leap forward which would have been unthinkable under the Italians; and yet, if any Eritrean fell about with delight at the news, I did not come across him. Chatting here and there while doing my rounds I could find no enthusiasm for what we had done. What conceivable advice worth having would we get from the chiefs and bigwigs we had appointed to the Council, I would be asked. And did we really believe that this 'Native Court' would dispense Justice? Didn't I know that Moslems would favour Moslems and Christians Christians and that, even if religious differences did not enter the picture, tribal, clan and family prejudices certainly would? Why couldn't we leave well alone, Negassi asked. What was to be gained by setting up these Councils and Courts? I tried to explain. We were attempting to train Eritreans to take on the responsibilities they would have to shoulder when they eventually gained self-government, I told him. And what made me think that they wanted self-government? But didn't he? Not if it meant finding himself under a Moslem Government! That was how everyone seemed to feel. Christians did not want to risk finding themselves under Moslems and vice versa. No one wanted to take a great leap forward into the dark.

What Eritreans wanted and would willingly have sold their immortal souls for was Education: the 'Open Sesame' to jobs, status and power. What the Italians had bequeathed us in the way of Eritrean education was a scandal. They had never taken it seriously or, to put it another way, they had taken it sufficiently seriously to make sure that Eritreans did not get more of the stuff than was good for them. They needed a few literate and numerate Eritrean hacks to work in their offices, not Doctors of Politics and Economics who would have wanted to take over the country. That was why the Swedish Evangelical Mission, which had been licenced to operate a few schools in the '20s, had been ordered to close down in 1932. It had committed the unforgivable sin of taking its pupils into forbidden intellectual territory. After that, Eritrean education had been rationed to the Three Rs and a smattering of arts and crafts. It had only been provided at a handful of schools and to a handful of pupils. Eritrean Education was so notorious a scandal that we were bound to do something about it. Belatedly we now did: in the most modest possible way. What GHQ Cairo was pleased to give us for the purpose were a humble Captain and a Church mouse scale budget. It was a gesture if not a joke and no one meeting the new Director of Education, Captain Kyneston-Snell, could believe that Eritrean education was being taken seriously. He had been recruited from the British Council in Cairo and spoke in a disconcerting falsetto. Affecting the precious manner of an

Oscar Wilde, he had a supercilious way of firing off erudite 'bon mots' and 'avant garde' opinions which were guaranteed and, evidently, intended to embarrass and irritate his listeners. No one was immune from his insolent witticisms, not even the irascible General who was our Area Commander. Encountering the General in the street a few days after his arrival, Kyneston-Snell failed to give him a salute. 'Don't you know who I am?' the General barked. 'I think not,' came the unexpected reply. 'I don't think we've been introduced.'

There was, however, more to this strange, spinterish figure than a clown. Behind the poseur there was a paragon. Get Kynaston-Snell down to his educational business and he would immediately set those outre airs aside. The supercilious dilettante would be gone and in his place emerged a professional talking about teacher training, the languages of instruction to be used, the drafting of text books, the ratio of pupils to teachers, the size of class rooms, where classroom windows should be sited and all the other minutiae of the educational business. Visiting Keren, he told me that he took Education seriously and hoped that I did. If I merely sought to keep up appearances by dotting a few schools about the countryside as I would 'objets d'art' on a mantelpiece, then there was nothing that he could offer. After I had assured him that I was no educational philanderer, he suddenly looked up and said, 'Be sure of one thing, however. If you educate, you educate for discontent.' It was a saying I was not to forget.

By this time he had got hold of a Glaswegian Sergeant with Marxist leanings called Robinson, from the Education Corps, and a barrel-bellied Abyssinian of dignified appearance called Ishak Twoldemedhin. With their help, he had already started training a few potential teachers and all but completed drafting text books for use in the schools. Ishak, Kynaston-Snell explained, was doing sterling work translating them into Tigrinya. Tigrinya? The language of the Christian Abyssinians, a language written in the archaic Ethiopian script conserved by and associated with the Coptic Abyssinian Church? Was it really intended to instruct Moslem children in it? Kynaston-Snell cocked an eyebrow at the portly Ishak. Humming and haahing, Ishak begged to observe that Tigrinya was Eritrea's only written language and was, moreover, the language of the majority of Eritreans. Maybe, I said, but if Tigrinya was to be the language of instruction for Moslem boys I could assure him that precious few of them would go to school. Moslem boys would expect to be taught in Arabic. Ishak huffed and puffed a bit, saying that it hardly seemed worth upsetting everything just to humour Moslems who were, after all, only a lot of backward cowherds and shepherds. He was, however, overruled and did not look too happy about it.

How Kynaston-Snell proposed to put Education on the map with the slender budget he had been granted I could not imagine. And yet with funds intended for, say, half a dozen schools he managed to get four times that number on stream. If a Community wanted a school, he said, they would have to pay to have it built, equipped and maintained themselves. He would provide the teachers. But would the Communities cough up? They did so with enthusiasm, the reason being that fathers traditionally expected their sons to meet the cost of their old age and, naturally, believed that sons with a decent schooling would do so in a more lavish fashion than sons without one. As the funds came pouring in, a difficulty arose. Who was to administer them? The chiefs, of course. They were, after all, the local civil authorities. At this Sergeant Robinson let out a wail of republican bagpipe noise, saying that the money belonged to 'the People' and should be handled by the 'People'. Kynaston-Snell stressed the importance of getting local communities involved and urged the appointment of local School Committees. Ishak agreed, mumbling suspicions that, if the chiefs had anything to do with the funds, they would siphon part of them off for their own personal use. The Educationalists were not being unreasonable but the chiefs were chiefs and I could not believe that it would be right to exclude them totally from the picture. It would undermine their authority and, as things stood, if theirs was undermined so ours would be, too. In the end, we agreed on a compromise: School Committees were to be set up but with the chiefs as their Chairmen. As is the way with compromises, it pleased no one.

So I came to learn on the arrival one day of Shum Hummed, the Moslem chieftain of a considerable tribe called the Maria. Heavily perfumed and splendidly garbed, he came into my house looking as if he had stepped out of a miniature from Isfahan. Having greeted me unhurriedly, he paused for a while stroking his exquisitely manicured beard. As a friend of the British, might he speak freely, he asked. I would know, he continued, that the Prophet had forbidden the drinking of wine. Why? Because he knew that, in their ignorance, Moslems would get drunk.

Wasn't that so? I nodded. Well, then, did I not realise that fools could get drunk on ideas quite as easily as on wine and that, if I went ahead with this school business, every boy in the place would become a ranting menace? Then there was another thing: did I realise that some of the young men who had been taken off to be trained as teachers were serfs? Well, I could guess that the last thing they would be teaching their pupils would be respect for their betters! Shum Hummed's disenchantment with our educational essay was echoed by most of his Eritrean peers.

Kynaston-Snell was well pleased with the success of his enterprise but even so he could see disaster ahead. What, he asked, was the use of his giving Eritreans hopes of jobs in the top brackets if we did nothing to provide them? What was he fussing about? His schoolboys would not be in the market for jobs for another five or six years. I seemed to have over looked the hundreds of Eritreans graduating from his Adult Education Centre, he said. I had.

During this tricky menopausal state of the country, what Eritreans of the brighter sort were waiting to see was whether we would admit Eritreans into jobs hitherto reserved for Whites; or, to put it as Howar Sheikh, our Office Manager, so quaintly expressed himself, 'We have always been ants. Are we now to become butterflies?' And so, modest though the innovation was, the appointment of a few Eritreans as Police Inspectors was of revolutionary significance. Had there only been one Sam Browned Eritrean officer, Eritrean eyes would have goggled with disbelief. Since about a couple of dozen made their bow, they caused a sensation. For perhaps a month we glowed happily in the warmth of Eritrean smiles and then the frost set in. Cantankerous chiefs tabled complaints that these young Jacks in Office were interfering in their business. Moslems complained that Christian Inspectors were maltreating them, Christians that Moslem Inspectors were behaving improperly. And then there were complaints from all sides that Eritrean officers were showing favour to their friends and relations. Everything seemed to be going splendidly, Newbold wrote after receiving a letter of mine telling him of all this. If there had been no complaints it would have meant that we were keeping too tight a control on the Inspectors. I rather doubted whether Longrigg would have shared so eccentric a view.

My time was so taken up with one thing and another during those exciting days that I did not have much of it to offer Antonelli. When I did

Peace, Progress and a Little Prosperity

occasionally see him, the old man would wag a courteous head in regret at what we were doing. Schools, Eritrean Police Inspectors, Councils, Courts... he would let out a despairing laugh and say that he thought we must be mad. Just because the Italians had taught Eritreans to salute and say, 'Si, Signor' it did not mean that they were a civilised people. They were still savages and, if we carried on as we did, they would get out of control. Why were we doing all this? he asked. Why were we giving ourselves all this trouble? It didn't make sense!

It was just after one of these encounters that Last appeared with a sunny smile on his face. He was off to better things, he announced. Rommel's defeat in North Africa had brought Italy's two Libyan colonies of Cyrenaica and Tripolitania under British administration and he had been given the job of the Secretary of something high falutin' in one of them. For myself this was good news. Although I had, in fact, been running the district, my equivocal position had been an inconvenience and, sometimes, an embarrassment. To be the Senior Political Officer in charge of the District would make life very much easier. I had, of course, assumed that I would be succeeding Last. And why not? I was his obvious successor: I had spent two years in Keren during which I had virtually been in charge for one. I had explored every region, visited every tribal stamping ground and village, I was 'au fait' with the ramifications of tribal politics and knew most tribal clan and village leaders well. I had just written a two hundred page treatise on the history, way of life and customs of the people. As one of my colleagues laughingly called me, I was 'Mr Keren'.

Imagine then the upsurge of blood to my head when a letter arrived from Longrigg's Secretariat to tell me that an elderly officer called Stranger-Ford was to replace Last. It was a laughable appointment. The poor man was by background a business man from Cairo who had been running our Trade Office. Nobody could have been less suited for the job. Blind to the impropriety of what I was doing, I fired off a letter to Longrigg telling him so. My letter came back by return of post with a covering note from Longrigg. It said, 'I hereby return this missive which I have no desire to keep on my files.' A telephone call from the Secretariat followed, ordering me to transfer myself at once to Assab, Eritrea's 'Devil's Isle'. It was the last letter I ever wrote with my blood on the boil.

7

A WHIFF OF ETHIOPIAN IMPERIALISM IN THE AIR

IT TOOK ME NEARLY TWO HOURS rattling around in a Blenheim bomber to reach Assab. It was a bumpy ride over one of Nature's most spectacular disaster areas. Within minutes of leaving Asmara, we lost sight of the soft green and gold patches quilting the highlands and looked down on utter desolation. Stretched out below us was a moonscape fringed on one side by the shimmering haze shrouding the Red Sea and, on the other, by the dark flanks of the Ethiopian highland massif. Grim mountains stripped bare of life looked up at us out of a blistering sea of sand and gravel. Here and there extinct and some live volcanoes stood brooding apart within great untidy circles of congealed lava. The only hint of life in this barren, forsaken land was at the foot of the Ethiopian mountains where rainwater had slipped down to spawn a few patches of green. Appropriately this ghastly Devil's playground belonged to the most devilish of peoples, the Danakil, amongst whom murder, followed by castration of the deceased, was a national sport. The more dead men's testicles one of these savages was able to flaunt, the greater was his prestige.

After an hour's flight bouncing in the heat, we saw a small white speck appearing out of the haze hanging over the sea. It was Assab. The heat was stupefying, the humidity over the top and, at close quarters, I could see that Assab was a dump and a dead one at that. The little partially modernised port which was its sole 'raison d'etre' was cluttered up with scuttled Italian ships and was now usable only by dhows, and then only a few at a time. Its small commercial activity was in the hands of a couple of dozen Yemeni merchants who exported Ethiopian goods to Aden and imported Aden's goods for onward despatch to Ethiopia. They kept very much to themselves, drinking coffee with each other in the mornings and getting fuddled in the evenings chewing a narcotic shrub called 'qat'. Hovering around them was a little band of Greek, Italian and Levantine entrepreneurs who were usually to be found doing their business in or around Assab's one sleazy bar. Lower down the social scale there were a few Abyssinian hacks who tapped typewriters in the Arabs' offices and a couple of thousand Sudanese, Somalis and local detribalised Danakil who earned a precarious living as labourers and petty thieves. To complete the picture there was the customary troupe of Abyssinian harlots and their Madame.

Apart from these cheerful ladies, there was hardly a woman to be seen in the place. Nor were there any children. There was no such thing as an Assab community. It was nobody's home. It was a transit camp where people came to make what they could and then get out. No scope here for useful, exciting work, as Commandant of a transit camp! There was, it is true, also an Assab district for which I was responsible but one look at what it amounted to told me that it had even less to offer than Assab town. It was nothing more than a three hundred mile long and fifty mile wide coastal strip linking Assab with Eritrea proper. It was uninhabited and no one visited it. In the immediate vicinity of Assab, however, there were three small fishing villages and, in hopes of getting some satisfaction out of nannying them, I made a point of visiting them soon after my arrival. Calling in on the first I found almost everyone in a state of incoherent inebriation as a result of drinking a demon toddy made from the resin of palm trees. At the two others I received a sullen and surly welcome. Had they anything they would like to say to me? No. They wanted nothing from me. If they wanted anything they would go to their Sultan, the Sultan of Aussa. Emaciated and, with nothing more than ragged loin cloths round their middles, they eyed me, like so many little fiends, with utter loathing. I have never been made to feel so unwanted.

That wild, malevolent look of theirs was the look of the savage with his instinctive terror of the unknown and it was a reminder of just how little the Danakil had been touched by the changing world around them. They remained, as for centuries past, imprisoned in the total isolation of their deserts and few oases lying in the shadow of the Ethiopian highlands. After massacring three Italian exploratory expeditions to the interior, they had been able to ignore the outside world, disregarding those few Italians bottled up in Assab. They were able to carry on as they had always done, killing and castrating each other under the nominal aegis of the Sultan of Aussa. Neither the Sultan nor his subjects doubted that he was a sovereign ruler as he had always been; nobody had told them that, when the British, the French and the Italians divided amongst themselves the Somali coast at the turn of the century, the Emperor Menelik of Ethiopia had added the Danakil his Empire, together with the Somalis of Ogaden, the Arab-Somalis of the old Emirate of Harar and the Galla hordes far away in the South. That the Danakil and the rest had become Ethiopian subjects was fully evidenced by treaties, conventions and maps but, since neither the Sultan nor his subjects knew anything about them, they had no reason to believe that their relationship with their Abyssinian neighbours had been altered in any way. Why should they have? Nothing had changed. They continued as always to raid and be raided by them. No Abyssinians had ever approached any of them with pretensions to rule.

None of this would ever have crossed my mind had we not become closely tied up with the legendary Sultan Mohammed Yao, seated two hundred miles away to the south-west in his lush pastures of Aussa. Needing his help to mount a blockade by land against the faithless French in Djibuti, we had, with the agreement of his legal Sovereign, the Emperor Haile Selassie, taken him onto our pay-roll and, since the French eventually capitulated, it could said that we were well rewarded for doing so. But it created an awkward problem. Having served the British interest faithfully and well, the Sultan clearly believed that he now qualified to be His Majesty King George's generously paid ally for life, whereas the unpleasant truth of the matter was that he had worked himself out of his job. No one had cared to tell him so and since, in the absence of any reaction from Haile Selassie, we had carried on paying him his stipend, he could only have assumed that he had been accepted as our man for good. Obviously, this could not go on much longer. Nor did it. The Sultan was struck off our payroll during my last weeks at Assab and it was I who was given the job of breaking the bad news.

I had to break it to the Sultan's Representative who used to come to Assab each month to collect his stipend and a box or two of ammunition to go on with. He arrived as usual in an old Italian Army truck with an escort of ragged soldiery and a few near-naked slaves to hump any stores he might wish to pick up. He had a handsome Arab face with sad, heavily-lidded eyes and, on this occasion, he looked particularly downcast. They had had bad news, he said, giving me a letter from 'His Majesty King George's true friend and ally'. The Abyssinians were collecting an Army to invade Aussa and take it over, the Sultan had written, so would I please come and help them defend themselves. Help them? And here was I on the point of saying that our friendship was over, thank you very much, and that the Ambassador's master was off our payroll. To tell him this was a nightmare. When I tried to explain that the Emperor Haile Selassie was the Sultan's sovereign and that it had only been with his agreement that we had had our arrangement, his eyes opened up in a frenzy of despair. It was all lies, he wailed, all Abyssinian lies! Haile Selassie was not their ruler. He was their enemy. Having argued himself to a standstill, he departed, leaving me in a state of guilt-ridden confusion. The inevitable duly happened. Haile Selassie's troops invaded Aussa and took it over. Mohammad Yao was removed in chains to Addis Ababa where he died of unexplained causes in a prison cell.

Soon after the poor 'Ambassador's' visit, I was sent to Asmara on sick leave to recover from a rash of suppurating sores. I felt bad about the way we had let the Sultan down and made a point of calling on Longrigg to tell him so. I had no monopoly of sympathy for the Sultan, he asked me to remember in a cold, dry voice. Facts were facts and the fact was that, in law, the Sultan was the Emperor's subject and there was nothing we could do about it. Not only that, our relationship with Ethiopia was going dangerously sour and to quarrel over an unimportant savage like the Sultan over whom we had no claim whatsoever would have been unforgiveable folly. Seated in Longrigg's office, hundreds of miles away from Aussa, I could accept what he said. Had the 'Ambassador' with the sad eyes been there, it would have been another story.

As Longrigg explained, the Ethiopians were in a fractious mood. Having damned the Italians with the apparent blessing of the Allies as so many war criminals who had done such terrible things to poor little Ethiopia, they were now appalled to learn that the Allies had done a 'volte face'. The Italian geese had become swans. The reason for this was that the Italians had switched sides and, on coming over to us, had been instantly converted from enemies into 'co-belligerents' or allies by another name. There was no talk now of their being war criminals: it was the Fascists who were to blame. Indeed, by the same way of thinking, the Italian people themselves were to be considered victims of Fascist oppression and in need of special help and sympathy. So, with the Allies treating the Italians like prodigal sons, the Ethiopians began to suspect that they might be intending to hand Eritrea back to them. Having all along assumed that the Allies would back their claims to Eritrea as a matter of right, and extract compensation for what they had suffered, this was a shattering thought. In desperation they were turning to desperate measures, Longrigg believed. What they seemed to be planning was a massive pro-Ethiopia nationalist movement which would give warning of the strength of Eritrean feeling and preempt any pro-Italian decision. It was strange, Longrigg mused, how it was invariably with the onset of peace that political stability came under threat.

Now that an Ethiopian claim to take over Eritrea was likely to find a place on the agenda, I naturally wondered what the Eritreans would make of it. Ethiopia, one had to remember, was an empire shamelessly created by and run for the benefit of the Abyssinian imperial rulers. They—their Shoan branch in particular—got all the jobs, schools, hospitals and so on. Their colonial subjects—Danakil, Somalis, and Galla—existed only to be squeezed and clobbered for the Abyssinian good. I could see that, as members of the privileged imperial race, Eritrea's Abyssinian population might well find Ethiopian rule preferable to the return of an Italian regime but the same could not be said for the Moslem tribes. Unquestionably, they would have the same status as Ethiopia's other colonial subjects. As Ishak, the Educationalist had so condescendingly put it, they were only shepherds and herdsmen. In Abyssinian eyes they did not count. It was, of course, to spare them the horrors of Ethiopian rule and all that would flow from it that Newbold had come up with his partition proposals. I could see that we might be turning to them sooner than expected.

With the decks being cleared for action, I returned reluctantly to the backwoods of Assab. It was, however, not for long. A couple of weeks later I was told to take over Asmara's rural district, the Hamasien. It stood at the heart of Abyssinian Eritrea and I could not have asked for anything better.

8

ETHIOPIAN MISCHIEF

THE FAMILIAR BAYING of peasant protest welcomed me to the headquarters of the Senior Political Officer in charge of Asmara. A sizeable crowd of rustics and clergy were assembled at the entrance over which a solitary police constable stood guard. It was a familiar scene. 'Is this over a land dispute?' I asked. Yes, it was, the policeman replied. The Italians had stolen these poor people's land and [they] wanted it back. And then, giving me a sly look, he added, 'They say that, if they don't get justice from you, they'll get it from the Negus!' By the Negus he meant the Emperor Haile Selassie. Here was a straw in the wind and no mistake.

I found the Senior Political Officer at his desk nursing a careworn face. He was a gentle giant called Stanley Parker who had been Editor of the *Egyptian Gazette* before joining us and the experience of reporting the ups and more frequent downs of the Anglo-Egyptian relationship had left him with large, sad eyes. I understood that the Ethiopians were trying to stir things up, I said. That was quite untrue, he snapped, and just the sort of irresponsible talk that gave so much unnecessary offence. Wasn't he having any trouble, then? Yes, he was, but it was no fault of the Ethiopians. The fault was entirely ours. If I didn't know that, it was about time that I did! Our failure to hand Eritrea back to Ethiopia was a monumental and indefensible injustice. As everyone knew, Eritrea was a part of Ethiopia which the Italians had taken by force and it should have been handed back to our loyal ally, the Emperor, at the same time as we handed him back the rest of his Empire. That we were only doing what we had to do under International Law he dismissed with derision as 'Lawyers' window dressing' and, when I suggested that Ethiopia's claims to the whole of Eritrea might not be quite as clear cut as he believed, he said that I must have been reading Italian propaganda. He refused to countenance the thought that any Eritrean might object to Ethiopian rule, saying that the Eritreans knew that they were Ethiopians and were proud of it. He could almost have said the same about himself.

Clearly, this kindly old Teddy Bear was under a spell and no sharp eyes were needed to see that it had been cast by the bright-eyed young Abyssinian who hovered so courteously and considerately around him. This was Tedla Bairu, his interpreter-cum-adviser on Eritrean affairs and a very gifted one he was. A former protege of the Swedish Evangelical Mission, this exceptional young man was one of the very few Eritreans to have had anything in the way of higher education. Neat, well-spoken, superbly mannered, he was a gem. He knew the district like the back of his hand. Ask him the most out-of-the-way question and back would come the answer as if he were reading it off a computer. Nothing was too much trouble for this Admirable Crichton and, when it came to explaining how passionately Eritreans of every class and creed yearned for union with their Ethiopian Mother Country, he did not stint himself. That was what was so splendid about him, Stanley Parker would say. He was totally selfless, totally dedicated.

Now and again Tedla would send Stanley Parker into fits of excitement by announcing that the Eritrean Committee wished to come and see him. This Committee was a group of Abyssinians who had formerly held senior positions in the Italian Administration as chief clerks and interpreters but who were now out of work. Professing a patriotic concern for Eritrea's future, they spent their time passing resolutions in favour of union with Ethiopia and belabouring the Administration with protests which were mainly slanted against the Italians. They were all too evidently a bunch of self-appointed, self-seeking, mischief makers in Ethiopian pay, but to say anything of the kind would send Stanley Parker into wails of despair. Didn't I realise that the 'Eritrean Committee' was the Eritrean equivalent of the Indian Congress and its members were Eritrea's future leaders?

Life in the real world outside Stanley Parker's office was far from tranquil. Dark storm clouds were casting ominous shadows over Asmara and the Eritrean Plateau. The 'War projects' had already closed down and, with the gradual return of imports to the Middle East, some of Eritrea's new enterprises were beginning to falter. Since the great mass of less employable Italians had by this time been repatriated, the Italians did not as yet show any serious signs of wear and tear. Nor did the Moslem merchants and traders. It was the Abyssinian proletariat who had been hit and hit hard. They were the 'have nots'. The Italians and Moslems were the 'haves'. An agitator telling a crowd of Abyssinians that they were the victims of Italian and Moslem exploitation could count on their yelling their heads off for 'Mother Ethiopia'. Incidents of disorder multiplied and, each morning, Stanley Parker would look glumly at the daily reports with Tedla at his side. The answer was 'so very, very simple', he would sigh, we only had to announce that Eritrea was to be handed back to the Emperor and there would be instant peace. Tedla would concur with a melancholy wag of his head.

Asmara was not, of course, my beat. Mine was its rural district, the Hamasien. As I had expected, it closely resembled the 'Abyssinian districts' of Keren. Here, as there, peasants and priests had that same bizarre museum piece look of other-worldliness. There was, however, a difference. These people might look as if Solomon and Sheba were their near contemporaries but they did not talk like it. There was an unfamiliar air of townee sophistication about them and that, of course, came from Asmara, where thousands of their young men had worked or were still working. They were easily distinguishable by their grubby European clothes and total lack of Old World charm. And yet, no doubt about it, their elders treated these graceless youths with obvious respect—and this in a patriarchal set-up where Youth only spoke when spoken to. That was the general rule but here it was the young buckaroos from Asmara who did the talking while their elders gawked. The lad from the big city knew what was what and his grandfathers believed him.

And what were these young townsmen telling their grand-dads? A visit to the small village of Dekki Zeru gave me a pretty good idea. While sitting with the villagers gathered around bombarding me with requests and complaints, a youngish man in slacks and shirt relieved himself of a throatful of spittle and shouted 'I want a charcoal licence!' In a country ravaged by Man and goat, firewood was difficult to come by and since oil fuels were, at that time, in short supply, there was an insatiable demand for charcoal. Licences to make it, however, were given sparingly and only to those who had been approved by the Forestry Department. I told him that his application would be referred to the Forestry Department in the normal way. 'To the Forestry Department!' he guffawed, with a fine show of teeth and hilarity. Then, changing gear into gravel-voiced menace, he snapped, 'To those Italian officials who only give licences to their Italian friends!' This was the opening bar to a querulous recitative about the injustice of our letting the Italians have everything and the Eritreans nothing. He signed off snarling, 'If we can't find Justice here, we know where we can find it!' A murmur of sympathy rippled through the crowd like wind rustling through long grass. No votes there for British Justice.

That was the first of many similar episodes. Time and again I found myself being told that we were supporting Italian against Eritrean interests. Time and again I had an earful about looking for justice elsewhere. Time and again it was some young scamp from Asmara who did all the talking. To hear the wailing voices of protest, it seemed nothing was right. There was no wrong for which the British Administration was not responsible. Even the death of a child from measles was held against us because measles was said to be an Italian disease and it was our fault for letting the Italians go round spreading it. Nonsense such as this was spewed out for hours at a time and, everywhere, in the same form. Words, phrases, punchlines were almost identical—too nearly identical to be spontaneous. It was tub-thumping to order and it did not take an unusually perceptive eye to see that the orders were coming from the Eritrean Committee.

Now and again I would find members of the Committee being feted in some village to the accompaniment of popular demonstrations of filial love for Mother Ethiopia. Arriving once in Zazzega, one of the Hamasien's larger villages, I found the Committee's President, a loud-mouthed old reprobate called Gebremaskal Woldu, holding forth to a couple of thousand rustics. Whenever he delivered a punchline, the local schoolboys who were paraded in front of him would set up a chant of 'Ethiopia, Ethiopia!' under the direction of their school masters. The clergy, who were also on parade, signified assent by rattling rattles and drumming drums. And what had Gebrasmakal Woldu been talking about? He had been preaching about the 'promised land', he said with a bleary smile: yes, a promised land where Ethiopians came first and where there were no Italians or foreigners getting rich at their expense.

Stanley Parker refused to see anything in the least sinister about agitation of this kind. This was not a British Colony, he asked me to remember, and there was nothing treasonable in Eritreans wanting to be reunited with Ethiopia. Yes, but did he really believe that we should sit quietly back and do nothing while these Ethiopian agents pumped grievances into simple bucolic heads? Didn't he realise that they were stirring up hatred against the Italians and, for that matter, against ourselves? 'Yes, but whose fault is it?' Stanley Parker would ask. It was ours, of course. There was nothing we could do. We would just have to be patient. The patience of others, however, was beginning to wane. The Senior Political Officers of the other two districts of the Plateau, the Serae and Akkele Guzai, were demanding action against the mischievous Eritrean Committee. The Commissioner of Police was beginning to talk of subversive Ethiopian influences at work in his Force. Accusing eyes began to focus on Stanley Parker with demands to know what the blazes he was doing about the 'vipers' nest' in Asmara. At last, predictably, Longrigg had enough. Telling Stanley Parker that he proposed to deal with the mischief-maker in chief, he summoned the Abuna Marcos, the Coptic Bishop of Asmara.

'Mischief-maker in chief!' Stanley Parker was deeply shocked for he had an overweening regard for 'His Beatitude' whom he would sometimes describe as a 'Saint' and at others as a 'Cardinal Wolsey.' The Bishop made no secret that he shared his flock's longing for union with Ethiopia but was that wrong? Stanley Parker wished to know. Was it wrong that the Bishop should, from time to time, visit his Emperor in Addis Ababa and keep him informed of the state of the Church in Eritrea? The Church, after all, was indivisible and, though Bishop of Eritrea, the Abuna was a Bishop of the Church of all Ethiopia. Longrigg dismissed all such special pleading, saying that one only had to see how the tempo of agitation immediately heightened on the Bishop's return from a visit to Addis Ababa to know that he had come back with orders and cash. As far as he was concerned, the Bishop was the Root of all Evil.

For all his poor opinion of the Bishop, there was not very much that Longrigg could do about him. It was no crime to preach the Ethiopian gospel and Longrigg had no chance of nailing anything worse on him. He could and did appeal to whatever better nature lay hidden beneath the Bishop's flowing, black robes to exercise his influence to put a stop to demonstrations which could get out of hand. The Bishop gave Longrigg all the assurances he sought and, having bowed himself out gracefully, carried on just as before. Longrigg thereupon issued a proclamation forbidding public gatherings and the flying of 'foreign flags'. To sidestep this was child's play for the quick-footed Bishop. Pro-Ethiopian demonstrations continued as before but under ecclesiastical cover. The honouring of the Church's innumerable saints and the celebration of its limitless days were now devoted to preaching, praying and cheering for union with Ethiopia and, since the Ethiopian flag was also that of the Church, it flew proudly over the celebrants on all such lively occasions. That looked like checkmate for Longrigg.

Then things began to happen in the Asmara Police. The Eritrean Police Force had been recruited in a hurry soon after our arrival to replace the Italian Police on whom we had until then had to depend. Since perfection in instant policemen was not to be expected, no one had taken their many inadequacies too seriously. But now, here and there, I and others, too, began to notice something more than mere sloppiness. They seemed to be surly, chip-on-the-shoulderish and bloody-minded. They quarrelled continually with and complained about the few Italian Police Officers who had been retained for various reasons of convenience. It was, however, only when they showed an unmistakable reluctance to tangle with pro-Ethiopian thugs who beat up Italians and Moslem traders that the penny eventually dropped. They, too, were being got at by the Bishop's mischievous friends! Quite by coincidence at this point as a means of saving money their British Officers decided to give them sandals instead of boots. Sandals! Every tavern in the town exploded in outrage at this insult to Eritrean honour. Sandals were for the ignorant and uncivilised. To accept them was to accept the humiliation of racial inferiority. No constable with an ounce of natural pride could possibly submit to the indignity of being debooted. Inflammatory words led to action. The Asmara Police went on strike.

What was to be done? About three thousand Policemen were sulking in their quarters, half a dozen NCOs had defected to Ethiopia and Asmara was virtually unpoliced. Stanley Parker tied himself in knots of despair over this calamity saying that, of course, the Police were right and we should give them back their boots with a handsome apology. Longrigg took a more old-fashioned view of the situation. Four Inspectors, known to have been ring-leaders, were promptly imprisoned together with five pro-Ethiopian activists who had made the loudest and most inflammatory noises. The rest of the Force was ordered to return to duty on pain of instant dismissal. In the event, they returned at once and to a man. The strike was broken. The Police Force was thereupon purged of all known political nuisances and we breathed again.

Stanley Parker alone felt unhappy at the result. Reaching for the new 'in' word of enlightened liberalism—'counter-productive'—he wailed over the terrible mistake that had been made. While he was agonising over our handling of the affair, Tedla appeared with an undertaker's face to announce that the Bishop and a party of senior citizens had arrived to protest at the internment of their 'innocent sons'. To relieve his poor, tortured conscience of the pain of this further twist of the rack, Stanley Parker hurried to the door to greet his visitors with a flurry of bows and bumbling courtesies. He was deeply distressed by this most unpleasant affair, he said. He had, in fact, had no hand in it himself. It had come as a complete surprise and he could assure His Beatitude it hurt him just as much as it hurt them. Yes, of course, he would see what could be done about the internees. All this he said in lowered, funereal tones. Every word was true. Every word was pumped out from a bleeding heart. Every word was a declaration of impotence.

To the surprise, perhaps even disappointment, of the anguishing Stanley Parker, Eritrea did not explode with outrage at Longrigg's old-fashioned handling of the Police Mutiny. It could have been the Punjab after General Dyer's 'tour de force' at Amritsar. As if at a signal, the entire pro-Ethiopian circus closed down. There were no more demonstrations, no more strikes, no more protests. The Bishop left for Addis Ababa, the Eritrea Committee went into retreat. Stanley Parker mooched around, a picture of misery nursing a bleeding heart. Having, by this time, had my fill of him and his sorrows, I could not believe my good luck on suddenly being told to move on and take over the Serae district. The prospect of life without Stanley Parker and his shadow, Tedla, seemed too good to be true.

9

THE CHRISTIAN ABYSSINIANS AND ETHIOPIA'S CLAIMS TO ERITREA

THE SENIOR POLITICAL OFFICER of the Serae district whom I was to relieve was a schoolmasterly type called Crawford. Clear skinned, bright eyed and crisp of speech, he was the Public School Spirit incarnate: a living memorial to cold baths on frosty mornings and six of the best for slacking. To him, everything was black or white. Grey areas never bothered him. When asked a question, he expected a 'yes' or 'no'. 'Buts' he treated as impertinences. Loyalty to one's team was the cardinal duty in his schoolboy code; disloyalty the unforgiveable sin. In his district he expected loyalty from the Eritreans and he made sure that everyone knew it.

He had no real trouble from the Bishop and his pro-Ethiopian scallywags, he told me. There had been a bit of tomfoolery at first—Ethiopian flags going up in schools, pro-Ethiopian speeches at Church festivals and nonsense of that sort—but he had put a stop to it pretty damned quick. A tail twisted here and a good wigging there had very soon put matters right. And what about young malcontents from Asmara? Had they been stirring up any trouble in the villages? None whatsoever, he replied, for the very good reason that the chiefs were under orders to deport them on sight. He could assure me that I was unlikely to see any of their ugly faces in the district. Say what you like about Crawford's methods, there was nothing equivocal about them. Every one knew precisely where he stood.

The Christian Abyssinians and Ethiopia's Claims to Eritrea

Over dinner at Adi Ugri, the District Headquarters, on Crawford's last night I asked whether there was much support for the Ethiopian cause in the district. 'None worth mentioning,' he replied. 'A few smart Alecs talking nonsense in the bars and coffee shops, a mad monk or two, no one of importance.' The chiefs, he explained, were all a hundred percent loyal and that was because their traditional leader, an ancient called Ras Kidanemariam, was one hundred percent anti-Ethiopian. Why was that? That was simply explained. He had gone over to the Italians as a young man at the time when they invaded Eritrea and he had fought on their side against the Emperor Menelik at Adowa in 1896. The old Ras was no fool. He knew that the Ethiopians had long memories and that he would be for the high jump if they ever got their hands on him.

I set off to see this pillar of the Adi Ugri Establishment soon after Crawford's departure. He lived in a little castle on the top of a steep hill where I found him waiting for me outside his front door swaying in the light breeze. One look was enough to tell me that he was as drunk as a sailor on shore leave. He was a frail wisp of a man topped by a head of fluffy white curls. Under him were two quivering skeletal legs, long overdue for retirement. On seeing me, the rickety old creature gurgled an incoherent salutation and then dived gently into my arms. This unusual reception was followed by a further surprise. Over the castle entrance there were two flags: one Ethiopian, the other a Union Jack.

I received an explanation for this unexpected Anglo-Ethiopian display from my host's son, Laine, in the dyspeptic aftermath of a luncheon of richly red-peppered stew and hair-curling mead. To look at his father now, he said, it was hard to believe that he had once been an outstanding warrior. Did I know that he had fought at the side of the Emperor Menelik against the Italians on that glorious day at Adowa? I knew something very different but let him carry on. After Adowa, the young mountebank continued, I could imagine his father's anguish on discovering that he had been left on what had become the Italian side of the frontier. Anguish? The Italians had rewarded the old devil royally for standing by them. His castle, chieftainship, land and title had all come from them. The fairy story ended appropriately with a happy ending: his liberation from Italian tyranny by ourselves. 'And so,' the sly young man concluded, 'he can now go to the grave in peace under the protection of his mother and father.' Who? Mother Ethiopia and Father Great Britain! The Ras was playing it both ways. So here was Crawford's loyalist who would never have any truck with Ethiopia!

With me at the time was my assistant, a portly young man called Johannes who had been carefully groomed to be Crawford's most obedient servant. He had trotted pug-like along behind Crawford with a look of canine awe in his large, expressionless eyes. He knew Crawford's rules as well as Crawford himself. Laine had broken them and he was clearly upset that I had not given him a good slap across the wrist for his impudent talk about Mother Ethiopia. 'Forgive me, sir,' he said, with a diffident little cough as we plodded home. 'If you don't give him a good lesson, he might tell everyone to follow Ethiopia and that would be very dangerous.' I didn't like disappointing him but I was no Crawford. If there were agitators around stirring up trouble, I was more than ready to give them a bit of stick; but twisting the tails of poor, soft-headed old fools who wanted to unite with Ethiopia was definitely not my job. Johannes gaped with disbelief. I had committed the greatest sin in Crawford's book: I had condoned what he would call disloyalty.

Disloyal or not, the Ras and Laine had my sympathy. These were awkward times for the unfortunate chiefs and, watching them looking this way and that for the sight of some straw in the wind, it was easy to see what was going on in their poor, tortured minds. If they turned their backs on the Bishop and Haile Selassie later took over, it would be off to the scrap heap for them. If they signed up with the Bishop and we in fact stayed put, it could mean incurring the wrath of some tail-twisting Crawford. They could try and play it both ways, of course, and despite their protestations of loyalty to Crawford, I had no doubt that that was what most of them had been doing. The difficulty of playing the two-faced game, however, is that there comes the time when one must jump one way or the other. The secret of success is to know when that time has come: which is why, at the time of my arrival in Adi Ugri, the chiefs, their kinsmen and courtiers were hopping around in a state of high agitation. What with Longrigg slapping down the mutinous police and sending the Bishop and his friends scurrying for cover, everyone was telling everyone else that the British meant to keep Ethiopia out. Would Longrigg now issue a proclamation declaring Eritrea British? Would he perhaps float a pro-British party first to convince Britain's allies that a British solution had popular support? Or would the British Government simply hand Eritrea back to the Italians to please the apparently Italophil Americans? With questions such as these buzzing about in their heads, every chief was waiting to see what would happen next. Something did indeed happen but never in a life time could any of them have foreseen it. To put it simply, Longrigg took leave of his senses and acted completely out of character.

The bizarre development which ensued took place in the third of the Plateau's three districts, the Akkele Guzai, and its author was Fitarouri Abraha, son of the district's equivalent to Ras Kidanemariam, another fluffy-headed ancient called Dejazmatch Tesemma. Unlike Laine, Abraha was a man of the twentieth century with an education in metropolitan Italy at his back. Balding, donnish and with the appealing look of a well-travelled suitcase, there was nothing he enjoyed more than a philosophical discussion. So, too, as it happened, did the district's Senior Political Officer, a meditative, pipe-puffing product of the Sudan Education Department called Basil Lee. They talked particularly about the future of Eritrea and, on this, they were both agreed: come what may, Ethiopia had to be kept out. Having laboured diligently bringing schools, clinics, Native Courts and Advisory Councils to life, Lee for his part could not bear to think of some Ethiopian barbarian destroying all his good work. Like most of us, he wanted to stay on until some responsible Eritreans were ready to carry on our good work. Abraha had other, more compelling, reasons for keeping Ethiopia out. For him, as for his father, it was a matter of political life or death.

This was because they were kinsmen of Ras Seyum, hereditary ruler of Haile Selassie's ever-rebellious province of the Tigrai,[1] and grandson of his eminent predecessor, the Emperor John. In contemporary Ethiopia, as in mediaeval Europe, men of such menacing eminence could not safely be allowed to go free; and, true to his country's traditions, Haile Selassie had taken the precaution of putting Ras Seyum and a clutch of his kinsmen away. Since Abraha and his father were outspoken protagonists as well as kinsmen of this Bonnie Prince Charlie, and were moreover believed to have had a hand in a recent Tigrinyan revolt which had all but cut the Tigrai loose from imperial rule, there was no doubt what would happen to them if Haile Selassie were to get his hands on Eritrea. Abraha saw only one sure answer. That was to excise the Tigrai from Ethiopia, merge it with Eritrea and so create a Greater Tigrai which would become independent and free. Not independent and free immediately, Lee would explain. Abraha was not one of those empty-headed ninnies who thought a country could be run without proper training and experience; and he knew only too well that his Tigrinya kinsmen would be starting from scratch. Thus an essential postulate to his plan for a Greater Tigrai would be an initial period of, say, ten years' British Trusteeship. The great thing about this splendid fellow, Abraha, Lee would say, was that he really understood and appreciated what we were trying to do. No doubt, either, that Abraha also understood and appreciated the need to get the British involved if this bright idea of his was to stand a chance.

Fanciful nonsense though I thought it, the Greater Tigrai plan was an instant success. Lee raved about it, Longrigg's advisers drooled over it and, finally, Longrigg himself swallowed it. It had, one must say, compelling attractions. The Abyssinian inhabitants of Eritrea's three Plateau districts were ethnically Tigrinvans and historically the districts had been a part, albeit a special part, of the Tigrai. On its own, neither Eritrea nor the Tigrai was economically viable; together they would add up to a good going concern. Lastly, the plan could be sure of the Tigrinyans' fervent support. That said, the idea was moonshine—pure pie in the sky. This was 1944, not 1884 and to imagine that any British Government would contemplate annexing Ethiopia's most ancient province or that Ethiopia would ever agree to letting the Tigrai secede was pure fantasy. Of all people, a wise old bird like Longrigg should have known this. As it was, he not only backed Abraha's folly, he let the whole of Eritrea know it.

This does not mean that he had so far taken leave of his senses as to proclaim this publicly. He did so more subtly, by boosting the Tesemma family and leaving it to be inferred that he would only be doing so because the Greater Tigrai plan had his support. As a start, the venerable Dejazmatch Tesemma was wheeled out ceremonially and elevated from Dejazmatch to the lofty status of Ras. Elevation for Abraha, from Fitarauri to Dejazmatch, followed after a decent interval. These were exceptional honours and, since exceptional honours are only awarded to those who are held in the very highest esteem by their rulers, the newly elevated Ras and his distinguished son were promptly besieged by the aggrieved and ambitious seeking compensation or advancement. The more successful their advocacy the more followers and hangers on they acquired. From being backwoodsmen in the Akkele Guzai, the Tesemma family were now soon firmly established on the Eritrean map.

When I first heard of the Greater Tigrai plan, it seemed good for a laugh but little else. I said something of the sort at a dinner party in Asmara and immediately came under fire from a young woman of considerable attraction sitting next to me. 'You don't know what you are talking about!' she blared, in the steamrollering way of someone who did. Africa was in the melting pot, she explained. It was crippled with anachronisms which we, the colonial powers, had tolerated for far too long and unless something was done about them, the whole continent would boil over with African discontent. The greatest anachronism of all, she continued, was Ethiopia with its scandalous Shoan regime and millions of oppressed subjects. Did I want to see Eritrea gobbled up by this monstrosity? Very well, then, what was the alternative? Colonial rule? Out of the question! Colonial rule was obviously going to be phased out. An independent Eritrea? That was nonsense. Eritrea was itself an anachronism and, in any case, it was not viable. Surely I could see that a Greater Tigrai was the only possible solution to the problem of Eritrea's future. It was right, rational and what the people wanted. Stunning me with a brilliant smile she said, 'Good! Now you understand!' and then proceeded to give the rest of the company present an account of how she would like to reorganise the African continent. She had a way with her which made for compulsive listening.

Compulsive listening was, of course, the lot of her husband and, as anyone knowing that amiable man would have expected, it was she and not he who was doing his job. It was a job of some local consequence for Major Mumford was the local representative of the Ministry of Information which had just set up shop in Asmara and published the only newspapers permitted under war-time regulations. Mrs Mumford's 'de facto' monopoly of the local Press had possibilities which did not escape Abraha's perceptive eye and, on discovering that her immediate ambition was to set herself up as an authority on Eritrea, he introduced her to a highly erudite young protege of his called Woldeab Woldemariam. A more charming or more informative tutor would have been hard to find and, to no one's surprise, Woldeab was very soon to the Mumfords what Tedla was to Stanley Parker. Having installed himself as the Ministry of Information office's officer in charge of Eritrean affairs, he quickly took over the editorship of its Eritrean newspapers and, of course, used them to boost the Greater Tigrai project. Offering his readers a great debate on the country's future in their correspondence columns, he would first publish poorly phrased and weakly argued letters in favour of union with Ethiopia, written under various pseudonyms by himself, and then follow these up with a further bunch of letters, also written by himself, arguing the case for a Greater Tigrai with great force and clarity. It was not a very subtle ploy and no doubt the pantomime was widely recognised for what it was. That did not matter. What mattered was that the British Ministry of Information's very own newspapers were backing the Greater Tigrai project. Who then could doubt that Britain was after the trusteeship of a Greater Tigrai?

Not many perhaps but one who was not quite sure was the faithful Johannes. Having met Tedla on a visit to Asmara and been told, on the authority of Stanley Parker, that the British Government had expressed an interest in the Greater Tigrai project, he was in a state of querulous anxiety. Could he please be told what British policy was, he wailed. How could he be expected to do his job if he did not know? Well, what was British policy? We could only hope that, when the time came to make a decision about Eritrea's future, Eritrean wishes would be taken into consideration. That was the official line. 'Yes, yes, yes!' poor Johannes moaned. But what did we want? Did we want to run Eritrea ourselves as a trusteeship? Did we want to hand it back to the Italians? Did we want a Greater Tigrai or did we want to give Eritrea to the Ethiopians? We must have some policy! He found it impossible to believe that we had none and so, no doubt, did the Serae's Vicars of Bray who were impatiently awaiting his advice.

Following this unsatisfactory discussion, the Serae's Noblesse came along to see how the land lay. One of the first was Laine with the doddering old Ras Kidanemarian in tow. His father wishes to assure the British Government of his fullest loyalty, Laine purred. Whatever was demanded of him he would do it: so long, of course, as it was consistent with his honour. I said that we had no demands to make on him other than that he should do his duty as a chief. Did that mean participating in 'this affair' of Tesemma's in the Akhele Guzai, he asked, eyes flickering with suspicion. Having received no instructions to back the Greater Tigrai project, I was able to give him an unequivocal 'No'. He seemed happier for that but left with the look of somebody who still had something on his mind. What was upsetting him and most of the other chiefs, Johannes later told me, was the rumour that we intended to make Ras Tesemma overlord for the whole Plateau. That was something which even the most craven Vicar would have found near impossible to swallow.

An unexpected visitor of a very different kind was the venerable head of Eritrea's Abyssinian Moslems, a merchant prince named Dejazmatch Hassan Ali. Since the 'Jiberti'[2] had always been treated as pariahs in Ethiopia, there had never been any doubt, except perhaps in poor Stanley Parker's imagination, that the last thing they would vote for would be union with Ethiopia. He and his Jiberti brothers were in a state of some confusion, the Dejazmatch confessed. This Greater Tigrai project was, of course, preferable to any form of union with Ethiopia, not least because there would be an initial spell of British trusteeship; but, however admirable, it had one grave defect. If Eritrea and the Tigrai were united, the Christians would have an overwhelming majority, and that would bode no good for the Moslems. Did I want the truth? he asked. I nodded. The truth was this, he continued. If the British did not want Eritrea, he and his brothers would like to have the Italians back. It was the first time that I had heard an Eritrean say that.

With speculation about the future running wild all around me, I naturally had a think about Douglas Newbold's proposals for Eritrea's partition. Seen from Adi Ugri in the Serae just after Hassan Ali had had his say about the Jiberti, they did not seem anything like as agreeable as they had when I had been seated in Keren. It was not that I saw any objection to slicing off Western Eritrea and handing it to the Sudan. Far from it. That made every kind of sense. What did not make any sense at all was letting Ethiopia take over the Moslems in other parts of Eritrea. Apart from Hassan Ali's Jiberti on the Plateau, there was the Moslem coastal district of Massawa; there were the Danakil's kinsmen, the Saho[3] tribes and, for what they were worth, there were the Danakil themselves. In total, almost one third of Eritrea's Moslems lived outside Western Eritrea and that was a lot to abandon. The way to look at it, Newbold argued in a persuasive reply to a little outburst of mine, was that we would be doing the decent thing by two thirds of Eritrea's Moslems and ensuring future peace. To exclude Ethiopia from other Moslem areas would mean excluding her from the port of Massawa and, were that to happen, there would be no peace for anyone, the Moslems of Western Eritrea included. In an avuncular postscript he warned me that I would have to learn to swallow the unpleasant truth: that politics was the art of the possible.

The Deluge

Not surprisingly, echoes of the Greater Tigrai bombshell made Addis Ababa sit up and take anxious notice of what had every appearance of being a most sinister development. Up to this point, they had been quiescent in an effort to humour us after the Police affair. The Bishop had lain low, agitation had diminished. Ghebramaskal and members of his Eritrean Committee had adopted a low profile. All this now changed. The doves gave way to hawks, the Bishop was summoned to Addis Ababa and, on his return, the trouble makers went back to work. A glum-faced Johannes began to appear Job-like each day with reports of mischief in the wind. Agitators from Asmara had been seen in this village and that and, contrary to standing orders, the local chiefs had failed to deport them. Would I please give them a wigging? Or I would be told that some chief or other had slipped off to Asmara and signed up with the Bishop. Should I not tell him to watch his step? Again and again and with growing exasperation, I told the obtuse little man that there was nothing doing. It was not illegal for people from Asmara to visit the Serae or for chiefs to sign up with the Bishop and, unless someone acted illegally, I could not intervene. I knew, of course, that I was right but after a while I began to wonder whether Johannes was entirely wrong. I had an uncomfortable feeling that the trouble might be getting out of hand.

It came to a head one morning when half a dozen anxious-eyed Italians turned up in a palpable state of the jitters. They were market gardeners who had been settled by Crawford on a few small patches of Crown Land as part of a scheme for vegetable and fruit production promoted by Longrigg to meet the needs of Asmara's Europeans. Having resisted a similar scheme in Keren on the grounds that, what the Law saw as Crown Land, villagers saw as theirs, I had asked Crawford whether he had had any trouble from the locals. None to speak of, he had told me. One or two hotheads had done a bit of blathering but a good dose of 'the cooler' had quickly shut them up. Now, I could see from the frightened faces before me that the effects of Crawford's tranquiliser had obviously worn off.

They were in fear of their lives, a bearded little man with a face like a walnut stammered. They begged me for protection. Everyone then spoke at once. One said that his crops had been destroyed at night; another that his horse had had its throat slit; and yet another that his dogs had been poisoned. All had been insulted and threatened by local villagers.

Poor wretches, they presented a heart-rending sight. These were not Colonel Grogans sitting on great domains but little peasants working small market gardens mainly with their own hands. But what could I do? To give them the Police protection they wanted was out of the question. I simply hadn't the men. I could have a word with the local chiefs and headmen, I said. A wail of anguish went up. They were the very ones behind their persecution, they moaned. It was no good having a word with such people, Johannes hissed at me. The only answer was to lock them up. That was what Crawford would have done. No, I replied. I would have a word with them first, and see how they reacted. 'But, but, but...' Johannes blabbered. Nothing doing, I refused to be panicked.

In the event, I never had time for a word with the chiefs or head men. That very night one of the little market gardeners was murdered in bed with his wife. Murdered? They were butchered! They were chopped up into small pieces. Their wretched little room was littered with bits of bone and flesh and washed crimson with fresh Italian blood. It was a ghastly sight and made ghastlier still for me by Johannes's cold, accusing eyes. If only I had been a Crawford, they said. Yes, he was right. If I had not been a dithering fool, telling myself that I must play everything with a decent straight bat, those two little Italians would still have been alive. It was a black thought at the blackest of moments. Returning from this obscenity, I found a letter waiting for me. Middle East Command required officers who had served for more than three years abroad to take leave in the United Kingdom. Since I had by this time been six years away from home, I was to hand over the district and proceed at once to Cairo for embarkation. I got home late in 1944, just before the last Christmas of the long War.

NOTES

[1] *Tigrai*: the northernmost province of Abyssinia and sharing a common frontier with Eritrea, had a long history of rebellion against the central authority in Addis Ababa.
[2] *Jiberti*: was the name under which the Moslem traders living in Abyssinia were collectively known. They lived mainly in the towns.
[3] The *Saho* tribes were a small grouping of semi-nomadic tribes in the district of Akkele Guzai, on the foothills of the Plateau fringing the Danakil desert.

10

AS THE WAR ENDS, THE ALLIES TURN THEIR ATTENTION TO THE ITALIAN COLONIES

MY SIX WEEKS' LEAVE was up and I was waiting for embarkation back to the Middle East feeling like a Glaswegian on the morning after Burns' Night. The Colonel in charge of our party came briskly up to where I was sitting, tut-tutted, marched off and returned with a medico. 'No convoy for you!' the latter announced, eyeing the thermometer. '105°. Off you go to bed!' God knows what was wrong with me. No one ever found out, and that was not for want of treating me like a guinea pig. I went in and out of military hospitals, had two sets of sick leave and was only passed fit for duty nine months later. I had never had so much time on my hands since my days as a Prisoner of War. I even managed to get myself married.

With Eritrea so very far out of sight and for so long and the possibility that I might not be returning there, it might be thought that my interest in it would have faded away. It didn't. One reason was that bloody spectacle of the unfortunate butchered Italians near Adi Ugri; another, the sad demise of our little ally, the Sultan of Aussa. Above all else, Newbold had made me feel duty bound to ensure that Ethiopia did not get her callous hands on our Moslems. We knew that the thought of Christian Ethiopian rule was anathema to them and we knew that the Ethiopians would badger, bully and, if necessary, butcher them. Our duty could not have been clearer. I was still young enough to believe that no British Government would neglect it.

But not for long. While mooching around killing time I suddenly received an invitation to call on some official in the Foreign Office dealing with Eritrea. How were things, he asked. I told him and while I was rattling along about our duty to keep the Moslems out of Ethiopia's clutches, he brought me to a halt with a 'quite so'. Yes, they knew all about the Moslems' feelings, he said. Newbold had made the point and so had Longrigg; and both had proposed partition. One had to face the fact, however, that the Italian Colonies were likely to become pawns in the game of diplomatic chess which would almost certainly be played once the War had come to an end. And what did that mean? The face on the other side of the desk let out a sigh, it meant that Eritrean, let alone Eritrean Moslem, wishes were unlikely to count for very much. The way things were going it looked as if the question of Eritrea would be a straightforward contest between Ethiopia and Italy. But what about the Atlantic Charter, self determination and all that? My guess was as good as his, my host smiled, showing me the door.

What this harbinger of gloom was saying was near enough the truth. Though the Italian Colonies hardly qualified for the headlines at that time, they were beginning to edge their way into the news. This was because a pressure group of unusual stridency was blaring away about Ethiopia's claims and a handful of Italophils were reacting to it.

The Italophils did not worry me. The pro-Ethiopian clique did. Evidently well endowed with Ethiopian cash, this was a group of defenders of lost causes and colour-prejudiced Left Wingers headed by Sylvia, the flamboyant and self-satisfied daughter of Emmeline Pankhurst, the Queen of the Suffragettes. Like her mother, this elderly virago was a compulsive agitator and when not lobbying Parliamentarians, haranguing public meetings, organising demonstrations, or writing letters to the newspapers, she was editing a propagandist periodical of singular crudity called *New Times and Ethiopian News*. Its message was the Bishop's message, the Eritrean Committee's message and the message all their stooges had been broadcasting. There was nothing new about it. What was so alarming was that here in Britain it was the only message about Eritrea anyone ever heard. Eritrea's Moslems could have been so many Trappist monks for all the publicity they generated, and there was no way that anyone could know that at least fifty per cent of all Eritreans were Moslems for whom Ethiopia was the principal Enemy.

Brooding over this I suddenly remembered Newbold saying that he had corresponded with the formidable Margery Perham over his partition plan and that she had given it her blessing. She was, I knew, just the person I ought to see and so, using Newbold's name by way of reintroduction, I hared off to see her in Oxford. She welcomed me with a tired nod, explaining that she was 'a bit pushed'. All the colonial problems which had been put on ice at the outbreak of war were now beginning to thaw out. The Gold Coast, the Sudan, Kenya and the Rhodesias were all heading for crises of one kind or another. That was why she had done so little about Newbold's plan for Eritrea. The plan was not perfect but, since it was the best we could expect for the Eritreans, she would do what she could to push it along. Perhaps Rita Hinden would do so as well. Rita Hinden? Didn't I know her? Why, she was Secretary to the Fabian Society's Colonial Bureau, the Labour Party's 'Think Tank' on colonial affairs. A word with her might be helpful. As she stood up to send me on my way, she asked if I had heard the sad news about Douglas. No, I hadn't. Douglas Newbold had just died in Khartoum. I felt as if I had lost an uncle.

I had never heard of Rita Hinden but I knew of the Fabian Colonial Bureau and, knowing that there was a possibility of a Labour Government being elected to office when the War ended I could see every advantage in putting this lady clearly into the Eritrean picture. We met for luncheon in a small and very austere cafe near Victoria Station. My hostess was small and sparrowlike with a brisk, inquisitorial manner. What she wanted, she said, were the facts about Eritrea. 'Facts, facts, facts!' she repeated to make sure that I understood what she was after. I gave them to her. She shot out the questions, I fired back the answers and all the time she scribbled away at her notes. When I had finished she left me to take a stroll round Vincent Square while she studied the facts I had given her. Yes, she said, on my return: partition seemed the only feasible solution to the Eritrean problem. With the great majority of Abyssinians so ardently pro-Ethiopia, it would be madness to deny them union with Ethiopia. Equally, it would be madness to let Ethiopia take over the great bloc of Moslem tribes in Western Eritrea. So, what were we left with? Partition.

As the War Ends, the Allies Turn Their Attention to the Italian Colonies

She got in touch a little later to say that Arthur Creech-Jones, who was then the Labour Party's recognised colonial expert, had agreed that partition was the right answer and had asked her to produce a paper on the subject for publication. Since I knew Eritrea and, unlike her, knew the subject in depth, would I write the paper? No, I could not agree. It was against the rules and I was still an obedient servant. 'It's up to you!' she snapped, buttoning herself up without a smile. She shut her notebook and that was that.

A few weeks later, in that glorious May of 1945 the flags were flying and the bells ringing in a joyous outburst of triumphalism to celebrate the defeat of Nazi Germany. With Japan's defeat now a certainty, the Allies got down to the job of peacemaking. In July, at Potsdam they took the first step by deciding to set up a Council of their Foreign Ministers to draft a Peace Treaty with Italy and a number of other former enemies. In September, the Council met and, for the first time, the Allies gave their views on the Italian Colonies an airing. For the Ethiopians, they were nothing less than a humiliating slap in the face.

An initial humiliation for the Ethiopians was to be told that no delegation of theirs might attend the discussions on the Italian colonies. And yet, how was it that Italy, the criminal and aggressor, should be given a right of attendance, Miss Pankhurst demanded in an outburst of purple-passaged tirades? How was it that Ethiopia, the victim of Italian aggression should be denied the right to state her case? Since the whole purpose of the Council's meeting was to draft an Italian Peace treaty, Italian representation at it was, of course, essential. Ethiopia, on the other hand, had no recognised right of representation at all unless hers was to be treated as a special case. And that the Foreign Ministers were not prepared to allow. Nothing could have hit Ethiopian 'hubris' more hardly.

More startling still was what the Allies had to say about the Colonies. With the sole exception of Britain, not one of them wasted so much as a word on Ethiopia or her claims to Eritrea. With sublime contempt for the Atlantic Charter and the democratic pieties to which they had variously subscribed, they all favoured putting Eritrea under some form of international trusteeship. The Americans and French agreed that Italy should be the Administering Authority for all four colonies until the Americans suddenly had second thoughts. The Russians, with an almost endearing cynicism, cut the cackle by proposing that the Allies should take a colony apiece under trusteeship (of course) and be done with it. We alone took sympathetic note of Ethiopia's claims, but only to the extent of putting forward proposals for Eritrea's partition on Newbold's lines. Hardly had Miss Pankhurst finished damning this as a sinister imperialist move to extend our Sudanese dominions when Ernest Bevin, our new Foreign Secretary, came up with the thought that we and the Ethiopians should each hand over our Somali colonies to merge with Italian Somaliland into a Greater Somalia. It was an admirable, indeed an altruistic suggestion which could have given the unfortunate Somalis a chance of living happily ever afterwards. The Ethiopians, however, denounced and damned it. They denounced and damned us, too, as 'perfidious Albion'. They were there to acquire territory, not give it away.

Agreement to disagree was the predictable outcome of the Foreign Ministers' jamboree. Because of the 'complexity' of the colonial problem it was handed down to their Deputies with instructions to report back in a year's time. I could not believe my luck. So much for my fears that our Moslems would lose out by default. Thanks, perhaps, to that backroom girl, Rita Hinden, our new Labour Government had recognised our Moslems' feelings by proposing the Newbold partition plan. None of the Allies had given a thought to Ethiopia's claims. So far so good.

11

THE MOSLEM AWAKENING

CRAWFORD MET ME at the airport on my return to Asmara in the Autumn of 1945 looking as carefree as a curate on a Monday. He had just taken over Asmara from the anguishing Stanley Parker and was happy to say that the political barometer was pointing firmly to 'Fair'. It was the Allies' total and contemptuous disregard of Ethiopia that had done the trick, he explained. The Bishop and his chums had managed to fool people into believing that Ethiopia had become a power that mattered but they would fool them no more. Everyone knew that Ethiopia was still the same tinpot little country it had always been. The Bishop and his friends had had it.

Eritrea was now under new management. Longrigg had gone and the new Military Administrator was a regular soldier called Brigadier Benoy. 'Made in Sandhurst and Camberley' was written all over him. What he said came from a head uncluttered by too many ideas. It was never ambiguous. It was always to the point. He came quickly to business when I called on him, saying that he was not at all happy with what he had seen since coming to Eritrea. Too many people were out of step, he said; not that he was blaming them. No one had set the step. Anyhow, he was setting it now and he would accept no excuses if anyone put the wrong foot forward in future. He then went on to say that there were two things we had to get firmly into our heads. First, Eritrea was not a British Colony. We were caretakers and our job was to hand it over as we had found it. Nothing more, nothing less. Secondly, we had to 'play fair' and keep our noses clean. We were British officers and had to behave as British officers should. He took a poor view of Eritreans being bullied and badgered for saying that they wanted union with Ethiopia and, as for that childish tomfoolery about a Greater Tigrai, the less said about it the better. 'Do I make myself plain?' he asked, pinning me down with a pair of unblinking eyes. If he had drawn a straight line on a clean sheet of paper he could not have presented me with anything plainer.

It was a straight talk from a straight little man but where did it leave me and my anxieties about the future of our Moslems? I did not share Crawford's airy belief that pro-Ethiopianism was in terminal decline. Since the Council of Foreign Ministers had chosen to believe that Eritrea's pro-Ethiopians did not matter, the Bishop and his friends would now almost certainly react by going flat out to capture the headlines by showing them that they did. And, given that war-time restrictions against political activities were now being relaxed, one could be sure that the Bishop would make a good job of it. That was what worried me. With La Pankhurst feeding the World Press with tidbits from Eritrea about pro-Ethiopian riots and demonstrations, World and British opinion would naturally assume that the Eritreans as a whole were passionately pro-Ethiopia. In other words, the Moslems could lose out by default. Did that mean that I should sit back and do nothing about it? By Benoy's rules, it did.

All this was very much on my mind when I was sent back to take over Keren. It was just as I had left it. Tribal serf and aristocrat were still snarling at each other; Abyssinian peasants were still throwing sporadic fits over land; and Antonelli was still schooling his horses. Everyone was doing his own thing as if nothing else in the world mattered. Negassi, our Abyssinian Chief, told me that some of his schoolboys had been waving Ethiopian flags about but, otherwise, no one seemed to have given the future a thought. Even the Qadhi did not seem to have done so. What did he make of the Council of Foreign Ministers' meeting, I asked him. He gave me a benign smile in reply, saying that he did not make anything of it. Who were these Americans, Russians and Frenchmen? What did they know about Eritrea? No, he and the Moslem faithful were quite content to leave themselves in the hands of their good friends, the British.

Though oblivious to the menacing facts of political life beyond their horizons, the Moslems were in a ferment over the one political issue which mattered to them. The serfs, or 'Tigrey' as they were collectively known, had suddenly risen up in a state of undeclared revolt against their overlords, or 'Shumagalle'. Longrigg, it will be remembered, had rapped my knuckles for failing to support the chiefs over the collection of feudal dues, arguing (quite rightly) that, unless we supported them—feudal warts and all—their authority would disintegrate and that would mean anarchy. Since then, Stranger-Ford had managed to calm things down but, with my return, everything flared up again. I was, after all, known as the Political Officer who had said 'No' to feudal dues. Within a few weeks all payment ceased. After a short interlude I was overwhelmed by multiplying howls for help.

Even if I had had my heart in the business of squeezing serfs to indulge their overlords, there was not much that I could have done. I could, at a pinch, have dealt with two or three rebellious cases but not with dozens at a time. I did not have enough Police. This, of course, meant nothing to the Kantibai and his friends and they arrived one day to see me in the form of a Grand Remonstrance. They came as 'Chiefs in the service of the Government', the Kantibai announced. Then, giving me a fierce, red-eyed look, he demanded to know where they stood. Were they chiefs worthy of our support and respect or mere nobodies to be insulted and humiliated? If we had no need of them, let us say so and set them free to make other arrangements. What could I say? We had not the Police to work miracles, I said. The Kantibai listened, tapping my office floor with a petulant slippered foot. When I had eventually limped to a halt, he left with barely a gesture of farewell.

Soon after this, Benoy turned up with a 'bombe surprise'. He wanted me to take over the neighbouring Agordat district as well as Keren owing to his difficulty in finding staff to man the two Districts which were now to be called the Western Province. What this meant was that I was to be in charge of Eritrea's Moslem West, the very region which Newbold had earmarked for the Sudan. 'You don't seem very pleased,' sniffed Benoy. Not pleased? I was over the moon!

Yes, I was over the moon but I had no illusions about what I was taking on. It was a king-size headache. The Agordat district was the stamping ground of Eritrea's largest Moslem tribe, the 80,000 strong Beni Amer, and following an ugly spate of fighting between them and their neighbours, the Sudanese Hadendowa, there was an awkward mess to be cleared up. Feuding and fighting between these cheerful savages had been an unchanging feature of the local scene but the fighting which had just ended had not been the usual tribal knock-about. It had been brutish and bloody. It had been a little war. This was largely because the Beni Amer had managed to get their hands on arms the Italians had abandoned during their retreat and because, during the fighting between ourselves and the Italians, they had got completely out of hand. In the event, since our newly-formed Administration had been quite incapable of dealing with the situation, it had looked to the Sudan for help. We were still living with the consequences.

To bring the Beni Amer to heel, the Sudan had despatched that hardened old campaigner, Hugh Boustead, with a brigade of Sudanese troops. Boustead's remarkable career spoke for itself. He was an Olympian but even Olympians have their weaknesses. Achilles had a vulnerable heel: Boustead had a blind enthusiasm which could run away with him, as it had during that visit to Keren. Whatever he did he saw as a crusade and so here he saw himself as leading a Sudanese punitive expedition against 'those Beni Amer bastards' for daring to molest 'our chaps', the Hadendowa. Boustead was too old a hand to waste time chasing bedouin around a countryside which they knew far better than he did. Instead, he went for their jugular: their livestock. The Beni Amer grazing area was swept and combed and when all the combing and sweeping had ended, he had picked up enough camels, cattle, goats and sheep to feed a division. The Beni Amer were told that if they wanted them back they would have to come in and make their peace. Since Boustead's troops were given full licence to butcher and devour as many Beni Amer animals as they wished, the unfortunate Beni Amer had the intolerable experience of watching their worldly assets vanishing like ice under a hot sun. It was more than they could bear. They gave in, handed in their arms and agreed to pay the Hadendowa compensation. His mission accomplished, Boustead and his men marched off well-pleased with themselves, leaving 80,000 bloody-minded Beni Amer on our hands.

The War was officially over but there was trouble in plenty to come. For the young Beni Amer bucks who had raided and looted and been told what fine fellows they were, the Hadendowa War had been fun. Peace was no fun at all. Inevitably, many of the young bloods hankered after the excitement and rewards of their old wartime life; inevitably, many of them went back to it: not just to fighting the Hadendowa but to an outlaw's life of raiding and looting as and where their fancy took them. The Police, who were themselves continually being raided for arms, were quite unable to cope and the Beni Amer chiefs were far too embittered by Bousteadism and the outcome of the Hadendowa War to lend them a hand. As insecurity spread, defaulting on the payments due to the Hadendowa as compensation increased. And so, what with straightforward banditry, tribal feuds and trying to badger the Beni Amer into paying up what they owed the Hadendowa, the Agordat district was in a pretty good mess.

Not that the Political Officer in charge of the district took it too hard. He was a solid, unflappable Arabist called Cleavely. Too unflappable by half, I thought when I paid Agordat my first visit and found him slippered and silk dressing-gowned on his verandah with a book of Arab poetry on his knee. Why was he lounging around at a time like this? Why wasn't he on the back of a camel getting in amongst the Beni Amer? He fielded my questioning with a lazy smile. Did I want us to look more foolish than we already did? One had to be a realist. There was no future chasing shadows. Well, what did he propose? There was only one answer, he replied, and his Eritrean assistant would give it to me. On this he introduced me to an effusive person who, as a compliment to his former Italian masters, had changed his name from Omar Hassan to Omar Hassano. 'The answer to our problem, sir,' he gushed, 'is money.' £500 would settle the whole affair. It would be enough to buy off the various gang leaders, pay the Hadendowa what was due to them and compensate the Beni Amer for the losses they had suffered at the hands of Boustead. If we did that, I snapped, we would have a hundred new gangs on the rampage the very next day! He shrugged his shoulders and said that if that was what I thought perhaps I should seek the advice of the Diglal. This was the old Sudanic title by which the paramount chief of the Beni Amer was known. A meeting with him was already on my agenda.

The Diglal was a Michelin man, as tall as he was wide, with what looked like a jester's three-cornered hat on the top of his head. He rose to his feet on my arrival and wheezed out none too cordial a greeting. What could he do for me, he asked, dispensing with further courtesies. He could bring the outlaws to heel for a start, I replied, and pay the Hadendowa what was owed to them. His face twitched, his belly bulged and his eyes pounced on me. He gurgled incoherently for a moment and then let me have it. 'You want me to rob my people to satisfy your Hadendowa!'

The Deluge

he raved. 'You want that after letting your Sudanese strip my people clean? You ask me to blacken my face and destroy my honour? Where is Justice?' He looked round the room as if Justice might be hiding in a corner. But there was only Cleavely there with that lazy smile on his face and Omar sitting a little apart. After the old gentleman had spluttered to a halt, Omar led him away to cool off. They sat talking in whispers for a while and then Omar rose to his feet to announce that the Diglal had agreed to do as I had asked. 'Excellent!' I said. He had, however, one small condition to make, Omar added. He would need £1,000. £1,000? Yes, it was more than his own estimate, he admitted, but then he had not taken into account what the Diglal and his chiefs would need for their trouble. I left on that, giving the Diglal a hard, cold look as I departed.

I did him an injustice, not knowing what this grizzly old bear had suffered through no fault of his own. He, poor fellow, had been put in an impossible position by the Hadendowa affair. His tribesmen had naturally expected him to behave as their chief and warlord: to beat his drums and lead them to victory. We, on the other hand, seeing him as our salaried surrogate, had expected him to bring his turbulent tribesmen to heel and disarm them. Poachers sometimes turn gamekeepers and gamekeepers poachers, but no one as far as I know has ever served as gamekeeper and poacher at the same time. The Diglal tried and, of course, failed. His tribesmen resented his half-heartedness, we his failure to do what we paid him to do. In the end we packed him off to 'residence forcée' in Khartoum where he languished until, his resistance eroded, he eventually gave us the assurances we needed. This had left him no way out of endorsing the peace settlement with the Hadendowa and, since every Beni Amer with a tongue in his head was denouncing this as a sell-out, that saddled him and the subordinate chiefs with the odium of accepting it. Unwittingly, we had torpedoed them all and, since we travelled on their backs, we had also torpedoed ourselves. I left Agordat with plenty to brood about.

Antonelli was waiting for me on my return to Keren looking as if he had swallowed an oyster when there had not been a R in the month. He was a picture of palpitating agitation. Italian lives were in danger! he quavered. Something had to be done! What on earth was the old boy flapping about? It took me a little time to discover that it was the pro-Ethiopian brigade who had given him the shakes. Shortly before this, Benoy had lifted the war-time ban on political parties and the pro-Ethiopians had

The Moslem Awakening

taken the field as the 'Eritrean-Ethiopian Union' or 'Unionist Party' for short, to the accompaniment of clamorous, flag-waving demonstrations. Predictably, the tone of the demonstrations had been anti-Italian and, predictably, they had resulted in some damage to the persons and property of a few Italians. And so, when the Unionists suddenly announced that they proposed to open a branch in Keren with a demonstration to mark the occasion, our Italians immediately feared the worst. The only thing to do, Antonelli insisted, was to ban the demonstration. Benoy would never have agreed and, in any event, Keren was not Asmara. It was all a fuss about nothing, I told him. If the Unionists could raise a couple of hundred Abyssinians for the occasion, they would be doing well. He left me with the look of a man about to walk the plank.

This was the prelude to the day of the Unionist Jamboree. It was certainly a day to remember. One moment Keren was its usual sleepy self, the next it was bouncing. Suddenly, out of the blue, there arrived a large convoy of buses from Asmara packed to their luggage racks with Unionist supporters. There must have been over two thousand of them, and to see and hear them as they drove slowly into the town, shouting slogans and waving flags, one might have thought they had come to liberate it. Their arrival was the signal for every Abyssinian in the district to pop up from nowhere in the wildest of wild welcomes: Abbots, priests, peasants and proletarians were all there, yelling themselves into ever greater convulsions of hysteria. Keren had never seen anything like it before but the biggest surprise of the lot came at the end of the revels. A crackling megaphonic voice suddenly demanded attention for an important announcement. It was sensational. The Kantibai and a number of other tribal chiefs had joined the Unionist cause!

The Unionists were in ecstasies and when the Diglal and some of his Beni Amer chiefs followed the Kantibai's example a few days later, Embaie Habte, Chairman of Keren's branch of the party, called with a face 'en fete' to tell me the good news. He was in rollicking form. So much for those lies about the Moslems opposing Ethiopia, he chuckled. He very much hoped that the British Government would now understand that Moslems and Christians were all united in demanding union with Ethiopia. The little dunderhead really believed this and so, I later discovered, did Tedla and those former Eritrean Committee loudmouths who had since become Unionist hierarchs. Such was their ignorance of the Moslem World that they had not the least idea of the harm that they had done themselves by their spectacular coup. Had they thought of a hundred and one different ways of arousing the dormant and apathetic Moslem tribes to a frenzy of anti-Ethiopian passion, they could not have hit on anything better. By publicly conferring their patronage on the Moslem chiefs, the Unionists had finally discredited them in the eyes of their rebellious Tigrey-speaking subjects.

I was given a fairly strong hint of what lay ahead while travelling in the hills near the Kantibai's seat at Nacfa. Descending into a narrow valley, I suddenly came upon a couple of hundred tribesmen brewing up. They had no tents, no livestock, no women and no children. Odder still, seated amongst these shaggy-headed bumpkins there was a small party of dignitaries gowned and turbanned with Pasha-like immaculacy. Who were these grandees and what were they doing in such improbable company? All was revealed over the coffee cups during the course of the next hour. What I had stumbled upon was a gathering of the family heads of the Asfeda: a tribe which had been conquered, cut up and parcelled out amongst the Kantibai's ancestors several centuries before. They were all Tigrey and so, by origin, were the laundered elite: who were, in fact, descendants of Tigrey who had escaped from the tribal world and later made good in the towns. What were they doing here? Advising their brothers what to do at this time of crisis, the most venerable of them replied. Now that the Kantibai was an ally of the Ethiopian Kaffirs,[1] they were naturally alarmed. They knew what everyone knew which was that, in return for giving them his support, the Kantibai expected the Kaffirs to help him whip them back to heel. And what advice were they giving their brothers? To look to Islam to defend them against the Kantibai and his Kaffir allies. It looked very much as if these grand gentlemen were stirring things up in the name of Islam.

That was, in fact, just what they were up to and just what dozens of others like them were up doing. Although resistance to the payment of feudal dues had become widespread, resistance to the authority of chiefs had, up to this point, been hesitant. Now it became near universal. It was the Islamic factor which did the trick, and it was these roving missionaries who were plugging the Islamic message. Nothing could have been simpler or more straightforward. The Kantibai, Diglal and other chiefs who had sold their souls to the Christian Kaffirs of Ethiopia had forfeited all right to authority over the Moslem faithful. For any Moslem to obey them would be a betrayal of Islam. As the message began to sink in, our whole system of rural government which depended on the chiefs, began to totter. Reports from Cleavely and other Political Officers told the same story. The Native Courts were barely functioning; taxes were not being collected; schools, health clinics and schemes of one kind and another were suffering from neglect. Every rule in the book, from deforestation to smuggling, was being broken with impunity. Humpty Dumpty was cracking into bits without any hope of repair. I should have been overwhelmed by depression. In fact, I could not have been happier. The seemingly impossible had happened. The Moslems had come to political life.

NOTES

[1] The term 'Kaffir' means unbeliever and is here applied to the Christian inhabitants of the Plateau.

12

THE EMANCIPATION OF THE MOSLEM TRIBAL SERFS AND THE BIRTH OF AN ANTI-ETHIOPIAN MOSLEM LEAGUE

IT WAS WHILE I was hunting around for some way out of our difficulties that the Qadhi ambled unannounced into my office with a seraphic smile and a delegation of Moslem worthies in tow. They had come, he said, to voice their anxieties over the deplorable Abyssinian invasion of Keren and the defection of their Chiefs to the enemies of Islam. Naturally their people were alarmed by this Abyssinian propaganda about Ethiopia taking Eritrea over. So please would I put all their minds at rest by assuring them that we would never permit any Moslem to be subjected to Ethiopian rule? Regretfully, I could give no such assurance. A collective gasp hissed round the room and the Qadhi asked if I was saying that the British Government would stand aside and let the Ethiopians take them over? That was possible, I admitted. It was up to the Allies to decide what should happen to Eritrea and for us to comply with their decision. Every face in the room except one registered wild-eyed consternation. The odd face out—a chubby, none too well shaven one—began to have a fit. 'You hypocrites!' its owner, a personage named Ibrahim Sultan, raved. 'You say you respect the Atlantic Charter and yet you look on us as nothing more than baggage in the caravans of our feudal oppressors!' A good deal more followed in tones of stinging insolence. I stood as much of

The Emancipation of the Moslem Tribal Serfs

it as I could and then rose to my feet, bade the Qadhi a curt goodbye and stalked off in dudgeon.

The Qadhi arrived at my house an hour later with a thousand apologies and a grovelling Ibrahim. After I had accepted Ibrahim's apologies and we had all exchanged handshakes and forced laughs, Ibrahim asked what they should do to avoid being taken over by the Ethiopians? How was I to answer that? Should I take the Benoy-caretaker line and say that that was nothing to do with me? Or should I say, 'For God's sake, wake up, follow the Abyssinian example, form a political party and let the world know how you feel!'? I had to play fair, though not by Benoy's rules. I had to put them wise as best I could. Ibrahim heard me out with a fat smile spreading across his face and said that, if I would do him one small favour, he would have an anti-Ethiopian Moslem party in the field within the week. And what was the small favour? All he asked was that I should formally and legally set the Tigray free of their overlords and chiefs. What the...? Didn't I understand, he asked impatiently. If I set the Tigray free, they would know that it was he who had negotiated their freedom and, knowing that, they would be his slaves for life. And then? With two hundred thousand Tigray at his back he would have a party and a political bandwagon which every Moslem in the country would want to join. All that was needed to unite all Eritrea's Moslems in one political party was this one small favour.

The one small favour Ibrahim was asking for was not one small favour at all. It was a revolution. He was asking me to dismantle the existing tribal set-up but for what? 'No problem!' Ibrahim chuckled. The Tigray would have their own chiefs. If he was thinking of my agreeing to a chief for every fifty Tigray he could think again, I said. Ibrahim chortled politely and said, 'No, no, no!' What he was proposing was a new set of tribes with their own chiefs. Tribes? What tribes? Why, the old Tigrey tribes which had existed before they had been conquered, carved up and distributed as serfs amongst the ancestors of the Kantibai, Diglal and all the rest of the feudal chiefs. God in Heaven! This was sheer fantasy! How could we conceivably dismantle the existing tribes and reorganise a quarter of a million wild tribesmen into a whole lot of tribes resurrected from the past? It would be impossible! 'Not at all!' Ibrahim protested. 'The problem had already been solved!' Those well-dressed delegations I had seen touring the countryside had been his emissaries and they had already prepared the ground for what I needed. Everywhere old tribes like the Asfeda, whose meeting of family heads I had seen, were coming together. For the first time in weeks I began to see daylight. Of all people, this fat, loud-mouthed lout had put forward what seemed to be a feasible alternative to anarchy.

To replace one tribal system with another was, however, no simple matter. It would entail the setting up of new tribal hierarchies, investing new chiefs and sub-chiefs with powers, reconstituting Courts, Councils and Committees, revising the fiscal system and drawing new tribal boundaries. In other words, this was not something I could do off my own bat. I would have to clear it with Benoy first. How would he react? One thing was certain which was that he would reject the whole idea and give me a flea in the ear for good measure, if he ever suspected that what I intended to do would boost Ibrahim's plans to set up a Moslem political party. Fortunately, no such suspicion crossed his mind but I could see that he did not like the proposal. It was not our job to turn everything upside down, however desirable, he said. It was not a question of desirability, I insisted: it was necessity. If we did nothing we would be faced with anarchy. Not if we supported the authority of the Chiefs who were already there, he rapped back. Their authority was non-existent, I argued. There was nothing to support. Benoy had by this time had enough. 'Well, we can't go on talking all day!' he said, looking at his watch. 'Put your case in writing. Full details, mind! No wishy-washy generalisations!' Full details? I could see from the look in his eye that every detail would mean a battle and a battle he intended to win.

At this point Providence made a dramatic intervention into our affairs. The balloon suddenly went up in Asmara. An explosion had, for some time, been predictable, for the Unionists had been hard at work exploiting proletarian discontent and with growing recession there was plenty of discontent to exploit. The anti-Italian drum was beaten and out came the mobs to give the 'Italian parasites' a lesson. And then—perhaps as a warning to Moslem merchants who were flirting with anti-Ethiopian ideas—the agitators beat a tattoo on an anti-Arab drum and, before you could say 'arson', Arab shops were going up in smoke.

Since the Police could not cope with disorders on such a scale, Sudanese troops were brought in and since Sudanese contempt for 'Abyssinian Kaffirs' was fairly matched by Abyssinian loathing for those 'black

The Emancipation of the Moslem Tribal Serfs

Moslem savages', racial antagonism acquired yet another ugly dimension. Incidents multiplied, leading like stepping stones to a shattering catastrophe. It came as a result of a market-place brawl in which an off-duty Sudanese private was stoned to death by an Abyssinian mob. Within the hour a company of Sudanese troops had broken out of barracks and taken their revenge: fifty-six Abyssinians were slaughtered and, also, by ill luck, ten Italians who got caught up in the cross fire.

I first heard of this hideous affair from Ibrahim who arrived with the news, grinning like a dog in a butcher's shop. He was delighted that we had acted with such exemplary firmness and said that the Moslems had been greatly encouraged by what we had done. Was this rascal saying that we had deliberately unleashed the Sudanese onto Asmara's Abyssinians? Yes, he was and so was every Abyssinian in Asmara. Benoy would have known this and he would have known that, unless the suspicion was scotched at once, mayhem might follow. And so, instead of playing it by the book and appointing a Court of Inquiry, he rushed ahead and did the decent thing. First, he broadcast an unreserved apology for 'the shameful and unforgivable behaviour' of our troops. Secondly, he attended the mass funeral of the victims and, with thirty thousand vengeful Abyssinian mourners present. That took more than ordinary guts. By doing so, he defused an unusually explosive situation. And what was his reward? The sack! The military mandarins in Khartoum were outraged that he should have 'let our chaps down'. Their superiors in Cairo agreed. Poor Benoy earned no marks for 'playing fair' by the Abyssinians—they were not 'our chaps'.

It was sickening but at least Benoy's unexpected departure relieved me of the need to do battle over my plans for tribal reorganisation. Instead, I now had to refer myself to his Chief Secretary who had assumed charge pending the arrival of his successor. This was an amiable, indolent and heavily moustachioed personage called Kenyon-Slaney who had cheerfully muddled through twenty years of colonial service by studiously evading anything awkward or irksome, his euphemism for passing the buck being 'delegation'. Delegation, he would tell you, was the hall mark of good administration. Since there was no one to whom he could conveniently delegate my tribal reorganisation plans, he delegated them back to me. 'You're the chap on the spot,' he said. 'You must know best.' That suited me: I had the green light.

When Ibrahim had said that the problem of tribal reorganisation had been solved, he had implied that the Tigrey had been neatly sorted out into clans and tribes and that all that remained was for me to give them my blessing. He was, of course, exaggerating. We were, in fact, nearer to Doomsday than to a new tribal system. Those fine friends of Ibrahim's who had stumped the countryside having get-togethers with their kinsmen had not been trying to resurrect their old Tigrey tribes. They had been trying to whip up tribal support. So we had to start again from scratch. We began by scouring the valleys and mountains and holding meetings at which were registered Tigray families and their vital statistics. This gave us pointers to where they slotted into the old Tigrey tribes but that did not mean that they would agree to be slotted into them! As Cleavely and Omar Hassano had predicted, every family head wanted to be a chief on his own and not one of them would agree to subordinate himself to another. We had registered more than five thousand families and there seemed no way that they would ever agree to grouping themselves together as tribes. What was the answer? Cleavely and Omar Hassano were too busy 'I told you so-ing' to offer any suggestions and Ibrahim (who was running around signing the Tigrey up) was rarely to be seen. There was, however, a possible way out, a quiet voice said one sultry evening after a hard day's wrangling in the desert. It came from Saleh Hinit, a bright-eyed young Eritrean with a degree from Gordon College in the Sudan whom I had recently taken on as an Administrative Assistant. The real reason why these family heads were refusing to unite together and form tribes, he explained, was that you could not have tribes without tribal chiefs and they did not want to find tribal chiefs over them. So? The reason for that was that they assumed the chiefs would be chosen from amongst themselves and they would find it demeaning to accept them as chiefs. So, what was the answer? It was to make those grand, Pasha-like emissaries of Ibrahim's chiefs. There would be nothing demeaning in accepting them. Yes, but would those city swells want to become involved in the hurly-burly of tribal life? I put it to Ibrahim. His eyes bulged with delight. Of course they would, he said. Didn't I understand? They were bourgeoisie and there was nothing they wanted more than to be gentry. He was absolutely right. It was a hard slog but slowly, piece by piece, new tribes were put together complete with clans, chiefs and fiscal obligations. Tempers in plenty were lost along the road but no

The Emancipation of the Moslem Tribal Serfs

lives. The Diglal, Kantibai and other pillars of the 'ancien regime' went down without fighting. Their pride and position were the only casualties.

It had been tough going but we had won through. Instead of certain anarchy, we now had a tribal system that worked. Ibrahim, having achieved a political reorganisation of the Tigrey, was now all set to form his Moslem party. The Tigrey had seen all their dreams come true. Everyone was happy. Everyone had what they wanted. Or had they? Talking to one of the new chiefs about some inter-family squabble in his tribe, he said that Ibrahim Sultan was dealing with it. As I did my rounds I got the same message, time and again. What about this? I would ask. Oh, that was with Ibrahim. And that? Yes, that was with him, too. No wonder the rascal had been so delighted to get his grand friends fixed up as chiefs. Through them he had the Tigrey tribes in his pocket. So long as we saw eye to eye, all would be well. But what if we should have any differences? I did not like it and when he once said with a smirk, 'You can call me Sultan Ibrahim Sultan now!', I found it difficult to smile.

With the Tigrey sorted out, Ibrahim formed his party. It was called 'The Moslem League' in imitation of Ali Jinnah's movement then agitating for the carve-up of India. What did I think of the name, Ibrahim asked. It seemed very appropriate, I replied. His followers were in much the same position as the Moslems in India, I explained. In India, the Moslems were afraid of domination by the Hindus; here, the threat was from the Abyssinians. So? Well, it seemed to me that the solution Jinnah wanted was the solution which would best answer his needs. Partition? I nodded. 'So you want to put Keren and Agordat into your Sudan,' he chuckled, wagging a finger at me. It was out of the question. What about the rest of Eritrea's Moslems? If the Moslems of Keren and Agordat were to go to the Sudan, they would be abandoning nearly two hundred thousand of their Moslem brothers. How could they possibly agree to that? May be, I replied, but it was all too possible that Ethiopia would get the Abyssinian highlands and, with them, outlets to the sea at Massawa and Assab. In that event, Massawa, Assab and the Saho tribes would go to Ethiopia anyway and, unless Keren and Agordat were slotted into the Sudan, they would obviously follow suit. Ibrahim remained unmoved. In any event, after what Boustead had done to the Beni Amir, did I really believe that the tribes would ever agree to go to the Sudan? To that I had no answer. Partition, I could see, was going to be impossible to sell.

What Ibrahim had in mind for Eritrea he did not reveal. He had won over Keren and Agordat and his energies were now directed to winning over the Moslems in the rest of the country. He was away a lot canvassing support and he would drop in now and again to tell me what progress he had made. Diving a hand into the left hand pocket of his bell tent of a gown, which he described as his 'in-tray', he would produce bits of paper signed by families who had joined the League and announce that that was another so many thousand new party members. As he had foretold, there was little Moslem reluctance to take a seat on the bandwagon he now had to offer. Even so, there were times when he was not his usual sunny self. 'Yes,' he would say, 'we have a Moslem League but what is it?' Then he would stab his chest with his forefinger and exclaim, 'It's me!' It was nothing, he would wail, except himself and those bits of paper which travelled from his left hand pocket to his 'out-tray' in the right hand pocket. The party had no offices, no employees, no organisation and no funds. When he asked for subscriptions, everyone prevaricated and asked what they would get in return. Why he killed himself trying to help such people he really didn't know. Turning to me with a sly look on one occasion, he suddenly asked if I thought the British Government would finance the party, adding that, if it did, he would get it to ask for a British Protectorate. Out of the question, I replied. He shrugged and sighed. The next day he left for Egypt.

He returned with little to show for the cost of his fare except a ragbag of anti-imperialist ideas. Egyptian anti-imperialism tickled him but it did not give him the cash he needed to bring the League to life. Where was he to get it, he would ask in tones bordering on desperation. Surely the British Government could at least give him a secret loan? How could they refuse if they knew that without it the Moslems would be handed over to those Ethiopian Kaffirs? 'So we are finished,' he said in a graveyard voice after I had told him for the umpteenth time that he would get nothing from us. It was almost immediately after this that he received a kiss of life given, incredibly, by the Unionists.

As was to be expected, the Unionists greeted the emergence of the Moslem League with howls of outrage. Tedla Bairu, who had by this time left Government service to become the Unionist Party's first Secretary General, wagged a sanctimonious head in disapproval of Ibrahim Sultan's chicanery and demanded the immediate proscription of the League on the

The Emancipation of the Moslem Tribal Serfs

grounds that Ibrahim was exploiting religion for his own malign political purposes. And this from the leader of a party which had shamelessly campaigned under the banners of the Ethiopian Coptic Church! He got the answer he deserved and so, having failed to strangle the Moslem League at birth by passably fair means, the Unionists resorted to foul. Which is to say that they set out to intimidate Moslems who had shown an interest in joining the Moslem League and, since the only Moslems within their reach were the Jiberti, it was the Jiberti merchants they set out to intimidate. They could not have made a greater mistake. Fortified by a new sense of Moslem solidarity, the Jiberti did not cave in as their tormentors had expected. Instead, they turned to the League for protection and willingly signed cheques to get it. Having already made Ibrahim a present of the Tigrey by signing up a handful of burnt-out tribal chiefs, the ham fisted Unionists now provided him with the funds to get his party off the ground.

With almost every Moslem in the country enrolled as a member and funds in the Bank, the League was now in business. It had however still to give itself an objective. Everyone knew what they did NOT want: Ethiopian rule and partition were out. When it came to discussing what they DID want, Ibrahim complained, they all wanted something different. The Tigrey could think only of their newly-won freedom and, since they had won it with British help, they wanted us to stay. The merchants from Asmara and Massawa hankered after a return to Italian rule because times had been good under the Italians and were bad under ourselves. While as for the Saho tribes, they had tiresomely got hooked on Dejazmatch Abraha's mad dream of a Greater Tigrai. And what did he himself want, I asked Ibrahim. A smirk hovered round his thick lips. 'Independence!' he said with a touch of defiance in his eyes. 'Yes, yes!' he went on as if I had disagreed with him. They were no better than infants in a primary school and needed a good long spell of British rule before taking over. But that was beside the point. What mattered was international support to keep Haile Selassie and his Kaffirs out of Eritrea and the only way of getting it was by demanding independence! Surely I saw his point? If you asked for colonial rule today, you would be thought mad or bad. You only had to look at India or Egypt to know that to win friends you had to shout for independence. I could see that his trip to Egypt had not been wasted.

The Deluge

It did not take the crafty Ibrahim too long to badger his fellows into agreeing [to] his formulation of the League's objective. He turned up one day, all grins and bonhomie, to announce that the League would demand independence but—and this was a sop to his pro-British followers—if the Allies should feel that Eritrea needed a spell of trusteeship first, their preference would be for it to be British. Now that this was out of the way, he guffawed, the League would be inaugurated with a show of strength that would give those Kaffirs in Asmara something to think about. He was as good as his word. He put on a Hollywood style spectacular. Two thousand sword-waving, camel-born Bedouin led a procession of ten thousand slowly round the streets of Keren chanting 'Hurriya, Hurriya'—'Independence, Independence!' It was the right thing to shout even if those who shouted it meant independence from their feudal overlords and not independence for Eritrea. There was only one minor hiccough. The Mirghani, who had been elected President of the League out of respect for his name and position, did not turn up. An Abyssinian lady of singular charm had, so it was whispered, captivated him the evening before and got him to sign up with the Unionists.

These Moslem high jinks took place in January 1947. A month later the Italian Peace Treaty was signed. Since the Italian Colonial question still remained unresolved, it was decided that the Americans, French, Russians and ourselves—grandiosely labelled 'The Big Four'—should reach a decision within a year after 15 September or, if we failed, leave the matter to the United Nations. In the meantime, a Commission of Investigation was to visit the territory to report on conditions in it and also on the wishes of its inhabitants. Things were moving at last.

13

A DIVIDED ERITREA
AWAITS A DECISION

WE WERE TRAVELLING in an open truck across a shimmering plain with a fiery sun beating down upon us. A line of palm trees strung along a wadi bed danced in the haze a mile or so ahead. My companion looked at his watch and said, 'It's ten to... time to call a halt.' 'Certainly,' I replied, 'but let's carry on to the shade of those palm trees.' 'No. We must stick to the rules.' Rules? 'Surely you know the rules of the march? Troops are required to halt for a rest at ten minutes to the hour. Well, it's ten to now!' My companion was Brigadier Drew, Benoy's successor.

This was the man who was to captain our ship when every straw in the wind pointed to tempests if not typhoons ahead. Long service in the Indian Army had trained him to live and work to rule. He knew every rule in the book. You didn't talk 'Shop' in the Mess; you never drank water unless it had been boiled; you took your anti-malaria tablets at dinner each evening. So long as you obeyed the rules you could never go wrong. But what was he to do now that there were no rules to tell him how to deal with the capricious and unreasonable people who dominated Eritrean life? His answer was to do nothing. 'Better be safe than sorry' he would say in a paternally knowing way. 'We'd best mark time.' Even when one had answered his every objection to a proposal, he would suddenly look up and come out with his favourite discussion stopper. 'Yes, yes, that's all very fine and large, a bit too fine and large if you ask me. Too perfect, if you know what I mean. Always remember that the

Best is the Enemy of the Good!' Yes, we had got ourselves a bumble-wit when we needed a Bismarck. While everyone else was in a state of feverish speculation about the Commission to which we would soon be playing host, this simple soldier remained a picture of disinterested 'sang froid'. What were our plans? Why, we had none and the reason for that should be plain enough. Drawing up plans for the Commission was not our business. It was the Commission's. And so, if we would be good enough to get on with our job, the Commission would no doubt let us know what its intentions were in its own good time; then, if there was anything it wanted from ourselves, we would do it. This Drew would say with a weary, paternal sigh, followed by a suitable homily about keeping your eye on the ball, your bat straight or something equally fatuous. For one who had Ibrahim banging on his door demanding to know how the Commission proposed to proceed, it did not make life any easier! Not that this mattered. What did matter was that the Commission should be given a fair chance of sizing up the comparative strength of the political parties and the popular support for their nostra. The more I thought about things, the clearer it became that, if we left the Commission to muddle along on its own, the Unionists would monopolise its attention.

I could all too easily visualise what would happen if we left the Commission to itself. It would, of course, base itself on Asmara and, since Asmara was the very heart of Abyssinian Eritrea and overwhelmingly Unionist, it would certainly be serenaded by massive Unionist demonstrations. The untutored Commissioners could hardly be expected to know that they were only seeing one side of the Eritrean picture and would naturally assume that, if the territory's capital was ablaze with pro-Ethiopian enthusiasm, the rest of it was as well. Nor, even if they paid flying visits to Eritrea's other principal towns, did it seem likely that they would change their minds. Though the League was, as I had already seen, capable of laying on a massive demonstration, it needed a great deal of time to assemble its widely scattered supporters; and clearly the chances of its presenting the Commission with anything more than a medium sized demonstration at any of its places of call were minimal. As against this, the Unionists would demonstrate en masse wherever the Commission went. If they were capable of bussing two thousand supporters into Keren for the opening of a party branch office, they would surely see to it that as many or more paraded before the Commission, even if it meant sending them to the Sudan frontier. With their Ethiopian cash and great concentration of supporters in Asmara, the Unionists would be unassailable in a contest of demonstrations. If the Moslems were to have a chance of catching the Commission's attention, it would have to be a contest of something else.

The thought niggled away at the back of my mind but I was far too busy dealing with problems arising out of our new tribal set-up to do anything about it. There seemed to be no end to the difficulties which needed resolving, and the worst of the lot was Ibrahim Sultan himself. With funds now at his disposal, he was in the habit of flying off every now and again to canvass support from his 'Moslem brothers', so he said; and, since during the course of his travels he would occasionally be given five minutes of some reasonably well-known figure's time, he began to acquire those swaggering airs which constitute what might be called 'big-shotitis'. Insolence was part of the disease and there seemed to be nothing that this puffed up lout enjoyed so much as poking fun at the signs of our imperial decline to which his attention was drawn by the various distinguished personages he met. We had as good as given up India, he would say; we had agreed to withdraw from Egypt; everyone knew that we would not be staying in Palestine or the Sudan for very much longer; so what did I make of that? He would then pin me down with an oily leer and say that he would tell me. The British lion was no longer anything to be afraid of. It had become a weary old cat.

I did not find it easy to tolerate these crude impertinences and when Ibrahim turned up with an impudent grin on his face to offer the Moslem League's congratulations on our granting Palestine and Indian independence on that red—or should one say black—letter day in August 1947, I could have thrown everything within reach at him. Independence for the Indian continent was, of course, inevitable and had been ever since Baldwin got his Government of India Act through after so much clamour and commotion in 1935. Even so, because the War had delayed the inevitable, it was a shock when it came: and by no means a pleasant shock. There was no good pretending that in India and Pakistan we now had two loyal Dominions which would take their place in the Commonwealth beside Canada, Australia, New Zealand and South Africa. What we had were two totally independent Asiatic republics which, though agreeable to joining the Commonwealth, made it plain that they felt no loyalty to it, let alone any to Britain. By their loss the heart of the Empire had been ripped out and we would now have to face the consequences of that monumental change.

Though rarely gracious, Ibrahim's manner became perceptibly more disrespectful after our loss of India and Pakistan. It was not his little digs at our imperial decline that bothered me so much as the offhand way in which he began to treat me. When he had let slip that little joke about calling him Sultan Ibrahim Sultan he had not, as I now discovered, been joking at all. Nothing was said but he clearly regarded the management of the Tigrey tribe as his business and mine as being that of a rubber stamp available for his use. 'Kindly approve this'. 'Issue a licence to so and so', 'A present to somebody else', and 'Sign the following orders' he would say, breezing into my office in a way that even the Kantibai would never have done. Not wanting a rumpus with this powerful rascal, I would grit my teeth and so far as my conscience would allow, try to accommodate him. Inevitably, however, the day would come when he would expect too much and in the event it came. So-and-so, the chief of Such-and-such a tribe, had proved totally unsatisfactory, Ibrahim said, and so would I please sign this piece of paper dismissing him and appointing this excellent fellow for whom he could vouch in his place? What had this chief done? That was his business, Ibrahim said in a voice of high insolence. I begged to differ. Did I mean that I would not agree to dismiss him? I certainly did. I showed him the door.

I regretted it a few minutes later. After this I would get no cooperation from Ibrahim and, if I got none from him, I would get none from the tribes. What a mess I had got myself into! I had been overhasty, I confessed to young Saleh Hinit. He looked at me in blank-faced amazement and then burst out laughing. I had got it all wrong, he said: it was Ibrahim who was at my mercy, not I at his. Why did I think the tribes followed him? It was because they saw him as their go-between with us. They had won their independence through us and they looked to us to preserve it. They only looked to Ibrahim as their friend at Court. What he said was so obvious that I couldn't think how I had overlooked it. Anyhow, I now knew how to bring the insufferable Ibrahim to heel. All I needed was to give a hint that I might be looking away from him to somebody else. That was easily done. He had as his senior lieutenant an agreeable but ambitious merchant of considerable influence called Mohammad Ali

A Divided Eritrea Awaits a Decision

Radas. He was just the man for my purpose. To have him up to my house for a cup of tea and a chat now and again was all that was required to bring a gushing Ibrahim along with offers to be my most obedient servant. Divide and rule? Yes, I suppose you could call it that.

A chastened Ibrahim now took pains to call in very much more frequently than in the past to let me know what he was up to. With every Moslem in the country signed up with the League, bar a feudal has-been or two, he could not see how a Commission could fail to honour its wishes and give Eritrea its independence. I could not believe that any Commission would be likely to honour the wishes of the Moslems alone. But they were in the majority, Ibrahim protested. That was questionable, I said, and if he really wanted to get the Commissioners' sympathy I thought that he would do well to get himself some Christian allies. Ibrahim pulled a face saying that his Moslems would not like that at all. For what it was worth that was my advice. I could see that he had taken my point but somehow wished that he hadn't.

In the meantime, while Ibrahim and his friends were resting on their oars after successfully launching the League, the Ethiopians were working overtime on Eritrea during this run-up to the arrival of the Commission and, judging by the expense-account life being led by Unionist topdogs, they were not stinting the cash. The key figure in this flurry of activity was an adopted son of the Emperor called Colonel Negga Haile Selassie who had recently installed himself in Asmara as 'Ethiopian Liaison Officer'. To have called him a 'Consul', the Ethiopian Foreign Minister explained, would have been wrong. Consuls serve in foreign countries and Eritrea was, of course, Ethiopian. Well, what's in a name? We knew and the Ethiopians knew that we knew that the Colonel would not be performing any consular functions and that, even if there were anything to liaise about, he would not waste much time on liaising. His job was to direct the Unionist campaign and act as the link man between the Unionists and the Ethiopian Government. He was rather a grand young man: rather too grand, I thought, to do the job very well. He obviously enjoyed walking up and down red carpets and making little speeches on ceremonial occasions but seeing Tedla Bairu, as I sometimes did when visiting Asmara, hanging about his residence waiting for him to wake up as late as midday, I could hardly believe that there was much get-up-and-go about him. Nevertheless, the sight of this haughty, uniformed figure driving around in a large limousine with an Ethiopian flag on its bonnet was good for Unionist morale and what was good for Unionist morale was no help to the League.

Ibrahim watched Negga's activities with increasing anxiety and then one day he came tumbling into my office in a state of spluttering protest to say that this young 'bastard' of Haile Selassie's was forming a private army. Yes, and he was spending hundreds of thousands of dollars on it! More than a thousand young ne'er-do-wells had been recruited and put into uniform and now they were being drilled. Could I guess why, Ibrahim asked with a querulous snap. It was obvious! They were going to be used to give a lead in demonstrations and riots. Yes, that was undoubtedly the Unionist plan: to capture the Commission's attention by staging a series of riots and demonstrations. So what did he expect me to do about it? Get the Administration to ban this Unionist Youth League, he replied as quick as a flash. How could we possibly tolerate the Unionists forming a private army?

I knew that I would get no change out of Drew and I didn't. To compare these young fellows with the Fascist youth was really going a bit too far, he thought. He preferred to think of them as something more in the nature of Boy Scouts. Whether they were to be called Boy Scouts, Fascist Youth or Unionist Militia was not the problem. The problem, as I had already concluded, was that unless we could present it with an alternative, the Commission would certainly draw its conclusions from a political contest by demonstration which the Unionists would win hands down. The Moslem League simply would not get a look in, I told Drew, and that wouldn't be fair. For this I got a good natured, schoolmasterly rebuke. I had no right to assume that the Commissioners would be a team of blind fools, Drew said in tones of mild disapproval. They were bound to be men of experience who would certainly know how to get the full facts about the League. In any case, that was their business, not ours.

Dejazmatch Tesemma, who had fathered the Greater Tigrai project, was also watching Negga's antics with finger-tapping alarm. His followers had, by this time, formed themselves into what he had unaccountably labelled 'The Liberal Progressive Party' but they were now embarrassingly thin on the ground. The defection of the Moslem Saho tribes to the League had hit them badly and now, so Abraha explained, Negga was at work bribing his more luke-warm supporters to change sides.

Not that this mattered, he admitted with a shrug of the shoulders, for when the Commission came it would see Unionists in their thousands and no one else. The Commission would not even know that the Liberal Progressive Party existed and, even though it would probably hear of the Moslem League, it would have no notion of its strength. 'C'est la vie!' he murmured, airing his sophistication.

By chance, one of the new Tigrey chiefs died soon after this and I was landed with the task of deciding on a successor. Who was it to be? Ibrahim naturally had a candidate up his sleeve and so had the deceased's family. I could not agree to either. When we formed the new Tigrey tribes, we had let the family heads in each tribe elect their chief and, though the elections had in most cases been formalities, the principle that family heads had a right to elect their chiefs had been established. And so I turned to the family heads of the tribe in this case to elect a successor to their late chief. No one objected. A new chief was elected and it was 'hear hears' all round. Why, I cannot imagine, but this little episode suddenly triggered off a thought in my head. Suppose, I thought to myself, we got the family heads throughout Eritrea to turn up before the Commission in their own localities and say what they wanted? Yes, that would do the trick! It would give the Commission a chance of hearing what every family in the country wanted and rule out demonstrations as a reliable guide to a party's strength. I put it to Drew with predictable results. 'Dear me, dear me!' he said. How often had he got to say that how the Commission tackled its job was no business of ours!

Up to this point I had seen the contest ahead of us as a straight fight between the League and the Unionists with Abraha's Liberal Progressives on the fringe. I had never given a thought to the possibility of an Italian comeback. And that was very odd indeed, a sun-baked old Italian settler called De Ponti said to me one day when I let this slip. I was young, he said, implying that I was too young to know what the Italians had done for Eritrea. Puffing slowly at his curly meerschaum pipe, he told me about the Eritrea he had first known nearly fifty years before. There had been no security then. He could remember having to bribe half a dozen petty chiefs for protection to get himself down from Asmara to Keren! Everywhere people had been afraid and that meant hunger because they were too frightened to cultivate. Everyone was hungry because, cultivation apart, rinderpest and other animal diseases would wipe out thousands of their animals. Come to that, there was precious little they could do about the diseases which cut hundreds, sometimes thousands, of people down at different seasons of the year. As for infants, barely one out of two could expect to survive. I would never believe that this was the same country, he said, and then, prodding me in the chest, he added, 'Yes, and don't forget what has happened to Eritrea is an Italian miracle!' And that, he asked me to take note, was something the Eritreans all knew.

What the old gentleman did not let on was that the Italian Government had just demonstrated a touching urge to honour Italy's debt to the many thousands of Eritreans who had served in her colonial forces. All pensions and gratuities would be paid in full, was the message which now came out from Rome. It would be helpful, the message continued, if Eritrean ex-soldiers would form a Veterans' Association to help the Italian Government trace and verify the credentials of would-be beneficiaries. The message had barely reached Eritrea when a Veterans' Association was established in offices conveniently provided for it by Italian well-wishers in Keren and, within hours, hundreds of jolly old soldiers were hobbling along to sign up.

The President of this organisation was an ex–Sergeant Major of majestic appearance called Kafel Hassenebi. All six feet six inches of him came to a thunderous attention before me soon after this. Might he have permission to speak? Certainly. Taking a piece of paper out of one pocket and a pair of spectacles out of another, the ancient warrior proceeded to read out what was on the piece of paper in the slowest of slow time. The message he had to convey was that the Veterans' Association looked on themselves as 'sons of Italy' and, being Italy's sons, they wanted to be with Italy, their mother. Was there any objection to their saying they wanted the Italians back? None whatsoever, I replied; everyone was free to say whatever he liked. He gave me a courteous bow and clumped off, shoulders back, head in the air. The next day the Italian Press had hosannahs for headlines: Eritreans were rallying in their thousands to the dear old flag, they boasted. The loyal old soldiers were leading the way.

I did not expect Ibrahim to throw his turban in the air on hearing the news or Tedla Bairu to clap his hands. Nor did they! They expressed themselves shocked, disgusted and otherwise outraged by this monstrous piece of Italian chicanery and lost no time in demanding that the Veterans be made to shut up and go home. Surprisingly, Drew—who, on normal form, would never have given the Veterans a passing thought—went off like a rocket in spluttering rage on hearing what had happened. The British Legion did not indulge in politics so why should the Eritrean Veterans? And why, for that matter, had I queered the pitch by saying that these charlatans could say whatever they liked? The whole thing was a shameless Italian racket and he was damned if they were going to get away with it. Would I kindly tell Kafel and company that they were not to indulge in politics? To soften the embarrassment of the occasion, I told Kafel that, if he and his friends wanted to play at politics, they would have to form a political party. An application to form one was on my desk the very next day. It had to be approved by Drew but that, I told Kafel, was a formality. The Moslem League's application had been approved within the week. Almost two months went by before the 'New Eritrean Pro-Italy Party' was eventually licenced but, by then, it had little time left to canvass support. The Commission of Inquiry was already heading our way.

In advance of it there now arrived Frank Stafford, the British Commissioner, to make arrangements for its visit. Formerly an Adviser to the Ethiopian Government in the aftermath of the Italians' defeat, Stafford had no difficulty in sizing up the situation. He quickly saw my point about the dangers of leading the Commission to draw its own conclusions from a contest of demonstrations though, unlike myself, it was not Unionist demonstrations that bothered him. It was the pro-Italians. Yes, I agreed, with the money the Italians seemed to be spending, they would have no difficulty in putting several thousands onto the streets and yet, if one got down to fundamentals, one would unquestionably find that their actual support was not very great. Let every family in the country elect a head, I suggested, and let the Commission hear what each had to say and the truth would be known. Stafford was enchanted with my proposal. Drew mumbled misgivings but gave in. The go-ahead was given and within the next few weeks every family in the country had presented us with a spokesman to tell the Commission what it wanted. I had got away with it at the eleventh hour. Nor was that all. Stafford subsequently invited me to join him on the Commission as a member of the British Delegation. I could not have asked for anything I wanted more.

14

THE FOUR POWERS
AGREE TO DISAGREE

'Have you no respect for my feelings?' Gianfillipi, Asmara's leading hotelier, shrilled. He was upset because the Commission was to be billeted on him and he objected to sharing a roof with 'the Bolshevisti' of the Russian delegation. He was not the only prima donna to test my nerves during those bustling weeks before the Commission's arrival. Every arrangement had critics and every critic was a potential spanner in the works. At one end of the scale were Ibrahim and Tedla Bairu, each complaining that the arrangements I had made favoured the other. At the other were Political Officers' wives upset either because they had been given the onus of entertaining the Commission at some point in their travels or because they had not. It was a headache a minute and for what purpose? To enable a Commission to establish a set of facts which were already well known.

So, that was what I thought, was it? Stafford gave me an avuncular smile. It was, also, the smile of a Man of the World who had been around far beyond the provincial bounds within which colonial hicks like myself were penned. As debonair and spruce as a dandy promenading along the Rue St Honore, Stafford could never have been lost in a crowd. With a twinkle and usually a monocle in his eye and, invariably, with a carnation in his buttonhole, this captivating person looked like someone who was accustomed to broad vistas and dealing with mandarins. Not surprisingly so, for that is just what he was. And so, when he seemed to question my remark on the absurdity of despatching a Commission to find out what

The Four Powers Agree to Disagree

was already well known, I sat up. What did he mean? That, if I imagined the Commission was out to get at the truth, I had got it all wrong.

He was not, in fact, talking about the Commission as a whole. He was talking about the French and Russians who, for their own different reasons, were apparently set on giving the Italians a trusteeship over Eritrea. The French, Stafford explained, were suffering from a colonial menopause after their recent loss of Syria and clearly believed that their position in Djibuti would be made more secure if Italian colonial rule was re-established in Eritrea. That I could understand, but the Russians? What were those sermonising high priests of anti-colonialism doing in such company? Couldn't I guess? As I knew, the Russians were going flat out to get Communist governments installed in as many European countries as possible and Italy, with its large Communist party, was of course one of their principal targets. Naturally, then, they would look on the elections which would shortly take place in Italy as crucial and since the Italians—Communists, Socialists, Christian Democrats and the rest—had all gone wild over the return of their colonies, they were bound to take a pro-Italian colonialist line. After all, when Italy was the prize, why should they worry about keeping their hands clean over a few African colonies?

And what was our line? Stafford took off his monocle and polished it before replying and then said, 'To get shot of Eritrea before things get too expensive and too hot.' He did not, of course, mean at any price. Our Labour Government, who had just brought about India's independence, liked to believe that they had won the moral leadership of the world by doing so. They were not going to jeopardise that reputation by taking a pro-Italian colonialist line and, in any event, they felt morally bound to do something for Ethiopia. What that meant, Stafford said, was that we must try to prevent the French and Russians from distorting the facts and at least get the truth about Eritrea on record. And the Americans? Stafford smiled. They really did not know whether they were coming or going! Like the Russians, their eyes were on Italy but, because of the anti-colonialist lobby in the States, it was less easy for them to be pro-Italian. On the whole, he thought they would go along with us and try to get at the truth. So that was how the scene was set. Ourselves and very probably the Americans pro-truth, the French and Russians anti. It was nice to know that we would be on the side of the angels.

One had only to look at the Russians to know there was nothing angelic about them. An earthier, shabbier, drabber lot would have been hard to imagine. Their features, like their clothes, seemed to have been dyed a dull proletarian grey. The head of their delegation was a General Feodorov who was a large, ungainly man with hands like shovels and arms and legs that seemed to have run away with the rest of him. His face was as hard and creased as a Siberian landscape but every now and again one could detect a smile pleading to be let out from behind the stern defences of his jaw line. He released it on me one day during our morning coffee break. 'Colonel Trevaski,' he said, giving me a little bow, 'you have a very interesting name.' Interesting, he said, because it was a Baltic name. Alas, I couldn't claim the honour, I replied, my name was Cornish. The General bared a set of strong teeth in a playful grin to say that, as a native of the Baltic, he knew a Baltic name when he heard one. He very much hoped that he would see me one day back where I belonged. 'As our guest, of course!' said his minder, with a thin smile. This was a bespectacled, professional person called Meier, the possessor of a cold, expressionless voice and an excellent command of English. Seeing him once after he had been on the sick list for a couple of days, I asked him how he was feeling. 'Like a King,' he replied, giving me the bleakest of looks. 'Yes, like a king... in a republic.'

The Russian I came to know best was a man of about my own age called Nikolai Klimov. Slight of build and delicately featured, he wore the mournful expression of a Victorian curate crossed in love. He rarely smiled, he never laughed: he took life seriously and he also took me seriously which I found flattering. He would spend hours questioning me about Eritrea and the Eritreans, holding me in his large, sad eyes as if he could not bear to lose sight of me. What a mine of information I was, he said one day. What a pity I had not put the results of my researches on record. Oh, but I had, I said, rushing off to get him various treatises I had written on tribal histories, customs and so on. Having read them and said that they exceeded all his expectations, he asked whether he could buy copies of them. Copies? What copies? But surely they had been published? Did I mean to say that my Government had not had works of this exceptional scientific value published? I did. 'My poor, poor Ken!' he said, looking tearfully out of the window, 'we'll have to do something about this!' A couple of days later he turned up with something approaching a smile to say that Feodorov had been in touch with Moscow University and that they had agreed to publish my works in the interests of science. I could not, of course, accept this but imagine my feelings! Neither Longrigg, Benoy nor Drew had given me a thank you for my opera, let alone read them!

Sometimes Nikolai would change the subject from Eritrea to my private life. 'Now, tell me about yourself,' he would say and then lead me on with questions about my pay and prospects. He could not believe that anyone as talented as I was could have been treated so scurvily. Befuddled though I was by Nikolai's sugared compliments, it was at about this point that I began wondering what he was up to. When he began preaching sermons according to the gospel of St Joseph Stalin, I knew. It was nice to be wanted but not if it meant going to bed with the Reds.

Even sitting down at the same table with the Russians sent distress signals across the aristocratic countenance of the French Commissioner, Burin des Roziers. Later to be a Gaullist pillar, he was as different from them as Burgundy from beer. To see him was to see a world of pre-war elegance when the smart set had raced at Chantilly, sunned themselves at Cap Ferrat and put on white ties and long dresses to dine at Maxime's. It was a long, long way from the crude, rude world from which the Russians had come and yet, surprisingly, the gulf between them was happily bridged by John Utter, the head of the American team who was later to serve the Duchess of Windsor as her personal secretary to the end of her life. The secret of his success was that he was an American who had lived for many years in Paris. The earthy American side of him could understand the Russians, his Parisian self Burin des Roziers. He was the perfect go-between. I once asked to what he attributed his success in dealing with us all so well. It was not too difficult, he replied, so long as you observed certain rules. 'Treat the French as if Louis XIV is still alive,' he said, 'and don't let on to the British that you know Queen Victoria is dead!' And the Russians? 'Buy 'em a drink!'

Knowing that the French and Russians wanted to conceal anything which suggested that the Eritreans were less than enthusiastic about a return of Italian colonial rule, I was not surprised that they should give our plans for the Commission a frosty reception: the fact being that they were nicely designed to reveal what the Eritreans wanted down to the very last man. All in all, we had registered 3,336 elected family heads and, since we had also registered how many members there were in each of their families, all the Commission had to do to work out how many Eritreans wanted what was to get each family head to state his preference. Nothing, it might be thought, could have been simpler. Nothing less objectionable.

After Stafford and I had explained what we had arranged, Feodorov cleared his throat and registered disenchantment to a 'hear, hear' or two from Burin des Rozier. Could he please have copies of the Electorial Law and Electoral Roll for these elections, he asked. What? There weren't any! So, these were customary elections held in customary fashion, Burin des Rozier's silken voice purred. That being so, these people would have been elected for customary purposes, not to express views on the future of Eritrea. What! Was I really saying that these people had been elected to say what their families wanted for Eritrea's future as well as for the family's customary needs? I was. Very well, then, could they please have copies of the election results: which was to say, could they be told how many votes had been cast for each candidate. Good Heavens! Surely, I was not saying that every family head had been elected unanimously? That was customary, was it? Burin des Rozier's eyeballs rolled around in a pantomime of disbelief while Feodorov said that he was far from convinced that there had been any elections at all. Having no other plans, the French and Russians eventually had to go along with ours. Not that it mattered. Having discredited our plans in advance, they could discredit their findings when necessary.

The French and the Russians were not the only ones with an interest in concealing the truth. The Unionists who claimed that ninety nine per cent of all Eritreans were behind them were naturally anxious to sabotage our plans; and so it was not surprising that throughout these preliminary discussions Tedla Bairu should have been popping in and out of our offices, trying to do just that. 'Believe me, sir,' he would invariably gasp, all breathless and agitated on arrival, and then out would come all kinds of scare stories. The Moslems had got hold of some arms and were plotting to bump off Unionist supporters, the Italians were bribing thugs to start riots and make it look as if the Unionists had started them; the Moslems were up to this, the Italians were up to that. Impassioned appeals to call off the meetings of family heads would be followed by warnings of bloodshed and disorders which were likely to take place if we did not do so.

Since Tedla had been careful to spell out his anxieties in letter after letter to Drew, we had him hopping around too adding to our difficulties. It was all very well laying on these meetings of family heads, he grumbled, but first things first and what came first? Law and order. In any event, the Commission did not want the meetings so why have them? What did I think? Stafford asked. I thought we would be taking a fair sized risk if we went ahead but I didn't say so. Having come as far down the road as this, I was damned if I was going to let the truth about the Moslem opposition to an Ethiopian take-over be suppressed. It was a Unionist try-on, I said, and in any event to cancel the meetings would play into the hands of the French and Russians. Stafford agreed, and Drew reluctantly piped down. Naturally I was pleased but could have done without all those butterflies flitting about in my stomach.

I need not have worried. We could not have had much easier a ride. The family heads were assembled, according to their locations, at fifteen different places and there the Commission asked each head individually what he and his family wanted. All this was done without any serious interruption. There was a scuffle or two here and there but, apart from a few sore heads—including those of a couple of turbulent abbots at Adi Ugri—there was no damage. We had, of course, taken precautions. Unionist efforts to bus supporters to the venues of the meetings were preempted; known Unionist agitators were picked up and put on ice and riot acts were read repeatedly to all concerned. Drew himself attributed the peaceful outcome of this exercise to Tedla Bairu's 'good sense' and wrote him a letter of thanks for making the Commission's visit such a success. In reply he received a Grand Remonstrance with copies for the Commission at the high handed and unwarranted behaviour of myself and our Political Officers. This had the poor man babbling with anxiety lest the Commission should 'make a stink'. What should we do? A Court of Inquiry, perhaps? No, an Inquiry carried out by himself might be better. Since my own behaviour would have been an object of inquiry, I was naturally 'anti' inquiries of any kind. Perhaps it would be best to do nothing, I suggested. Nothing at all? Drew started up with surprise and then suddenly clouds lifted and out came a slow, sunny smile. Yes, he said, there was that Prime Minister Thingummy Bob whose policy was always to do nothing in a crisis on the principle that it would blow away and, dash it, it always did. So he did nothing. The crisis blew away, 'just as I thought it would' Drew said a little smugly.

It was, of course, too much to expect that Feodorov and Burin des Roziers would allow the referendum by family heads to proceed according to plan. The first thing they did was to question the population figures we had given them. The figures given for the number of people in each family were ours, Feodorov said, and, as far as he was concerned, they were unacceptable. They would prefer to get the figures from the family heads themselves, Burin des Roziers said with persuasive guile. And so, as he had no doubt foreseen, on being asked how many people he represented, each family head gave an exaggerated figure, the slicker Unionist exaggerating most. Despite this, the results which emerged were not too far from the truth. The figures showed that the Eritreans were clearly split between the Unionists and Moslem League, less a handful apiece for the Pro-Italy and Liberal Progressive parties. Yes, that was what the figures showed, Burin des Roziers agreed, but who could trust the figures? If you added up the figures given by the family heads, the total came to more than twice the known total of Eritrea's population. So what did that mean? That the results were meaningless, he replied, with a cultivated little sigh.

To discredit the outcome still further, Burin des Roziers argued that, while the family heads might have given the Commission a vague though highly inaccurate idea of the support each political party enjoyed, that was not the same thing as telling it what the people wanted. Quite so, Feodorov agreed. It was his impression that the great majority of Eritreans had formed political parties for social and religious reasons which had nothing whatsoever to do with the future of Eritrea. Having a tongue like a trip wire, Burin des Rozier had no difficulty in getting guileless family heads to substantiate what he and Feodorov had been saying and even the clumsy Feodorov was able to get quite a few of the bumpkins to say that they were ready to accept whatever the Allies decided. There it was, they had proved their point... or had they? Grill peasants from the Russian Communist party or even French Gaullists and the chances were that they would have reacted in much the same way. The unthinking classes invariably leave their political leaders to do their thinking for them. Having smeared the results of the referendum with doubt, the

The Four Powers Agree to Disagree

French and Russians went on to demonstrate how uniquely qualified the Italians were to run Eritrea. They did so by concocting an Italian success story out of the huge sums the Italians had invested in roads, railways and other public works, leaving the Americans and ourselves to point out their near-total neglect of Eritrean welfare. Nikolai asked if we had any proof of this. Proof? It was well known! No one, not even the Italians, would deny it. Well, if we had no proof of our allegations, he had proof positive that the Italians had, in fact, made a major contribution in the sphere of Health. On that, he slapped an Italian publication down on the table before us and pointed a quivering finger at an article in it. It was written in the 'braggadocio' style of a Fascist propagandist and gave a self-congratulatory account of Italy's civilising mission in Africa. As an example of what Italy was doing, it referred to the construction of an ultra-modern sanitorium at a village near Asmara for Italian and Eritrean use. Well, what had we to say to that? I enlightened him. No such sanitorium existed. The article was nothing more than Fascist propaganda. That sent him mouthing around in search of a reply but he quickly recovered to say that he did not believe me. If that was so, would he take a half-hour's drive to the village in question and see whether I or the writer of that article was right? No, he wouldn't. The article was good enough for him. That was too much! I lost my temper and could have kicked myself for doing so.

Not surprisingly, the Commission's report was so much waste paper and, after receiving it, the Council of Foreign Ministers agreed to disagree. We alone came anywhere near to giving the Ethiopians what they wanted: with, however, the most curiously impracticable proposal imaginable. Ethiopia should take over Eritrea for a probationary spell of ten years, we suggested, at the end of which the United Nations would either confirm her in her tenure of Eritrea or decide otherwise. The Americans had an equally absurd proposal: to give Ethiopia Assab and half the Plateau and to defer a decision on the rest of the country for a year. The French and the Russians both opted for trusteeships: the French for an Italian and the Russians for a collective international one. And so, at the cost of Heaven knows how many millions of dollars, the Four Great Powers came up with nothing. On 15th September 1948 the Italian Colonial question was handed over to the United Nations.

15

STRUGGLE AND STRIFE

I HAD BARELY HEARD what the Council of Ministers had said about Eritrea when the Qadhi appeared at my door with a smooth smile on his face and a posse of long-faced Moslem grandees as an escort. An unsmiling Ibrahim Sultan brought up the rear. A most alarming rumour was going round, the Qadhi said, and they had come to ask for my assurances that it was not true. Perhaps I had heard it myself? It was that the British Government wanted to hand the whole of Eritrea over to Ethiopia. I deplored it as much as he did but what could I say? Yes, I feared it was true but I had been given to understand that our Government had, in fact, suggested that an Advisory Council should be set up to safeguard Moslem interests. The Qadhi and his entourage gaped disbelief. Ibrahim let out a vulgar guffaw. Advisory Council! His voice pealed with mockery. 'Words, words, words: what use are words?' Turning a hot, hostile look on me he then asked all present to remember that the British had just betrayed their Arab brothers in Palestine. They had abandoned them to the Jewish invaders. We were not to be trusted, he thundered, and it was no good their thinking that they could expect any honest help from us. That hurt, but I could not blame him.

The Unionists were no happier. Bumping into Tedla Bairu one day in Asmara, I found him with a face like an undertaker's. He was still querulous about our handling of the Commission's visit but what had chased the smiles off his face was the inescapable truth that the Italians had very much more political clout in the world at large than Ethiopia. He knew, as we all knew, that with the Latin Americans as allies the Italians could count on very much more support in the United Nations and, since they had now taken over the Italian Colonial question, that was bad news. Tedla did not mention this directly, preferring to denounce Italian chicanery and corruption and complain that we did nothing to stop it. It was intolerable, he grizzled, and unless we did something about it, he really could not be responsible for the consequences. I was by this time an old enough hand to know that this meant he was cooking something up.

If Tedla and Ibrahim were upset by what had come out of the Council of Ministers, so was I. I had had no warning that we intended to back down on partition and I knew quite as well as Ibrahim that even if there were a hundred and one advisory councils set up to safeguard Moslem interests, the Ethiopians would do just as they pleased once they got their hands on Eritrea. What puzzled me was that, during a short leave at home after the Commission had gone, Rita Hinden had expressed no doubts about Bevin sticking to partition. He was like a bulldog, she said, and, having got his teeth into partition, he would never let go. Nevertheless, she had seemed anxious that the case for partition should be well publicised and had pressed me once again to write an article in depth about Eritrea for the Fabian Colonial Bureau. Being a less obedient servant by this time, I did so (though anonymously). So what had gone wrong? Why had Bull Dog Bevin let partition go?

I never resolved the mystery but, to make it even more mysterious, Bevin reverted to partition soon afterwards. This came about during talks he had with Count Sforza, the Italian Foreign Minister, in an effort to cook up a solution to the Italian Colonial question which the United Nations would accept. Their proposed solution was to give Italy trusteeship in Somalia and Tripolitania and ourselves one in Cyrenaica. Eritrea was to be partitioned between Ethiopia and the Sudan. Having received the blessing of its First Committee, the Bevin-Sforza proposals seemed all set to be approved by the United Nations' General Assembly. Voting first took place on the proposals for each territory with favourable results, Eritrea's partition being approved by a solid majority of 39 votes to 11. To get the Assembly's formal approval, however, the proposals had to be accepted as a whole and, incredibly, they were rejected by a thumping 37 votes to 14. This was due not to caprice but to the outbreak of violent anti-Italian riots in Tripoli after it had become known that an Italian trusteeship for Tripolitania had been proposed. And so, though approved by the General Assembly one day, the partition of Eritrea was rejected the next for reasons which had nothing whatsoever to do with Eritrea. I could hardly believe that Providence could be so cruel.

He imagined that I would be disappointed at the collapse of the Bevin-Sforza plan? The speaker was Italy's answer to Colonel Negga, Count di Grapello, the newly arrived Italian Liaison Officer. Suited, shirted and shod with discreet refinement and wearing a signet ring the size of a quail's egg, the Count was an eye-catching addition to the local scene. Speaking personally, he observed, he had never thought very much of our 'crazy' partition plan and that was why he found the news from Lake Success so encouraging. What news? Hadn't I heard? Why, the representatives of the anti-Unionist organisation, who had gone to Lake Success to hear the Bevin-Sforza proposals debated, had got together after their rejection and agreed to combine as a Bloc to demand immediate independence for Eritrea. That was a straightforward, sensible objective, in complete conformity with the times, wouldn't I say? His own Government was giving it their full backing and, since it would undoubtedly have the support of most Eritreans, he thought we could take it that it would get the United Nations' approval. I had a feeling that he might be right.

The news of the Independence Bloc brought the Qadhi and Ali Radas trotting along looking decidedly flustered and fussed. They had been holding the Moslem League fort in Ibrahim's absence at Lake Success and were very put out that he should have committed the League to joining the Bloc without consulting them first. Anyone could see that this Bloc was an Italian affair, Ali said, and it would be wrong for the League to get involved in it. For a start it would upset the Tigray tribes who associated the Italians with the Diglal, Kantibai and their feudal past. The Tigray tribes were, admittedly, as wild-eyed and suspicious as the wildest of wolf packs but if the Qadhi, Ali and all their other leaders assured them that their fears were unfounded they would, in the end, believe them. So what was bothering this sombre-faced pair? The League wanted independence and now, with the Italians and their friends behind them, they had the best possible chance of getting it. That was true, the Qadhi admitted, but independence with the Moslem League in the chair was one thing, with Italy in it was another. The Italians would see to it that their friends had most of the ministries and important positions in the Administration. So that was it! With the Italians and their friends as allies, there would be fewer jobs for the boys of the Moslem League.

Since the United Nations had announced that it would be sending a fact-finding Commission to Eritrea after their rejection of the Bevin-Sforza proposal, Ibrahim was far too busy on his return to take the grumbling anxieties of the Qadhi and Ali seriously. Having taken a plunge in the international pool, he affected a statesmanlike contempt for their provincialism and complained that having to educate such blockheads in the basics of political life took up more time than he could properly afford. There was such a lot to be done! He had to show the flag in Cairo and Karachi, have discussions with the Italian Government in Rome and tie up a lot of loose ends with the Italians and pro-Italy party here in Eritrea! It was no business of mine, I said, but had he thought of what the Tigray tribes would be thinking now that they knew that he had taken the Italians on as allies? What did it matter what wild nonsense entered their stinking, rancid heads? Ibrahim hoiked up some phlegm in his throat and expectorated into a grubby handkerchief. Where else could they go? They were stuck with the League which meant that they were stuck with him. They could presumably get him voted out of the League's Secretary Generalship, I pointed out. What? With a new United Nations Commission arriving in a matter of weeks? The Tribesmen might be dense but they were not suicidal idiots! A couple of days later he swanned off to Pakistan.

Despite Ibrahim's pretentious posturing, it was easy enough to see that the Qadhi had been right. The Italians were in the Bloc's driving seat, not Ibrahim. The Italians in question were a small group of the colonial elite settlers in and around Keren who had set up an 'Italo-Eritrean Association' with an Italian-cum-halfcaste membership as big brothers to the Eritrean pro-Italy party. They were deceiving themselves, Antonelli said, and letting that smooth-tongued di Grapello put silly ideas into their heads. Would I credit it but these fools seriously believed that if Eritrea got its independence they would be left to run it? They thought that they were making use of Ibrahim Sultan but the truth of the matter was that Ibrahim Sultan was making use of them. The old pipe-puffing de Ponti, who was a founder member of the Association, thought differently. Of course they would run Eritrea once it became independent, he insisted. You could not leave it to loud mouths like Ibrahim Sultan and they knew it. What the Italians were doing was criminal, Colonel Negga begged me to understand and, unless something was done about it, he could see blood baths ahead for which, of course, he would not be responsible.

Since the League and the Bloc were Keren-based and had most of their supporters in the Western Province, it was reasonable to suppose that we would be the target of Ethiopian wrath. And we were. The first hint of trouble was the desertion of an Abyssinian security guard called Hagos Tamnou from a cotton scheme at a place called Tessenei. Other Abyssinian security guards followed and then a few Police Constables. Within the week Hagos had an armed gang under his command and within another they had raided the estate of Filippo Casciani, Eritrea's premier Italian settler and founding father of the Italo-Eritrea Association. Fruit trees were destroyed, cattle seized and a letter left to explain that these 'friends of Ethiopia' had done what they had done to punish Casciani for supporting that evil of all evils, the Independence Bloc.

The raid brought Antonelli with a sealed and ribboned document to my door. It was a remonstrance from 'the Keren Italian Residents'. One pace behind him was Filippo Casciani with a further remonstrance from 'the Italo-Eritrean Association'. What they were remonstrating about was our failure to protect Italian lives and property. The Administration was doing nothing, Antonelli said, breathless with agitation. Here in Keren they had watched events on the Plateau with increasing anxiety and now the trouble had come here. What did I propose to do about this? There was nothing I could do except my best with what I had. I was, I realised unhappily, in the same position that I had been when those murders took place at Adi Ugri. When I explained this as best I could, Casciani heaved with hiccoughs of laughter. The truth of the matter was that we did not attach importance to Italian lives, he quavered. Now, if British lives were being lost then there would be action all right. Casciani was no rough neck rancher but very much the sophisticated young Seigneur, a little aloof, a little grand. 'We appreciate, of course, that Great Britain has interests in this matter just as our country has,' he said. 'Unfortunately, they do not appear to be the same.' He looked me slowly up and down, inviting an answer, but I said nothing. Giving a little sigh he went on to say that the Italians resident in Eritrea had roots in the country and wanted to remain partners with the Eritreans in an independent Eritrea. That, of course, was against British policy and, for that matter, against Ethiopian policy also. You could say then that Britain and Ethiopia were on the same side. He paused to fix a cigarette in a long holder and, having lit it, gave me a long, quizzical look and said, 'Need I say more?' What was he getting at? Was he suggesting that we were encouraging the Ethiopians to terrorise the Italians and looking the other way? Yes, he replied, he was.

The raid on Casciani's plantation was the overture to a sequence of other raids which kept our police continually on the hop—if invariably a dozen hours or more behind the raiders. Suddenly, however, late one night I had a hot tip that Hagos was on his way back to give Casciani another going over. And so, having aroused a sleepy-eyed posse of police, I hurried off to Casciani's and deployed them in the hills behind his place across the track which we expected Hagos to use. Dawn came without any sign of him. An hour passed and still no sign. Two more hours went by and then a small boy came trotting up with a letter in his hand. 'This is for you!' he said. It was from Hagos. Addressing me in the name of 'God the Father, the Son and the Holy Ghost,' he asked why I was trying to stop him killing Italians. They were the enemies of King George and they were the enemies of his sovreign, the Emperor Haile Selassie. If I wanted any further proof of his friendship he would have me know that he had had me in his sights not a hundred yards from where I had been sitting but had done nothing, so would I please let him do his duty? I visited Casciani on my way back to find that Hagos had got round behind us and damaged a few more acres of his fruit trees. Casciani was breakfasting on a verandah shrouded by bougainvillea. He greeted me with a mock bow. 'What a pity that you should have chosen to remove your police from here just before the bandits turned up!' I could feel the bite in his voice as he spoke. Even the finest Police forces are at a disadvantage when faced with elusive Hagoses. Ours was by no means the finest but, to add to our difficulties, Drew had only recently responded to a Whitehall appeal for economies by reducing the Police establishment by one third; and this at a time when the Sudanese brigade which had formed our garrison had been replaced by nothing more than a solitary battalion of British troops. If we were to get anywhere we needed at least a thousand more Police. Drew chuckled with avuncular indulgence at the very idea when I put it to him. 'No, no!' he said, wagging his finger at me. 'You are thinking yourself into a sense of crisis!' This was too much! I had not imagined Hagos. I had not thought up the raids and murders that had

The Deluge

taken place. Men had been killed, property had been damaged. These were not dreams. They were facts. Drew listened as a nanny might to a child in a tantrum and assured me that things were nothing like as bad as I supposed. Nevertheless, he would give some thought to what I had said and see what could be done. A week later he issued a circular to say that it was up to British officers to dispel the quite unjustifiable mood of alarm and despondency which was taking hold of the civil population. They could best do this, he thought, by setting an example of normal, relaxed behaviour: for example, by going out on picnic parties in the countryside. He was not joking. He really meant it!

The next round in the saga developed when the Moslem tribesmen grazing in the shadow of the Plateau on the fringe of Abyssinian territory came under fire. This was wild, inaccessible country and our efforts to throw out the invaders were laughably inadequate. Abyssinian terror rampaged about these frontier lands. Killings and looting went on unabated. In one of the worst incidents, seven tribesmen were tied up and beheaded in front of their own families. To spell out what all this was about, the marauders left crude pamphlets everywhere telling the Moslems that this and worse to come was what they could expect if they did not leave the Moslem League and the accursed Italian Bloc. Ibrahim was away playing politics somewhere or other and so it was Ali, accompanied by the Qadhi as usual, who came to appeal for help. A couple of dozen greybeards stood on the verandah outside as grim faced as a bunch of coal miners on picket duty. What could I possibly do for them? No more than I had been able to do for the Italians. That was the embarrassing truth. I could do nothing. Searching frantically for the right words to convey this message to my visitors, I suddenly remembered that I had a hundred rifles in my store. A hundred rifles! Heavens above, here was the answer to my problem. With all their accusing eyes focussed on me, I did not pause to look before I leaped. They could have the rifles to defend themselves with, I announced. Ali and the Qadhi left showering me with benedictions. About a week later they came back glistening with delight. The tribesmen had smashed the Kaffirs, they reported. They had ransacked their villages and carried off their livestock. I was aghast. I hadn't given these scallywags rifles to start a war. They had been given to them for self defence. Goose pimples popped up along my back as I listened to the horrifying news. Worse was to come. They had beheaded seven Abyssinians. Another two or three who had been carried off as prisoners had died of gangrene as a result of being tied up too tightly. Ali could not understand my objections to what had been done. Self defence? Retaliation was the only sure form of self defence, he protested. Maybe he was right but enough was enough. I withdrew the rifles without further delay. In the event, however, there wasn't another cheep from the Abyssinians for a long time to come.

This murderous episode was soon taken over by other events but indirectly it precipitated a political drama of exceptional magnitude. In effect it did what Colonel Negga, Tedla Bairu and all the thugs in their pay had tried and failed to do. It bust the Bloc. It was those anti-Bloc pamphlets which the Unionist raiders had been scattering around the countryside that did the trick. Every tribesman now knew that the League had joined an Italian organisation called an Independence Bloc. An Italian organisation! Suspicions flared up with encouragement, no doubt, from the Qadhi, Ali and other Moslem bigwigs who had grown disenchanted with Ibrahim and his overbearing ways. As excited tittle-tattling travelled from valley to valley and mountain to plain, Tigray tribesmen gathered together to ponder what involvement in this Bloc could mean. Ibrahim was unmoved. These people were mere sheep, he told me, and he had no time to exchange baas with them. In a couple of weeks' time they would have forgotten all about this. He was wrong. After a couple of weeks Ali called to say that the Tigray tribes had decided to secede from Ibrahim's Moslem League and form a new party of which he had the honour to be President. The Party was to be called 'The Moslem League of the Western Province'.

Stafford, who was to be Liaison Officer to the United Nations Commission with my assistance, arrived monocled and full of smiles just after Ali had made this startling announcement. 'Praise be...!' he laughed on hearing the news. If that did not put paid to the Bloc he would buy a hat and eat it. His reaction surprised me. Why, I wondered, had he not expressed delight at the Moslems of the West seceding from the League and so removing one of the main obstacles to partition? And why, for that matter, did he feel so strongly about the Bloc? I asked him. He did not like bribery and corruption, he said, and the Italians were bribing and corrupting as if there were no tomorrow. But so were the Ethiopians, I reminded him, and that was not all, the Ethiopians were sponsoring murder. He clearly did not want to pursue the argument and before I knew it he had slipped neatly out of it under cover of badinage.

And what did 'the Moslem League of the Western Province' want, I asked Ali and a delegation of the party's leaders. 'Independence!' they said. Independence for the Western Province? Yes, they replied in one voice. This was absurd. Economically, the Province was unviable and in any case it was far too small to stand on its own. They would look to their friends, the British, for help, Ali said with an effulgent smile, and with their help all would be well. But why did they imagine that our Government would help them in this impractical enterprise of theirs when they had already made it plain that the best thing for them would be to join the Sudan? But they did not want to join the Sudan, Ali said apologetically. Not after what Boustead had done. After all, could I really expect the Tigray to become the Hadendowa's slaves? This reaction was all too predictable but I was very far from being dismayed. Once we had made it clear beyond question that we would have nothing whatsoever to do with an independent Western Province, even the thickest headed Tigray would be bound to pause and think and, if we then found ways and means of guaranteeing them against Bousteadism and Hadendowa domination on their joining the Sudan, I felt they could be persuaded to join it. If we leaned on them good and hard, I told Stafford, I was sure that they would come round to partition. He murmured his assent but with a faraway look in his eye.

What was in his mind was the prospect of banging another nail into the Independence Bloc's coffin. Having loosely allied themselves with the Moslem League at the time of the Four Power Commission, Dejazmatch Abraha's Liberal Progressives had drifted reluctantly into the Bloc. They were not at all happy about it, Abraha said, but what could they do? They could not join the Moslem League of the Western Province and they were too small a party to stand on their own. They could come to terms with the Unionists, Stafford suggested. Abraha let out a laugh like a burglar alarm. What? And submit themselves to Ethiopian rule? 'Never, never, never!' He hammered the words out. Of course not, Stafford said but, in political situations of this kind, one could not always expect to get what one wanted. Invariably there had to be resort to compromise. What compromise? What he was thinking about, Stafford explained, was some sort of conditional union with Ethiopia which would leave Eritrea self-governing. By curious coincidence, Abraha received a gracious invitation to visit His Imperial Majesty Haile Selassie a few days later. On his return the Liberal Progressives left the Bloc and opted for conditional union with Ethiopia. The Commission arrived a few days later.

16

THE UNITED NATIONS BRINGS THE CURTAIN DOWN ON ERITREA

'RATHER A MIXED BAG,' Stafford remarked as the five United Nations Commissioners descended onto the tarmac at Asmara Airport followed by their retinue of advisers, secretaries and whatever. First down the steps was a pocket-sized Guatemalan lawyer with a sallow face called Garcia Bauer and, following hard on his heels, a lawyer from Pakistan called Mian Zaud Din whose appearance was not so very dissimilar. Descending more ponderously several paces to their rear was a jolly, round-bellied Burmese judge called Aung Khine and following him there was another judge, a cadaverous Norwegian called Quale with hair and complexion of the snowiest white. Last to appear was a South African General of Huguenot descent called Theron, looking very British in what we used to call an 'Anthony Eden hat'. A mixed bag? They certainly were!

We had no doubt arranged matters to suit our own ends, Mian Zaud Din smirked; but if we had, he could assure me that he would see through it in no time at all. We should not forget that he had a long experience of British imperialist ways. Whatever we had arranged or otherwise, I replied, I could tell him that we had not arranged the riots which were rocking Asmara at that very moment. Unionist terror and intimidation against the Italians and supporters of the Bloc had multiplied horrifyingly in the run-up to the Commission's arrival and now the inevitable had happened.

As if we had not had dramas enough before, Asmara was staging a gala performance to welcome the Commission. The town was packed to

The United Nations Brings the Curtain Down on Eritrea

its roof tops with supporters of the rival parties and Drew, in a fatuous attempt to show the World how cool, calm and collected we all were, had instructed the Police to keep what we now call 'a low profile'. He was asking for trouble and he got it. Scuffling between Moslems and Christians led to fighting, fighting to the killing of a Moslem, his killing to his funeral and his funeral to mayhem. The fighting went on for five days in all and, throughout, rifle shots and exploding grenades provided a sinister obligato to the Commission's deliberations. He could see our imperialist hand in all this, Garcia Bauer said, pointing an accusing finger at me and Stafford. We were out to smash the Bloc and we had deliberately kept the Police looking the other way while the Unionist murderers did their dirty work. Imperialist hand? He never questioned that it was the bungling hand of the absurd Drew.

It did not take us more than a day or two to size up our visitors. From the moment of their arrival, Garcia Bauer and Mian Zaud Din blatantly boosted the Bloc as if every Eritrean citizen of probity and distinction was its most fervent supporter. Oh, so there were other political parties were there? Mian Zaud Din snorted when I mentioned them. Who did I mean? Those British stooges in the Western Province and those Ethiopian hirelings on the Plateau? Garcia Bauer leered and sneered his agreement, reminding us that, after the way we had stolen Belize from Guatemala, no one was able to recognise British colonial trickery quicker than a Guatemalan like himself. More amiable but with a mind as oysterlike as theirs was the elderly Norwegian, Quale. When I told him that the curse of Eritrea was the split between its Christians and Moslems, he closed his eyes and said that he was totally unaware of it. All he could see was a united people praying for reunion with Ethiopia. Since the Pakistani and Guatemalan spent most of their time off with the big boys of the Bloc and the Norwegian his with the Unionist establishment, we did not see too much of them. That suited us well enough. Neither Stafford nor I were partial to banging our heads against concrete.

That left us free to hobnob with Theron and Aung Khine. Theron was a Smuts man and spoke of Malan, the apostle of apartheid who had just come to power in South Africa, with lofty contempt. His Burmese colleague made it plain with disarming frankness that he had only one real care in the world and that was to go on getting comfortable, well-paid jobs with the United Nations. Theron said he had nothing to conceal.

South Africa wanted African stability and he would back whatever solution seemed most likely to realise it. Aung Khine admitted with a rueful grin that he was rather differently placed. His instructions were to stand by Mian Zaud Din in the interests of Asian solidarity. No matter what Mian Zaud Din proposed? Well, he supposed that his Government would think differently if it could be shown that his Pakistani friend was making proposals which were not in Asian interests. Such as backing a Bloc which was a cover for Italian neo-colonialism? Stafford interjected, flashing him a grin. Well, yes, Aung Khine smiled back. Put like that, he thought his Government might change its mind. A few days later he was happy to report that it had.

The Commission tackled its job much as the previous Commission had and 'deja vu' just about sums up its activities. The same old family representatives turned up, mostly saying the same old things: which were not, of course, always what they were supposed to say, seeing that the political allegiances of so many of their leaders had changed since they were last on parade. This gave Mian Zaud Din and Garcia Bauer scope in plenty to use their legal tricks to trip up these simpletons, twirl them around their little fingers, tie them in knots and, otherwise, get them to say that what they said was in fact not at all what they meant. Theron did not think this was quite cricket, Aung Khine thought it lacking in respect for 'personal dignity', Quale registered disgust at what he considered conduct unworthy of the United Nations. So affected was the formerly tight-lipped Quale that he slowly crawled out of his shell and became chummier by the minute with Messrs Theron and Aung Khine. As a result, he began to take a more flexible view of the Eritrean scene, admitting that, contrary to what he had thought at first, Moslem opposition to union with Ethiopia was genuine while Theron and Aung Khine, who had up to then looked on the Unionists as nothing more than Ethiopian stooges, now accepted that they had the Plateau in their pockets. This led Theron to say that there could be no hope of stability unless Ethiopia and the Unionists were kept sweet. Yes, Quale agreed, but to keep them sweet by uniting Eritrea with Ethiopia might upset the Moslems and jeopardise stability. That was why we had favoured partition, I explained. But no one wanted partition, Aung Khine argued, not even the Moslems of the Western Province. That I could not deny.

1. *Sir Kennedy Trevaskis*

2. *Trevaskis in uniform as a member of the Northern Rhodesian Regiment, 1939–41*

3. *POWs, c. 1940. Trevaskis is in the top row, left.*

4. *Sudanese Beja tribesman*

5. *Feudal dignitary*

6. *Trevaskis on home leave with family, 1944–45*

7. *Trevaskis with friends and family*

8. *Trevaskis with Sir Douglas Newbold in Sudan*

9. *Local government in Eritrea*

10. *Trevaskis as political secretary in Eritrea, 1949–50*

11. *Trevaskis as chief secretary*

12. *Tribal gathering, Radfan, Yemen*

13. *Trevaskis with Sultan Fadhel bin Ali, Minister of Defence*

14. *Northern Yemenis*

15. *Trevaskis with British Army commander*

Alas, the truth of the matter was that Ali Radas and his Tigray had not budged. They had remained hooked on their inane belief that independence for the Western Province could be taken seriously. I had done my best to dissuade the idiots but I needed Stafford with his greater rank and known links with London to get them to see sense. So, would he please help me rub it into their silly fat heads that their only alternative to Ethiopian rule or rule by an Italian-dominated Bloc was to go over to the Sudan? Of course he would, Stafford replied in a distrait voice. He would have to handle it carefully, however, to make sure that he did not frighten them into going over to the Bloc. A few days later he told me that he had done Ali Radas and his lot the best of good turns and that they could not thank him enough. He had got the Unionists to say that, if the Moslem League of the Western Province did not want to join Ethiopia, they would not press for it. Not bad? He gave me a cheery smile. It could not have been worse. Having, as they now believed, no reason to fear an Ethiopian take-over, Ali Radas and his friends would never give partition a second thought. Partition was a dead duck.

Stafford, as I now saw, had never cared for partition; maybe because his stint as an adviser to the Ethiopian government and the Ethiopian friends in high places he had thus acquired had left him with a sympathy with Ethiopian pretensions which I had begun to notice since the arrival of the Commission. And so, I was not surprised that he should discreetly but persistently encourage Theron, Aung Khine and Quale in their belief that there could be no stability if Ethiopia remained unsatisfied. Yes, but what about the Moslems? The answer to that, Stafford believed, was conditional union with Ethiopia on the lines that Abraha and his Liberals were suggesting. By 'conditional union' he meant a self-governing Eritrea within a federal Ethiopian framework. Theron and Aung Khine lapped this up as a happy compromise between Independence and union with Ethiopia. Quale thought the Ethiopians would resent being denied full control of what they insisted on calling their 'last province'. If necessary, he was prepared to leave the fate of the Moslem Western Province in abeyance for a year but he could not agree to anything but a full unconditional Ethiopian take-over. And so, predictable from the outset, the Commission left Eritrea as divided as they had been on arrival. Garcia Bauer and Mian Zaud Din were arguing for independence, Quale for union with Ethiopia and Theron and Aung Khine for conditional union. Reasonable men usually opt for the middle way and, though reasonableness was not always the United Nations' General Assembly's most notable quality, they voted for the compromise solution urged by Theron and Aung Khine. Eritrea was declared to be 'an autonomous state federated to Ethiopia'. A beaming Stafford met me in London after the news had come through. As the back room architect of the decision he naturally had a paternal pride in it and remarked that, when all was said and done, it took care of everybody, Ethiopia got Eritrea within its fold, the Unionists would now become Ethiopians and the Moslems would have the next best thing to independence within Eritrea. Didn't I agree? I was not sure that I did. If Ethiopia allowed Eritrea to remain autonomous, the Tigray, Ogaden and goodness only knew what other resentful and rebellious provinces would be shouting for autonomy, too. Quite apart from the natural possessiveness of Ethiopia's rulers, I could not see how they could risk the almost certain consequences of Eritrean autonomy. Stafford bubbled over with merriment at the mere thought of little Ethiopia daring to tamper with a United Nations decision, I need have no fear, he said: my precious Moslems would be all right.

That was the end of the Eritrean question. It was, also, the end of the Italian question. Tripolitania and Cyrenaica became independent as Libya, and Somalia was put under Italian trusteeship as a prelude to independence in ten years' time. The Italian Empire was dead and now being buried. Having no appetite for the Eritrean obsequies, I took myself to the Colonial Office and reported back for duty. No one there had the least notion of what I had been doing or of my involvement in the region. My welcome, if not cold, was unenthusiastic. Been having a jolly time? some Assistant Secretary asked, eyebrows raised, as if I had been playing truant. 'Well, well, well,' I would have to get used to doing a proper job of work again in Northern Rhodesia. But I did not want to go back to Northern Rhodesia. My experience in Eritrea could be far better used elsewhere, say in Aden. It was no good. I had to learn to do what I was told. It was back to Northern Rhodesia.

17

ERITREAN POSTSCRIPT

ALL THAT THE FAR-SIGHTED Douglas Newbold foresaw and much more has happened. The Sudan is being ravaged by civil war and overrun by Eritrean refugees; Somalia has been shattered by war and rebellion; the Ethiopian Empire is falling apart; and Eritrea, the cause of it all, is a battle field.

What lies behind all these calamities was Ethiopia's all too foreseeable contempt for the United Nations' decision and her high-handed liquidation of 'the autonomous state of Eritrea'. Disenchanted as they by then were with Ethiopia's bad faith and her intolerable behaviour, Eritrea's Christians, once her most fervent supporters, quickly went over to their rebellious Moslem neighbours. A popular uprising followed and, despite continual bombardment from the air and the deployment of 150,000 Ethiopian troops in Eritrea, the Eritrean revolutionaries have remained as full of fight as ever. Apart from stampeding tens of thousands of Eritrean refugees into the Sudan and both sacrificing and taking lives with ever greater desperation, the Ethiopians have nothing to show for their efforts.

The Sudan, too, is suffering just as Newbold predicted. As he envisaged, a regular flow of warlike stores (provided by sympathetic Arab states) has been passing through the Sudan to sustain the Eritrean revolution, in retaliation for which the Ethiopians have been aiding and abetting the Christians and pagans of the South Sudan to wage war against the Sudan's Moslem Government in the North. Step by ominous step this has saddled the unfortunate Sudanese with a devastating civil war to add to the ghastly incubus of the hordes of starving Eritrean refugees who are now settled within their frontiers.

What Newbold could never have guessed was that the rot would also spread to Somalia. The reason for this is that the Somalis hoped to take advantage of Ethiopia's difficulties in Eritrea to take over the Ogaden. Having first stirred up a rebellion there, they later invaded it but without success. Forced to withdraw by Soviet, Cuban and East German intervention, they have continued to fight the Ethiopians on and off but, in the meantime, the Ethiopians all but crippled the Somali Government by exploiting Somali tribal jealousies to promote rebellion against it. All in all, battered and shattered Somalia is in much the same horrifying state as the Sudan.

It remains to be said that Ethiopia, whose maltreatment of Eritrea is the principal cause of all these horrors, is in the long run likely to suffer most. The Ethiopians' failure to quash the Eritrean revolution has encouraged other provinces and peoples to revolt and, with the Tigray scoring success after success, it may well be that the disintegration of Ethiopia's unlovely Empire is in sight.

No one, not even Newbold, the prophet, could ever have imagined that the United Nations' thoughtless handling of the Eritrean question would bring such chaos to the Sudan and the Horn of Africa. If only we had got our partition plans through! So much of my life has been dominated by damned 'ifs'.

V

NORTHERN RHODESIA
(ZAMBIA) REVISITED

I LEFT FOR NORTHERN RHODESIA UNDER PROTEST AND I continued to protest having arrived there. Eleven months after, I was given the posting to Aden—or, to be exact, the Aden Protectorate—that I wanted. Eleven months wasted? In the sense that I never became involved in Northern Rhodesia or made any contribution to its affairs, yes. And yet it was no bad thing that I should have had a chance to sit back in a state of detachment after so long a spell on the whirligig of Eritrean politics. In that sense I could not have gone to a better place. Northern Rhodesia and Eritrea were different worlds and they were moons apart.

Arriving at Broken Hill, the mining dump to which I found myself posted, I felt as if I had stepped through the looking glass so different was it from what I had just left. I could not, at first, say quite what it was that made it so different and then I knew. In Eritrea it had not been possible to escape the blowing and bluster of what Harold MacMillan was to call the 'Wind of Change'. It could be felt in local reactions to the British loss of India, to the French and Dutch retreats from the Far East and most of all in the depressing news from Palestine and Egypt. But here? Hardly a single prejudice had been shattered.

Who, for example, would seriously have believed that here, in a British colony in the year 1950, a full blown colour bar would be flourishing? But it was. Segregation was total. Africans were not even allowed to enter White-owned shops. Wasn't this pretty shame-making? I put it to the local Provincial Commissioner, James Murray, for whom I was working as an Assistant. He looked surprised and said that he supposed it was a matter of what you were used to. I found it shocking, no doubt, because I was not used to it. He, on the other hand, did not even notice it and he could assure me that the Africans did not resent it in the least. Since every one was content with things as they were, why upset them? Let sleeping dogs lie...

This was indolence speaking and, persuasive though its argument was, it overlooked the real damage that the colour bar was doing. Forget moral iniquity, affronts to human dignity and all the rest of it; the inescapable fact was that, to live with a colour bar is to acquire a colour bar mentality and a colour bar mentality was a crippling handicap for anyone trying to do what we should have been doing as colonial trustees. I had only to compare the way Facey, Broken Hill's District Commissioner, went about his business with the way Political Officers like myself had gone about ours in Eritrea to know that he was no more in tune with the spirit of colonial trusteeship than one of Cecil Rhodes' Native Commissioners. Where we had lived cheek by jowl with Eritreans, coffee-housing with them and having them in and out of our houses at all times of day and night, the impassive Facey saw Africans only from behind a desk and a barrier of schoolmasterish condescension. And as for Murray, who was by no means illiberal in outlook, I never once saw an African visit his office in the four months that I was with him.

An offshoot of the colour bar was the ghastly 'Colonialitis' which Fox-Pitt had so detested and, as so often, it thrived in its most ludicrous forms amongst the underemployed ladies of the British officials. Of these, Mrs Murray, Broken Hill's Queen Bee, was in a class of her own. Of this I received the earliest warning. Arriving at Murray's house, where we had been invited to spend our first night, my wife suddenly collapsed with a high fever and went to bed. On being told what had happened, Mrs Murray (who was out at the time of our arrival) went off to see how my wife was. On entering the bedroom she froze and then let out an anguished squawk. 'They have given you the VIP blankets!' she shrieked and, on that, she ripped them off the bed, sparing neither a glance nor a word for my fever-stricken wife.

Though British officialdom seemed to be on autopilot for endless decades of British colonial rule, the prospect had no appeal for the Whites and, as so often before, they looked to union with White-ruled Southern Rhodesia as a means of escaping it. Getting together with their fellow Whites from Southern Rhodesia and Nyasaland they had, in fact, hatched out proposals for a union of the three territories in a Central African Federation two years before. Though Arthur Creech-Jones, the Colonial Secretary, put a swift stopper on them with an inflexible 'No', his successor, a fellow Labourite called James Griffiths, decided to have another look at them. He arrived in Ndola, the commercial hub of Northern Rhodesia's Copper Belt, to start doing so shortly after I had arrived there as District Commissioner. He was attended by six foot six of lofty arrogance in the person of Andrew Cohen, the head of the Colonial Office's African Department. Attended by? Hardly. You could see at a glance that Griffiths was the puppet and Cohen was pulling the strings.

With me to greet the Colonial Secretary was my Provincial Commissioner, a barrel-bellied bullfrog called Billing with a voice to match. They wanted to get some idea of what Africans thought about federation, Cohen said. Indeed, if they even knew what it meant. 'Very well,' Billing boomed. They had better have a meeting with the African Advisory Council. Appointed members? 'Well, yes, but…' Billing blustered. 'No, thanks!' Cohen snapped. They hadn't much time to spare and they did not want to waste the little they had. Could Billing please rustle up a few Trades Unionists and some of the leaders of the African National Congress? Billing could but wished them to understand that the Trades Unionists and African National Congressmen were in no way representative of the Africans as a whole. They would do far better to see the Advisory Council. Cohen did not even trouble to give him a reply. 'Let us know when you have fixed the meeting,' he said and, collecting his long arms and legs together, he gathered up the Colonial Secretary and took him off.

The meeting was no more than a bizarre formality. The Trades Unionists and Congressmen spent their time trying to outdo each other in assaulting Griffiths with crude impertinences while that poor little man responded by fawning, cringing and abasing himself as if he had been one of the Kantibai's serfs in the bad old days. Cohen, seated a little to one side with his long legs sprawled across a desk, looked on disdainfully through half-closed eyes, interrupting every now and again to fire a question at some African and then giggling with open contempt at the answer he received. 'A very useful meeting,' Griffiths observed when our disagreeable visitors eventually left. 'Very!' Cohen snapped. It made one thing clear and that was that no one present knew anything about federations. Well, it did seem to him that these Africans were against any form of union with Southern Rhodesia, Griffiths mumbled. Expelling an impatient sigh, Cohen asked him to realise that the views of people who knew nothing about federation and federating with Southern Rhodesia were valueless. 'You do agree, don't you, Secretary of State?' he asked, giving the little man the eye. 'Yes, yes, of course,' he dutifully replied.

Cohen, as we now knew, was a Left Wing intellectual who had found favour with Arthur Creech-Jones as a dedicated anti-colonialist and, ironically, no one seems to have done more to sabotage the Colonial Empire than this eminent Colonial Office hierarch. Why then did he favour the proposals for a Central African Federation which liberals, everywhere, opposed on the grounds that Southern Rhodesian Whites would dominate it? Cohen was kind enough to give us the answer. Anyone with any sense, he argued, would know that in a partnership between two African-dominated territories and one that was dominated by Whites, the latter would eventually fall into line with the former. It was for that reason and because he thought a solid and economically strong British Dominion in Central Africa would be an effective counter to the malign influence of a Nationalist South Africa that he backed the Federation proposals which almost every other Left Winger opposed.

We were to explain the Federation proposals to the Africans and sound them out, the Colonial Office wished us to note after Griffiths' return. What did I do? For a start I took myself off to the African Advisory Council which Billing had advised Griffiths to consult. It was an uninspiring body of near-total inarticulacy presided over by the confidant of a former District Commissioner who called himself Adam Frog. And what did they think about the Federation proposals, I asked.

They had no views at all. Whatever I thought, they said, would suit them fine. Having drawn a blank there, I next invited Africans to meet me in the Native Compound's recreation hall. This produced some lively meetings but no serious debate. Provided with a platform, glib-tongued young African show-offs ranted away about the wickedness of the Southern Rhodesian Whites and, striking heroic attitudes, declared themselves ready to die rather than submit to them. This was received with outbursts of clapping and bibulous yells. Opposition to federation was 100%. Ignorance of what it meant was about the same.

When I reported this to Billing he put on the poest of po-faces. Did I seriously mean that this was what Adam Frog and the Council had said? No, I didn't. Adam Frog and his friends had simply said that they would agree with whatever I thought was right. Well, then, what was I talking about? I was talking about the Africans I had sounded out. Oh, indeed, Billing said, and how many Africans had I in fact sounded out? Fifty? A hundred? I thought about a hundred or so. 'A hundred!' He wheezed and heaved with merriment. 'Well, well!' he gasped, recharging his lungs. He scarcely thought that the views of the hundred Africans I happened to have talked to could be taken to represent the view of the fifteen thousand Africans living in Ndola! Surely he did not expect me to question all fifteen thousand? 'Of course not!' Billing replied with a condescending seigneurial smile. That was why we had an Advisory Council. It was their job to tell us what Africans thought. They were not the sort to be influenced by those big mouths from the Trades Unions and the National Congress. They spoke for the silent African majority.

And did I now see what he had meant? I could not believe it but there, standing before me, was Fox-Pitt! After a final spell as a Provincial Commissioner who had been in voluble disagreement with the Government on almost every aspect of policy, he had reached retiring age but, to the consternation of higher authority, had stayed on in Northern Rhodesia to advise the African National Congress. Billing had been outraged. It was not cricket! You did not expect this sort of thing from someone who had been treated as 'one of us'. Perhaps a good talking to would fix him, he mused. In the end he did nothing, but the Northern Rhodesian Government eventually lost patience with their rebellious ex-colleague and deported him some years later as an 'undesirable alien'.

Unlike Murray, who was too indolent to shake himself free of 'colonialitis', Billing was steeped in it. How steeped I only discovered just before leaving for Aden. Poking his head through my office door, he casually announced that India had appointed a High Commissioner to British East and Central Africa called Pandit Pant and that 'the fellow' would be visiting Ndola and staying the night. Our instructions were to look after him and that meant me. Me? But he was the senior Government representative and in any event my house was all packed up and I could not have put up a hair shirted monk, let alone a High Commissioner. 'I am sure you will find some way round your difficulties,' Billing said, giving me a cracked smile and ambling off.

The best I could do was to get the local hotel to have our distinguished visitor—which it agreed to do—so long as he did not offend the White riff-raff lodging in it by using any of the public rooms. How could I tell this to a High Commissioner? Surely, he could spare us all the hideous embarrassment of doing so by putting up the High Commissioner himself? Billing would not budge so there was nothing for it but to come clean. I did so and Pant smiled all embarrassment away rather as Shocket Hyatt Khan had done when he encountered South Africans in the Prisoner of War Camp at Adi Ugri. Many years later when Pandit Pant was Ambassador in London I found myself sitting next to him at a luncheon in the Savoy. 'It is very pleasant here,' Pant remarked, 'and they let me use the public rooms!'

VI

THE END OF ADEN AND THE RAJ

1

A CHIP OFF THE OLD BRITISH INDIAN BLOCK

IN NOVEMBER 1951, as the BOAC Dakota chugged slowly across the smiling highlands of East Africa towards Aden's 'barren rocks', my mind went back to a day when a lean, leathery type with a face tanned the colour of Scotch whisky popped up in Keren. He was a Political Officer on leave from the Aden Protectorate called Davey and he had come to see how our tribal administrations worked. What could we possibly tell him? After more than a hundred years of British rule I would have thought that Aden had a great deal more to tell us than we had to tell them. Aden no doubt. Davey said, but not the Aden Protectorate. Why, weren't they all part of the same show? Davey paused with a puzzled look on his face before replying and then said, well, yes, they were part of the same show but they were totally different. It was quite a long story. He kept me up half the night listening to it.

What I had to realise, he began by telling me, was that the Imams, who were rulers of the Yemen and, as heads of the Islamic Zeidi sect, the spiritual leaders of most Yemenis, believed that Aden and almost all of Southern Arabia were theirs by Divine Right and that they had a God-given duty to recover them. That, he said with a sigh, had been the curse with which we had always had to live and, alas, were still doing so. That was why what appeared at the time to be a simple matter of taking over Aden for use as a coaling station had led to our involvement in the tribal bear garden that was Aden's back yard. It was the last thing we had wanted but, with a hostile Imam as a neighbour, we had to make him keep his distance and that meant cultivating a friendly, not to say dependent, hinterland as a buffer between him and ourselves. By the best of good luck the hinterland tribes were of the Shafi'i Islamic sect and did not look on the Zeidi Imam as their spiritual leader. Having no wish to find themselves subjected to the Imam's rule they had happily signed Treaties of Protection or Protectorate Treaties with us on the clear understanding, however, that we would not interfere in their turbulent affairs. The upshot of all this was that we got just what we were after: a 'cordon sanitaire' between ourselves and the Imam at next to no cost.

That had been fine but, in the cold, liberal, post-War light it did not look so good and there was a growing feeling that we should be doing something to improve conditions in our shamefully neglected Protectorate. But to improve conditions we would have to intervene and since we had no right of intervention what could we do? An answer had been produced by a dedicated genius called Harold Ingrams. If we tried to intervene as the Aden Government, the Arabs would never accept us, he argued. If we presented ourselves as advisers who were anxious to help, he thought they would. He had been proved right. Signing what were called Advisory Treaties with the rulers in the Hadhramaut, far away in the Eastern part of the Protectorate, Ingrams introduced law and order where there had been chaos and, in time, had a conventional Administration with schools and health clinics in good working order. He had performed a miracle which it was hoped would be repeated in Aden's hinterland away to the West. That was what Davey had been trying to do when I met him. Unhappily, he was stabbed to death soon afterwards.

Quite by chance, the legendary Ingrams paid Ndola a visit shortly before I left for Aden. He was a tall Old Testament figure with an untidy head of grey hair and [a] wild look in his eye. I would find dealing with Arabs very different from dealing with Africans, he warned. Even the meanest Arab thought himself as good, if not better, than ourselves and, however courteous they might be, there was no doubt that almost all Arabs despised us for being infidels. Nevertheless, they valued us for the know-how we had and they hadn't and it was for this reason that that he had been able to get the Advisory system accepted in the Hadhramaut. Even so, he had had to watch his step to allay Arab suspicions that the whole thing was a ploy for us to get control and that was why, to make our presence less obtrusive and provocative, he had

A Chip off the Old British Indian Block

always insisted on his Political Officers dressing and, as far as possible, behaving as Arabs. Some of them had not cared too much for it, he murmured with a grim look. No drink and that sort of thing. He might have added that they did not always take his injunctions too seriously. One of his many 'musts' was that his officers should relieve themselves Arab fashion, squatting and not standing up. To make sure that a new recruit knew the form, he asked him if he knew how to pee. 'I should hope so,' came the reply, 'I have been peeing without any difficulty for the past twenty five years!'

Since Ingrams' and poor Davey's day, the Protectorate had been divided into two with a British Agent in charge of each half. That splendid old warrior, Hugh Boustead, who had left such a mark on Eritrea, was in charge of the Eastern Protectorate, and another colourful old soldier called Major Seager was in charge of the Western. It was to the latter that I was due to report. He had been a contemporary of Ingrams, Davey had said, and had had an unusually swashbuckling and adventurous time in the wilder parts of the Western Protectorate. He was not much of an office man, he told me, but he was just the sort of wily old fellow to have around if one got into tribal difficulties. I was curious to meet him.

As we approached Aden I wondered what I would find when I got there. I could hardly believe that it would be a peaceful and relaxed atmosphere, for I had just received a letter from my mother saying 'poor Bobbie is having a dreadful time with those awful Egyptians'. 'Bobbie' Erskine[1] was our cousin and, as Commander-in-Chief in Egypt, he was being severely harassed at the time by a guerrilla campaign which was being sponsored by the Egyptian Government to ease us out of our Suez base. The Egyptians had already abrogated their Defence Treaty with us, torn up our Condominium Agreement over the Sudan and rejected an invitation we and our Allies had made for them to join an organisation for the defence of the Middle East. As if the Egyptians' total rejection of us was not bad enough, Mussadiq, the aged madcap Prime Minister of Iran, had just closed our Anglo-Iranian Oil Company down and taken it over. You did not need second sight to know that we were in for a tough time in the Middle East.

And so, expecting Aden to be bedevilled with riots and demonstrations in support of the Egyptian and Iranian revolt against British imperialism, I was astonished to find it as calm as some lazy sea in the Doldrums.

The Deluge

There was not a sign of excitement, nor a hint of anxiety, anywhere—least of all in the demeanour of John Allen, the Deputy British Agent for the Western Aden Protectorate who took charge of me in the absence of Seager on leave. He was a thin scarecrow of a man with a nervous laugh and a monocle. He must be having a worrying time, I said. Worrying? He let out a high-pitched cackle to say that every minute of every day in the Protectorate was a worry. If I was afraid of being worried, I had best apply for a job elsewhere. No, I meant worried by local reactions to what was happening in Egypt and Iran, I explained. Another cackle followed as he told me that no one gave a hoot for what 'Gyppos' and Persians were up to. They had quite enough local worries to concern them.

My immediate assumption that Allen was an oddity who was not firing on too many cylinders was quickly dispelled when he took me round to meet some of the 'chaps' at the Club. So I thought the Arabs here were anti-British did I, someone laughed. They were loyal 'through and through', a solemn Pink Gin assured me. Gins and Tonics, Whiskies and Sodas and other hearty souls all gulped agreement. Aden, they said, was different. There was no bloody nationalist nonsense here. Well, I had heard British bar room braggadocio of this kind often enough not to take it seriously; but astonishingly what I was being told was not too far from the truth. There really were Arabs here who proudly called themselves 'the King's Arabs'.

Taking a stroll in one of Aden's dusty bazaars, I stopped of a sudden and thought to myself, 'Surely...?' Yes, the pungent aroma of urine and spices hovering around me came straight out of my Punjabi past. I had known it at Gurgaon, Rhotak, Rupar, Kalabagh and Heaven knows where else. And then, with my thoughts racing back to India, I suddenly realised how very Indian Aden was. There were Indians everywhere: walking about the streets, selling almost anything from cooking pots to tinned milk in shops and from stalls and offering their services as lawyers, dentists, barbers or whatever to the public at large. Although outnumbered by the Arabs, they were much to the forefront of the Aden scene. The firms of the longest standing were almost all Indian; Indian accountants, cashiers and clerks dominated the banks and commercial offices; every Government department was as good as run by Indians; Indian doctors and dressers were the mainspring of the Health Service. To put it in a single phrase, it was the Indians who made Aden tick.

A Chip off the Old British Indian Block

This was not too surprising. We had governed Aden from Bombay as an outpost of British India for nearly a hundred years and from the start the Indians had been our partners in what was, in fact if not in name, an Anglo-Indian colony. As an elderly Parsee merchant put it to me, Aden was 'a chip off the good old British Indian block'. Certainly, my mother and father would have felt at home there and my father would immediately have noticed that these Adeni Indians were of the good old fashioned pre-Gandhian type: loyal, respectful and anxious to please. You could safely say there was not a rebellious itch in any one of them. Maybe they remembered that they owed us their chances of making good in Aden and were grateful.

It would be stretching the truth to say that the British and Indian communities were bound together by anything in the way of hoops of fraternity. All the same, there was a rapport between them which, I have to admit, took me by surprise. From having had a quick look at Aden's exclusively British club, its Anglican church, statue of Queen Victoria and the genteel isolation in which the British seemed to live, I had written them off as obvious cases of acute colonialitis. In fact I wronged them. Forget the Indian merchant princes who entertained and were entertained by the top British, there was a good deal of Anglo-Indian mixing and mingling lower down the scale and that was no doubt because so many British and Indians were working closely together in Government and other offices. Also, the British community at the time amounted to only three or four hundred and had not the same ability to withdraw and live apart in isolation as was the case with much larger communities. 'Believe me, sir, we are one big happy family here,' an Indian lawyer said to me. He clearly believed it. More probably, they knew that if we went they would go too.

I could see that the news from the Middle East was not going to get the Indians out onto the streets. But what about the Arabs? Surely, they would respond to the Arab nationalist noises roaring out of Cairo? Curiously, it seemed that they would not. The majority of Aden's Arabs did not, in fact, belong to Aden. They were temporary immigrants from the Yemen who came down for stints of a year or so to earn a bit of cash and, since they were entirely dependent on our good will, it was hardly likely that they would risk forfeiting it. In any event, coming as they did from a country which was cocooned in mediaevalism and just about as cut off from the world as Tibet, they were far too blinkered by provincialism to know or care about what was happening in the Middle East. It was much the same with the 'Adeni Arabs': the Arabs resident in Aden and mostly from families of old and respectable Adeni vintages. Having become, as it were, honorary members of the Indian community and inclined to look Indiawards because of Aden's past links with India, they too had little natural interest in the Middle East. Also, they knew that they were our creatures and that, without us, they would be for the dustbin.

A summons from Bill (later Sir William) Goode, the Chief Secretary of Aden, reached me just as I was beginning to understand the Aden set-up. For a former prisoner of war of the Japanese who had been working on the Burma railway only six years before, he looked remarkably serene. He never spoke about his time as a prisoner and it was, perhaps, because he treated that traumatic episode as a book that had been closed once and for all that he was able to maintain such a remarkable equanimity. Having listened to the impressions I had formed, he said that I had overlooked the most important fact of all and that was the Yemeni Imam's claim to Aden and South Arabia. 'Ah, yes!' I said, remembering what Davey had told me. That was the curse with which we had to live. Goode smiled and, looking out of his window at the shipping in the Port for a few moments, said that as far as Aden was concerned it was a blessing. Blood-chilling stories of the Imam's savage ways—his chopping off of heads, lopping off of limbs and indescribable tortures—were always buzzing around Aden like flies in an abattoir. No one hearing them would sleep peacefully at night if he believed that we were on the way out. No one had done more than the Imam to make Aden pro-British.

Having made this interesting point, Goode said he felt he should give me a warning. The fact of the matter was that Sir Tom Hickinbotham, our new Governor, was not at all happy about Seager, my British Agent. That was because he suspected him of encouraging intrigues against the Imam which were doing very great damage to our relations with the Yemen. As I probably knew, we had ended years of misunderstanding and open warfare by signing the Treaty of San'a[2] with the previous Imam, Yahya, in 1934 and after that all had gone reasonably well between us until the 1940s. It was then that various intrigues against the Imam, mounted by a group of Aden-based Yemeni merchants calling themselves 'the Free Yemenis', had taken place, culminating in his assassination and replacement by their candidate, Seyid Abdulla al Wazir. That was not, however, the end of the affair for the old Imam's demoniacal son, Ahmed, had successfully hit back and, after beheading Seyid Abdulla, had become Imam himself. So that was the position, Goode said with a weary sigh. We had a new, reputedly paranoiac, Imam who firmly believed that we had encouraged the Free Yemeni to do away with his father. Since then, we had, it was true, just recently managed to get the Yemenis to reaffirm the Treaty of San'a with what was known as the 'Modus Vivendi' Agreement[3] but the fact remained that the Imam was intensely bitter and suspicious. And 'H.E.' believed that this was entirely due to Seager.

Having given me time to take in this startling information, Goode went on to say that the real culprit in all this seemed to have been one of the rulers: that was to say, Sherif Hussein of Beihan, descendant of the Prophet, kinsman of Jordan's royal family and proprietor of South Arabia's sharpest wit and cleverest tongue. He was a man of inordinate ambition and was known to have been in close touch with the Free Yemenis and their revolutionary friends, his obvious purpose being to get some territorial or other advantage when the Imam fell. Surely this was a little far-fetched? Goode assured me that it was not. But what possible interest could any Yemeni revolutionary have had in a small Protectorate chief? That was where Seager came in. The Sherif would assure his revolutionary friends that he could get them British sympathy and help and he would then take them along to Seager who would whisper sufficiently encouraging things into their ears to lead them to believe that he could. But why had Seager allowed himself to be used in this way? Because Sherif Hussein had persuaded him that, unless we got rid of the Imam, he would get rid of us. And what was the position with the new Imam, Ahmed? Goode shrugged his shoulders. Not at all good, he admitted. He was giving us a lot of trouble and H.E. was convinced that it was all Seager's fault. So, to judge from his expression, did Goode.

If Seager was to blame, how was it that he had been free to indulge in all this cloak and daggery? Surely he should have been under some sort of control? Goode agreed but said that the men on the spot in the Protectorate had always been left pretty free to do as they pleased. In any event, it would not have been easy to control an Arab expert who claimed to know everything worth knowing about the Protectorate. You could not judge things here by normal standards, Goode asked me to believe.

We might be in the twentieth century but Aden and the Protectorate were still in the nineteenth century India and what Seager was doing was only what Nicholson, Abbot, Mackeson and other imperial Titans had all being doing on the North West Frontier of India. As the sagacious old Parsee whom I encountered had said, this was all a 'chip off the good old British India block'.

NOTES

[1] General Sir George Erskine, who had formerly commanded the 7th Armoured Division (the Desert Rats).
[2] The Treaty of San'a of 1934 prescribed that both parties should preserve the 'status quo' on the 'frontiers' for a period of forty years. The word used for 'frontiers' in the Arabic text could be interpreted to mean not the line of the frontiers but what lay inside them.
[3] The 'Modus Vivendi' Agreement of 1951 reaffirmed the Treaty of San'a and prescribed that a joint Anglo Yemeni Commission should agree the 'status quo' on the ground.

2

MARKING TIME

ARRIVING ONE DAY at the crumbling antique in Aden's 'Crater' which was the British Agency for the Western Aden Protectorate, I was met by Allen, hair on end and monocle awry. The cause of his agitation was a telegram which he handed me. It was from Seager and read, 'Tell the tribes Seager is coming on Thursday.' But he had said it would be Saturday, Allen moaned. How on earth they would get everything done in time before his arrival he really didn't know. It was panic stations and then some. I cannot imagine why, for when Seager eventually arrived he showed no interest in any of the things which had so excited Allen. He never even visited the Agency. He never did, Allen said in what was almost a whisper. His work was so very hush-hush. If you wanted to see him you had to visit him at home.

This I did, arriving to find fifty or so near-naked savages sitting on their hunkers outside his house. All of them were painted a startling bright blue. They were daubed with indigo as ancient Britons were daubed with woad. Though not painted blue himself, Seager was no more elaborately dressed. A loin cloth was his sole article of clothing. Tall, lean and fitted out with a pointed Captain Kettle beard, he was smoking a cigarette in a holder the size of a drum stick. Even without the ugly weal which a tribesman's dagger had scrawled across his face and chest, he made an arresting picture. He rose to greet me with a 'Ha!' like a Sergeant Major's bark, adding for good measure 'Ha!' once again. After we had sat down he changed his tune to 'Well, well, well!' Since he seemed lost for something to talk about, I asked what job he had in mind for me. He was immediately uncorked. He understood I was good at 'Administrative Bunk', so he wanted me to be the 'administrative chap' in the Agency while he handled 'the tribes'. The idea, he explained, was that I should be his Deputy but I would have to wait a bit to be formally promoted since Allen, who had fallen foul of the Governor, had first to be posted elsewhere. In the event I only had to wait a couple of months but two months waiting to move into a dying man's shoes, with the dying man looking accusingly at me through his monocle, were not the most comfortable I have known.

Though Administrative Bunk was my official lot, Seager made it plain that I would be lost if I did not know what was going on with 'the tribes': by which he meant all the strange goings on between ourselves and the Yemen and their bearing on tribal politics. And so, not so much to brief me as I suspect to let off a little steam, Seager would have me round every other evening to fill me in: his invariable routine being to start by knocking back three pink gins in a row, letting out a self-satisfied sigh and then saying, 'Now where was I?'

If I was ever to understand 'the tribes', he said, the first thing I would have to realise was that we and the Yemen were at war. Yes, these were critical times, the most critical in the whole history of South Arabia and by South Arabia he meant the whole shebang—Aden, the Protectorate, the Yemen, the lot. Anything could happen anywhere, at any time. Events were boiling inexorably up to a climax which would seal South Arabia's fate for generations to come. All this would be said in mysterious tones of high theatre to the accompaniment of vigorous gesticulation and ocular acrobatics. To see the strange bearded figure, half naked and scarred, waving his long cigarette holder about and talking, as it were, in capital letters, was a bizarre experience. He was half moving, half ludicrous.

Stripping all that he said of the histrionics and hyperbole with which it was habitually shrouded, the picture was clear enough. Unlike Ingrams, who had used the Advisory System as a means of helping our proteges to order their affairs and improve conditions, Seager saw it mainly as a device for installing a British presence in the Protectorate to keep the Imam out. As he rightly said, with no British presence there, there was nothing to stop the Imam moving in, as indeed the Imam Yahya had to an alarming degree after the First World War.[1] And so Seager's declared objective was to persuade all the rulers who mattered to sign Advisory

Treaties, it being understood that, once a ruler had signed, a Political Officer would move in to 'advise' accompanied by a detachment of our gendarmerie, known as 'the Government Guards'. As one would expect, neither the Imam Yahya nor his son, Ahmed, had taken this lying down and so, while Seager was pressing ahead trying to get rulers to sign up, the Imams had been doing their devilish best to dissuade them from doing so, not forgetting to make life difficult for those who had already signed 'pour encourager les autres'. That was what all the troubles were about. Seager was trying to press ahead with what he called the 'Forward Policy',[2] the Imam was doing his best to halt him, and Seager was hitting back where and when he could to put a stopper on the Imam.

The real and imagined tricks and wiles of the Imam seemed to hold Seager's mind firmly captive. What the Imam was working for was a general tribal uprising which would throw us out of the Protectorate, he would thunder. Yes, any moment now, we could be faced with a 'major explosion'. And so it seemed, for every now and again Seager would telephone in a voice of quivering excitement to say that a crisis of 'the first magnitude' had arisen and would I come round 'pronto' to talk about it. On arrival I would invariably find his right hand man, an old faithful called Abdulla Hassan, telling him about some Yemeni plot someone had reported. All the while Seager would listen with bulging eyes, interjecting occasional 'hah's' and 'ho's' and then, as like as not, he would eventually leap to his feet crying out that, if what he had heard was true, it meant this and this meant that and that... why, Good God, this could be it! This could be the major explosion he had been waiting for. Whereupon he would seize pencil and paper and fire off a report, shrieking disaster in capital letters. No one in the Government Secretariat took these colourful missives seriously. He had cried 'Wolf' too often.

I was naturally curious to know how Sir Tom Hickinbotham and Seager would get on together in the light of what Goode had told me. I was of course curious, too, to see what sort of person our Governor was. By chance, I was given a close up of him which told me all. One of our quainter local customs was to require Protectorate rulers to pay their respects to the Governor once a year and so, when a Sultan turned up to make his annual obeisance at a time when Seager was away travelling, the job of escorting him to Government House fell to me. 'And don't forget to bring an interpreter!' the Governor's ADC telephoned.

The Deluge

That was easily arranged. I gave the job to our office workhorse, an Arab Assistant Political Officer called Ali Qassim. Did I really mean that he was to go to Government House? He quivered with delight at the unbelievable honour being done him. Would he need a new suit? No need whatsoever, I assured him. Nevertheless, when our little party set out for Government House the next day, there he was in the shiniest new white suit imaginable. But that was not all. That relic of Ottoman days, a fez, was perched on top of his head. No one could have looked happier, no one more bizarre.

At first everything went according to plan. We drove in through the gates of Government House as the clock struck nine, an eight gun salute boomed out from a headland nearby and a red turbanned Guard of Honour from the Aden Armed Police gave the Sultan a crashing 'Present'. These formalities done, I escorted the Sultan through the front door of Government House with Ali walking on air behind us, up to where Sir Tom was waiting for us in the hall. Having shaken the Sultan by the hand and saluted me with a curt 'Good morning!', his face froze as his eyes came to rest on Ali whose fez had, by the time, tilted jauntily over to one side of his head. 'And who might this gentleman be?' Sir Tom demanded to know in a voice of haughty distaste. After I had introduced the palpitating Ali, Sir Tom looked him coldly up and down. 'I won't be needing this!' he said, giving Ali the sight of his back. His fez sliding down over his eyes, his coat and trousers as taut as sausage skins, Ali gawped helplessly. 'Come, come, Trevaskis!' Sir Tom snapped. 'Get this creature out of here! We haven't got all day to waste!' Poor, poor Ali. That was the humiliating end to the day he had hoped to remember with pride.

This was my first real sight of the man in charge of our affairs. He was a strange, unlovable man and the better I came to know him, the stranger and more unlovable I found him. He was a boor with a petty schoolmaster's delight in twisting tails, rapping knuckles and stamping on corns. Give him sight of anyone's feelings and he would be sure to dance all over them. Having recently read Churchill's *History of the Second World War*, he was going all Churchillian: his favourite ploy being to fire off two-line minutes to half a dozen officials a day demanding to know why, what or when, with an introductory 'pray', about whatever trivia happened to come to his head. His purpose was not, of course, to inform himself. It was to harass and embarrass his addressees. And this he invariably did for he was remarkably well informed about what his officials were up to. Like so many ageing bachelors gay in countries where servants were cheap and plentiful, he treated his servants as so many surrogate sons whom he encouraged to feed him with tidbits of gossip about his officials. In other words, he had reared a nest of mischievous spies around himself and, in nine cases out of ten, those he tormented had them to thank for it.

Up to this point Sir Tom had been too tied up with Aden to give us much of his attention. The first sign that he was likely to give more of it came with his appearance at our office one morning on the dot of eight. This was opening time and though most of the office staff were all present and correct, the usual bunch of stragglers came dawdling along a few minutes late. They did so to be met by a blistering governatorial glare. Having berated each and written the delinquents' names down in a notebook, he demanded to know where Seager was. He was at home, was he? His lips curled. And when, pray, did we expect him to turn up? Oh, so he worked in his home all day, did he? Having registered this with something between a sniff and a snort, he asked if I was in charge of the office. Yes, I was. Well, then, why did I encourage the staff to arrive late? Encourage? Of course I was encouraging them! To let them come as they pleased amounted to encouragement!

Soon after this Sir Tom cross-examined Seager with myself in attendance. He would be glad to know what was happening in the Western Protectorate. Seager cleared his throat and had just changed into top gear when Sir Tom brought him to a halt. He did not want to hear what a pack of Yemeni informers had had to tell him about the Imam, 'thank you very much indeed.' He wanted to know what Seager was doing in the Western Protectorate. Doing? Yes. What was his policy? Seager brightened and said he was, of course, carrying on with the Forward Policy. And what might that be? Well, the idea was for us to go forward into the Protectorate so as to keep the Imam out. Indeed! And what about the Advisory System? Wasn't he supposed to be introducing it to the Western Protectorate? Yes, of course, Seager babbled uneasily, the idea was for us and the Advisory System to go forward together. Sir Tom's face registered a few twitches of irritation and he then desired Seager to be good enough to explain how far forward we and the Advisory System had gone. Well, we now had Advisory Treaties with... Seager began. But Sir Tom had had enough.

'Now look here, my friend,' he said in a decidedly unfriendly tone, 'I am well aware of the states with Advisory Treaties. What I want to know is what progress has been made with the Advisory System!' Seager looked wildly round the room for inspiration but could only come up with a stuttering of 'buts'. At that point Sir Tom moved in for the kill. It was as plain as a pikestaff, he said, that the Advisory System had been so grossly mismanaged that no ruler now wanted a Treaty. If he was not very much mistaken, the fact of the matter was that the Advisory System had made no progress at all. Treaties had been signed but not kept. Wasn't that so? He withered Seager with a Grand Inquisitorial look. Would Seager care to have the details? Whether he did or not, he got them.

Happening to pass by in his car while I was out for a walk a week or two later, Sir Tom stopped and asked how I was getting on with 'Major Cigar'. He paused to let his little joke sink in and then said that the Advisory System had got to be made to work properly. It was all very fine and large for Seager to say that things were not quite as they should be because of Yemeni interference but why was there Yemeni interference? It was because of Seager's interference in the Yemen! If Seager behaved himself, the Imam would do so as well. I did not want to tangle with this pugnacious little man but I could not agree. Sir Tom saluted my reservations with an explosion of 'Indeeds!' I had presumably heard of the Treaty of San'a? Yes, I had. Well, then, did I really think that the Yemenis would have signed it if they had been intending to make trouble? Of course they wouldn't have! All would have been well if Seager had not involved himself with the Free Yemenis and other Yemeni mischief makers. Anyhow, now that the 'Modus Vivendi' Agreement had been signed we had a chance of making a fresh start. He trusted that I would see to it that Seager stuck to making the Advisory System work and kept his nose out of the Yemen.

It was at this point that Cousin Bobbie fortuitously set off the devastating explosion in Cairo which was to bring Gamil Abdul Nasser to power, with all the terrible upheavals and calamities that were to ensue. What brought this about was, in the context of all that followed, a comparatively minor incident. Having trained, armed and directed guerilla gangs to attack our troops and installations in the Suez Canal Base, the Egyptian Government stepped up the pressure in the closing days of 1951 and, eventually, provoked Bobbie into hitting back. Short of packing up and leaving the Base he had no alternative, for the guerillas were by then attacking our water supplies with the help and from the cover of Egyptian Police stations just outside our boundaries. Having neutralised two Police Stations, his men met with fierce and courageous resistance from a third in Ismalia. Forty-three Egyptian Police were killed before it gave in. As soon as the news got out, Cairo went up in smoke against a background of mayhem and the way was cleared for the Nasserite Revolution. For his part in this grim historic episode, the Egyptian propagandists labelled Bobbie 'the butcher of Cairo'.

This Middle East if, perhaps, not world-shattering event made little impression in Aden. Seager dismissed it as a 'nine days' wonder' and Sir Tom merely raised his eyebrows as if it was an irrelevance when I mentioned it. We clearly had more important matters on which to concentrate our minds and it was back to seeing what could be done to revive the Advisory System. Whether Sir Tom's belief that we had Seager to thank for all our troubles was valid or otherwise, any blue-bottomed tribesman could have told him that, so long as Fadhl Abdulkarim, the Sultan of Lahej, held aloof from the Advisory System it would never get off the ground. Though he was not their overlord, the hinterland rulers tended to take a lead from the Sultans of Lahej whose ancestors had been sovereigns of Aden before the British took it from them and who, unlike themselves, were princes of repute throughout the Arab World. And so, when rulers and tribal bigwigs came to learn that the Sultan would have nothing to do with the System and then took note that four of five rulers who had signed Treaties were in serious trouble, it was not surprising that they turned their backs on Seager and the System and that, as a consequence, the Forward Policy was brought to a halt. Anyone with sufficient patience to look at the scene with unblinkered eyes would have known that to expect the Advisory System to take root without the support of the Sultan of Lahej was tantamount to expecting a harvest without any rain.

But why, when the Sultan's Hadhrami peer, the Qaiti Sultan, had happily signed an Advisory Treaty with Ingrams did Sultan Fadhl Abdulkarim hold aloof? Because the fellow was as mad as a March hare, Seager grunted. He was mad and bad. Drink, drugs, women and every conceivable depravity: he indulged in them all. He was a hopeless case and, as if this deplorable behaviour was not bad enough, the rascal had taken to surrounding himself with a pack of Egyptian pimps who were stuffing him up with a lot of anti-British nonsense. The only thing to be said for his style of life, Seager mused with a flicker of a smile, was that 'His Highness' would almost certainly drink himself into an early grave.

Very different from this disreputable debauchee was his younger brother, Ali. Nowhere in Southern Arabia would you have found anyone quite like him. Looking as if he had just stepped out of Savile Row and Bond Street, he was spectacularly elegant and, being well travelled, intelligent and perceptive and having an ability to speak pure Oxford English, he was an attractive and stimulating companion. A chat with him was a tonic which I enjoyed as often as I could. One of the subjects we discussed was, of course, his brother's refusal to have anything to do with the Advisory System. What I had to realise, he asked me to understand, was that no Sultan of Lahej could conceivably sign a Treaty to subject himself to colonial rule. Surely that was going a bit far, I argued. To accept advice on how to run his government would scarcely amount to the Sultan bowing to colonial rule! In any event, the Qaiti Sultan in the Hadhramaut—who was on a par with the Lahej Sultan—had signed up and it was inconceivable that he would have done so if he had believed that he was submitting to colonial rule. Ali listened with a lazy smile on his face and then, giving a gurgling little laugh, said that what I had overlooked was that the Qaiti had dealt with Ingrams. Here his brother had to deal with Seager and the way that Seager had managed the Advisory System was nothing short of colonial rule.

I found this difficult to dispute for the truth of the matter was that, except in Beihan where Seager seemed more disposed to take orders from the mischievous Sherif Hussein than to give him any advice, he and his Political officers seemed to have thrown their weight about in a way which would have made Ingrams blench in despair. Incredible though it may seem, Seager had even used those Treaties with us to advise three rulers to surrender all their powers to nominees of his and, in the case of two of them, had also advised them to go off into exile. What was wrong about the whole business, Ali said, was that Seager's sole interest in these Treaties was to use them to get control. The last thing he and his Political Officers ever bothered their heads about was giving advice about administration. Since none of them knew anything about it, that was hardly surprising. Seager, I felt, would have been the first to agree.

Marking Time

And what did I think of the future, Ali asked one day. He was worried about the future, he explained. He had the impression that, since we had left India, the Empire no longer meant as much to us as it once had and that, if we got into serious difficulties as we had, say, in Ireland, we would now very probably withdraw rather than fight. So? So, he could see that there was now every chance of our facing increasingly grave trouble from the Imam and, then, deciding to abandon Aden and the Protectorate to him just as we had abandoned Palestine to the Jews. So what did he suggest? He shrugged his shoulders and then said that, since our present colonial set-up could hardly be expected to last for very much longer, he thought we should be thinking of something to supersede it. He could only mean that we should be planning to give Aden and four dozen or so states and sheikhdoms independence. Ali wagged his head. There was a much simpler solution to the problem. We could hand the whole lot back to Lahej and sign a treaty with the Sultan to safeguard our interests. That, he could assure me, was a treaty he would sign without hesitation.

NOTES

[1] After the end of the First World War, the Imam Yahya invaded and occupied the Amirate of Dhala, most of the Audhali Sultanate, the Quteibi, Alowi, Shaibi and Sabeihi Sheikhdoms and parts of the Upper Yafa highlands. He was eventually forced to withdraw after the RAF had bombed the Yemeni town of Taiz in 1928.

[2] British efforts to thrust British influence into India's frontier regions during the latter part of the nineteenth century became known as the 'Forward Policy'.

3

FORWARD WITH THE FORWARD POLICY

I KNEW THAT SEAGER was not too happy about my seeing so much of that 'smart Alec, Ali' but l was more than a little surprised when, after a bout of nose blowing and throat clearing, he suddenly said that I should give him a miss for a while. But why? He had had information that Ali was stirring things up in Lahej and he did not want it to be thought that we had anything to do with it. Ali, he explained, seemed to be cooking up a revolt in hopes of throwing out his brother and getting the job of Sultan for himself. It all sounded a bit far fetched but it was not for me to argue.

In fact rather more was going on in Lahej than even Seager had suspected. Harassed by plots, intrigue and rumours of further plots or intrigue, Sultan Fadhl ran amok and personally executed three of his cousins with a pistol. As soon as the news reached Aden, Ali was on the telephone shouting for action. Everyone was terrified, he bawled. Refugees were pouring into Aden. It was imperative that we intervened before things got any worse. That had Seager up on his feet, dancing around and slapping his thigh with delight. This was splendid news, he chortled. What was so splendid about it? Didn't I see? He seemed surprised that I did not. Why, we had got Fadhl by 'the short and curlies', he explained. Unless we went to his rescue, he was for the chop and he knew it. So, all we had to do was to bolster up his authority with the backing of a Political Officer and some Government Guards and he would be our man for keeps. He would sign a Treaty and lick our boots if necessary. But surely... Surely what? But surely we should be getting rid of this disreputable character? Quite apart from all his other vices, he had committed murder! What did I mean by murder, Seager asked a little fiercely. Those three rascals had been in cahoots with Ali and got what was coming to them. It wasn't murder for a ruler to put traitors to death!

That, however, was not how Sir Tom saw it. Summoning us to Government House he asked Seager how he proposed to deal with the situation and heard what Seager had told me for an answer. Sir Tom was enchanted to be given such a Heaven-sent opportunity to pretend that his ears must have deceived him and, making a pantomime of discovering that they hadn't, showered the unhappy Seager with sneering contempt. So he wanted us to support a homicidal maniac, did he? Well, if he would be good enough to take careful note, he wished Seager to understand that he intended to do no such thing. Fadhl would have to go into exile and the Sultanic clan would then be persuaded to elect Ali as the new Sultan but only after he had agreed to sign an Advisory Treaty. Understood? We nodded.

A governatorial letter to Fadhl telling him in the politest language that, if he did not come in to Aden and explain what he had been up to Sir Tom would come out to Lahej was enough to send him helter-skeltering off to the Yemen with his family, retainers and bagpipe band. Sir Tom received the news in a matter of fact way and then asked Seager what he had done about Lahej. He had done nothing. Nothing? Good God, he should have taken Lahej over to maintain public order! But all was quiet there... Sir Tom snorted, saying that he had no doubt it was and, no doubt, that if he didn't take the place over pretty damn quick the Sultanic clan would be electing a Sultan we didn't want. So would Seager be good enough to wake up and do something about it!

Seager and I left immediately for Lahej. Seager was a little on edge, saying that we were bound to run into trouble and then, as if to prove him right, a wild-eyed creature waving a pistol suddenly bounded out from behind a bush on the side of the road. 'This is it!' Seager yapped. 'Drive like hell!' I did as I was told but there was no cause for panic. Our apparent assailant watched us go, screaming nonsense but without firing a shot. Seager seemed disappointed but cheered himself up with the thought that we might be welcomed by a riot on our arrival at Lahej. In the event, the townsmen greeted us 'en masse' with unctuous smiles.

They had a request to make, their spokesman said. They wanted British rule. They had had more than enough of Sultans.

After visiting Fadhl's abandoned palace, I could understand how they felt. It reeked of depravity and worse. Outside in the forecourt the newly-dug graves of Fadhl's murdered kinsmen stood under the twitching nose of an emaciated caged tiger which he had been given on a visit to India. Inside all was litter and chaos. Crumpled women's clothing, boxes and bags bursting with costume jewellery and dozens and dozens of broken and open bottles of nauseating scent were strewn about the dirty divans and tumbledown beds gracing the harem. Pornographic magazines and cigarette ends were scattered all over the floor. In the main reception room hubble-bubbles, spittoons, drums and percussion instruments lay higgledy-piggledy amid heaps of dirty dishes and plates. A broken-down cinema screen hung from a peeling wall in an adjoining room and, in the dining and kitchen areas, half-opened cartons of cigarettes and cases of whisky stood like islands in a sea of filthy cooking pots and broken electrical gadgets. Even Seager was appalled by what he saw. 'There you are!' he said. 'I told you he was as mad as a hatter!'

During our absence Sir Tom had rounded up the Sultanic clan and, having persuaded them that an Advisory Treaty would give them an effective safeguard against arbitrary rule, he had further persuaded them to elect Ali as their new Sultan but only if he agreed to sign one. Would he agree to sign? I asked him the same evening. He confirmed that he would. And yet he had only recently told me that no Sultan of Lahej would ever sign a Treaty. Maybe, but the fact of the matter was that his People needed him as their Sultan and, because of the Sultanic clan's condition, he could only do his duty by them by signing up. So he would be signing of his own free will? Yes, that would be so. And he would not later complain that we had tricked him into signing? But he had been tricked. Hickenbotham had tricked him by persuading the Sultanic clan to make this condition. That was hard to dispute.

With Ali signed up and bedded nicely down in our Advisory fold, Seager predicted a howl of protest from the Yemen and sure enough it arrived in the person of Qadhi Muhammed Abdulla Asshami, the ancient Yemeni dignitary responsible for 'frontier affairs', through whom our business affecting that region was normally conducted. We had agreed to respect the 'status quo' he complained, and here, by interfering in Lahej,

Forward with the Forward Policy

we had flagrantly disregarded it. No, no, we had agreed to respect the 'status quo' ON the frontier, we argued, and in Lahej we had interfered INSIDE the frontier, not ON it. We argued at cross purposes knowing that it was an exercise in futility. The foundations of misunderstanding on which the Treaty of San'a had been built had left us with an Agreement that was no agreement. In the old days the Arabs had always respected an 'Englishman's word', Asshami said, wagging his head in a mournful way, but now... He left us mumbling predictions of woe and worse.

Sir Tom made it plain with a couple of yawns that he was not interested in Seager's encounter with this 'old busybody'. What he wanted to know was what were Seager's plans for getting on with the Forward Policy. This was not something you could plan, Seager tried to explain. You had to wait for opportunities, in the same way that a batsman waited for a loose ball before hitting out. Sir Tom told Seager what he thought of this in his own unequivocal way and then said that he would be obliged if Seager would do as he was told and produce some plans. 'Well, yes...' Seager muttered and then suddenly rushed forward in a stumbling stammer to say that he thought we ought to go slow for a bit. Go slow? Sir Tom seemed to rise up out of his chair in outraged surprise. Well, the point was this, Seager croaked. He didn't think it would be wise to panic the Yemenis. It would be best to let them calm down after this Lahej affair. And how did he explain that, Sir Tom snorted. Well, if you looked at it through tribal eyes, Seager babbled. This was too much for Sir Tom. Damning tribal eyes and Seager's eyes, too, he said that he would put up with no more prevarication. We were going to go ahead and the first item on the agenda would be the Upper Aulaqi Sheikhdom.

The Upper Aulaqi Sheikhdom was remote, inaccessible and wild. Its tribes were notoriously turbulent and mostly lived along a Wadi described by Lord Belhaven, a contemporary of Davey's, as 'Murder Valley'. That anyone living in such a place would give a post-prandial belch for British advice to set up an administration seemed laughable and one can safely say that neither the bedridden, nonagenarian Sheikh, nor his two sons, Abdulla and Farid, who managed his affairs, would have given the matter a thought had Farid's Westernised young son, Mohammed, who was an Assistant Political Officer with us, not let slip the interesting possibility of a British subsidy accompanying a Treaty. If the British were prepared

The Deluge

to hand out subsidies, they were obviously squeezable for more, their old tribal minds would have told them. And so the bargaining began.

It started with Abdulla and Farid wishing to know how much they could expect as a subsidy. It was hard to say, they were told, because to begin with it would depend on the cost of setting up and running an Administration. But since they proposed to set up an Administration straight away, they needed the money straight away. They could not possibly sign the Treaty until that had been done. Why not? Before signing they needed to win over public opinion and they could not do that without first setting up an Administration and giving jobs to the people who mattered. This specious argument appealed to Seager's tribal mind and since Sir Tom was not in charge at the time, it was accepted. Once the subsidy had come and an Administration had been set up, Abdulla and Farid confirmed, they would sign the Treaty.

All too predictably, they did no such thing. The subsidy was totally inadequate, they regretted to say, and unless it was substantially increased there could be no question of their signing up. Deadlock followed and then, when the 'unheavenly twins' (as they were known to the Agency) finally got the message that they hadn't a hope of getting a larger subsidy, they came up with a fresh idea for raising additional revenue. What they had in mind was the extension of the road or motorable track linking Aden and a region called Dathina to the Sheikhdom and then on to Beihan and the Yemeni frontier. If there were such a road, they pointed out, all traffic from Aden bound for North Yemen would use it and in doing so would pay customs dues to the Sheikhdom en route. There was, of course, one point in need of a mention and that was that they would have to look to us for help to build the road. Astonishingly, they got it. The road was made and still they did not sign. No wonder, then, that Sir Tom should place the Sheikhdom at the top of his agenda. No wonder that he should now send me off to the Sheikhdom saying that I was on no account to return without a Treaty.

Said, the Sheikhdom's capital, was 'en fete' to receive me. Female ululations echoed around the surrounding hills in welcome as did occasional rifle shots from eminences overlooking my approach. On the outskirts of the little town several hundred tribesmen were drawn up in a long straggling line with Abdulla and Farid and other members of the Sheikhly family in their midst. All, I noticed, were armed with rifles.

Forward with the Forward Policy

Walking towards them, I noticed something else. Every rifle was going up and there I was looking down the barrels of two or three hundred apparently aimed straight at my head. Within seconds, every man of them was banging away with a will. I had not known anything like it since the battle of Tug Argan. This punishing welcome was followed by a stupefying banquet of boiled mutton as a prelude to the business of the day. We would be glad to know when they were going to sign the Treaty, I said as an opener. Abdulla looked at Farid and Farid looked at Abdulla. Public opinion was insufficiently prepared for a Treaty, Abdulla said. Now, if only the subsidy could be increased, Farid observed. It was not even worth talking about, I said, a bit sharpish. In any event, they already had a subsidy and a new road. Surely that was enough to get public opinion on their side? 'Ha, Ha!' crowed Farid. 'Ho, Ho!' gurgled Abdulla. I had to be joking. No, I was not joking. We had nothing more to offer. There was a long muttering pause and then Farid said that it might be possible to get public opinion in the right mood if we undertook to restore their lost territory. What lost territory? Why, the territory we had taken from them—Dathina! He could not be serious? Oh, yes he was. Dathina was theirs and they wanted it back.

Dathina was one of our problem children. It was a smallish tribal district lying outside the recognised jurisdiction of any Treaty Chief and was coveted by a ruler called the Audhali Sultan as well as by the Upper Aulaqi Sheikh. To prevent these two coming to blows, Seager had taken the precaution of occupying Dathina himself and putting a Political Officer in charge. This was not an arrangement which fitted very happily into our Protectorate set-up but, pragmatically, it made sense and there could be no question of upsetting it to placate the Aulaqis. I said as much to Farid, smiling my regrets. Sheikhly indignation promptly blared like a factory hooter and then subsided. Farid looked at Abdulla and grinned. They both grinned. No Dathina, no Treaty! The message behind the laughter in their eyes was that they had me over a barrel. Certainly I was in a fix but there was just a chance that I could wipe those insolent grins off their faces. If they did not want to go ahead with the Treaty, that was fine by us, I said. We would call the whole thing off. The money we were giving them as a subsidy could be used elsewhere and so could Marsack, the Political Officer we had made available to advise them. The two Sheikhs looked puzzled. I wasn't surely suggesting…? Yes, what I was saying was

The Deluge

that, if they didn't want a Treaty, the subsidy would cease at once and Marsack would return with me to Aden that very evening. Their bluff had been called. They signed up.

Sir Tom met me with a couple of grunts of satisfaction and said that he now wanted me to get on with the Dathina project. What Seager had done with Dathina was quite unacceptable. You could not have bits of the Protectorate left uncovered by any Treaty at all. It was anomalous and the position had to be regularised. So would I be good enough to draw up plans for the inclusion of Dathina into the Audhali Sultanate? Seager let out a wail of despair when I told him of this, saying that to give Dathina to the Audhali would be utter madness. The Dathina tribes would revolt with the help of the Aulaqis and then the whole bang shoot would go up in smoke leaving the Imam to walk in and pick up the pieces. He looked gloomily out of the window and then said that he did not know how to put this but we were up against a very special difficulty in this matter. The fact of the matter was that the Audhali Sultan was a nice, attractive, bright-eyed young man and Sir Tom was obsessed by him. It seemed hard to believe but this tough, irascible, hard-headed fellow was as wet as water when it came to dealing with the young Audhali. Yes, and I could take it from him that Sir Tom would already have promised Dathina to the Audhali and since you could hardly expect him to go back on his word it looked as if we could look forward to fireworks.

A visit to Dathina told me that Seager was unquestionably right. Apart from a Political Officer of doubtful worth, whom I discovered with a whisky and soda in his hand at eight o'clock in the morning, everyone I spoke to made it clear that, if we handed Dathina over to the Audhalis or even to the Aulaqis, come to that, there would be bigger trouble than we had seen in years. The Political Officer's view that this was balderdash did not impress me but then I was not all that surprised after the glass I had seen in his hand. So, on my return, I advised that Sir Tom's Dathina project be called off and received an earful of abuse for doing so. I had been instructed to draw up plans for including Dathina in the Audhali Sultanate, Sir Tom glared. Where were they? Did I mean to say that I had disobeyed his instructions? I stood about as much of this outburst as I could but I was not a schoolboy at Summer Fields any more and was forced to indicate that enough was enough. I told him that, if he was unwilling to accept my advice, I would go ahead as he wished but I would first, however, like his instructions in writing which I thought should be filed together with my own opinion in the matter. I got a blistering glare for my impudence but nothing more. Dathina was shelved. We did not talk about it any more.

This was a relief but there was a hangover. Had I realised that the Audhali had probably agreed to sign an Advisory Treaty in return for Dathina? Seager asked. No chance of that now. Nor, I imagined, was there any of having a friend for life in the Audhali Sultan. I did not know him too well and when he suddenly walked into my office I felt awkward and uncomfortable. 'So, you don't think we should have Dathina?' he asked, smiling in a surprisingly friendly way. No, I didn't. I told him why and I told him that, if handing Dathina over to him caused half the trouble I thought it would, we were doing him a favour. He laughed, asking if I really expected him to agree. No matter, he went on, the responsibility was mine and if that was what I had decided on he would accept it but… He smiled, saying his was quite a big 'but'. As I would have guessed, everyone knew that Sir Tom had promised him Dathina and so, if he did not get it, it would be thought that he and the British had fallen out and that could do a lot of harm. If he signed an Advisory Treaty, no one could say that, I suggested. No, but it could be said that he had been bullied into it and that would 'blacken his face'. So what did he propose? He proposed that we should help his Sultanate undertake a very special project, so special that his 'face' would be left unquestionably 'white'. He then told me what he had in mind.

Showing me a map, he pointed out that the shortest route from Aden to Beihan and North Yemen lay though his Sultanate and then over the mountains to its north and down into a Wadi Hatib. After that it would be easy going over gravelly plains all the way to Beihan. What he needed, he explained, was help to make a road over the mountains and down into the Wadi Hatib. His proposal made unquestionable sense but I could see that there was rather more to that gleam in the young man's eye than the prospect of having a road. Behind it there also undoubtedly lay the happy thought that, if his road materialised, the traffic from Aden would switch to it from the much longer road we had helped the Aulaqis build and that the customs revenue the Aulaqis were getting would then come over to him. In other words, if he got his road, he would double his revenue and at the same time deliver the Aulaqis a kick in the teeth for doing him out of Dathina. After the run-around the Aulaqis had given us, I was not going to let this inhibit me. The Audhali's proposal could not be faulted and that was good enough for me. I backed it and so did Sir Tom. Shortly afterward the Audhali signed an Advisory Treaty.

This brought Sir Tom out of his sulks and back to the Forward Policy. He was glad to say that, apart from the Upper Aulaqi Sultanate, we had now got everywhere that mattered reasonably under control. So what was Seager doing about the Upper Aulaqi Sheikhdom? Seager was, of course, doing nothing: which set Sir Tom off with his customary pantomime of expressing astonishment and displeasure as a prelude to reducing Seager to a state of gibbering incoherence. The Sultan was a raving lunatic, Seager tried to explain, and he would have nothing to do with us. 'Us?' Sir Tom thrust an inquiring jaw at Seager. 'Or you?' Having thus established by innuendo that, far from being a raving lunatic, the Sultan had sufficient good sense not to want to have any dealings with Seager, he said that, in the circumstances, he would like me to deal with the Sultan and the sooner I got on the move and extracted a Treaty out of him the better. I set off a few days later with Marsack, the Political Officer from the Upper Aulaqi Sheikhdom, as my companion. We were wasting our time, he said in a matter of fact way. The Sultan would almost certainly try to shoot us.

Nisab, the Sultan's seat, was a small market town of crumbling mud houses standing isolated and alone in a shimmering plain of near-desert. We arrived in the heat of the early afternoon to find the place deserted and dead. There was not even a bark from a stray cur to greet us. A scarecrow with a rifle guarding the door of the Sultan's dilapidated residence said that his master was asleep and could not see us. We hung around twiddling our thumbs for a couple of hours but the Sultan reportedly slept on. There was nothing we could do about it except go home and report failure to a frosty Sir Tom.

I was invited to lunch at Ali's splendid Rajahesque palace on my return and there I met for the first time some of his modern and fashionable, but not Westernised, young friends. Talkative and bursting with bright ideas, they could be called an intelligentsia but not one of the usual penurious and seedy kind. These young men came from the privileged 'jeunesse d'or' with all the time in the world to air their views, which they were doing in no mean fashion on this particular occasion. They were, in fact, in a delirium of speculation. The nice pipe-smoking General Neguib had just removed King Farouk and taken over on behalf of the Free Officers in Egypt, and no one quite knew what to expect next. This was not an Egyptian Revolution but an Arab Revolution which would unite the Arabs, one young man announced with shining eyes. Yes, but it was a a republican and secular revolution and what would that lead to? a glum voice enquired. After everyone had had their say and, eventually, left, Ali said that whatever shape the future took we were obviously in for change and, as foreigners, he did not think we would find it easy to negotiate our way through it. 'And so,' he lowered his voice, 'please remember that, as an Arab, I am better placed to do it for you.' What did he mean by that? I wondered. Make him King of South Arabia and sign a treaty with him? Maybe that was what was in his mind.

4

DRAFTING A BLUEPRINT FOR THE FUTURE

'IT'S ABOUT TIME you people realised that times are changing!' Ali said with a show of petulance. He was upset because I had to cancel an appointment with him at the last moment on account of a summons from Sir Tom. This was not 1852 and he was not a petty tribal Sheikh, he grumbled. He expected to be treated with proper civility, not with old fashioned colonialist arrogance. Times were changing and changing fast. No one living in Aden could have thought otherwise for a new Aden was shooting up all around us. No longer the sleepy hollow it had been on my arrival from Ndola only eighteen months before, it was more like a Klondike or a Rand: all bustle, new buildings, new faces and much more of everything. What had brought this about was the massive oil refinery British Petroleum were building to replace the one they had lost at Abadan in Iran. This had already spawned innumerable small and medium sized enterprises. Aden's traditional entrepot trade had rocketed and its port had become one of the busiest in the world. Perhaps the most noticeable change was in the population. Thousands of Yemenis had come pouring in to meet the ever growing demand for labour and hundreds more had come to cater for their needs. Europeans, Levantines and other Middle Eastern entrepreneurs were arriving by the 'planeload to serve the mushrooming new enterprises and collect the rich pickings sharp-eyed cut-throat opportunism could expect to win. Everywhere as much money was being earned and spent in a week as had been earned and spent in a year not so long before. Everywhere, the old Colonial Aden of 'Sahibs and Memsahibs' was on the way out.

A welcome bonus of all this was that we saw rather less of Sir Tom. He was now far too engrossed in Aden's impressive affairs to give us so much of his time and, in any event, having new butts for his nasty little witticisms in the Aden officials responsible for them, he seemed to find us less interesting. Even when Seager and I were occasionally summoned for a discussion on some subject he would, as often as not, switch from whatever we had come to talk about to what was at the top of the Aden agenda and so at the top of his mind. Throughout, his unchanging refrain was that it was time we in the Protectorate understood what was happening in Aden. It was becoming a modern city and, to flourish, modern cities needed modern environments. So what was Seager doing about modernising the Western Protectorate? Having nothing to disclose, Seager had to withdraw—as so often with Sir Tom's malevolent eyes in hot pursuit.

During the course of his 'tours d'horizon' on the subject of Aden Sir Tom would not infrequently remark that, in its new prosperity, we had the best possible insurance against political discontent. Full bellies did not make good rebels, he would say. Rebels had 'lean and hungry looks'. This was not what Eritrea had taught me nor what Wylie had taught me at Marlborough. Suddenly, seeing Kynaston-Snell running around with his eyes shining like fairy lights, I knew for sure that Sir Tom was deluding himself. He had come here from Eritrea as Aden's first Director of Education and had already set about 'blowing the cobwebs away'. A 'School for the sons of Chiefs' which Ingrams had set up he had closed down as something 'too laughably elitist' to take seriously and, with it there had been banished most of the old 'fuddy duddies' who had previously manned Aden's modest Department of Education. Now, with his old trusty, Robertson, the Glaswegian Red, at his side he was, he said, giving Aden the educational set-up it deserved. He had funds for all the schools it needed and, maybe, for a University, too, in God's good time. Come what may, he could assure me that he would be turning out a new generation of young Adenis 'with lively twentieth century ideas'. Remembering how lively his Eritrean students had been, I did not doubt it.

How long Aden's Victorian calm would last was anyone's guess but, even without the revolutionary antics of Kynaston-Snell's young men, it seemed all too obviously drawing to an end. It was plain to see that the far-sighted Newbold's predictions were coming true. We were fighting Communists in Malaya and the Mau Man rebels in Kenya; in Egypt and the Sudan we were under notice to quit; in Cyprus, a revolutionary liberation movement was already taking ominous shape; the French, too, were being thrown out of Indo-China and harassed by national revolts in North Africa. Almost overnight 'Colonialism' had become the dirtiest of dirty words and colonial environments everywhere time bombs ticking their way to disaster. The writing on the wall spelt havoc; the warning of a coming Deluge could not have been clearer. And, at this critical time, what were we in the Western Protectorate doing? Exactly what the old Empire builders had been doing a hundred years before. We were a hundred years behind the times.

When I first toured the Western Protectorate I could not imagine how anything recognisable as state government could ever exist in its unusually robust tribal climate. I was, of course, no stranger to tribal people and, apart from language and appearance, there was only one difference between the tribes here and in Eritrea. It was, however, a difference with the force of a hundred differences. Every tribesman here had a rifle slung across his shoulder and a bandolier of bullets around his belly. Every bloody minded, blood thirsty, little tribe was nothing more than a gang of armed outlaws. To rule them in the sense of taxing them and getting them to accept the authority of his courts was something no Ruler could pretend to do: which was why the tribes were largely left to their own sanguinary and unsavoury devices. Though usually described as a Ruler's 'followers'—never as his 'subjects'—the tribes were in fact a blend between mercenaries on call and protection racketeers. When they did their Ruler a specific service they expected to be rewarded for it. When they did nothing in particular, they expected occasional sweeteners and privileges for being good enough not to misbehave. They would have regarded as an outrage anything in the nature of a demand for tax; though, without knowing it, they contributed handsomely if indirectly to the state's excise revenues by purchasing supplies in the local markets.

Fortunately, though spread across the greater part of the map, the tribes did not dominate the whole of it. Here and there were to be found a few havens of comparative tranquillity where non-tribesmen—agricultural tenants, merchants, artisans, labourers and hangers-on—lived under the protection of their Rulers on land belonging to the ruling class. It was in these oases that we had helped the Rulers to set up Administrations which, at first glance, looked respectable enough. In each there was a Treasury, Courts, and local gendarmerie called the Tribal Guards. In some, schools and health clinics were also beginning to appear. There was nothing wrong with the principle, but everything with the practice. The Administrations were being run unashamedly as family businesses in the interests of the ruling class. They were seen not as the machinery of government but as collections of jobs to be shared out among sons, brothers, cousins, uncles and varying degrees of in-laws. If there was anything to be made on the side, no one objected. Bribery and corruption were the recognised 'perks' that went with the job.

My introduction to this tribal concept of government occurred when I found myself helping the Upper Aulaqi Sheikh's two sons, Abdulla and Farid, with their budget. We were at cross-purposes from the start for, whereas I was trying to determine what was necessary to enable the Administration to function, they were solely concerned to devise sufficient sinecures with impressive titles to ensure that everyone who mattered was squared. To complicate matters, the traditional rivals to the Sheikh's family in the ruling clan, the Ahl Bubakr, objected to jobs being distributed 'ad personam'. Each family within the clan, they insisted, should have its cut and then share the jobs amongst themselves. And how would the cuts be determined? Nothing could be simpler, said Muhammad, the burly leader of the Ahl Bubakr. The entitlement of every family was well known. It followed the traditional entitlement to a share of the loot after a tribal raid. Thus a family entitled to two rustled goats out of every ten would get one fifth of the jobs on offer. This seemed to make sense to everyone except me.

It was on an inaugural visit to Beihan that I had my first close look at an Administration in action. Received in customary fashion by a thunderous three hundred or so rifle salute, I was welcomed with grave formality by the tall, black-bearded Sherif. He had a lot to tell me about what the Imam was planning, he said in a lowered voice as we walked towards his palace. Seager would no doubt be interested to hear about it, I replied, but the object of my visit was to inspect his Administration. His eyes popped with surprise. His Administration? That would be difficult, he thought. He had had no opportunity to warn them. Another time, perhaps. There was no need to warn them, I assured him. I just wanted to see them working normally. A quick run through what might be termed the 'staff list' revealed that most of those on it were of the nature of non-executive directors with no functions at all. The Islamic Court was closed during my visit because the Qadhi, or Judge, had gone to Aden on private business. No one knew when he was likely to return. The non-Islamic or customary Court was operating, however, and we arrived at the end of a case to find the litigants being made to pay their fees—not, however, Court fees alone but fees also to the Judge himself. Why was this? How could the Judge he expected to give good service if he wasn't compensated, the Sherif asked. But he was compensated. He received a salary. No, that did not count. He got that as a right, for being a member of the family. After that it was no surprise to find the Treasury safe as bare as Mother Hubbard's cupboard, because members of the family had all helped themselves to loans from it; or to discover that half a dozen near bed-ridden geriatrics were receiving salaries as gendarmes in the 'Tribal Guards'.

A final shock awaited me when we adjourned for lunch after I had done my rounds. Luncheon was a banquet of boiled goat and rice to which about fifty of us sat down cross-legged on the floor. We had barely lowered ourselves when a strange sound of clanking heralded the arrival of three youths manacled and chained to each other. Exchanging greetings in a matter of fact way with the Sherif and others present, they sat themselves down and joined us in the repast. Who were they, I asked the Sherif. They were the sons of three 'Aqils' or tribal lords, he explained, and, since their tribes had been threatening to cause trouble, he had taken them as hostages against their tribes' good behaviour. And how long had they been chained up like this? He stroked his beard in an off-hand way and said it would be about eighteen months. Eighteen months! I was appalled. I really thought it was time that he released them, I said. What! And have their tribes on the loose once again? The Sherif chuckled with contempt for my naivete. However, I stuck to my guns and said that, since this was my first visit to Beihan, I would very much appreciate that he should do me the favour of granting my request for their release. He wriggled but, finding no escape route, graciously gave in. The hostages were released and within the week their tribes were shooting up traffic on the roads.

Not all Administrations were as cheerfully unorthodox as Beihan's. Two of them were, in fact, comparatively elaborate and impressive affairs. First, there was Lahej where an elementary 'government' of sorts had operated from our earliest days and where, with our help, Ali was now trying to knock it into more reputable shape. Then there was Abyan, the scene of the Western Protectorate's one glittering success. This was a hundred and fifty square mile patch of coastal plain lying at the foot of a 7,000 foot massif upon which heavy rains descended for a few months each year. During them, cascades of water tumbled down the mountainside and flooded across the Abyan plain, leaving behind a rich deposit of silt. Here, in the middle of nowhere, was a potential Garden of Eden where anything from bananas to bamboo shoots could be grown. Left to themselves, Abyan's factious and feckless inhabitants never grew much of anything nor ever would have done so had not Aden gone dangerously short of cereals during the War. In this situation, one of those strong, silent men who revel in making bricks without straw was sent there with a Government loan of £25,000. His name was Hartley and he had no difficulty in starting a flourishing cereal production scheme and, once the War was over, in switching from cereals to cotton. Fortified with a further loan of £250,000, he could not go wrong. Production and profits shot through the roof. An ever growing network of dams, canals, and irrigation channels spread across the plain; a scientific research centre was set up to study and combat diseases and pests; large quantities of stores and equipment were installed, together with a ginnery. To administer and direct the Scheme's operations a management team of British technocrats was established under the control of a tough, no nonsense Cornish agriculturist called Congdon who had trod on any number of toes in Eritrea in the past, including mine. Nothing like this dazzling Abyan scheme had been seen in South Arabia since the days of Sheba and the Mareb dam.

So far from being favoured with an agreeable political environment, Hartley could hardly have had worse. Abyan unfortunately did not fall within the borders of single state, but straddled two Sultanates—the Fadhli and Lower Yafa—and since every square yard of cultivated land was increasing in value by the minute, there were endless commotions and affrays about boundaries and water rights. The greatest difficulty of all was the blind rapacity of the two Sultans and their ruling class.

The Deluge

When Hartley put aside profits to finance the running of the scheme and development, they threw fits of hysterical rage, claiming he was taking money which by right was theirs. When money was deducted as tax and paid over to these states to be used for state purposes, they put their heads back and howled that they had been robbed. Seager had battled away trying to persuade, cajole, threaten and otherwise silence these maniacs in what he described as 'shouting matches' and would no doubt have gone on doing so had they not begun to interfere with the irrigation system by switching water off each other's land and onto their own. Enough was enough. Seager intervened decisively. The two Sultans were removed from the scene by the instrument of advice issued under their treaties and Abyan was put under a thinly veiled colonial regime firmly in charge of one of our Political Officers. This action saved Abyan but, in what were supposed to be Advisory Treaty States, the result did look a little bit odd.

At this point some hidden button seemed to have been pressed which was marked 'Full speed ahead!' Suddenly everything seemed to be hustle, bustle and activity. The Administrations were extended and made more elaborate while staff were trained to run them; Education and Health both made a great leap forward; irrigation pumps were issued to farmers to grow fruit and vegetables to exploit Aden's demands for them; a marketing scheme was set on the stocks and tentative plans for a fisheries project were drafted. What had been a barely inhabited desert less than ten years before had become the most prosperous region in South Arabia outside Aden. By Sir Tom's reckoning, its prosperity was a prescription for a golden era of unbroken political tranquility.

This was not Seager's forecast of things to come. In a farewell chat before handing over to me and leaving on retirement in the early Summer of 1953, he repeated his ritual warning of the imminence of the great 'explosion' the Imam was planning for our discomfiture. What I had to bear in mind, he said, was that the Imam was sitting on a powder keg and that, unless he dealt with us, it might go off. In the Yemen he was only acceptable to the Shi'ite minority, the Zeidis, and that was because he was their spiritual leader. The Sunni majority, the Shafi'is, were itching to rebel and join our fellows in the Protectorate who were Sunni and Shafi'is like themselves. Even so, they were not idiots and were unlikely to make a move until they were sure that the Protectorate was in reasonably good order. That was why the Imam was bound to [do] his damnedest to sabotage what we were doing, quite apart from his divine mission to get South Arabia back. That, said Seager, solemn-eyed and in Doomlike tones, was the position. An explosion was inevitable.

He had, of course, been saying this for nearly two years and even though we had gone successfully ahead with the 'Forward Policy' the Imam had done nothing worth talking about. How did he explain that? It was obvious enough. After all, the Imam had taken over in a counter coup after his father's murder and, with the country in an uproar, he had had his work cut out to get things under control again. Also, thanks to the intrigues of the Sherif's friends, he had had serious misunderstandings with some of his brothers, including Prince Hassan—the brightest of the lot. Yes, we had been lucky, Seager reflected, damned lucky, but we could not expect to go on avoiding trouble for ever.

It was some time after this that I welcomed Ali back from London where he had been one of the guests at the Queen's Coronation. The visit was not a success, so I gathered. Everything had gone wrong and what appeared to lie at the root of Ali's querulous ill humour was his belief that he had been treated with 'colonialist' disdain. He had not been received by anyone of suitable rank, he had been lodged in a down-market hotel, time and again he had been kept waiting and hanging about. And then, to add to all the other indignities, he had had to share a carriage with that great black she-elephant of a woman, the Queen of Tonga, in the Royal procession! Listening to his litany of grievances, I thought it as well that he had not heard Noel Coward's 'bon mot' about himself. 'Who is that little chap with the Queen of Tonga?' someone had wanted to know as they stood watching the procession. 'Her lunch!' came Coward's reply.

Nevertheless, if we British had treated him with unseemly indifference, Ali made a point of letting me know that he had received the utmost courtesy and consideration from a number of well-known figures attending the Coronation including, in particular, Pandit Nehru. And could I guess what Nehru had said to him? Nehru had said that he and his fellow Arabs in South Arabia had only to give a push on the door and they would be free. The British people had lost all interest in the Empire and the old imperialist classes were thoroughly demoralised. And so, was he proposing to push at that door? What, and get taken over by the Imam? Ali laughed and, reminding me that he had already offered to help us negotiate ourselves a relationship with a new South Arabia when the time came, said that the situation was still far too obscure to make any plans. What was to be done about this impossible old savage, the Imam? What would happen in Egypt now that General Abdul Nasser had taken over from Mohammed Neguib? Were we going to remain in Egypt or would we withdraw? Shrugging his shoulders, Ali said that only a fool would waste any time planning for the future while questions such as these remained unanswered. Not that he had any reason to complain, he laughed, waving a hand out towards the distant squalor of his capital. He had plenty to do in the meantime reorganising Lahej.

We, also, had plenty to do in the smaller Advisory Treaty States where, as in Beihan, the tribal mentality had been allowed far too much scope. 'Administrative bunk' and State Administrations had meant nothing to Seager and his Political Officers had followed his lead, subordinating everything to tribal politics and leaving the State Administrations to their Rulers' strange devices. Though a tough lot of ex-Chindits, Paratroopers and such like, they were no fools and, apart from a couple who had taken to the bottle and had to go, they were easily persuaded that 'good government' was something worth working for. They were only too glad to be shown how to set about it and I very soon had a willing and useful little team at work. Gradually, almost imperceptibly, what had happened in Abyan began to happen on a smaller scale and in a lesser degree amongst its neighbours. We even got cotton schemes going in some of them with help from Abyan and, here and there, a start was being made with growing fruit and vegetables with irrigation pumps. In the phrase Harold MacMillan was to coin some years later, we had 'never had it so good'.

So I would think at times in a self-satisfied way but some article about what was being described as Egypt's 'Revolution' would quickly remind me of Newbold's predictions and that we were living in a dream world. 'The Forward Policy' and our efforts to build a buffer of well-ordered little states to keep out the Imam was a nineteenth century device to deal with a nineteenth century situation. It defied all reason to imagine that we could long continue living in a nineteenth century style when we were already half way through the twentieth. We would clearly have to adapt ourselves to a twentieth century situation where colonial regimes were being phased out and colonies were becoming independent. In other words, the sane, sensible thing for us to do would be to prepare the ground for South Arabian independence now and then arrange to safeguard our position and interests in Aden by negotiating a treaty with… with whom exactly? With an independent Aden and a collection of independent little Protectorate states?

I needed time to brood but I was leading a full and wonderfully exhilarating life which held me captive for most of my waking hours. What with rushing around on tours of inspection, supervising and guiding Political Officers and state officials, handling rulers with tantrums, grievances and outrageous demands, dealing with a hundred and one problems at a time, to which a hundred and one impatient people were demanding instant replies and, not least, keeping an aggressive and inquisitorial Sir Tom at bay, I was hard put to set aside an hour of thinking time. Even when I did, my mind would be so cluttered with what was going on all around me that I had difficulty in switching over to what seemed remote and a little unreal. This, I imagine, is why it took me so long to see the obvious, for the answer to my problem could not have been plainer had it been written down for me in capital letters. Since the Protectorate states were each too small to be independent on their own, they would have to be united by either merging or federating them together. Since merger would only be feasible if the rulers were prepared to liquidate themselves and their states, federation was the answer. That was all there was to it.

I had no difficulty in drawing up a federal plan and, with the draft constitution of the stillborn Indian Federation[1] as a model, I was able to draw up detailed constitutional proposals without too much delay. The question now was how to present them to Sir Tom. The easy, innocuous way would have been to present them as a next step to the Forward Policy by explaining that the States' need for common Health, Education and other services demanded some super-state authority which a federation could best provide. But what about my plan for independence and a treaty to safeguard our position and interests in Aden? That was the real purpose of my proposals but, certain though I was that they offered the best hope of our surviving the future, I was all too uncomfortably aware that bright ideas about independence did not come too well from a British Agent of only a few months' standing. It was awkward and could well give Sir Tom a field day but, having got so far, I could not contemplate backing down.

The Deluge

And so what I now proposed was the setting up of a Federation of Western Protectorate states as a first step followed by its merger or federation with Aden and, then, full independence. The Treaty safeguarding our position and interests would be negotiated and signed on the eve of independence. Although I proposed setting up an all-Arab Government for the Federation with an Arab Premier and Ministers, I had to assume that we would make British officers available as Advisers, Permanent Secretaries and Heads of Department. Arabs who were still incapable of running their states without our help could hardly be expected to handle a federation on their own. Having completed my proposals, I sent them off to Sir Tom and then sat tight waiting for a barrage of thunderbolts. Astonishingly, none came. More astonishingly still, Sir Tom actually congratulated me on my proposals with the back-handed compliment that, had he had the amount of free time I evidently had, he would very probably have drafted proposals on much the same lines. He had nothing to say about independence or the Treaty. He saw no point in talking about Aden until after the Western Protectorate Federation had been set up. He purred on for a while in a self-congratulatory way and then said that as soon as he and Goode had gone through my proposals in detail and made such minor amendments as might be necessary, he would clear them with the Colonial Office and then convene a meeting of chiefs at Government House and get them to agree to federate. There was to be no dragging of feet. What he wanted was immediate action.

NOTES

[1] The 1935 Government of India Act, which introduced self-government in the Provinces, also envisaged federation at the centre. The Viceroy dispatched five senior officers of the Political Service to persuade the princes to come into the Federation but, perhaps because they did not persuade hard enough, their mission was unsuccessful.

5

A HIDEOUS SELF-INFLICTED WOUND

I FOUND SIR TOM padding around his garden puffing his pipe as if he had not a care in the world. Everything was going very nicely according to plan, he said, releasing a smile. That was just as it should be but there could be no slacking off. Delay was the great saboteur of success so we had to keep up the momentum. That brought him to the next item on his agenda. The Colonial Office had now approved our federation proposals for the Western Protectorate, he was glad to inform me, and so the sooner we got the Rulers to accept them and began setting up the federation the better. Would I, then, please summon the Rulers to Government House in, say, a couple of weeks' time? All being well, he thought we could count on getting their agreement within the day. That seemed a little optimistic, I thought. Well, how long would I say, Sir Tom bristled. I would give it a month. 'Thank you for being so very helpful!' he said, leading me to the door.

Although I had no doubt that the Rulers would agree to federation in the end, it was not a concept that they could be expected to understand too easily and, so, I had taken the precaution of sending my proposals to Ali in advance in the hope that he would give them a lead. I sold them but by no means as easily as I had expected. He could see no sense in drawing up a complicated constitution for a lot of bedouin chiefs who would not understand a word of it, he said, smiling disdain. All we had to do to decolonise was to hand Aden back to him and then leave him to do the rest. I could not believe that would be feasible and, since it

The Deluge

looked as if my proposals had a good chance of being accepted. I said I thought it would be wiser for him to go alone with us, rather than start an argument which he would almost certainly lose. He chewed this over for a while and then said he would agree provided I made one minor amendment to my proposals. Instead of having an elected President of the Federation, he wished the Presidency to be reserved exclusively for the Sultan of Lahej. I would surely agree that it would be quite unthinkable for a Sultan of Lahej to take second place to one of those tribal chiefs whom we now described as rulers. I saw his point but could not believe that what were, in effect, feudal claims to preeminence would count for very much in these enlightened days. In any event, since his prestige and standing would ensure that he was elected President, was this, I asked, worth arguing about? He agreed though with rather a glum smile.

Glancing through the copy of the finally approved federation proposals after leaving Sir Tom, I felt my blood turning to ice. I could not believe that what I was seeing was true. But it was. My proposals, I had been told, remained virtually unchanged. Unchanged? They had been turned inside out, stood on their head and made to say the very opposite of what I had intended. My autonomous Arab Federation with its Arab President and Ministers had been replaced by a Federation with the Governor as its Head and British officials as the equivalent of ministers. Far from preparing the ground for early independence, the proposals as they now stood would give the Western Protectorate a carbon copy of the Aden Government. And to think that I had been jollying Ali along with talk of early independence!

As I took in the hideous implications of what was now being proposed, I realised that unless the federation project was scrapped we would be asking for trouble. And so I hurried back to Government House to beard Sir Tom. Indeed!! He snorted exclamation marks at me when he heard what I had to say. And what did I think was wrong with the proposals in their present form? Oh, so I did not think he was up to the job, was that it? This ghastly, ludicrous and totally irrelevant pantomime dragged on for a few agonising minutes but I could not get through. It was like trying to argue with an answering machine. I left with Sir Tom telling me that he had not much patience to spare for young men who were getting too big for their boots. His opinion of me was, by this time, the least of my worries.

A Hideous Self-inflicted Wound

The farcical charade of a Rulers' Conference at Government House was duly played out early in the New Year of 1954. Shortly before the proceedings were due to begin, Sir Tom demanded to see the seating plan. He glared at it for a while and asked what criteria I had used for establishing the rulers' precedence as against each other. With the exception of Lahej, which I regarded as a special case, I had listed them according to the dates of their treaties, I said. What treaties? The Advisory Treaties, since they were the ones that mattered. Sir Tom disagreed. I should have used the Protection Treaties. On that, he removed his 'bete noire', Sherif Hussein, from the front row to the back and his friend, the Audhali Sultan, from the back to the front row. And so, to add to our difficulties, we would now have an apoplectic Sherif Hussein on our hands!

And we did. Throughout the proceedings, the Sherif yawned, scratched himself, stretched his legs, looked at the ceiling, coughed and cleared his throat in a calculated display of contempt for the proceedings. In the meantime, Sir Tom led the rest of his audience through our federal proposals paragraph by paragraph and the further he advanced down the road the glassier-eyed and stiffer-faced did Ali become. Reaching the end, Sir Tom asked if anyone would like to ask any questions. Ali rose to his feet and said that he and his brothers would first like a little time to study the proposals. Very well, then, Sir Tom agreed to adjourn and reconvene the meeting in the evening. Ali squeezed out a courteous smile of regret, saying that would be too soon. They would let His Excellency know when they were ready to participate in further discussion. They never did. The project was dead. It was a long time before federation was mentioned again.

6

A SURROGATE WAR WITH THE YEMEN

ON THE DAY AFTER that catastrophic Conference I looked in on Ali to see what I could do to repair the damage. He was naturally cross and spoke bitterly of our proposals as 'peace terms dictated to a defeated enemy'. He made it plain, however, that he harboured no hard feelings against me since he knew very well that I must have been over-ruled. But where did all this leave him, he asked. The Colonial Office had now made it plain that it was not interested in any moves towards independence but, whether they liked it or not, the People were bound to start agitating for it. Could I see what this meant? He would be left having to make a choice between siding with his People against ourselves or siding with us against his People. Nonsense! I said, summoning up a laugh. It would never come to that. In my heart of hearts I knew that it very likely would.

Happily, the sour anti-climax of the federation affair was almost immediately sweetened by the arrival of our new Queen and Prince Philip on a visit to Aden. The occasion detonated a quite unbelievable explosion of popular euphoria and, in the midst of it all, a purring Ali was dubbed a Knight of St Michael and St George. It was a heartening little interlude which briefly masked my worries but the Royal Yacht Britannia had hardly weighed anchor and sailed away when I received a rather disturbing message which sent me scurrying off to see the Audhali Sultan. Work had by this time begun on the road for which he had asked our help as his price for signing an Advisory Treaty and it had already reached the top of the mountain ridge looking down onto the Upper Aulaqi plains. All that now remained to be done was to take the road on down the Wadi Hatib and out into the rolling plains. There was, however, a little difficulty, the Audhali said. The two small tribes through whose territory the road would run—the Rabizis and Dammanis—had written to warn us that, if we tried to carry on with the road, they would stop us by force. Their letters were identically and rather curiously phrased. Informing us that they had placed themselves and their territories under the protection of the Arab League, they ordered us to keep off their land on pain of attack by the 'Arab nation'. The letters each ended with the ringing exhortation, 'Death to the Colonial Oppressors'. George Henderson, the tough and experienced Political Officer on the spot, dismissed this as nothing more than a try-on to get a sweetener out of us. The Audhali was inclined to agree, saying that since the tribes could barely muster a few dozen old Turkish blunderbusses, he did not think there was anything much to worry about. We agreed to ignore them and carry on. Within the week our working parties were being shot up: not by old Turkish blunderbusses but by British .303s. The rifles had been given to them by Asshami who was seated just over the frontier in the Yemen at his seat of office, Beidha, the 'White City'.

The news had Sir Tom trumpeting down the telephone, demanding to know what I was doing about the Dammanis and Rabizis and expressing his astonishment that I had not seen fit to rush off and give Asshami 'a rap on the knuckles for his impertinence'. There was not much that I could do about the two tribes but a meeting with Asshami on the Audhali frontier was easily arranged. He arrived looking strangely mediaeval with his thin wisp of a beard and top-heavy turban seated on his diminutive head. Gathering his shabby old sheepskin coat around his frail little person and peering at the Audhali and myself, he snivelled a greeting. And what could it be that had made us want to see him at such short notice? he asked with feigned surprise. He knew very well what it was, the Audhali retorted. He had been arming our tribes to cause trouble. Asshami gave a little hiccoughing laugh, saying that the Audhali had misunderstood the position. What he had done was to respond to a call from his 'Arab brothers' for help to defend their territory against us. Turning to me, he insisted that the Yemen wanted peace but asked how there could be peace if we illegally invaded Arab territory that was not ours. We had agreed to respect the 'status quo' but had immediately broken it by invading Audhali, Dathina and the Aulaqis and occupying them with our Government Guards. So who were we to complain, he asked, looking to his retainers for support. We were the aggressors and he would speak frankly. He knew that we were plotting an ever bigger aggression! What was that? Why were we building those roads up to the North through the occupied territories? 'Heh, heh, heh!' he cackled, wagging a knowing finger at us. It was to link our new refinery in Aden with the oil in Shabwa![1]

Sir Tom had hardly had time to tell me off for letting Asshami 'get away with it' when the trouble began to spread from the Dammanis and Rabizis to a number of other small tribes scattered about Audhali, Dathina and the Aulaqis. In every case, we received near identical letters informing us that the tribes were under the protection of the Arab League and ordering us to remove our Government Guards and keep off their land under pain of attack by the 'Arab nation'. These warnings were promptly followed by attacks on our Government Guard forts and transport on the roads. Was this the big bang Seager had been prophesying for so long? It looked very much as if it might be. 'Stuff and nonsense!' Sir Tom snorted. Just because a few tribesmen got playful it didn't mean that the end of the world had come. Anyhow, what was I doing about the situation? What political action was I taking? There was nothing very much I could do. I could make a start by negotiating with some of the dissident tribal leaders, Sir Tom snapped. Negotiate about what? Sir Tom rolled his eyes around in a gesture of agonised impatience and wished to know if he had to spell out the obvious to me. What he expected me to do was to make these idiots see some sense by reading them the Riot Act and telling them 'or else'!

To arrange meetings with rebel tribal leaders was none too easy but, with the help of the Audhali, I eventually persuaded the Aqil of Dathina's Hassani tribe to meet me. I was to come unarmed, he said, and without escort. The Audhali did not like this. Better forget about it, he advised. No, I thought to myself, better face the consequences than a cantankerous Sir Tom wishing to know why I had not obeyed his instructions! I agreed to the meeting and turned up unarmed and with only the Audhali and our wise old tribal adviser, Mubarak Assahm. The Aqil arrived, head in the air, with a posse of fifty armed warriors dancing and singing their contempt for our small party. Having greeted us courteously enough, the Aqil announced that he was willing to make peace with Great Britain. His conditions were that we should sign a treaty with him recognising his independence and agreeing to withdraw from his country. This was absurd! I had to say it and instantly there was a clicking of rifle bolts and an outbreak of snarls from his followers. Would I please repeat what I had said, the Aqil asked in tones cold with menace. Before I could do so, the Audhali chipped in to say that what I had meant to say was that I agreed in principle to discuss these important matters but that the discussion would have to take place later in more appropriate circumstances. 'Lies, lies, colonialist lies!' yelled the Aqil's followers. Let me agree now and at once... It was a nasty, awkward moment. We were three unarmed men and those facing us were the Aqil and fifty raving savages. Without a tremor the Audhali gave the Aqil a long, friendly smile and a farewell handshake. God willing, we would meet again soon, he said. I followed suit. The Aqil blinked and mouthed his farewells. We then legged it for safety.

We were, of course, indebted to Asshami for all the commotions erupting around the countryside and Asshami, I could see, was on to a winner. Offer tribesmen arms and they would sell their grandmothers to get them. So, all Asshami had had to do was to let it be known that arms were on offer to any gallant tribesman willing to wage war against Colonialism and he had been inundated with would-be warriors in the Arab cause. None of them, it is true, had any quarrel with us and, left to themselves, they would all have gone home with their booty and done nothing. The wily Asshami naturally knew this and, to make sure that he got value for his arms, he made the tribes leave hostages behind against their taking action against us. In the event, he had no difficulty in getting what he wanted. Within a few weeks, hundreds of tribesmen were shooting away at our Government Guard forts and Political Officers' houses. Increasingly, too, they were making the roads unusable. We had a military situation on our hands without the soldiery to deal with it. The Forward Policy had led to all our surplus Government Guards being used to man new posts. Now, without any reserves left, we could only look to the 'Military' for help.

Military support? Sir Tom could not believe that he had heard me correctly. Was I seriously asking for military support? Yes, I was. What had the Air Officer Commanding to say to that? Sir Tom turned to an Air Marshal Bufton at his side who sat comfortably back in his chair and said that the situation as I had described it did not concern him. He was ready to repel Yemeni troops invading the Protectorate but, when it came to dealing with our own tribes who were, for some reason, discontented, that was a political matter outside his sphere. It needed a political not a military solution. Sir Tom cordially agreed and asked what political solution I had in mind. I had none, short of giving in to the tribes' demands and withdrawing. If I could do no better than that, Sir Tom said somewhat testily, perhaps he could give me some advice. Tribes had to buy and sell to live and, since they used particular merchants and markets to do so, the proven way of dealing with them if they made trouble was to stop using their markets. So, if I would find out what market the Dammanis and Rabizis used for a start and took it over, we would be well on our way to bringing them to heel. He and the Air Marshal thereupon exchanged appreciative looks and I left with my tail between my legs.

The market used by our errant tribes was a small hamlet buried away in the Wadi Hatib called Robat and it was with some difficulty that we moved down there and installed the last of our Government Guards as a garrison. Since they immediately came under siege and since the merchants with whom the outlaw tribes dealt merely moved a couple of miles out of Robat and carried on business as usual with their clients, all we got out of Sir Tom's helpful advice was an unnecessary additional Government Guard fort under siege to maintain and supply. Even Sir Tom had to accept that we no longer had the resources to convoy supplies down insecure roads to Robat and the many other Government Guard forts under siege. Reluctantly, he had to agree that we were in need of military support. We needed it for convoy work and, also, to deal with the rebels.

Aden had been a Royal Air Force Command since the First World War, and the soldiery available was not impressive. Apart from a troop of Gunners to fire salutes on ceremonial occasions, the only men we had were the Aden Protectorate Levies—a British-officered Arab force five hundred strong. Though originally raised as Aden's answer to those colourful regular irregular Scouts, Levies and the like who had kept the flag flying on India's North West Frontier, our Levies had become Aden-bound, parade ground soldiers without experience of or interest in climbing around mountains. They had in fact become a subsidiary of the RAF Regiment and were mainly trained to guard and defend aerodromes. So it may be imagined how well my request for military support was received.

Support? The Levies' Commanding Officer, Group Captain Godfrey, raised an eyebrow. Precisely what form of support did I need? We needed the working parties on the Wadi Hatib road protected against attack and Levies available to go to the rescue of the Government Guards where necessary. The Group Captain smiled the smile of an indulgent schoolmaster. That was not possible, he said. If I would give him a specific task he would do it. For example, if the Enemy were occupying a particular position and I wanted them removed, he would remove them. He talked as if I were in a position to say that the Rabizis would be on such and such a hilltop at 6am the morning after next. How could I be? We were up against will o' the wisps who were here one minute and gone the next. What we wanted were men in the field; a fire brigade, you might say, which would be ready to rush off to wherever there was a fire and extinguish it. Out of the question, the Group Captain said. If I had my way, his force would be dispersed in penny packets all over the place and that would never do. The impasse between us took us to Government House.

The issue was quickly settled. It was not for me to dictate to the Group Captain, Sir Tom pronounced. It was up to him to say what he was prepared to do and for me to fall in with his views. Air Marshal Bufton wagged his head in agreement and Godfrey simpered satisfaction. I had lost the argument in the first five minutes. But Sir Tom had not finished with me yet. Why, he asked, had I not considered the idea of a 'flag march'? Yes, showing the flag. We had not had a man and a boy available to do anything of the kind, I replied a little huffily. Well, I had now, Sir Tom snorted, and he would like to see me accompanying a Levy force up the Dathina-Mahfid stretch of the Upper Aulaqi road which had, so he understood, been closed to all traffic for the last few weeks. I could think of a hundred better ways of employing a force of Levies but I said nothing. I had lost my appetite for further argument.

When I arrived at Mudia, the capital of Dathina, to join the 'flag march', the air was vibrant with what sounded like a concert of cicadas. It was, in fact, the hum and burr of dozens of new cheap radio transistors that had recently appeared on the market and one and all were switched on to Cairo's 'Voice of the Arabs': the voice, one could have said, of General Abdul Nasser, the smiling revolutionary who had just ousted the complacent Mohammad Neguib. It was poisoning the people's minds, Ahmed Hassan Mudhaffer, our Assistant Political Officer, complained. It was, in fact, applying Dr Goebbels' dictum that the more often a lie is repeated, the more likely are people to believe it. Regularly on the half hour the Voice would deliver its message in short, sharp simple phrases. Colonialism was organised robbery, collaboration with it was treason. Now, with Nasser at their head, the Arab masses were on the march. Victory over Colonialism was assured. The Levies' Officer commanding the convoy detailed to carry out the flag march greeted me with a weary grin. 'It's just a new toy,' he said dismissively. 'These Arabs are like children. They'll soon forget it.' He was large, middle-aged and heavily whiskered. He hoped there was going to be no 'fart-arsing' around, he said. Come what may, he had to be back in Aden within a week. I had no idea how long our mission would take but what was it that made it so necessary for him to get back so soon? There was the Levies' Annual Ball, he said. That was a must.

This was the prelude to none too happy an adventure. With two dozen trucks and a couple of jeeps snaking their way slowly through the wild countryside, we were sitting ducks. A platoon of one-eyed and one-armed men could have cut us to bits. As it was, we got off lightly. After bumbling along for about five miles, we ran into trouble. Bullets began pinging and cracking all around us. Shouting and confusion followed. No one knew where the Enemy was. No orders were given. Everyone fired when and where they thought fit. When the firing eventually stopped, our Convoy Commander said that two of his chaps had copped it. Three others had been wounded. That was sobering news but there was also the sobering thought that the Enemy could hit us again and again with complete impunity. Fortunately for us, we were left alone. The Enemy had hurried home to celebrate.

This sickening experience was a foretaste of endless similar episodes to come. With dozens of widely scattered Government Guard posts to keep supplied, convoys were continually on the move to and from them and every convoy was a suicide mission. As one gloomy report after another came in, Godfrey and Bufton began to complain that we 'Politicals' were not being sufficiently cooperative. How, they asked, could they possibly take precautions against ambushes if we did not find out where they were going to take place? Sir Tom naturally agreed and asked what I had to say. What I had to say was that we needed armoured cars and that for convoys to travel without armoured escorts seemed to me to be asking for trouble. There weren't any armoured cars, Bufton snapped, so there was no point in pursuing the matter. But surely we could send for some? 'I will repeat,' Bufton said in a firm, slow-motion voice, 'there are no armoured cars.' 'What! Nowhere?' Bufton nodded. And that, Sir Tom said, was that. It was not for me to question the Air Officer Commanding on military matters.

I did not believe Bufton, but how could I disprove him? Quite easily, as it happened. Cousin 'Bobbie' had by this time moved on from Egypt and was waging war against the Mau Mau as Commander in Chief in Kenya. A letter to him brought me the answer I wanted. Of course we had armoured cars, he replied, but when Bufton said we had none he presumably meant that the RAF Regiment had none. So that was it! If we were to have armoured cars it would mean turning to the Army for them and to let the Army in might be the thin end of a wedge which could upset the RAF's control over Aden. I showed Bobbie's letter to Sir Tom. He read it with a face like a coffin lid but said nothing. Some time later a squadron of Blues and Royals arrived—with their Ferrets.

In the meantime things continued to go from bad to worse. It was all hit and miss. For the Levies, who were repeatedly peppered running supplies out to the Government Guard forts, it was a tough and taxing time. A time when officers with stiff upper lips were needed and not, as was the case, a grumbling and querulous bunch of RAF Regiment officers who went around saying that this was not their job and, anyhow, why didn't the bloody 'politicos' clear up their own 'bloody mess'? Querulous officers made for querulous, near-mutinous men. Why should they risk their lives taking supplies to the Government Guards in the Wadi Hatib, a Levy Corporal asked me in a voice sharp with truculence. The Wadi Hatib did not belong to us. It belonged to the Dammanis and Rabizis. It was our colonialism that was causing all this trouble. Mutinous muttering was the prelude to a steady stream of deserters leaving the Force and leaving it at such a rate that replacements could barely be recruited fast enough to fill the gaps. It was at this point that our Political Officers began to look anxious and say that the Levies had become dangerously subversive and should be removed from the Protectorate. The Audhali and Sherif Hussein complained that their rebellious attitude was infecting their people. Group Captain Godfrey trumpeted outrage at this insult to the honour of his Regiment, the Air Officer Commanding wished to know whether he or my Political Officers were better judges of his Regiment's morale and Sir Tom said that if I and my Political Officers would be good enough to mind our own business we would all be the better for it. Almost immediately afterwards a company of Levies refused to obey orders.

Our masters were just beginning to comprehend the gravity of the situation when news of the Anglo-Egyptian Agreement[2] gave them the wildly misleading impression that the crisis was over. The Agreement, which was promptly hailed as a triumph for commonsense, an act of masterly statesmanship and so on was in reality nothing more than the peace terms we had been forced to sign after failing to withstand the clever campaign of guerilla operations the Egyptians had conducted against us in the Suez Canal Zone. This meant 'peace in our time' in South Arabia, Sir Tom said with glowing satisfaction and he hoped that would put an end to the 'alarm and despondency' I spent my time spreading around. Peace in our time? I could not understand what he was talking about. If the Imam were to see any message in the Anglo-Egyptian Agreement, it could only be that so long as he kept up the pressure against us he would be bound to win in the end. On my saying as much Sir Tom let out a petulant sigh and remarked that I did not seem to have grasped the fact that the Imam treasured the 'status quo' agreement above everything else and would never risk jeopardising it by carrying on with his subversive operations against ourselves. If that were so, why had he been making all this mischief? He would have thought it was obvious enough, Sir Tom retorted. He had been under pressure from the Egyptians and had not liked to risk offending them by refusing to cooperate. So, now that we were at peace with Egypt we would be at peace with the Imam as well. Looking at the cast iron self-confidence in which Sir Tom's features were set, I could not detect so much as a niggling doubt that this nonsense of his might be less than a hundred per cent true.

A meeting with Asshami soon afterwards brought me quickly back to earth. The ostensible reason for the meeting, which was at Asshami's request, was to discuss some minor incidents on the Beihan and Audhali frontiers. Its real purpose, however, was to see how we were taking our punishment. Mumbling his regrets at our troubles, he repeated his charge that we had brought them upon ourselves by breaking the 'status quo' agreement. He had not, however, come to indulge in recriminations, he said. He had come to offer us 'bliss'. Yes, what he had to offer was the equivalent of iced water on a hot Summer's day. He tapped my knee and, favouring me with an ingratiating smirk, said that the Imam now accepted that we had legitimate interests in Aden and was prepared to sign a treaty recognising Aden as a British possession if we in return withdrew from the Protectorate. That was out of the question, I replied. It would mean breaking our treaties with the Protectorate rulers. Supportive noises came from the Sherif and the Audhali, who were also present, but Asshami immediately cut them short with a sardonic laugh. Turning to me he threw out a question. 'But if they don't want their treaties, will you let them go?' Without waiting for an answer he immediately set about trying to suborn our two rulers right under my nose.

He had powerful arguments to put forward and he used them, jabbing away with a long, boney finger as he made his points. Surely they could see that the British were withdrawing from their old possessions, he gabbled a little breathlessly, and since we had now agreed to leave Egypt and the Sudan, could they really believe that we would remain in South Arabia indefinitely? So why did they choose to take the side of foreigners and Christians against their fellow Moslems and Arab brothers? Why did they expose themselves to the humiliation of being called traitors to Arabism and of finding their own people turning against them? He begged them to see reason and join their Arab brothers before it was too late. When he finally came to a teetering halt the Sherif piped up and said that he would give him an answer. It was 'No, no, no'. The Audhali laughed and said that 'No, no, no' was his answer too and, to save Asshami the trouble of finding out how they felt, he would tell him now that that was the answer he would get from every other Protectorate ruler. Unabashed, Asshami insisted on having a private chat with the two but to no purpose. He had offered them millions to defect, the Audhali said on their return, but... Well, what was money if you had a ruler who was likely to chop your head off at any time, the Sherif asked with a playful little smile. That said it all.

Curiously, perhaps shamefully, it was only at this meeting with Asshami that I first felt uneasy about our friends and allies, the Protectorate rulers. In saying that they were taking exceptional risks by siding with us Asshami was right but might he also be right in saying that we were bound to abandon Aden and, in the process, them? I had no idea how much Aden meant to the British Government. I had always supposed that our Suez base had meant a good deal to them but in the end they had agreed to leave it. Would they do the same and, if I thought they would, would I be right in encouraging the rulers to stand by us? My unease heightened soon afterwards when the Audhali and the Sherif called round to ask what British intentions were. If we had it in mind to withdraw from Aden as we had from so many other places, they would not blame us, they said, but as old friends they would expect us to warn them in advance so that they could 'make other arrangements'. So what were our intentions? The Audhali put the question to me direct, looking me straight in the eye. There was only one honest answer I could give him and I gave it. I believed that we intended to hold onto Aden but I did not know for sure. They would have to ask someone who could speak directly for the British Government.

Quite by chance Henry Hopkinson (later Lord Colyton), who was a Junior Minister at the Colonial Office, paid us a visit soon afterwards. How could he help, he asked. He could, for a start, set the rulers' minds at rest by assuring them that the British Government would not let them down, I told him. That was easily and happily done during a tour which took him to most of the rulers. The last on the list was the Sherif who put on a spectacular and sonorous reception for the Minister during which runaway horses and shaggy looking bedouins firing their rifles with uninhibited delight competed for attention. And what were the British Government's intentions, the Sherif asked as we sat recovering from the usual feast of boiled goat. The British Government would honour their treaty obligations to the full, Hopkinson assured him. The Sherif thanked him, saying that, with Britain abandoning so many of its responsibilities in different parts of the world, he and his friends were naturally anxious to know how they stood. If they had any further doubts. Hopkinson assured him, they should remember that the British Government had just invested several million pounds in the new refinery at Aden and they would certainly not have done that had they any intention of withdrawing. The Sherif smiled his thanks and then, just as Hopkinson rose to leave, he cleared his throat. 'As a matter of interest,' he asked, 'how many million pounds had the British Government invested in the Suez Canal?'

With Hopkinson as a companion for two or three days, I had a rare chance of saying what I thought to someone on the captain's bridge without having to say it through Sir Tom and other custodians of the 'usual channels'. What was needed above everything, I told him, was a theme which could inspire. What did I mean? The theme I had in mind was South Arabian nationalism, and an independent South Arabia in treaty relations with ourselves was the objective towards which I thought we should be working. Was I saying that we should revive the federation project? Yes, I was. But what was the use? The rulers had clearly rejected it. Of course, because the proposals we had put to them would have placed them under direct colonial rule. If we let the rulers decide on the sort of federation they wanted, I felt their reactions would be different. And how soon did I visualise independence? The sooner the better, I thought, but I doubted whether it would be feasible in less than two years. He was not sure how HMG would take it, he said, but he would see what he could do.

In the meantime, Sir Tom's pipe dreams of 'peace in our time' went the way of so many soap bubbles. Things went from bad to worse and had we been forced to rely on the Levies alone we would have been out of business in no time at all. Our saviours were the Government Guards who stood reasonably firm throughout that testing time of mounting crisis and that was because a great bull of a man called Fadhl Abdulla had them all tightly sewn up in his pocket. A cadet of the Upper Aulaqis' ruling clan, he had God's own opinion of himself. There was thunder in his voice and swagger in his manner. He could uplift with a smile and crush with a snarl. He had panache and was brimming over with bubbling ambition. James, the Force's quietly-spoken and unobtrusive Commandant, had the good sense to see that here was a man capable of delivering the goods but only if you gave him a free hand and subsequently spent most of your time looking the other way. So he made Fadhl his Deputy and, reserving the 'administrative bunk' for himself, let Fadhl do much as he pleased with the Force which Fadhl did in uninhibited Arab fashion. Recruitment, appointment, promotion: everything was directed to one end alone and that was to ensure that the Force was loyal to Fadhl. And they were. With few exceptions, they would have done anything for him. Certainly they would cheerfully have slit our throats had that been his wish.

In the meantime it was anybody's guess how much longer the Levies would be able to carry on. Their morale was in ribbons and the little that was left was reduced to mere dust in the wind after a major disaster in June 1955. A Levy convoy to Robat in the Wadi Hatib was scuppered. Two British officers, an Arab officer and six Levies were killed and eleven more Levies wounded. This was the end. After that the Levies had to be withdrawn for treatment. If they had not been, they would probably have scampered off of their own accord.

We were now in a real fix. Without the Levies we had no means of supplying the Government Guard outposts. We would have to withdraw some of them at least so as to free men to run convoys in place of the Levies. That was sheer defeatism, Sir Tom sneered. Imagining difficulties created difficulties! Why couldn't I look on the bright side for a change? Might he make a suggestion? A firm unruffled voice spoke and the speaker was a firm, unruffled man. He was our new Air Officer Commanding, Air Marshal Lawrence (later Sir Lawrence) Sinclair, GM. There was no need to have convoys, he told us. In fact, there was no need for us to use the roads at all. We could do everything that we wanted to do by air. We could, without difficulty, hack out landing strips next to our Government Guard posts and, once we had done so, we could supply the whole bally lot without the risk of losing a man. Sir Tom scratched a pensive chin. He seemed overwhelmed. This was the first worthwhile suggestion anyone had made for months.

It was, in fact, rather more worthwhile than any of us could have guessed at the time. That wise old bird, our tribal adviser, Mubarak Assahmi, got it in one. Did I see what this meant? Why yes, it meant that Asshami would have failed to get us to withdraw! Yes, but that was not all, Mubarak laughed. It also meant that the tribes would now all make peace. And how was that? If there was nothing to shoot at on the roads, Mubarak explained, then tribal rebels would have nothing to do. If they did nothing they would get nothing from Asshami. And that was what happened. Rebellion slowly petered out.

By coincidence, this welcome development took place just as a major crisis paralysed the Yemen. The Imam's two querulous half-brothers, the Princes Abdulla and Abbas, staged a 'coup' which landed the Imam in prison and gave every promise of success until the Imam's son, Mohammed al Badr, rallied the Zeidi tribes and came to his rescue. The 'coup' immediately collapsed and, to lend colour to the occasion, the Imam personally stormed his way out of prison firing a Bren gun. Abdulla and Abbas paid with their heads for their treachery and so did a number of others who had climbed onto their bandwagon. The crisis came and went in a matter of days but there is mopping up to be done after crises of this kind and then one is talking of months, not days. And so, for us, it meant peace.

NOTES

[1] The discovery of significant reserves of oil in the Marib region, near the borders with Saudi Arabia and South Yemen, was formally announced only in 1984 but their existence had long been suspected. The natural route for exporting this oil would be through Aden.

[2] The Anglo-Egyptian Agreement, in settlement of claims arising from the Suez crisis, was signed in February 1959. But the cease fire leading to withdrawal of British and French troops from the area had taken place more than two years earlier.

7

A COUP THAT FAILED

WHEN I CALLED to welcome him home, I found Ali holding court in the Victorian grandeur of his Aden palace. He was lounging on a sofa as radiant as a Sun King with a half-circle of silk-turbanned heads deployed in front of him. There was neither sight nor sound of the scowls and growls with which he had greeted me a little earlier in England where he had been on a visit and I on leave. As before, the Colonial Office had upset him. No official car, down-market hotel, no one dancing attendance... the same old complaints had been trotted out with the same heavy breathing. But now he was in the best of good humours. He had just been on the pilgrimage to Mecca where, he was happy to tell me, his Saudi hosts had given him the sort of treatment Sultans of Lahej expected. 'Oh, and by the way...' he teased me with a little smile, 'I met President Nasser while I was there. We had a very interesting talk about things!' I gulped down my surprise and asked how he had found Nasser. What did I expect? Nasser was an Arab, he was an Arab and he liked Arabs.

What was I to make of all this? Ali was a ruler in treaty relations with ourselves. Nasser was out to destroy us as a Middle Eastern Power. Encouraged by Pandit Nehru to see himself as the Middle East's future liberator and spurred on by the anti-colonialist battle cries of the Afro-Asian Emperors, Kings and Presidents gathered together at Bandoeng,[1] Nasser was doing his damnedest to make our position in the Middle East untenable. To prepare the ground for the Arab nationalist uprisings which would eventually sweep us away, he had opened heavy fire on the

A Coup that Failed

'shameless regiment' of British 'stooges' and 'puppets' upon whom we depended to maintain our position in the Middle East. The Hashimite Kings of Jordan and Iraq who had treaties with us he denounced as traitors for having them, as did the rulers in South Arabia and the Gulf. Those who collaborated with them or directly with ourselves he similarly denounced, our close friend and ally, the Sultan of Oman[2] the most severely of all. So what was Ali, our friend, doing hobnobbing with Nasser, our enemy, and what was Nasser doing passing the time of day with a British Treaty chief like Ali?

Since the meeting would certainly have been at Nasser's request, there would have been something about Ali which had interested Nasser and, since Nasser was in no need of a charming and cultivated companion, it could only have been Ali's potential as South Arabia's future leader. And what about Ali? For him to meet a rising international star like Nasser would have enchanted him, whatever the reason for their meeting, but had Nasser so much as let out a hint that he was thinking of backing him to be South Arabia's future supremo he would have been in ecstasies. And who could blame him? He believed and had reason to believe that he had legitimate claims to receive the suzerainty of Aden and a position of paramountcy in the Western Protectorate. So, knowing that he could expect no support from us, was it likely that he would have told Nasser that, as a ruler in treaty relations with the British, this was something he would prefer not to discuss? Of course he would have discussed it and, of course, he would have let Nasser understand that, depending on this, that and the other, he would hope to play a part in the future decolonisation of South Arabia. Anyone in his position would have done the same.

Of one thing I was sure—that he was, for the present at least, up to nothing sinister. Whenever I saw him, he was full of plans and blueprints for the greater good of Lahej. One had to think ahead and move fast these days, he would tell me. Lahej was not some bedouin backwater. Its people read newspapers, listened to the radio and knew what was going on in the world. People like that could not be neglected. They wanted what other twentieth century people had—education, health facilities, proper water, electricity, housing and so forth—and unless something was done to satisfy them there was bound to be trouble. To hear him talk about his plans for Lahej was a tonic. We had not a ruler with a fraction of his capabilities or public spirit. He was a paragon.

That, in fact, was how Robin Young, the Political Officer who now sat at his elbow in Lahej, described him; and since Robin was as solid and hard to please a product of the Sudan Political Service as any 'Sheikh' Lea, that was no casual compliment. Yes, Robin would say, the fellow was a 'gent' and 'gents' were above board. He could not believe that Ali was up to any hanky panky with Nasser. Not even if Nasser offered to back him to be South Arabia's future monarch? Giving a couple of meditative puffs at his pipe, Robin was inclined to think 'no'. Quite apart from anything else, Ali was no fool. Why should he blot his copybook with us when the chances were that we would be here for a good long time to come? But supposing he thought what the Afro-Asians at Bandoeng and many others thought: that our days might be numbered? A few more meditative puffs at his pipe had Robin saying that in such an event he would probably keep his options open. I was inclined to agree.

Someone who did not seem to see any need for keeping his options open was Ali's close friend and counsellor, a personage with wide flashing eyes and a film star's smile, Seyid Mohammed Ali al Jifri. Descendants of the Prophet, the Jifri Seyids were a well known family of religious teachers based on the Upper Aulaqi Sheikhdom and it was from there that Seyid Mohammed's immediate ancestors had migrated to serve the Sultans of Lahej as religious instructors and state councillors. Of them all, Seyid Mohammed, popularly known as 'the Jifri', was far and away the most erudite and impressive. Toqued and gowned in the distinctive style of a Doctor of Egypt's ancient seat of Islamic learning, al Azhar, he captured immediate attention in a part of the world where old Azharis were as rare as Old Etonians. His commanding intellect, gift of language and sonorous voice made for compulsive listening and he had for some time had a captive audience of wide-eyed young men whom he inducted into a society he called 'the Sons of the South'. He was a self-proclaimed Arab nationalist and, having spent some years decrying the Balfour Declaration,[3] he was now echoing Nasser's demands for our immediate withdrawal from every corner of the Middle East, including South Arabia. I did not see him very often but when I did he was all courtesy and good manners. Were his 'sons of the South' a political party, I once asked him. 'No,' he said. Political parties agitated. 'The Sons'' function was to educate, that was to say to liberate Arabs from the ignorance in which Colonialism had imprisoned them. He meant well, Ali would say with a paternal smile, and if he followed the fashion and used extremist language I should not take that too seriously. Given time, he thought he was someone with whom I would find it possible to work.

Soon after his return Ali called to say that he had good news to report. Egypt was sending him a team of school teachers, free of all cost. Had he told me that a family of rattlesnakes was on the way I couldn't have felt less enchanted. I didn't seem very pleased, he grumbled. I could not say that I was, I replied. If Egypt provided school teachers, it would be for propagandist purposes. That would upset us and embarrass him. Ali put his head back and laughed, saying that we British were really getting a bit paranoiac about Egyptians. We seemed to think that there was no such thing as a harmless Egyptian. In any case, since we had not provided Lahej with funds for education, it was hardly fair to expect him to refuse an offer of cost-free teachers simply because they came from Egypt. He had a point there. I said no more. And why not, Sir Tom wanted to know. Surely I realised that this 'young gentleman' had been having dealings with the Egyptian Government in breach of his treaty? 'Well?' He glared at me through the monocle he had recently come to affect. He was quite right but where education was concerned, we had to watch our step. Sir Tom demanded to know why. I tried to explain. Since one of the principal anti-colonialist themes was that we deliberately starved our proteges of education to keep them subservient, he could imagine what the Egyptian media would say if we rapped Ali's knuckles for agreeing to have Egyptian teachers. Sir Tom sat back in his chair, stroking his chin and then, looking sharply up, snapped, 'Well, we've wasted enough time on that! What's next?'

The Egyptian teachers duly arrived to a rapturous welcome from the 'Sons of the South' which the Jifri honoured with a passionate outburst of nationalist exhortations; and, duty-bound to show their nationalist worth, the teachers piped up a few days later to say that the syllabus used in the Lahej schools was not at all suitable. It was 'colonialist' and they proposed to replace it with the syllabus used in Egypt. The syllabus to which they objected was in fact the one used in Aden and the other schools we had set up in the Protectorate. To call it 'colonialist' was laughable. There was nothing political about it at all. And what did Ali have to say about all this? He did not claim to be an educational expert, he said, but what the teachers said sounded all right. Nonsense! It was political tomfoolery! Ali smiled indulgently at my little outburst and said I was being unreasonable. What I was saying was that Arab boys should direct their steps towards Oxford and Cambridge when common sense said that they should head for universities in Egypt, Syria and Iraq. The fact remained that every school in Aden and the Protectorate used the Aden syllabus, I pointed out, and it made nonsense for Lahej to step out of line and go Egyptian on its own. Ali smiled through half-closed eyes and said, 'Well, it would of course if the others followed our lead!'

Our little contretemps over the Egyptian teachers was quickly overtaken by news that Hopkinson had prodded the Government into having second thoughts about federation. The rulers were now to be left free to set up a federation in whatever form they wished: it being understood that the federation would be self-governing and would not aspire to independence. I could not imagine Ali taking very kindly to that sting in the tail. Since the Protectorate States had always been self-governing, he would at least have expected a cautious hint of 'eventual independence'. Never would he have imagined that independence would be banned from the agenda 'sine die'. He would not like it, I told Sir Tom. And why not? I explained. Thanking me with frigid sarcasm for being 'so very helpful', Sir Tom then said that he would discuss the matter with the rulers and I could spare myself the trouble of coming to the meeting. He could manage very well on his own, 'thank you very much indeed'.

There was no discussion at the meeting, Ali later told me. Sir Tom explained what was on offer and the rulers then withdrew to consider it. Since then he—Ali—had formed a Committee of Rulers and its first act had been to pass a resolution declaring 'immediate independence' to be the proposed federation's objective. A copy of it had been sent to Sir Tom. What Sir Tom thought of it I was privileged to hear within the next couple of hours. This was all Ali's doing, he snapped, and he would be glad if I would tell 'the young gentleman' that he would be getting into trouble if he didn't mind his manners. It was time he remembered he had a duty to honour his treaty with us. I, of course, did nothing of the kind. Though clearly upset over HMG'S attitude, Ali was still on good terms with us. He needed humouring, not harassment.

Sherif Hussein came sauntering in a few days later with his beard combed out and his turban set jauntily on the side of his head. Had I seen 'His Majesty', he asked in a voice heavy with sarcasm. 'His Majesty?'

'Yes, His Majesty Sultan Ali of Lahej, the King of South Arabia.' He had formed a Committee, he explained, and had got them all to sign a piece of paper demanding independence. Independence! He spat the word out with a look of disgust. Were Ali to get away with his little game, he would hand Aden and the Protectorate over to Nasser within the week! I mumbled disbelief. Didn't I know that Ali was the Jifri's slave and that the Jifri was Nasser's, he asked, eyebrows erect. How could I possibly trust the slave of a slave? In any case, how could rulers, who had only recently begged Hopkinson to confirm that Britain would not be withdrawing, now demand independence? The Audhali and the little Emir or Dhala sidled up to me a few days later and said much the same thing. Nothing more was heard of Ali's Committee. The Sherif had evidently sabotaged it.

Ali did not seem unduly put out. To get all the rulers to agree to federate at one and the same time he thought impracticable. After all, how could one deal simultaneously with rulers who differed so widely in sophistication and intelligence? It would be better, he thought, to set up an embryo federation of, say, Lahej and the two Abyan states for a start and then move outwards progressively to include the others later. By happy coincidence, the Jifri had the same bright idea and, having already converted the Sons of the South into a political party called The South Arabian League, he launched them into a lively profederation campaign. Large, raucous demonstrations took place in Lahej and Abyan at which the Jifri and other orators fired popular passions in the new style of the Voice of the Arabs. Although ostensibly pro-federation, the tone of all this activity was in fact mostly anti-British. The biggest and most fiery demonstration of the lot developed into a triumphal celebration of General Glubb's dismissal by King Hussein under Nasserite pressure.[4] Glubb had been the last great symbol of British Middle East power. His fall was a disaster.

Ali was all sympathy and understanding when I called in to say that I thought the Jifri was taking a highly offensive line and couldn't he please get him to moderate his tone. What was needed at this time more than anything else, Ali replied, hands folded and soft voiced, was patience. I had to remember that these were probably the most revolutionary times in all the Middle East's history. The Egyptians had got us out of Suez and the Sudan; they had sabotaged the Baghdad pact; and now they had made Hussein dismiss Glubb. That, of course, was not all. The Arabs had also all but removed the French from North Africa. Tunisia and Morocco had both won their independence and the French in Algeria were under siege. Naturally, Arabs everywhere were wild with excitement at what they saw as great victories for Arabism and surely I could see that the Jifri had to adapt himself to the mood of the moment if he was to be taken seriously. When passions and emotions subsided, as they certainly would, we could expect him to be less extreme. In the meantime he held his hands out in a mute appeal for understanding. I understood him from A to Z but I did not feel too happy about it.

Nor, I must admit, did I feel too happy on hearing what the South Arabian League was up to. The Party was based on Lahej, Ali explained, because Lahej was the traditional centre of South Arabia. That did not mean that it was a Lahej party. Very far from it. It was a South Arabian party and branches were being set up in Aden and all the Protectorate states. And what a sensation the appearance of the Jifri's young men in the Protectorate states was causing! They quickly set the whole barnyard of Protectorate life clucking and squawking with excitement. Never having seen a political party before, no one knew quite what to make of the League. The rulers tended to view it with suspicion as a possible rival to their authority, the families in the ruling classes (who were busy intriguing against their rulers) looked on it as a possible ally to aid them in their ambitions. The tribes, in their own uncomplicated fashion, merely wondered what they could expect to get in return for giving it their support. No one really cared what it stood for. Quite a number of solid citizens, however, appeared anxious to know what we thought of it. I had no reason to object to it, I would say, and that was true enough. Had I cared to tell the whole truth, I would have said that, if that gleam of ambition in the Jifri's eye meant what I thought it did, we would not be on friendly terms with him for very much longer. Nor were we.

The first hint of trouble had come some time before from Mohammed Aidrus, the son of the Lower Yafa Sultan whom Sir Tom had so happily appointed Naib to run his father's Administration. He was a handsome, cold-faced young chieftain with a double dose of not unbecoming blue-blooded arrogance and at first looked as though he would do well. And then, as suddenly as if someone had turned on a switch, he went sour. Marching into my office, head high and haughty, he demanded Justice in the name of 'the People' and by Justice, he explained, he meant the prompt expulsion of the Abyan Scheme's British Management which was stealing the cotton cultivators' money. This was a gross canard and easily refuted. The Management collected and sold the cultivators' cotton, I explained, and then paid them the proceeds less the running and development costs. Nothing could be more straightforward or simple. Mohammed Aidrus signalled disbelief and then, sitting up sharply like a card player about to produce a trump, he asked how it was that the cultivators in Lahej were being paid more for their cotton than in Abyan. He would tell me. The Lahej scheme was run by Arabs! In Abyan the thieving colonialist British were in charge. This was news to me. It was a bombshell.

Since the Lahej scheme was very much smaller and simpler than Abyan's and cost far less to run, it had always been in a position to pay its cultivators more. We had, however, persuaded Ali to pay out at the same rate as in Abyan and use what he saved to finance his various schemes for Lahej's betterment. So what had gone wrong? Why had he gone back on his word and, by paying the Lahej cultivators more, landed us with a first class crisis in Abyan? He was full of apologies when I tackled him, saying that he was no longer controlling the Lahej scheme. It was now in the charge of a Board representing the cotton cultivators. Maybe it was, but the Jifri sat on the Board and there was no Board, Council or Committee on which he sat which he did not enslave.

In the meantime, Abyan was in an uproar of demonstrations variously demanding justice for the cultivators, the expulsion of Abyan's British Management and federation with Lahej. All this was being set up by the Jifri's grinning emissaries and almost every demonstration was being graced by gangs of cheer-leading schoolboys from Lahej. At the height of the furore, Mohammed Aidrus turned up with the Lower Yafa State Council. He had come to abrogate the Lower Yafa's treaties with us, he announced, lighting a cigarette, and he would be obliged if we would withdraw the Abyan scheme's British Management forthwith. Treaties were no business of his, I told him sharply. He was a Naib, not a Sultan. So I refused? Turning on his heel, he marched off with his councillors trotting along behind him. They arrived in Lahej that evening to an ecstatic welcome from the South Arabian League as 'refugees from Colonialism'. Their wild-eyed Sultan turned up in Lahej the following morning to give Mohammed Aidrus and the Councillors his blessing. So we were faced

The Deluge

with the entire Lower Yafa Government in Lahej demanding an end to their British connection. It was about as awkward a situation to find oneself in as ever I could have imagined.

And yet far worse was to come, if the South Arabian League's chatterers were to be believed. Now that the Lower Yafa had joined their 'brothers' in Lahej, the Fadhli Sultan, so they said, was bound to follow suit. When he did, the three states—Lahej, Lower Yafa and Fadhli—would form an independent federation and the Arab League would guarantee it. Laughable nonsense? Far from it. It only needed the Fadhli Sultan to report in to Lahej for this ghastly nightmare to come true; and it was a thousand to one that he would do so. Ever since Sir Tom had bullied him into handing over his Administration to that young gentleman jockey, Ahmed bin Abdulla, he had divided his time between shooting fish from a coracle floating off the coast and plotting to get rid of Ahmed. Well, here was his chance. All he had to do was to report to Lahej, sign up for a federation and Ahmed would be out and he would be back in the chair. Ahmed was, of course, on full alert but nevertheless he was surprisingly unperturbed. Oh yes, the Sultan was desperate to take the Council to Lahej, he chuckled, but he was stuck. He couldn't move. For him to appear in Lahej alone without the State Council in attendance would be a humiliation which even a Sultan with a pumpkin for a head could never contemplate. But why wouldn't the State Council accompany him? 'Because I pay them!' Ahmed grinned. He was quite right. The Councillors would not budge. The Sultan returned to shooting fish.

That was the end of this agonising drama. Once the Jifri's federation plans had flopped, the Lower Yafais trickled quietly back home. The Jifri's coup had failed. Not that this gave us anything to crow about for the humiliating fact remained that we had been publicly rejected by our proteges and at a time when our presence in South Arabia was under critical attack. It was an excruciating experience but, at least, we now knew where we stood with the Jifri. We could forget about Ali's special pleading on his behalf, knowing that we could never expect to do business with someone who had tried to wreck the Abyan scheme and suborned one of our Protectorate's State governments. We now knew the Jifri for what he was. He was in Nasser's service and he was out to destroy us.

During these troubles, an outburst of strikes and commotions in Aden had spared us much help or harassment from Sir Tom. He was, however, back on the telephone firing off 'what's, how's and when's' almost as soon as the Lower Yafais had gone home. And what did I propose to do about the Jifri, he wished to know. There was nothing I could do except ask Ali to restrain him and I had done that often enough to no purpose. Well, then, what did I propose to do about that 'tiresome young gentleman', he asked in a voice rattling with impatience. What could I do except talk to him? 'Yes, yes, yes!' Sir Tom rapped out, but what we needed was firm, uncompromising talk—not amiable sweet nothings. He was absolutely right. I had not as yet steeled myself to have it out with Ali and so, with a recent report from Robin Young in my pocket saying that he suspected Ali of encouraging anti-British demonstrations, I set out for Lahej to do so.

Egyptian flags were flying over every house and hovel in Lahej and Nasser's face was projected at me from every wall and doorway. 'The Voice of the Arabs' was whining and booming from a thousand transistor sets. To reach Ali I had to run a gauntlet of angry shouts and insults on my way to his palace but thankfully nothing worse. The whole place was awash with Nasserism and, as if to show me that we no longer belonged there, the Police, who had always given me a salute in the past, looked me up and down with calculated disdain with their hands in their pockets. I had no idea how much the mood of the place had changed since I had last visited it only a few weeks before.

Ali welcomed me with an amiable enough smile but quickly put it to bed when I told him the reason for my visit. What did I expect him to do, he asked, choking with indignation. Arrest the Jifri? Did we arrest those young Trades Unionists in Aden for shouting anti-British slogans? No, we liked to say that we allowed free speech. So why should we expect him to do what we did not do ourselves? They had free speech in Lahej, too. To shout against us but not, I felt sure, to agitate against his Sultanic regime. He dismissed this with a petulant pout but, softening of a sudden, he asked me to try and understand how he was placed. He was Sultan but that did not mean he could openly go against his own people and I could see for myself how his people were thinking. If I thought he could, I should remember what had happened to the Bey of Tunis[5] who had acted as a French puppet. So, did that mean that he saw himself as another Sultan of Morocco who had refused to stand by the French? That was going to the other extreme, Ali smiled. He saw himself rather as a go-between trying to reconcile differences between one side and the other. I could have said that, if that was what he was, he had not done too well up to date but I left it at that.

Sir Tom was far from pleased with the way that I had handled Ali but he was too busy preparing for the arrival of Lord Lloyd, the Parliamentary Under Secretary at the Colonial Office, to pursue the matter. It was, as it turned out, none too happy a visit. It began with a turbulent Nasserite demonstration headed by the Jifri at the airport to greet the Minister and, if our friends in the Protectorate later took heart from his robust confirmation of Hopkinson's assurances, he effectively alienated almost all our friends in Aden. The solid, traditionally pro-British Adenis had by this time formed themselves into a political party called the Aden Association and, having seen off the Nasserites of the rival United National Front in elections for the few seats on offer in the Legislative Council only a few months before, they were now contemplating the future with acute anxiety. The reason for this was the scale and extent of the disturbances the Nasserites were causing and their fear that the British Government would give in to the Nasserite agitation and extend the franchise to the immigrant Yemeni Trades Unionists, who were Nasserites to a man. To preempt this and win some popular applause to the bargain they were demanding immediate independence for Aden: it being understood that their independent Aden would be fortified by some treaty with ourselves. What they got in return from Lloyd was a slap in the face. Aden, he informed them, could forget about independence and, indeed, about any further constitutional advance for the time being. 'They don't really want independence,' he said over a pre-lunch gin and tonic. 'All they want is to know that we will stand firm.' Taking his cue from this tough talk, Sir Tom clamped down on the Jifri. He banned him from Aden and, since he did so just after the Jifri had flown off to Cairo, this meant that he would find it difficult to find his way back to South Arabia. 'But not impossible,' Ali said on hearing what had happened.

This was Sir Tom's final act before leaving Aden for good on retirement. For us in the Western Protectorate it was sighs of relief all round.

NOTES

[1] The Bandoeng Conference of 1955 brought together states unwilling to align themselves with either the USA or USSR. President Nasser of Egypt was one of the architects of this movement, in which Islamic countries were strongly represented.

[2] In 1950 the Saudis occupied Buraymi Oasis in territory disputed between them and Oman but withdrew in 1955. Following this the Omani Sultan, Sa'id, imposed his authority on the interior of the country with the help of his British-trained forces and received further assistance from British SAS troops in pacifying Jebel Akdhar.

[3] During World War I the Allied Powers made a number of arrangements for partitioning the Ottoman Empire. The Balfour Declaration (November 1917) stated that the British Government favoured the establishment in Palestine of a national home for the Jewish people.

[4] General Glubb had been Chief of Staff to King Hussein of Jordan, the early years of whose reign were disturbed by demonstrations sponsored by Syria and Egypt. 'Glubb Pasha', as he was known, formed and commanded this Jordanian Desert Patrol and his dismissal in 1955 was regarded as a serious setback to British interests.

[5] In March 1956 a nationalist movement under Habib Bourguiba took effective control of an independent Tunisia, which had been a French Protectorate since 1881. Shortly afterwards, the hereditary Bey was deposed.

8

THE LAHEJ CONSPIRACY

I WAS AT HOME on leave when the Suez fiasco took place and so returned to Aden curious and anxious to know what effect it had had in South Arabia. Surprisingly, I could see very little change. Our Arab friends were disappointed but not dismayed by our failure to finish the job and polish off Nasser. Our enemies were damning and denouncing us as usual. But what about Ali? I could scarcely believe that Suez would have left him unmoved; and so it was with some apprehension that I set out for Lahej on receiving an invitation from him to luncheon.

When I entered the town it seemed to be alive with saluting policemen who most obligingly cleared a way for my car through the crowd. I had a comfortable insult-free drive down to his palace where he received me with the warmest of smiles and handshakes. After an elegant European-style luncheon off the best Crown Derby at which half a dozen of his frock coated courtiers were present, Ali took me aside for a chat. Suez was a terrible mistake, he said, but it was no good thinking about it. What had been done had been done. We had to forget the past and think of the future and how we could cooperate for the best. My sentiments to the letter, I replied, but what suggestions had he? Finger tips pressed together, his face grave, Ali asked if he might speak, perhaps, with 'hurtful frankness'. I nodded and was given a revealing little homily in return.

We had had too many misunderstandings in the past, he was sorry to say, and basically they all arose from the fact that Seager had saddled us with a whole lot of stooges who had no popular support and we had expected him to align himself with them. Surely I realised that he couldn't do that? It was more than his job was worth to oppose the People's wishes. And what were the People's wishes? Well, they were obvious enough: they wanted to see our stooges removed and replaced by their true leaders. Could he be more specific? Certainly! In Dhala, for example, no one wanted our little stooge, Sha'aful: the People wanted Haidera whom Seager had expelled to the Yemen. In Fadhli, they wanted the Sultan—not that corrupt Ahmed bin Abdulla whom we had made his Naib. In the Upper Aulaqi Sheikhdom Mohammad Bubakr, the old Sheikh's nephew, was the People's choice—not our ludicrous proteges, Abdulla and Farid, his sons. And what about Muhammad Aidrus? Yes, the People backed him but we clearly did not. And the Sheriff and Audhali? Ali's voice chilled with contempt. That bearded friend of ours, the Sheriff, was a fraud. That whole gang of Sheriffs were nothing more than a pack of penniless preachers who had tricked us into signing a treaty with them when we knew little or nothing about the Protectorate. The Audhali was different. His voice softened. He had the People behind him but, unless he adapted himself to the modern world, he would lose their support. Was that all? That was all that really mattered. And what did he expect us to do, I asked. Sack our so-called stooges and replace them with the men he said had popular backing? No, Ali laughed, that would be going too far! All he was asked that we should stand back and let the people have their way. In other words, if the People rose up against, say, Sha'aful or Ahmed bin Abdulla, he would ask us not to send in the Levies and Guards to their rescue. Did I see his point? All too clearly, I thought to myself. He wanted a free hand for himself and his allies to topple our friends!

Though the local scene was little changed, the same could not be said about our capricious and bellicose neighbour, the Imam. Having reasserted his authority after depriving Prince Abdulla of his head, he was back in fighting form but, on this occasion, he turned to Nasser for advice before going into action. The outcome of his overture was the Jedda Pact, which is to say an anti-British alliance jointly signed by the Imam, Nasser and King Saud of Saudi Arabia, with whom we were then in conflict far away in Oman.[1] What this amounted to was that Egypt and Saudi Arabia would now equip and finance the Yemen to wage war against us. $40 million of Saudi cash was duly paid into the Imam's Treasury at Taiz. At the same time, by arrangement with Egypt, Russian ships were soon unloading military hardware at the little Yemeni port of Salif. At a calculated guess we could expect two months' breathing space before the balloon went up.

It was none too happy a prospect but I did not get those sensations of leaden-hearted gloom which had afflicted me so often at times like this in the past: and that was because Sir Tom, who was always at his most intolerable during times of crisis, was several thousand miles away spending his retirement in England, looking for someone to bully. And, even more to the point, in his successor, Sir William Luce, we had a gem. He was the best of the best from that cradle of excellence, the Sudan Political Service. He spoke the same language as we did, he saw things as we saw them and his mind ticked over in the same way as ours. He never barked, he never bullied. He did not domineer—he led.

Since the Imam had already been roughing up Beihan and Audhali, I paid each a quick visit. Bizarrely attired in a black dinner jacket, the Sheriff bade me welcome on the blistering gravel of the Beihan landing strip. And how did I like his new suit, he asked with a smirk. It was modern, wasn't it? Now that that little 'who do you call him, Nasser' was going around saying that Arab rulers were antiquated relics from the days of 'the thousand and one nights', it was important to show that one was modern. Having made his joke, he put me aboard a gigantic vehicle which Wendel Phillips, the American explorer-cum-archaeologist, had given him. Formerly known as 'Eisenhower' in recognition of its American origin, the Sheriff had renamed it 'Churchill' following President Eisenhower's treachery over Suez and it was in this that we made our way across the sands to his Disneyland palace.

I had barely entered it and shaken a few hands when a thunderous crash of musketry from the courtyard outside announced that we had visitors. Almost immediately a wild-eyed creature with a beard like a Guardsman's bearskin came tumbling into the room bellowing for attention. He was a Balharith Sheikh, he roared, and he had been raided by the Yemenis. He wanted help. This was the cue for the Sheriff to rise mournfully to his feet semaphoring distress. What help could he give? He had no money and no arms! All he had was a treaty with the British and that was worthless! A banquet of mutton and rice followed this little pantomime; and then, the eating done, the Sheriff left his guests belching their satisfaction and took me off to a smaller room for a 'tête à tête'.

He was calmer now and, soothed by a couple of lungfuls of cigarette smoke, he asked me to remember that we were no longer up against a mad, mediaeval monarch but against Nasser and his Russian patrons and they had that camel, King Saud of Saudi Arabia, tethered up to pay their bills. That was what the Jedda Pact had done. Nasser was now all set to grab South Arabia and the Gulf. To get South Arabia he would use the Yemen and his resident slaves here. What slaves? Why, Ali of Lahej, his servant the Jifri and the street boys feeding at their expense. Yes, from now on Ali and his friends would cooperate with the Yemen and the Yemen would be receiving Russian arms and Saudi cash. What did l think of that? The Sheriff slowly blew out a chain of smoke rings. I found it hard to believe that Ali would cooperate with the Yemen, I said. Ali wanted an independent South Arabia! The Imam wanted to take it over. The Sheriff looked at me with laughing eyes. Surely I realised how Nasser would deal with the matter? He would tell Ali that, at an opportune moment, he would ditch the Imam and give him his independent South Arabia. In the meanwhile, he would tell the Imam that he would ditch Ali and give South Arabia to him. Hadn't I been here long enough to know the Arab way of doing things?

The Audhali came to the point in his usual direct fashion without any Sheriffian pantomime. Wasn't it true that Asshami had concentrated most of his attacks on himself and the Sheriff, he asked. And why? I knew very well why. It was because, unlike Ali who had no trouble from the Yemen at all, they had been loyal to us. Surely then they were entitled to the protection we had promised them in their treaties with us? He looked me full in the face, holding my eyes captive. And yet he was sorry to say that we had given no effective help whatsoever. Asshami had done as he liked and they had had the humiliation of seeing their tribes desert over to the Yemen. Didn't we realise that, if we continued to do nothing, they would be left without any tribes at all? And what good would rulers without tribes be to us, he would like to know. He signed off with a smile saying, 'Think on that, my friend!' That smile hit me in the conscience far harder than any outburst of spluttering rage. There was no denying it. Our friends had stood by us and we had not stood by them.

So now, with the storm clouds rolling down towards us, what should we do? Anyone with Protectorate sand in his hair knew that there was only one sure answer to what the Yemenis were doing and that was to do to them what they were doing to us... with interest. Ask the Audhali, Sheriff, 'Mister' Fadhl of the Guards; ask any of our Political Officers and that was what they would all tell you. We could get Yemeni tribes across the frontier to cause trouble for Asshami just as easily as he could get ours to upset us. And then one should remember also we only had to give our tribes bigger and better douceurs to stop them running off to Beidha. There was, however, a tiresome snag. To do what we wanted to do we needed arms and, in Establishment circles, 'arms' was a dirty word. Even Boustead—comfortably seated four hundred miles from the Yemeni frontier, it is true—thought giving arms to 'bare arsed bedouin' definitely 'off side'. And so did Horace (later Sir Horace) Phillips who had recently been seconded to us by the Foreign Office as a form of political minder. Yes, yes, Phillips said, like a nanny soothing a fractious child, he fully understood how I felt but the fact of the matter was that HMG wanted to defuse the situation. What I was proposing would escalate it. Escalate it? How could you escalate an erupting volcano? Phillips ha-haed sympathy and said he was quite sure that things were nothing like as bad as I seemed to think. Luce said that that was precisely what the Foreign and Colonial Offices would say and there was no point in our putting up proposals if we knew that they would be shot down. We needed more ammunition before making a move. A week or so later the balloon went up.

It went up in the most unexpected of places. It went up in Dhala which had been a haven of peace throughout our past troubles. There had, I now remembered, been a hint of possible trouble there in the lecture Ali had read me. 'The People' wanted Haidera, the late ruler's son, as their ruler, he had said, not our little 'stooge', Sha'aful. And that was what we were now expected to believe, for Haidera, who had been living as an exile in the Yemen, had all of a sudden raised his standard at the Yemeni frontier town of Qataba and the Dhala tribes were falling over each other to join him. Where Asshami had been handing out a few hundred rifles in the past, Haidera now handed out over 2,000, so plentiful had the stocks of his Yemeni patrons become. It was not Haidera's cause, the Arab nationalist cause or any other cause that sent all those tribesmen galloping off to Qataba but the lure of the rifles Haidera had that had them all buzzing around him like moths around a lantern and, as I took care to tell Luce, had our little 'stooge', Sha'aful, had what

Haidera had, we would not nave been running around ringing alarm bells. He did not disagree.

As it was, Haidera had a clear field and, within days, the whole countryside from the Qataba plains to the mountains of Radfan was in revolt. We had never had to face up to a rebellion on such a scale before; but, happily, we were now in very much better shape to do so. The Levies were no longer a demoralised ragbag of incompetent and mutinous soldiery. The Army had retrained and reequipped them as a fighting brigade under a team of keen-eyed British officers. The Government Guards had increased in size and improved in quality. And so, though the crisis lasted some weeks, the outcome was never in doubt. No matter that Yemeni troops took the field against us for the first time, neither they nor Haidera's supporters could stand up to us. Time and time again they were routed and often pursued across the frontier right up to the gates of Qataba. It did not take long to remove the sting from the revolt. It took months to repair the damage.

In recognition of the unwelcome improvement in the quality of our troops, our enemies now devoted themselves mostly to trying to sabotage their morale. 'The Voice of the Arabs', the 'Robata' and the Jifri all reminded them of their Arab duty and exhorted them to mutiny against their colonialist masters. More dramatic, however, were the antics of the Lahej mob which now took to halting every military convoy passing through the town on its way to Dhala and reviling our troops for betraying their Moslem brothers. As full-blooded tribesmen with old fashioned views about their honour and prestige and equally old fashioned views about urban riff raff respecting their tribal betters, our men did not take at all kindly to this treatment. And so it came as no surprise when 'Mister Fadhl' flipped his lid. Giving an 'up Guards and at 'em' on being halted in the middle of Lahej, he released his troops onto the mob and in seconds it scampered off without a shot being fired to help it on its way.

So much for the mob but I had an apoplectic Ali on my hands as a result of 'Mr Fadhl's' 'tour de force'. Accusing us of breaching Lahej's sovreignty and breaking our treaty he demanded that I keep my 'Gestapo' under proper control. Seeing him choking with indignation, I began to wonder whether I had perhaps misjudged him. It seemed hard to believe that he had been privy to our troops' harassment. But I changed my views a few evenings later when 'The Voice of the Arabs' let its listeners know that General Erskine, 'the Butcher of Egypt', was my cousin and that as 'the Butcher of South Arabia' I was following faithfully in his bloodstained footsteps, Since Ali was the only person who knew of my relationship to Cousin 'Bobbie' it could only have been from him that 'the Voice' had got this tidbit. There could be little doubt now that Ali was playing Nasser's game.

Luce agreed but reminded me that Ali was not a Fadhli Sultan or Muhammed Aidrus. He was His Highness Sultan Sir Ali Abdulkarim, KCMG, and there could be no question of our taking any action against him without the approval of the Colonial Secretary and, very likely, the Prime Minister as well. To get their approval, he explained, we would clearly need good, hard evidence of Ali's knavery and since what we so far had was flimsy and circumstantial, to say the least, there was nothing we could hope to do for the time being. That was disappointing but to make up for it Luce had managed to get a qualified 'go ahead' from London for the distribution of arms. In view of the large number of arms the Yemen was now giving insurgents, he said, the Colonial Office was agreeable to our issuing arms for self defence. Self defence? We had no need to take the term too literally, he smiled, if I knew what he meant. I did.

Haidera's invasion of Dhala was not the only crisis to hit us. An ugly situation, also, blew up in the Fadhli Sultanate where a clearly coordinated Laheji-Yemeni plan to oust Ahmed bin Abdulla, the Naib, and replace him with the Sultan was being carried out. Denouncing him for land grabbing, corruption and multiple injustices, the 'Voice of the Arabs' and the 'Robata' called upon the Fadhli to revolt against this 'criminal British stooge'. Anti-British and anti-Ahmed demonstrations thereupon erupted in Abyan and, at the same time, following a massive distribution of Yemeni rifles, some of the Fadhli tribes broke out in revolt, ostensibly against Ahmed's 'oppression'. Well, what did I expect? Ali clucked sympathy with our predicament but reminded me that he had given fair warning of Ahmed's unacceptability. Our only hope of peace and stability, he asked me to understand, was to respect the wishes of 'the People' and that meant getting rid of Ahmed and letting the Sultan take over. In the event, it only took the time Ahmed needed to round up half a dozen South Arabian League agitators from Lahej to restore peace to Abyan. It took rather longer to pacify the tribes but, with the rifles we could now distribute, they gradually quietened down. All was well and then, just as we were breathing normally again, Ahmed went off his head.

What he did was unforgivable. Finding that a lorry driver, who was said to be the worse for drink, had killed a newly-born foal of his, the hot-headed idiot had had the ruffian grabbed, tied to the back of a lorry and dragged through the streets of his capital, Zinjibar. Since the streets were, in fact, covered with a thick carpet of sand, the man came to no harm. Even so, as Robin said with a solemn puff of his pipe, 'It was a pretty bad show.' That was putting it mildly and no one was quicker off the mark to tell me what an outrage it was than the Sultan. Ali was there, too, I-told-you-soing and begging me 'in the name of the People' to rid the Fadhli of this vicious and dissipated little tyrant. What was I to do? By every criterion of good or even passable government, Ahmed should have been dismissed with ignominy but... If he went, what then? The Sultan would take over and, since he was Ali's stooge, and since Ali's other stooge, Muhammad Aidrus, was in control of Lower Yafa, Ali would have control over Lahej, Lower Yafa and Fadhli and so would be in a position to bring the Jifri's federation plan back to life. If that went through, our position would be disastrously, perhaps irreparably, damaged. Even so I could not bring myself to exculpate Ahmed. It was for the State Council to look into the matter and decide what to do, I told Ali. But that was absurd, he protested. They would back Ahmed. That was up to them, I replied, and as I knew they would, back Ahmed they did.

We had barely got over this crisis when that ancient monument the nonagenarian Sheikh of the Upper Aulaqi most inconsiderately died, leaving the awkward question of who was to succeed him at the top of our agenda. The candidates for the job were the old man's son, Abdulla, who had been running the Administration in harness with his belligerent brother, Farid, and their inveterate enemy and rival, Muhammad Bubakr, nephew of the departed Muhammad Bubakr who had been in a state of open rebellion against the Administration ever since there had been one. He enjoyed the enthusiastic support of the South Arabian League while Abdulla, if not our favourite friend, was at least committed to us. Not surprisingly, then, Ali hurried along to remind me that the 'People' execrated Abdulla and looked on Muhammad as their father. If we were to get Abdulla made Sheikh, he warned me, we would have every Aulaqi up in arms against us. He could equally well have said that the Upper

Aulaqi Sheikhdom would defect to Lahej and the South Arabian League if Muhammad got the job.

Though naturally anxious to be spared such a disaster, I felt I had to stick to the rules and the rules said that it was for the Sheikhly clan to elect a successor. Since each candidate suspected his rival of buying the clan up, neither would agree to submit to its judgement. So what were we to do? Why not ask Rufus, the Upper Aulaqi Sultan, to visit Said, the Sheikhdom's capital, and decide the issue, George Henderson, our resourceful Political Officer, suggested. He was, after all, recognised as 'father of all the Aulaqis'. Rufus agreed, the two candidates agreed and we all sat anxiously back to see what would happen. And then suddenly, on the eve of decision day, Muhammad Bubakr got it into his head that his rival had nobbled Rufus. Things were getting very hot indeed, George signalled. Muhammad's men were picketing the approaches to Said with the intention of stopping Rufus by force while the supporters of Abdulla and Farid were moving up to provide them with an escort.

D-Day dawned with George squawking excitedly down the radio telephone to say that Rufus had done a bunk during the night! With no Rufus available to give judgement, he decided to set out for Said 'to play it by ear'. I waited anxiously for him to report back when he arrived. It was a long, tense wait and the longer it became the more certain I was that something hideous and sanguinous had happened. What did in fact happen I could never have guessed. Arriving at the approaches to Said. George found the two factions looking menacingly down each other's rifle barrels and then suddenly a miracle took place. 'The People'—everybody who was anybody and a great many nobodies besides—rushed in between the rival armies and, while George was still rubbing his eyes, they had made Muhammad Bubakr and Abdulla kiss and make friends. In the ensuing love feast, Abdulla was proclaimed Sheikh and Muhammad Bubakr and Farid joint deputies. Our man was in: Ali's was out.

Though banned from Aden, the Jifri had not been banned from Lahej and, following a prolonged visit to Cairo, he was now back to find that everything had gone wrong in his absence and nothing right. Failure in Dhala, Fadhli and the Upper Aulaqi Sheikhdom and not a success to put on the other side of the ledger. He could not have returned to a more depressing scene and being a 'never say die' type he hit back as best he could.

One of the first things he did was to reactivate Muhammad Aidrus and all too soon it was back to the 'status quo ante' with Muhammad harassing the Management of the Abyan scheme in between organising demonstrations for our discomfiture. Cheered on by the 'Voice of the Arabs', the 'Robata' and the Jifri himself, Muhammad became increasingly stiff necked and big headed. Hailed as a great revolutionary hero of the Arab people, he became increasingly cavalier in his treatment of the little nobodies who sat on the Lower Yafa State Council. Rumours of their grumbling discontent began to float our way and then one day Muhammad trod heavily on the toes of a tubby little Councillor with a voice like a ratchet called Billeil: and Billeil took himself off in protest to the mountains. The first I heard of this was when Muhammad came strutting into my office. Billeil had rebelled, he said, lighting a cigarette; and so would I please get the RAF to bomb him. Could I have the facts? They did not concern me, came the haughty reply. Had Billeil killed anyone or done any damage? No, but that was not the point. He had rebelled and had to be punished. I tried to explain that we only took air action as a last resort in extreme cases but Muhammad dismissed this with a heavy sarcastic laugh. So, I refused his request? I could not agree to air action, I replied. In that case, I had broken the treaty, he retorted, rising to his feet. He shook me coldly by the hand and did a slow march out of the room. That evening he, too, went off to the mountains. Had his State Councillors decamped with him, we would have been in a fix. Emissaries from the Jifri came hurrying over from Lahej to remind them of their Arab duty. Ali even offered them rifles as an inducement but they would not budge. They had had enough of Muhammad and his grand seigneural airs and were now beginning to make conciliatory noises in our direction.

We had done surprisingly well and we were doing well, too, on the old battle grounds of Audhali and Beihan. Now that the Sheriff and Audhali had rifles to hand out, Asshami no longer had things all his own way. He was attracting less recruits from our tribes and tribes now in receipt of rifles from the Sheriff and Audhali were beginning to chase his hirelings off. Our most potent weapon, however, was a lithe, spry young man with a choirboy's look of innocence, called Jabil. He was the Audhali's younger brother and one of Nature's bandits. Meeting Duncan Sandys, who paid us a visit at the time as Minister of Defence, he said that he did not care much for his title. What title would he prefer, Sandys asked. 'Minister of Attack!' he replied with a cherubic smile. And attack was his speciality. His popularity amongst the tribes was unrivalled and why? Because no one offered his supporters better chances of loot.

Off and on I met Asshami for an exchange of recriminations, usually with the Sheriff and Audhali in attendance. We could not hold him responsible for attacks on those frontier posts, he protested. If they worked for the Colonialists, it was only natural that Arabs should see their posts as colonialist and attack them. If only they would be sensible, he moaned, and join their Arab brothers they would have perfect peace. In one of the Imam's dungeons, the Sheriff laughed. They did not want to commit suicide, he chuckled, wiping his eyes. What did he mean? He meant that there was no future for the Imam and therefore no future for anyone foolish enough to join his caravan. Not one of the political parties in the South wanted anything to do with him. The Jifri wanted a separate South Arabia; the schoolboys in Aden, the United National Front, wanted to take the Yemen over and throw the Imam out; and the shopkeepers of Aden of the Aden Association wanted to be independent. Who in their right mind would want to be with the Imam? He was wrong, Asshami blustered. The Imam, he reminded us, had signed a pact with Nasser and King Saud of Saudi Arabia at Jedda. They were his friends. Friends? the Sheriff sneered. They would be the first to stab him in the back!

Asshami was continually reminding me that the Yemen was no longer defenceless and backward. Since the Jedda Pact it had become a respected Middle Eastern power and we could no longer expect to treat it with the colonialist contempt we had in the past. So why didn't we make peace before it was too late? he would ask, pulling earnestly at his little beard. Then, lowering his voice to a confidential mumble, he would tell me that the Imam had never been more willing to make peace and that was because there was a growing danger to both of us if we left matters between us unresolved. He would be referring to the radical influences entering the Yemen with the stream of Egyptian and Russian technicians and advisors flowing into the country. It was only because of the hostility between us, he would explain, that the Yemen needed them. If we could make peace, they could all be sent home and that would be better for both of us. The Foreign Office was being serenaded with similar tunes and so, when the

Yemen suddenly suggested that the Crown Prince Muhammad al Badr should visit London for official talks, they readily agreed. After a close look at his Egyptian and Russian allies, the Imam obviously realised that the British Devil he knew was best, Phillips chuckled. The official mood of the moment was that the Yemen was ready to do a deal at almost any reasonable price.

'The Voice of the Arabs' was telling its listeners something very different. With 'the People' in full revolt our position had become untenable, it proclaimed, and the sole purpose of 'the talks' was to agree on the timing of our withdrawal. And that, you might have thought, was what the Crown Prince believed, for why else should he have chosen to attack us in terms matching the 'Voice of the Arabs' at its most offensive on the very day before he set off to London? And so, in the event, the 'talks' were no more than a repeat of the dozens of talks I had had with Asshami. Selwyn Lloyd, our Foreign Secretary, looked down his long nose and with that practiced diplomat, Sir Harold Beeley[2] at his elbow, wearily trotted out all our old arguments while the Crown Prince recited all theirs with prompting from Asshami and the Yemeni Foreign Minister, Al Amri. Somewhat incongruously, the talks were adjourned at appropriate intervals to enable our visitors to say their prayers. Notwithstanding their ultra Islamic pretensions, our Foreign Secretary occasionally refreshed himself during our discussions from a bottle of whisky placed before him in surprising indifference to Islam's disapproval of alcohol. It was a gaucherie which visibly pained our interpreter, the distinguished Arabist, Sir Alec Kirkbride.[3]

This, however, was not our Foreign Secretary's only lapse. Although we had, as it happened, failed to honour our guests with any hospitality beyond the payment of their hotel bills at Claridges, the Crown Prince was considerate enough to hold a reception at the Savoy for Selwyn Lloyd. It was a courteous gesture and, whatever our differences, deserved a more courteous response than it received. Though the Guest of Honour, Selwyn Lloyd turned up an hour and a half late, just as the other guests were beginning to leave. Following this unforgivable lapse, the Crown Prince suddenly produced an Arab pony as a gift for Her Majesty the Queen. What a bore of a man, grumbled some Foreign Office hack. This meant that we would now have to find a present for Her Majesty to give in return! Had I any suggestions? Yes, I had. 'No, no, no!' the hack guffawed, we hadn't enough money in the kitty for fancy nonsense like that. Couldn't I think of something in the £25–30 bracket? Nothing suitable, I replied. What about a signed photograph of Her Majesty in a reasonably good frame? I didn't think that that would fit the bill. In the end we got an old cavalry sword, free of charge, from a museum. As I was to discover years later, the Crown Prince still had it in what had since become his home in Blackheath.

In the meantime Muhammad Aidrus was getting back into the news. On withdrawing to the mountains, he had taken care to instruct his Gendarmerie and the officials of his Administration to down tools and await his return: his purpose presumably being to blackmail us into begging him to come back on any terms he cared to name. Having won over the State Council to our side, we decided instead to get Muhammad dismissed and replaced as Naib by a Councillor of their choice. To do this we had to resort to the not very respectable device of issuing formal advice to the Sultan and it fell to me to issue it. Evidently under the impression that I was pleading for his help to get Muhammad back, I and the Sultan spoke at cross purposes for some little time. To say that he took it badly when he eventually got the message would be unpardonable meiosis. He exploded in a convulsion of incoherent rage and, literally frothing at the mouth, marched off looking like The Demon King.

No one knowing Muhammad would have imagined that he would take this slap in the face lying down. Nor did he. A week or two after his father had stumped off blowing bubbles, Muhammad suddenly descended from his highland home with a posse of wild tribesmen and, after doing a rip roaring haroush around his old parish, he returned home taking his Gendarmerie, Administration and the contents of the State Treasury with him. Again, he was unable to persuade the State Council to go too despite his threats, blandishments and tentative bribes. Once more, Ali's man was out and ours was in.

This was not to say that Muhammad went into immediate innocuous retirement. Though he scarcely justified the 'Voice of the Arab's' description of him as South Arabia's Ahmed ben Bella, he did make quite a considerable nuisance of himself by sending so-called 'Commandos' on occasional expeditions to raid Abyan and throw hand grenades about Aden. What he achieved was nothing very much but, thanks to the interest the Arab and, to some extent, the British media took in him, his name because sufficiently well known for Jack Profumo, who was then Minister of War, to ask me to take him by air to have a look at Mohammad's 'Eagle's Nest', al Qara. Perched on a pinnacle sticking boldly out of the clouds, his castle was a splendid sight and while I was all for our distinguished visitor having a good close look at it, it did seem to me that the pilot was descending far too close to it for safety. Our descent was in fact no fault of his but that of the failure of one of our ancient Dakota's two engines. Aden was only a hundred or so miles away but what with the Pilot wondering aloud whether we would reach it on one engine and Profumo telling me of the unpleasant experience he and his friends had had in comparable circumstances when he had been serving in the Oxford Air Squadron, it was one of the longest flights I have known.

It was at this point that we had news of Egypt's federation with Syria as 'the United Arab Republic' and then of the Yemen's improbable link with it as 'the United Arab States'. The news brought the Sheriff down to Aden with a grin on his face to say that, since federations were now the fashion, he and his friends the Audhali and Ahmed bin Abdulla, the Fadhli Naib, had agreed to federate. Sha'aful of Dhala had indicated his willingness to join them and he had no doubt that others would eventually follow suit. Once news of the Sheriff's federal intentions had got out the airwaves hummed with the growling and howling of indignant Arab patriots who issued repetitive warnings that the People would take merciless revenge on any traitor who joined the Sheriff's abominable 'federation of slaves'. As if to drive this point home, the Imam launched all-out attacks on the prospective federalists: Beihan, Audhali, Dhala and Fadhli. And, for the first time, Yemeni troops appeared on the scene equipped with the new heavy Russian weaponry. Coming to see how our troops were coping, General Templar, who was then Chief of Imperial General Staff, surprised the Commander of one of the Levy battalions by asking whether he was troubled by buggery amongst his men. 'No,' came the cool reply, 'our chaps are a little narrow minded about that kind of thing.'

As before, the Yemenis got a bloody nose and the rebel tribes were variously coaxed and harried into passivity. That, however, was not the end of the matter. Suddenly, Haidera, who had been leading the rampage in Dhala, made a dramatic comeback. Sweeping across the frontier, he occupied an extensive segment of the Amerate and in doing so encircled the Government Guard fort perched on top of Jebel Jihaf, the towering eminence which looks down on Dhala. Inside the fort there were about thirty Guards and one splendidly named Political Officer, Fitzroy Somerset. Outside there was a thousand of Haidera's cut-throats. It was a nasty situation and got nastier still after the local Levies' garrison had twice been forced to turn back while trying to go to the relief of the fort. Eventually, the Kings Own Shropshire Light Infantry got through and the fort was relieved just as the ammunition ran out. It was a nerve-wracking episode made memorable for me by the unflappable sang froid of Somerset. To hear him speaking on the Radio Telephone in impassive, almost bored, tones of his assailants' 'damned impertinence' was a tonic for jangling nerves.

By coincidence, this sensational affair took place in the immediate aftermath of high drama in Lahej. After months of indecision, we at last decided to put an end to the Jifri's seditious activities: not least because rumours were flying around that Ali proposed to abrogate his Treaty and join the United Arab States. If we marched into Lahej and grabbed the Jifri, we would, I believed, be rid of Ali as well. I could not believe that sensitive element in his being, his pride, would allow him to remain after we had breached his sovreignty and taken action against a friend under his protection. The humiliation would be too great. And so it proved. Though the Jifri got a tip off and bolted to the Yemen, we were rid of him. We were rid, also, of an outraged Ali who left for Milan in a flurry of protests to nurse his hurt feelings. Ali had gone but he was still Sultan and that was awkward, for while he continued to be its ruler we would get precious little cooperation out of Lahej even though he was sunning himself in Milan or wherever. Fortunately the problem was solved by Ali himself. A few weeks after he had gone he gave us good enough cause for withdrawing recognition from him by ordering 'the Lahej Army' to decamp to the Yemen with the contents of the State Treasury. The Colonial Secretary agreed and so did Harold MacMillan, the Prime Minister. And so ended the Lahej Conspiracy.

NOTES

[1] In 1952 the Saudis occupied the Buraimi Oasis which was jointly owned by our proteges, Oman and Abu Dhabi. After the breakdown of efforts to get the matter settled by arbitration, we expelled the Saudis by military force in 1955. Coincidentally, the Sultan of Muscat came into conflict with the Imam of Oman who, unlike his predecessor, refused to acknowledge the Sultan as his suzerain. In the civil war which followed, we supported the Sultan while the Imam got Saudi backing. The Imam was finally expelled in 1957.

[2] Sir Harold Beeley, KCMG, was one of our more experienced Middle Eastern hands. Having served on the Anglo-American Committee of Inquiry into Palestine, he spent five years in our Baghdad Embassy before being Ambassador in Saudi Arabia and, later, in the United Arab Republic.

[3] Sir Alec Kirkbride was the virtual founder and architect of Jordan. Having taken part in Lawrence's advance against the Turks, he was put in charge of what became our Protectorate of TransJordan as Resident and Advisor to its Arab ruler, the Amir Abdulla, son of Sheriff Hussein. When TransJordan became the Kingdom of Jordan after the end of the Second World War, Abdulla became King and Kirkbride the first British Ambassador.

9

THE ARAB EMIRATES OF THE SOUTH TAKE THE FLOOR

BAD NEWS IS good for business if you happen to be a journalist and, since we had been having a rough time in the aftermath of Suez, visiting journalists quickly became a feature of the local scene. And, for my part, none too welcome a one. When I could, I evaded them; when I couldn't, I got rid of them as speedily as good manners would allow. This was foolish, of course, and it was only a year or so later when I began to understand the sinister power of the Press that I came to realise that, if the Press influenced public opinion, the sensible thing to do was to try to influence the Press. By chance, I did so for a few months. Having discovered that the elderly Correspondent of the *Sunday Times* was invariably in a pother over what to say in his weekly article, I used to write it for him during his visits to Aden. It was a facility I was never to get again.

The only journalists I did not look on as licenced nuisances during those hectic months of the Lahej Conspiracy and Yemeni offensive were Randolph Churchill and David Holden.[1] Bottled, bellicose and bizarre (he came to dinner once in tennis shoes and a dinner jacket!), I found Churchill sadly appealing and, improbably, during a bibulous near all-night session in his hotel bedroom, he talked a great deal of interesting sense. Holden was perhaps a little calculating, a man of the times who had got the message that we were now a third-rate power and made ourselves look ridiculous by striking old fashioned imperialist attitudes. Churchill, by contrast, refused to accept that our greatness had anything to do with material strength. Unlike, say, the Russians with their big battalions, we had become great because of our genius, he said, and he insisted we could still remain great because of it. Needless to say, I found Churchill's views the more agreeable.

Holden's views, however, were the more thought-provoking. One look at the Middle Eastern scenario was enough to know we could never hang onto Aden, he would say. We had lost Suez, left the Sudan and now Jordan was no longer our ally. And so, since we were now negotiating our way out of the shambles into which Cyprus had dissolved, all we had left was a treaty with a very shaky Iraq. One had to remember, too, he said, that the French had been forced out of all their North African possessions except Algeria and who could seriously believe that they would be able to hold Algeria for very much longer? So what did that mean for Aden? It meant that, in the very near future, Aden and the Gulf would be the last outposts of imperialism in the Middle East and the entire force of Arab nationalism would be directed against them. How could Aden possibly survive? In any case, was Aden worth defending?

For someone as deeply immersed in South Arabia as I was, it seemed inconceivable that we might ever decide that Aden was not worth defending and rat on our treaties and Arab friends. Like every Political Officer in the Protectorate, I had lost sight of the fact that we were only where we were because HMG needed a friendly Protectorate to secure our position in Aden. We had, I suppose, become emotionally involved and saw ourselves as having a mission to defend our proteges against the horrors of a Yemeni take-over and help them get themselves into reasonable shape. What Holden was now saying was an uncomfortable reminder that, if the cost and effort of holding onto Aden added up to more than its worth to us, the chances of our trying to remain out of any sense of duty to our Arab friends would be negligible. So what was Aden worth to us? The Ministry of Defence saw it as a forward base for the protection of our oil interests in the Gulf and for giving support, when needed, in East Africa. Holden doubted whether it would serve either purpose very satisfactorily. Whether it would or wouldn't, we could be sure that the Russians would move in the minute we withdrew. That alone, I thought, made it vital for us to hang on. A loud enigmatic 'h'mm' was his only reply.

Yes, but could we hang on? The rising tide of Arab nationalism, Nasserism or what you will had swept us out of nearly all the Middle East so what possible hope had we of resisting it here? It was only a matter of time, Holden was certain, before we would have the whole population against us. If we carried on in colonial fashion with a Colony of Aden and Protectorate, I had to agree that he was probably right. But that was not what I envisaged. It now seemed likely that the Western Protectorate rulers would set up a federation. If they did and, if their federation and Aden then wished to form an independent South Arabia, I thought it would get sufficient popular support to survive. And why? Because it would give South Arabians the independent South Arabia apart from the Yemen which most of them wanted. And what about our use of Aden as a military base? We could expect to acquire rights to that by treaty in return for the generous subsidy the South Arabian Federation would certainly need. 'Hm, hm, hm,' Holden murmured even more enigmatically than before.

Looking about me I could see nothing to justify Holden's pessimism. The departure of Ali and the Jifri and our successes against the Yemen had in fact generated a new mood of smiling cooperation. Even Lahej was now the most amiable and salaaming of places with hardly an Egyptian flag or portrait of Nasser to be seen. The climate was just right for the launch of the federation project and Luce agreed that this was the moment to tackle HMG and get their blessing before anything happened to persuade our friends to have second thoughts. Alan Lennox-Boyd, who was Colonial Secretary, was all for going ahead and go ahead we did. The sponsors of the federal project went, at his invitation, to London with Luce for discussions and returned with HMG's blessing and a promise of financial support. What we now had was what we should have had in 1953. Five precious years had been wasted and during that time we had lost every one of our principal Middle Eastern footholds except Iraq. By malign coincidence, our friend and ally, King Feisal of Iraq, was struck down by revolution within a couple of days of the federalists' return from London. All that was now left of our Middle Eastern 'empire' was Aden and the Gulf.

Now that Lennox-Boyd had given the 'go ahead' for federation, my first duty was to get the Rulers to agree [on] a federal constitution, and a very wearying business it was. And nothing wearied me more than the unhelpful demeanour of the Sherif. He fidgetted with matches and cigarettes, he stared at the ceiling, he closed his eyes, he scratched and yawned, he did everything he could to show his disdain for what I was trying to do. I stiffened my upper lip and tried to ignore his impertinences but it was no good. My patience in shreds, I eventually demanded to know what was wrong with him. He was unwell, he replied in a languid voice. What did he mean? He meant that he was sickened by my wasting time on trivialities when I should have been attending to what mattered. Such as? 'Money!' he hissed in a stage whisper. How could he want to talk about money? He knew very well that HMG had agreed to support the Federation with a Grant-in-Aid which was to be discussed with some Colonial Office official in the near future. 'No, no, no!' he snapped with an impatient toss of his head. That was money for the Federation. He was talking about money for the Rulers! Money for the Rulers? Surely they did not expect to be paid for agreeing to federate? Oh, yes, they did! Everyone at the table came at once to the alert and let out the equivalent of a resonant 'Hear Hear!' I was by no means amused and said so in plain language.

Half an hour later a quiet, persuasive voice told me that he thought I was misjudging the Rulers. By their standards they were not being unreasonable. The voice belonged to Mohammed, son of that Upper Aulaqi problem child, Farid, and it was a voice to which I was beginning to listen with some respect. With the exception of Ali, no South Arabian was as charmingly anglicised as Mohammed but, unlike Ali, Oxford had processed Mohammed into a thoroughgoing anglophile. As a go-between who could put across our ideas to Arabs and Arab ideas to ourselves, no one could have been better. So how was it that he should be trying to justify what I saw as nothing more than an exhibition of vulgar, opportunist greed? I had got it all wrong, Mohammed laughed. The fact of the matter was that, if the Rulers got nothing, they would be in trouble. He then patiently told me why. What I had to understand, he said, was that whenever a Ruler had some windfall his tribal leaders expected handouts in the same way that they had had a share of the loot after a tribal raid in the past. So, accustomed as they were to the Arab practice of superiors giving visiting inferiors presents, the tribal leaders would all assume that the Rulers had received very special gifts on such a very special occasion as a visit to London and perhaps even to the

The Deluge

Queen herself. So that was it! Having stopped looting each other, these old bandits had now turned to looting us!

Thanks to Lennox-Boyd's avuncular regard for them, the Rulers got their handouts in the end but there was a price to be paid for the favour. The Colonial Office officials were scandalised at having to make payments of this kind to what one of them described as 'those irresponsible scroungers' and, as a consequence, the Rulers and, later, their Federation were continually hobbled and hampered by official ill will. This was immediately apparent on the arrival of an unsmiling official called Kirkman to discuss the question of financial aid. To explain what was needed I had drafted a budget for the future Federation which Kirkman now inspected with unfriendly analytical eyes. Taking out his pen he set about lopping and chopping to such effect that he had very soon cut the budget by half. To my wails of protest he asked me to bear in mind that Grants-in-Aid were given on a basis of need, not desirability; and so, while he would not go so far as to say that what he had cut out was undesirable, he could say with certainty that none of it was needed. But this was absurd! Here we were trying to set up a federation which would have to stand up to all-out Nasserite assault. Surely he could understand that there was a real need to give it a look which would at least win it local respect? A political need, perhaps, Kirkman remarked, looking wearily out of the window. Politics were no concern of his.

In the meantime, I was labouring away at what daily seemed to be the increasingly impossible task of getting the Rulers to agree a federal constitution. Knowing their Seagarian disinterest in 'administrative bunk', I had imagined that they would happily accept the constitution I had drafted with a yawn and a nod. But I was wrong. It did not take my friends long to discover that what we were talking about was not so much boring old 'administrative bunk' as power, and next to arms and money nothing set their pulses thumping as fast or as furiously as thoughts of power. And so, what I had thought would be an easy ride to agreement, was in fact a sequence of shuffles, stumbles and stops which were getting us nowhere.

At the root of our difficulties was the Rulers' total aversion to what we meant by federation. What they had pictured was some kind of Arab League which would meet every now and again and take decisions by consensus. What they had never dreamed possible was that we should lure them into an organisation where they would have to surrender some of their powers and subordinate themselves to the orders of others. Did I really imagine that he would agree to so-called federal ministers doing as they pleased in Beihan, the Sherif asked with a ringing laugh. Had I any idea what his people would think if he handed over powers to federal ministers? asked the Audhali. He would lose the last shred of their respect and that was all there was to it. You could only have one Ruler to a state, Sha'aful piped up and yet if every minister was free to give orders, as I was suggesting, there would be half a dozen at least. You might as well let another man get into bed with your wife as do what I wanted them to do, Ahmed the Fadhli quipped in his customarily earthy fashion.

The Rulers were right. To have more than one master in a state would be a recipe for disastrous conflict; to whittle down the Ruler's authority, one for chaos. And yet, if every Ruler went his own way without giving the federal government a thought, what sort of federation would we have? In the end we hit on a solution. The Rulers were to become the federal government executives in their states: which was to say that the federal government would only be able to act through them in the states and so implicitly with their consent. Having taken this step away from federal orthodoxy in the direction of wooly confederation, we became less inhibited about taking a step or two more. Thus every state was given equal representation on the Federal Legislature despite the variations in the size of their populations. Each state was also awarded a ministry and the right to appoint a minister to it, even though this would entail the creation of more ministries than were needed. While as for the Presidency, this would rotate with each Ruler holding it in turn for a month at a time. I argued forlornly for more respectable constitutional provisions but in vain. What I refused to understand, the Sherif continually complained, was that the Federation could only survive in an atmosphere of brotherly love and that, since brothers were equals, meant equal treatment for all.

The Colonial Office followed our antics with telexed bleats of astonishment and protest and even Luce was occasionally moved to say that this or that really was not good enough and would I please try and make the Rulers see more sense? Even if we had had all the time in the world to coax and curse and not a mere few months we would never have persuaded them to agree to anything else. The Colonial Office might very well have said that, if this was what the Rulers wanted, they need not expect any

British money to be invested in it. As it was, they merely grumbled and gave in. This was partly because they still did not realise quite how loose the Federation would be and partly because it would not have looked too good for HMG to back out only a few weeks before Lennox-Boyd was due to visit Aden for the Federation's inaugural ceremonies. And so, if hardly shipshape and Bristol fashion, we had a Federation ready for launching in time for the Colonial Secretary's visit. The happy event took place on 11th February, 1959.

It was a splendid occasion. Flags flew, bands blared and ten thousand or so spectators cheered and clapped. The centrepiece of the ceremonies was a dais on which the Rulers sat, gaily turbanned and scented. Luce and I were uniformed, Victorian imperial style in white, while Lennox-Boyd outshone us all in the most elegant of grey tail coats and a gleaming silk hat. The climax of the proceedings was to be the delivery of speeches by Lennox-Boyd and the Federation's first monthly President, Ahmed the Fadhli, followed by the signing of the treaty between the Federation and the United Kingdom. All went well up to the point when Lennox-Boyd stepped forward, speech in hand, to address the multitude. It was at this critical moment that an unexpected diversion took place. Unknown to us all, 'Mister' Fadhl, who was in command of several hundred Guards paraded before us, had momentarily nodded off and now, suddenly coming to, he jumped to the conclusion that the speeches were over, that the treaty had been signed and that everyone was waiting for him to march his men off. As a result, before Lennox-Boyd could so much as open his mouth, the Guards were stepping briskly off to the rousing strains of 'The Barren Rocks of Aden'. There could be no speeches now, no signing of the treaty: Fadhl's idiocy had wrecked the whole proceedings! Lennox-Boyd yammered something to Luce, Luce snapped at me, 'For God's sake, do something!' and I barked something to the same effect to James, the Guards' Commandant. And then, while we were all throwing mental fits, Fadhl unaccountably came to his senses. Having marched his men up to one end of the parade ground, he did a Duke of York and marched them all the way back again. For this unexpected and pointless manoeuvre, the crowd gave him and his men a handsome round of applause.

Following these jollities, Lennox-Boyd made a tour of the federal states, contriving throughout to look as if there was nothing he enjoyed

The Arab Emirates of the South Take the Floor

so much as sitting on the floor eating boiled goat with his fingers and having wild tribesmen loosing off their rifles around his ears. Everywhere he was welcomed in style and nowhere in greater style than in Beihan. Instead of the usual rifle salutes the unfortunate Lennox-Boyd was here saluted with bursts of machine gun fire. What with that, prancing ponies and trotting camels, it was quite a reception. The Sherif, however, had a very special surprise for his guest. Placed in the centre of the room where he was to spend the night in the Palace was a gigantic and hideously ornate bed, recently purchased by the Sheriff (so I was told) to celebrate his marriage to an Aden beauty known as 'the Golden Girl'. It was an unusual bed: how unusual Lennox-Boyd was to discover during the night. Half way through it, some catch or clip gave way and the bed suddenly folded up with Lennox-Boyd sandwiched between its lower and upper ends. Clambering out of this mantrap with some difficulty, the poor man clawed his way to the electric light switch—the electrical system having only recently been installed as a rush job—only to receive a lively shock for his pains. It was an unforgettable visit, he said to his host on leaving next morning.

The Federation we had thought and talked about for so long was in being at last. 'The Arab Emirates of the South' was on the map. It was on the map but that was about all. It was as yet nothing more than a piece of paper. It had no offices, no officials, no equipment. It did not even have a letterhead. We still had a long way to go.

NOTES

[1] David Holden was for many years the *Sunday Times* Middle Eastern Correspondent. Some while later, on a visit to Cairo, he vanished, never to be seen again, the presumption being that he had been abducted and murdered.

10

OUR ENEMIES CONFOUNDED

BY THE TIME that poor Lennox-Boyd was smiling his way through the unnerving ordeal of the Federation's inaugural ceremonies, the Middle East had lost that look of imminent disaster which it had worn when our young friend and ally, King Feisal of Iraq, had been sliced up by the Baghdad mob. Although still riding high on the crest of the Arab nationalist wave, Nasser was no longer having everything all his own way. The nakedness of his ambitions and his brashness in pursuing them aroused fear and thus opposition.

By a strange irony, this improvement in the political climate was largely due to President Eisenhower, who had humiliated and all but ruined us over Suez to save Nasser's skin. Having sabotaged our attempt to snuff out the menace of Nasserism he had since come to realise that it was a menace after all and was now offering American help to any power which felt itself to be threatened by it. So it happened that, when the Iraqi Revolution (which was understandably, if mistakenly, seen as a Nasserite coup) led to panicky 'cris de coeur' from Jordan and the Lebanon, these brought British troops to the one and American marines to the other just in time to preempt Nasserite take-overs. That what had so nearly happened in Jordan and the Lebanon might happen elsewhere was beginning to percolate the Arab ruling classes and even Saud, the Saudi King who was ostensibly Nasser's ally, was so afflicted by Nasserphobia that he tried to bribe Colonel Sarraj, Syria's Minister of the Interior, to have Nasser eliminated. Everywhere Nasser seemed to be at work plotting and planning popular insurrection. He was hard at work in the Yemen, too.

There he had had the facility of the all too anxious-to-please Crown Prince Mohammed al Badr. Eager to cut a popular Nasserite figure, this naive young man had opened the Yemen's doors to troupes of Egyptian advisers, technicians and the like, with any number of Soviet and Chinese auxiliaries into the bargain. Persuaded that this was the price to be paid for Soviet arms and technical help, the Imam had grudgingly tolerated this influx of undesirables but, predictably enough, they were very soon putting their own ideas into Yemeni heads. News of this filtered through to us in Aden but it was only when the sly face of Salem Arramah—a merchant-cum-courtier in the political-pimp class—appeared one day with an ingratiating smile that I realised how far the Nasserite rot had set in.

The Yemen was heading for revolution, Salem said in a low, conspiratorial voice. This was entirely due to al Badr's folly, he sighed. It was those mischievous Egyptian officers who had poisoned the minds of the riff raff in the towns. What the Egyptians were after was a Nasserite take-over with or without al Badr as their puppet. And the Imam? Salem sniggered. As I would know, he was the last person to compromise with opposition and if Nasser wanted a fight he would fight him. As it was, he was actively ordering his son's Egyptian friends out of the country and throwing their Yemeni stooges into his dungeons. Did he think that would restore the situation to normal? Salem shrugged his shoulders. He personally doubted it and that was why he had come. He wanted my assurance that we would give him asylum in Aden in the event of the Nasserites taking the Yemen over. I wouldn't regret it, he quavered; he would keep me fully informed about all that was happening in the Yemen and, as I knew, he had access to the Imamic circle itself. This was splendid news! It was not having an informer in Salem that delighted me, for informers were two a penny. It was knowing that this uppercrust Yemeni wanted a bolthole in Aden. That could only mean that the Yemen was in a bad way and would leave us alone. To be left alone to get on with the job of putting the Federation together was what we needed more than anything.

What Salem had said about the Yemen was confirmed soon afterwards by our amiable Charge d'affaires in the Yemen, Christopher Pirie-Gordon. Life in the Yemen was a Mad Hatter's tea party, he laughed, with the Imam running around like the Queen of Hearts shouting 'Off with their heads!' Yes, it was 'no ordinary brouhaha'. Seriously, though, he asked us to understand that we had a golden opportunity to clinch a lasting peace with the Yemen. The Imam now knew precisely what the Egyptians were up to and, with a little discreet nudging, he thought he could be persuaded to see that we were his natural allies. What was needed was a little 'quiet diplomacy', Horace Phillips explained. 'Yes, in-deed,' Pirie-Gordon agreed, adding that what was not needed was any 'funny business' on the part of our federal friends. Could I please ensure that they did not get up to their 'little games' on the frontier? If the Yemen behaved itself, I said, I felt sure that they would do the same.

True to his undertakings, Salem danced dutiful attendance serving up 'important' and occasionally 'very important' items of news. And then one day he turned up, his thin normally impassive face twitching with excitement. He had something 'very, very important' to tell me. Indeed he had. The Imam was leaving for Rome. Having regularly overdosed himself with morphine to dull the pain of arthritis, the old devil had the choice of taking his Italian doctors' advice and going to Rome for repair and refitment or of staying put and conking out. And so he was off to Rome, leaving his feckless son, al Badr, in charge. It was too bad, Phillips grumbled. Here was Christopher poised to win over the Imam as a friend and ally for keeps and now we would be back to Square One. Once al Badr was in the driver's seat, his Nasserite friends would wing their way back and then it would be goodbye to any hopes of a lasting peace.

A few weeks later the sunshine had come back into his eyes. Christopher had done it, he said, waving a piece of paper in my face. He had just had this telex from him saying that al Badr was desperately anxious for peace and, to ensure it, was sending Asshami down to Aden to settle the Yemen's various differences with our Rulers. 'Quiet diplomacy' had done the trick! This was good news but 'quiet diplomacy' had nothing to do with it. It was rather the mess which al Badr had brought about. Once the Imam had gone, he had flooded the Yemen's larger towns with Egyptians as part of a crash Nasserisation plan, and this had been generally seen as a Nasserite plot for him to replace his father as an Egyptian puppet. Not surprisingly, Conservative Yemen did not take at all kindly to the prospect of being dictated to by brash young Egyptians in trousers and dark glasses, and Conservative Yemen reacted in its own customary fashion. And so, beset by revolts, outbursts of indiscipline and officials of ever decreasing reliability, al Badr was in no position to tangle with us.

If he was to be left free to deal with his troubles, he had to have peace. He could not fight two wars at once.

The Rulers were not surprised to hear of Asshami's peace mission but it was to be a peace mission to whom? It was the Audhali who raised the question. They were a Federation now, he said, and Asshami should realise that he could no longer deal with them separately, making peace with one and not with another. From now on he would have to make peace with them all as a federation or with none of them. Phillips bubbled with exasperation on hearing of this 'petty minded' attitude, saying that to ask Asshami to deal with the Federation was to put him in an impossible position. For him to deal with it would be tantamount to his recognising it and that was something he obviously could not do. So what was he proposing? That we should pretend the Federation did not exist, to placate the Yemenis? That was not the point, Phillips protested. Couldn't I see that here was a chance of lasting peace which the Rulers were threatening to throw away for nothing of substance? I did not see it like that. Whether we signed a hundred agreements with Asshami or not, I knew very well that we would have peace with the Yemen just so long as it suited al Badr, and no longer.

Asshami came and, having failed to break through the Rulers' federal resolve, left in a fit of the grumbles. Before leaving, however, he gave me solemn-voiced assurances that he would not issue so much as one round of ammunition to any Protectorate tribesman and begged me to restrain that mischievous little 'Afrit', Jabel. Imagine my surprise, then, when, barely a week or so later, Salem turned up to report that Mohammed Bubakr, who had rebelled against the Upper Aulaqi Sheikh yet again, had just left Beidha with a large consignment of arms.

But Asshami had promised... Salem stopped me with a deferential smile to explain that it was not Asshami who had given them arms but King Saud of Saudi Arabia. He had sent them to Beidha for Mohammed Bubakr to collect. King Saud? Where did he come into this? Salem grinned like a conjuror about to explain how he had done his trick. What lay behind all this, he explained, was Egyptian disenchantment with the South Arabian League after Ali's failure to take the Protectorate over and Saud's fears that the Egyptians would now back the Young Socialist revolutionaries of the Aden Trades Union movement. The last thing the Saudis wanted was Socialist revolutionaries as their neighbours and so they were doing all they could to give the South Arabian League credibility by dressing up Mohammed Bubakr and his followers as a National Liberation Front. And Asshami expected us to sit twiddling our thumbs while Ali and the Saudis used Beidha as a base of operations to attack us? I left for Mukeiras the next day and got Asshami over from Beidha for a talk. I put it to him as straight as a slide rule. If Mohammed Bubakr received arms in the Yemen, I would look on them as coming from the Yemen and act accordingly. Whether King Saud, the Emperor of Japan or whoever had sent them left me totally disinterested. Asshami babbled 'buts' with senile despair and waved his poor spindly little arms about like a child in a pet but I gave him no change. A week or two later Mohammed Bubakr got a further consignment of arms but this time he had to go all the way to Nejran on the Saudi frontier to collect them. Asshami was toeing the line.

And then, while we were still wondering what Mohammed Bubakr would do next, we received sensational news. The Imam was on his way back fully restored, it was said, to his old rumbustuous self. We had no reason to doubt it. From the moment of his return the old ruffian was back at work retrieving what his feckless son had lost. Egyptians were packed off home and their Yemeni friends were variously deprived of their heads and their liberty. No one could deal with a Yemeni situation as effectively as this old veteran of the tribal political game. But on this occasion, contrary to all precedent, he suddenly went off the rails. Having invited Ibn al Ahmar, chief of the great Zeidi tribe, the Hashid, to come under safe conduct for a little chat about the large sum of money he had extorted by near blackmail out of al Badr, he had him seized and beheaded on arrival. This was unquestionably an act unbecoming a Defender of the Islamic Faith. Also it was political madness. At one stroke of his executioner's sword, the Imam had put one of the Yemen's two largest and most powerful tribes against him. When I heard what had happened, I could have thrown my hat in the air and danced a fandango of delight. After this the Imam would be hobbled and incapable of giving us any serious trouble. George Henderson, who was staying the night, turned up for dinner with a bottle of Veuve Cliquot procured from our enterprising provisioners, Messrs Bicasjee Cowasjee of Steamer Point.

Our federal friends were in a celebratory mood, too, but it was not just the Imam's self-inflicted discomfiture that gave the Sherif such a sparkle in his eye. It was the belief he shared with nine Arabs out of ten that the Imam was in terminal decline. What was the British Government's policy towards the Yemen, he asked thoughtfully, massaging his hands. Policy? We wanted peace. Nothing more. The Sherif rattled a matchbox with impatience and, lighting a cigarette with a show of fuss and flamboyance, explained that what he was talking about was the succession in the Yemen when the Imam died. Surely we had plans of some kind? Not as far as I knew. Was I seriously saying that at a time when Nasser was doing everything possible to arrange an Egyptian take-over we were doing nothing? Didn't we realise that the moment the Imam died al Badr would be on the telephone to Nasser who would immediately fly in the Egyptian Army to make sure that he became Imam? Was that what we wanted? Hoiking with apparent disgust into a spittoon, he rose and clattered noisily out of my office.

He was back in a better humour a few days later to say that Ahmed Muhammed Nauman, the leader of the Free Yemenis, had just arrived on a visit from Cairo and wanted to see me. Our visitor was an oldish man who looked more like a Victorian Bishop than a revolutionary. He had a soft-spoken intellectual manner and spoke slowly, seeming to caress each word before setting it free. As I would know, he said, the Yemen was the cradle of Arab civilisation and yet, today, it was the haven of mediaeval barbarity where ignorance and misrule flourished under the direction of that most barbarous of rulers, the Imam Ahmed. The Yemeni people had suffered enough and now they were ready to liberate themselves from his tyranny. Hands clasped, he gazed at me as if to make sure that I had understood what he had said. So, would we help our Yemeni friends? He smiled a benign, patriarchal benediction as if to say that Heaven would reward us if we did. What he did in fact say was that, in return for our help, he was ready then and there to sign a treaty recognising the Federation and our right to a military base in Aden. What did I think of that? I knew very well what Phillips, Pirie-Gordon and the Foreign Office would think of it but I kept that to myself and asked what form of government the Free Yemenis would favour in the event of their taking over from the Imam. He glowed good will saying that, as admirers of the British, they naturally wanted a British set-up: which was to say a democratically elected parliament and constitutional monarchy. Al Badr as monarch? He laughed politely and said no, it would have to be Prince Hassan. A democratic Yemen with a constitutional monarch? It did not make sense. I left, saying that I would report our conversation to my Government and let him know their reaction.

Their reaction, as conveyed by Phillips, endorsed by Pirie-Gordon and, to my disappointment, accepted by Luce, was that Nauman was of no great account and that to have any dealings with him could only upset the Imam at a time when we had every possibility of winning him over. I had best make it clear that we were not interested, Phillips said. In the event, I could not bring myself to go as far as that. But why did he come to us of all people for help, I asked Nauman. Why not look to his Arab brethren, the Egyptians? We, after all, were Christians, foreigners and imperialists. Nauman let out a sunlit smile. They did not want Egyptian help because the Egyptians were the new imperialists and would certainly want to take over the Yemen if they were given half a chance. As for us, he gave me the kindest of smiles, well, we had had our day. They had nothing to fear from us. We would be content with what we had. It was all good for a laugh, Phillips smiled. The old fellow probably hoped that a bit of flattery would get him a hand-out of arms and ammunition. In fact, this soft-spoken old man was almost certainly telling the truth. A few years later he became Prime Minister of the Yemen and was imprisoned in Cairo by Nasser for not doing as he was told.

The Sherif predictably threw tantrums in protest at our refusal to give Nauman our backing but, just as he was rising up to full throttle, he received an urgent call to go to Beihan. A few days later he asked me to join him as a matter of urgency. I arrived to find surly, black-turbanned Zeidi tribesmen lounging around, sipping coffee and picking their teeth. Inside the Sherif's palace their master, Sina'an abu al Hum, the head of the Bakil, sat demanding attention. He was a small, plump man with an enormous Semitic nose which gave him the appearance of a caricaturist's dormouse. They were fed up with the Imam's tyranny, he said. And what were they after if the Imam fell? He knew his lines. They wanted what we British had. And a King? Oh yes, of course. And who did they want as their King? He gave me a significant look and said that they wanted none other than their beloved friend, the Sherif. It must be a joke, I thought, and was about to laugh when, looking at abu al Hum's pop-eyed countenance, I realised that I was supposed to take him seriously. As for the Sherif, he was ecstatic. He really believed that this scallywag was telling the truth.

Phillips sighed sad-eyed disapproval at my meeting these dubious characters. They were men of no real account, he wished me to know, and 'playing around' with them could only jeopardise Christopher's efforts to win over the Imam. His gloomy forebodings were almost immediately allayed by the arrival of an unctuous invitation for Luce to visit Taiz and, even though his illustrious host was away taking the waters at the Yemeni spa of Sukhna during his visit, it was by Luce's account a love feast. I had a similar reception on a visit I paid to Beidha just then at the invitation of Asshami. It was all bugle salutes, Guards of Honour and gushing speeches of manifest insincerity. Since all this was in aid of detente and, possibly, an entente cordiale, nothing of substance was said which could have sullied the atmosphere of peace and unity. A few days after Luce's return, however, Pirie-Gordon sent us an urgent message to say that the Imam was greatly upset to hear that Nauman and a number of other Yemeni bad hats were using Aden to promote revolution in the Yemen and, as evidence of our desire for his friendship, he wanted us to kick them out. Phillips agreed with gusto and so, to my dismay, did Luce. What conceivable sense was there in trying to appease an old has-been in terminal decline to whom we owed nothing if it meant alienating the up and coming men of the Yemen's future? I argued long and loud but got nowhere. One had to be pragmatic, Luce said, and the irrefutable fact was this: if the Foreign Office was dead set on something within their own sphere of responsibility, it was a waste of time trying to do battle with them. And so Nauman and his friends were shown the door. A predictable display of pyrotechnical protest followed from the Sherif and his friends.

In the meantime, Mohammed Bubakr was banging his war drums and since he had Saudi rifles galore on offer recruits were signing on for his National Liberation Front as if they were buying tickets for a Gold Rush. Trouble in its ominous old form began to erupt and, as every old British hand could see, it was as clear as tracer bullets on a cloudless night that, if it were not stopped quickly, the Western Protectorate could go up in flames and the Federation with it. But what were to do? It was no good our thumping the Yemen: Mohammed Bubakr's godfather was King Saud, not the Imam. We could not out-bribe King Saud, nor could we hope to get very far by conventional means. If we had learned nothing else from our troubles in the past, we now knew that you might as well ask a blind cripple to catch the maddest of March hares as expect conventional soldiery to cope with Bedouin operating in their own country. So what were we to do? Our resident sage and tribal adviser, Mubarak Assahm, puckered his brow and said that, as I knew, Mohammed Bubakr moved his base from one remote tribal area to another and so depended on the good will and consent of the tribes concerned. That being the case, we had to persuade those tribes to withdraw their consent and deny him refuge in their tribal areas. But how? By hitting them from the air—after warnings, of course—whenever they harboured Mohammed Bubakr and his men. Hitting them from the air? I did not care for that but, seeing my doubts, Mubarak's old face wrinkled into a laugh as he explained that he had not visualised anything so shameful as hitting the tribes and their families. The target he had in mind were their goats. Let our planes shoot up a tribe's goats and he could assure me that it would ban Mohammed Bubakr from its tribal area within the hour. Remembering how Hugh Boustead had finished off the Beni Amer by depriving them of their cattle, I had no reason to doubt him. The Mubarak plan was a winner. Within a matter of a week Mohammed Bubakr had been expelled from one tribal area to another and out into the Yemen. Everywhere he had become 'persona non grata'. Without any hiding place he was impotent.

With his eclipse and with the Yemen in a state of rampant confusion, we found ourselves suddenly and surprisingly in what seemed to be an unreal world of smiling peace. On the frontier we were now the masters. Jabel could have taken over Beidha any time he wished and the Sherif had only to give the nearby Yemeni tribes a nod and he would have been lord of the Yemeni frontier town of Harib. It was the same away from the frontier. Rebels, dissident tribes and other dangerous nuisances had all suddenly melted away. For the first time in years we were able to get on with our jobs without fighting some minor war, revolt or incipient rebellion at the same time. This was the most timely of reprieves, for we had the Federation to set up and, though none of us had ever imagined that it would be easy, none of us had realised just how much would have to be done. Ministries had to be created, staff recruited, conditions of service drawn up, temporary accommodation found while a federal capital was being built... there seemed to be no end to what had to be done and all the time the fractious Rulers had to be taught how to be ministers and the British Civil Servants transferred to the Federation how to handle the 'prima donnas' who were their ministers. We had hitches, rumpuses and occasional ministerial walk-outs but no disasters. Bit by bit the Federation took shape. By the time that Harold MacMillan was making his 'Wind of Change' speech in Capetown, bar a hiccough or two, it was ticking over quite well.

Success brought its own reward. The remaining Advisory Treaty States clambered onto the federal bandwagon and Lahej's ruling clan dutifully deposed Ali and elected an amenable princeling of distinguished appearance called Fadhl bin Ali to replace him. Dining with this decorative newcomer soon after he had been 'turbanned', I made some remark about the great improvement in the political weather. Did I really believe that? he asked. I thought I had reason enough for doing so, I replied. Perhaps I would think differently if I looked over my shoulder at what was going on in Aden, he said with a silken smile. If I did I would see that Nasser had switched his support from the South Arabian League to the Aden Trades Unionists. I had to agree. Our troubles were far from over.

11

ADEN AND THE FEDERATION UNITE IN THE NICK OF TIME

WHEN I SCRIBBLED OUT those proposals which Sir Tom so brashly strangled at birth, I had felt that we should be doing something about preparing South Arabia for independence and that federation was the only feasible way of doing so. My motive, I must confess, was self interest, not idealism. If we made it plain that early independence was our aim, I believed we had a fair chance of keeping the good will of most Arabs. If we were seen to be dragging our feet I felt that even Arabs of the friendlier kind would drift away for, whatever the merits of our form of imperialism, this had become a dirty word and, to submit to it, a disreputable solecism. And so, envisaging a federation of Protectorate States which Aden would join as a prelude to early independence, I had looked forward to our being in treaty relations with an independent and friendly South Arabia within a matter of two or three years. As it was, seven years had drifted by since then and, far from holding out any hopes of independence, we had told the Adenis that the best they could hope for were occasional tidbits of 'constitutional advances'. That young Adenis from even the better known Anglophile families had been going Nasserite came as no surprise.

Nevertheless, now that we had our federation of Protectorate States we could make up for lost time. It only remained to get Aden to join it and then we could put out the flags for independence. When I said as much to Luce he hoisted an eyebrow in mild surprise. Independence? It was the last thing HMG would favour. Cyprus had gone, he reminded me, and Singapore and Kenya were going: which meant that Aden would be our only overseas military base. I did not see that this mattered. Our base would be more secure if we held it under a Treaty with a friendly Federation than if we left it within an increasingly rickety and vulnerable Colony. Luce smiled through half-closed eyes and said he didn't think HMG would agree. After all, it had only taken Hussein of Jordan to get a touch of cold feet for him to scrub his treaty with us and all our rights in Jordan with it.

This did not mean that he was against Aden joining the Federation. He was all for it. It was logical and, politically, it would mean that Aden's conservatives would be able to call on the support of the conservative federal Rulers against their Nasserite opponents. The problem, he said, was not whether but how Aden should join the Federation. It could join as another federal state or as an equal partner. These were only two of several possibilities. Having thought the matter over and over again, he had come to the conclusion that this was a matter which the Adenis should be left free to decide for themselves, so what he was proposing to London was that Aden should be converted from a Colony into a Protectorate state and left free to negotiate directly with the Federation on equal terms. That was fair, was it not? Perhaps it was but, left to themselves, I could see months if not years of inconclusive argument lying ahead and time was not on our side. The Yemen would not remain quiescent for ever. We had to make hay while the sun still shone.

Luce left us on a high tide of farewell parties and parades soon after we had this chat. His time as Governor was up and signing his proposals about Aden and the Federation was about the last thing he did. Arriving in London on leave shortly afterwards, I found that the Colonial Office had reacted coolly to his proposals. What we 'people in Aden' seemed to forget, Bill (later Sir William) Gorrel-Barnes grumbled, was that we were talking about a base worth millions of pounds, not to mention a prime political and strategic asset. So while there was in general a lot to be said for uniting Aden and the Federation, he really had to make it clear that there could be no question of HMG agreeing to union if it meant jeopardising the security of our base. No doubt converting Aden into a Protectorate state and letting it do a deal with the Federation was a very fair and proper way of getting the two together; but, in all frankness, as far as our base was concerned he could think of nothing more disastrous. It would mean withdrawing British sovreignty from Aden and without British sovreignty what security would we have? When I tried to argue that we would have more under a Treaty than as a Colony I was, predictably, invited to remember King Hussein.

Having put Luce's proposals on one side, Ian McLeod, who was now Colonial Secretary, asked his successor, Sir Charles Johnston, to think things over and let him have a report in a few months time. Johnston's was a curious appointment. He had been our Ambassador in Jordan and anyone in the know should have realised that one might as well put a General in charge of a battleship as make an Ambassador a governor. Ambassadors liaise and occupy themselves with writing reports. Governors rule and spend a large part of their time making decisions. Temperamentally, too, Johnston was not the man for the job. Scholarly, sensitive and gentle, he was handicapped by a crippling shyness against which he had been sustained in the past by the devastating charm of the Russian Princess who was his wife. That had been possible in the narrow circles of diplomatic life. Now he was much more exposed and to much rougher customers. His painful inadequacy did not go unnoticed. Coming away after meeting him for the first time, Sherif Hussein released a villainous laugh, took off his turban, kicked off his shoes and, throwing himself down on a divan, announced that 'Mr Johnston' was just the man we needed. He knew nothing and he knew that he knew nothing. He would do just what he was told.

There he was wrong. We of the federal interest were not the only ones after his ear. We had rivals. Those of the Aden interest were also after it, and poor Johnston rapidly assumed a look of mounting bewilderment as we told him one thing and our rivals told him another. Though they spoke in courteous officialese, Aden's Chief Secretary and its other British Mandarins dismissed any thought of Aden joining the Federation in the near future as premature and, perhaps, in any event, unthinkable. It would hardly be sensible, they said, to consign Aden with its sophisticated Administration and embryo democratic government to what was really a 'tribal bear garden under shotgun rule'. By the worst of bad luck, my efforts to pooh-pooh this were overtaken by a report in one of the local newspapers—which was almost certainly true—that Ahmed, the Fadhli Naib, had hired a gang of thugs to beat up Fadhli malcontents who had taken refuge from him in Aden. And this, its readers were reminded,

Aden and the Federation Unite in the Nick of Time

was the barbaric young Prince who had tied some unfortunate behind a Land Rover and dragged him round the streets. Clearly, a commentator was moved to write that life in the Federation was life not under one but under a dozen Imams.

What was uppermost in the minds of the little band of legislators who were recognised as the Adenis' official spokesmen was not, as it happened, federation but self government for Aden. Once Aden had been given self government, they said, they could start thinking about federation. On this they were all agreed but otherwise they were by no means united; and that was because the old Aden Association to which almost all good Adenis had belonged in the past had split and begun to splinter. As so often in such cases it was personalities, not principles, that had brought about the rupture. In this case, an ultra-ambitious thruster called Hassan Ali Bayumi had trod on the sensitive toes of the doddering old Mohammed Ali Lugman, the self-important newspaper proprietor who was President of the Aden Association. When the split came Lugman sulked off to found a 'People's Constitutional Congress' while Bayumi hoisted the standard of a less pretentiously described affair called the 'National Congress'. Though most former Aden Association members followed Bayumi, Lugman had the advantage of his newspapers which he used to stir up doubt and disaffection in the Bayumi camp. To make a confusing situation still more obscure, many Adenis floated between the two camps, giving their allegiance to neither.

If the federal rulers were to do business with any Adeni, Bayumi was obviously their man, not least because he had known most of them while serving as an Assistant Political Officer in the distant days of Seager. Also, having won golden opinions from Luce for crippling the Trades Unions by getting an Industrial Relations Ordinance enacted, he was a clear favourite to be appointed Aden's first Prime Minister when the time came. We would have no difficulty with Bayumi, the Sherif and Audhali assured me. He was their friend and, having hit the Trades Unions so hard, the Nasserites detested him. No one had more reason to want to get Aden into the Federation without delay. Bayumi did not hesitate to say so: in private, that is to say.

Bayumi did not look too impressive. He was small and scruffy, his hair a tangle of undisciplined curls, his suit crumpled, his shirt rumpled and his tie deplorable. And yet the moment he spoke in that harsh, cigarette-stricken voice of his, you could detect somebody out of the ordinary. He had elan, panache or whatever it is. Of course he wanted to join the Federation, he said. He did not trust HMG and if Aden continued to be a Colony he could see them giving in to Nasserite clamour and handing the Yemeni Trades Unionists the vote. If that happened, Aden would be finished. There was a snag, however: it would take time for Aden and the Federation to agree on terms and they had no time to spare. So what he and his friends—and all Adenis for that matter—were demanding was immediate self government. That would close the door on HMG giving in to the Nasserites and, once that had been done, they could get on with joining the Federation. So, would the federal Rulers back their demand for immediate self government? Throats were noisily cleared, glances exchanged and then the Sherif gave Bayumi a long, penetrating look and said, 'No.' If Aden got self government outside the Federation they would never join it, and that would be a disaster.

There was no bridging the gap. Bayumi and the Adenis insisted on self government for Aden before, the federal Rulers after federation. Aden's Chief Secretary and official establishment, though continuing to mumble reservations about federation, took the Adeni view about self government. I myself hammered on about the overriding importance of getting Aden into the Federation before it was too late but mine was a lone voice and I could hardly expect Johnston to give way to it. He didn't and his report went off to McLeod taking the Adeni line. McLeod would almost certainly accept his recommendations and that would be that unless... Yes, unless the federal Rulers had a chance of nobbling McLeod! They got it soon afterwards when McLeod decided to look in on Aden en route for East Africa in the Spring of 1961.

Johnston was, of course, arranging for them to see him during his visit but where would that get them? He knew what they thought and to be told what he already knew, however vociferously, was unlikely to do them any particular good. What was far more to the point was that he should be made to feel that they were worth backing. Once he felt that, he would listen to them more attentively. The fact was that the Nasserite smear that they were feudal reactionaries and British puppets without any popular support was leaving a mark even, as I had noticed, in the Colonial Office. This had to be corrected and I could think of no better way of doing so than staging a parade-cum-jamboree such as we had laid on for Lennox-Boyd. An excuse for one was easily found in the inauguration of the Federation's capital on a site which it had just acquired in a minor Sheikhdom on Aden's borders. It was a splendid occasion. Despite the Trades Unions' strident demands that 'the People' boycott this 'empty farce' presented by the 'false Federation', 10,000 or more jolly, appreciative souls rolled up and with flags flying and trombones blaring. The federal Rulers' stock stood high. Though hardly a demonstrative person, McLeod was clearly impressed. So far so good. We had realised our first objective.

And very evidently so, for soon after McLeod's departure we were told that the federal Rulers had been invited to visit London as guests of HMG and that I was to accompany them. This was unquestionably a compliment but why was it being paid? Why were the Rulers to be received and treated with such VIP consideration? We soon knew. McLeod's object was to soften them up as a prelude to getting them to agree that Aden should get self government before joining the Federation. A couple of meetings should do the trick, McLeod thought. I doubted it. Well, we would see, he said with the knowing smile of someone who had done quite a few tricks in his time.

Though happy enough with their treatment, the federal Rulers were not bowled over by it and when it came to discussing Aden and the Federation, they stuck like limpets to their view that Aden should get self government only after it had joined the Federation. McLeod, poor man, who was simultaneously carrying on discussions with the West Indies Federation and delegations from Kenya, Uganda and Mauritius, began to lose his sang froid. If they were not prepared to be reasonable, he told me, it would be best for them to go home. He could not go on talking to them indefinitely to no purpose. Let him throw them out if he wished, the Sherif responded when I passed this on. They were not prepared to give in. Though I was with him, I knew that now the choice was between compromise or a fiasco which would do my friends no good. Compromise? What compromise, the Sherif and the others wished to know when I begged them to be sensible. Strident emotional argument followed but, in the end, they agreed to Aden getting 'a measure of constitutional advance' at once provided that it got full self government only after joining the Federation. McLeod all too thankfully agreed. To clinch matters, my federal friends demanded that Johnston and the Adenis be brought to London immediately to subscribe to what had been agreed. They came and they subscribed. Aden seemed to be as good as in the Federation.

Now that the basic differences between the two sides had been settled, McLeod expected Johnston to get full agreement between them within the next few months. A spate of hot and heavy argument after our return to Aden showed that we were not going to float easily along to agreement on a flood stream of mutual good will. In situations such as this I had learned that there was only one way of getting results which was to take the initiative and press relentlessly ahead towards the objective. In other words, we should decide what we thought were the right solutions to the various problems and then press hard on the two sides to accept them. Johnston did not care for this 'arm twisting approach' and, reminding me that he had spent a large part of his working life at negotiating tables, said that the art of successful negotiation was to create a 'climate of agreement'. The way to do that, he explained, was to deal with non-controversial matters first and leave what was more difficult to the end. To ensure that the non-controversial honeymoon was sufficiently prolonged he then set up committees to examine future financial arrangements and the Federal Administration's conditions of service: subjects about which the Adenis and federal Rulers knew nothing and cared even less and which were anyway being most competently handled by experts. Alas, for Johnston's hopes of creating a 'climate of agreement' which would lead to smiling accord on the more contentious subjects, howls of uncompromising argument broke out as soon as they were broached. In the end it was only discreet arm twisting that brought matters to a tardy conclusion. By then it was June 1962. A whole, long year had drifted by since our discussion with McLeod.

That protracted spell in the doldrums had done us no good at all. During it the Federation's stock steadily declined. Nothing, as they say, succeeds like success and, after defeating the Lahej conspiracy and defying Nasser's huffing and puffing to launch their Federation, the federal Rulers had at the outset won an unexpected degree of public interest and support. To keep it, however, they needed more successes and, above all, they needed Aden in the Federation. But, as month after month went by and nothing happened, public interest in the Federation waned, as did public support. Inevitably that gave a boost to the Nasserites, who now claimed they had thwarted the Federation's colonialist plot to kidnap Aden. After a period of depression in 1961 when Nasser's prestige suffered because of Syria's defection from the United Arab Republic, the Nasserites were now back on the top of their form. The year we had thrown away in fatuous and largely play-acting discussions had done them unbelievably well.

Above all else, it gave them time and opportunity to help build a new political party of considerable strength, to which Cairo transferred its support once the South Arabian League had all too evidently flopped. With this support the hard core Trades Unionists, who were the Union office-holders, set up a 'People's Socialist Party' (PSP) as the political wing of the Trades Union movement in apparently flattering imitation of the British Labour Party. Fraternal and cordial relations with leading members of the Labour Party duly followed and before long the PSP came to be recognised as the voice of the South Arabian people in Labour Party circles. The credit for enlisting the Labour Party as an ally was very largely due to its Secretary General, Abdulla al Asnaj, the Trades Unions' Generalissimo. Tubby, pop-eyed and blessed with an engaging smile and silvery tongue, he could speak the language of democratic socialism with just the same facility as he could the intimidatory patois of the professional agitator. He had, Kynaston-Snell told me, been one of his more promising pupils.

At the time, none of us realised how damaging the PSP's rapport with the Labour Party could be. If a few starry-eyed 'lefties' thought al Asnaj and his fellow thugs a little band of angels, who cared? Who cared if soft-headed Labourites asked fatuous Parliamentary questions which were so clearly based on mischievous misinformation? Had we been less naive, we would have known that what was being repeatedly said or implied in Parliament was bound to leave a smear on ourselves and the Federation. We should, also, have known that this would lead to critical interest being taken in our affairs and to critical articles appearing in the Press. And once that happened we should have known that hardly anyone in Britain would be inclined to give us the benefit of any doubt. After Palestine, Suez, Cyprus and other milestones along our retreat from Empire, the British Public no longer had much time for what was left of the Empire and none for imperial trouble spots. Sitting next to some man in the Underground while last home on leave, I had had my first glimpse of the growing disillusionment with Empire when he looked up from his newspaper and muttered, 'Cyprus! Why don't they give the bloody place up?' Now that al Asnaj had so successfully employed the Labour Party to bring Aden and the Federation into the limelight, I had no doubt what men in the Underground, on buses or wherever else would be saying about them.

It was, however, nearer home that the damage first became noticeable. By carefully arranging for newspapers in Aden friendly to the Nasserite cause to quote everything said in Parliament or written in the British Press critical of the Federation, al Asnaj managed to convey a creeping impression that British backing for the Federation might perhaps be fading away. Nothing gave his campaign a bigger boost than the sudden appearance in Aden of two Labour Members of Parliament as the PSP's guests. They were Robert Edwards, General Secretary of the Chemical Workers' Union, and George (later Lord) Thomson, Adviser to the Educational Institute of Scotland. The Man in Aden's Streets was easily persuaded that these eminent personages had come as representatives of Parliament to see what was going on and so when, to oblige their hosts, they dutifully appeared at a mass rally of Trades Unionists and denounced the Federation and what we were trying to do, there was considerable disquiet amongst our federal friends. Was I sure that the British Government was not about to change its mind, the Audhali asked. I was sure. Why then did they let these two do all this mischief? When I produced our democratic attachment to the principle of freedom of speech as an answer, his face clouded over with doubt. No principle, he said, could justify a true friend allowing an ally to be attacked in the way these two had been attacking them.

This was my first experience of anything of the kind and I must admit to being more than a little shocked. Parliamentary opposition was one thing: incitement of what was so obviously revolutionary resistance to our authority was, to my mind, unquestionably another. Was I saying that they should tell the Adenis they agreed with our foolish and indefensible policy, Thomson asked, his hackles rising. I thought it wrong that they should come out here at the expense of our declared enemies and incite them against us, I replied. Surely they realised that what they were doing could lead to violence and loss of life? It could, also, lead to a return to sanity on our part, Edwards snapped. It was only right that the Adenis should know that there were some British who were on their side. There was no arguing with them. They probably thought there was no arguing with me.

As so often in colonial political parties of the dying imperial days, the respectable, democratic face of the PSP which had so much appeal for Labour Party worthies was a mask behind which lurked the political bandit: the dealer in death threats, the hit man, and professional harasser. Even while Edwards and Thomson were being fawned upon and feted, the PSP was engaged in an attempt to bully the Aden Ministers into abandoning their talks with the Federation. They were assailed by jeering schoolboys, stones peppered their windows and front doors: almost all received death threats. Serious violence was fortunately limited to an assassination attempt on Aden's one Indian Minister, an imperturbable lawyer called Joshi, and to the wrecking of a printing press owned by Abdulrahman Girgirah, a Minister of unusual intellect and urbanity. Greatly to their credit, the Aden ministers stood up to this campaign of intimidation surprisingly well. Two ministers who were in any event no friends of his resigned but, thanks to his pugnacious tenacity, Bayumi kept the rest of his colleagues in line. And so the PSP failed in their objective. The Aden–Federation talks were not abandoned.

Save for two or three points of what nobody thought of any great importance, all was agreed and so off we all went to London to get the Colonial Secretary's blessing. Thinking that we would be seeing Reginald Maudling, who had taken over from McLeod the previous October, we found instead that we were to see Duncan Sandys who had become Colonial Secretary overnight as a result of the cabinet reshuffle which was to be known as Harold MacMillan's 'Night of the Long Knives'. At a time when the Colonial problems were at their most vexatious and when continuity at ministerial level was of overriding importance, we had four Colonial Secretaries—Lennox-Boyd, McLeod, Maudling and now Sandys—in less than three years. Hardly the way to run an Empire.

Nevertheless, Sandys' appointment was good news. His bulldog demeanour and confident, gruff expressions of support when he visited us as Minister of Defence during the troubles of 1957 had greatly impressed our federal friends. So, on hearing that he was to be in the Chair, they were all sparkling eyes and 'praise be's'. It was, however, with diminishing enthusiasm, if not respect, that they came to look on him once our talks had begun for, greatly to their dismay, he subjected them to a process he called 'negotiation by exhaustion'. By talking all day and then, after a brief break for dinner, keeping them up to three, four and, on one occasion, five o'clock in the morning, he hoped to get them to capitulate and agree. The federal team were no strangers to late hours but they had strong views about how to spend them and having, in almost every case, made elaborate arrangements for evenings of sybaritic delights, they were not at all pleased to be summoned back to spend them at the negotiating table. What accounted for the Minister's uncivilised behaviour, the Sherif wished to know. Had he no wife at home to amuse him? Told that this was his way of trying to exhaust him and his friends into agreement, the Sherif's eyes became incandescent with mischief and when evening came he and his friends resorted to every conceivable trick to protract the discussions until, eventually, Sandys said that he thought it was about time to adjourn. What? Adjourn? The Sheriff clamoured surprise. Why, the cool of the morning had come! But still, he conceded with a shrug of his shoulders, if the Minister was feeling tired... Sandys had met his match. There were no more late nights after that.

Agreement between the federal and Aden ministers was eventually reached, albeit with rather more difficulty than we had expected, and we returned to Aden for the final formalities: the Agreements ratification by the Federal and Aden Legislative Councils. Since the Federal Council were bound to ratify it, the PSP's only hope of aborting the operation was to intimidate the Legislative Council into refusing to ratify and, predictably, they did everything in their power to do so. A general strike was called and every weapon in the ugly armoury of intimidation was used with ruthless abandon to bully the unfortunate Councillors into voting 'No'. Once again, the indefatigable Bayumi rose to the occasion and, despite a tumultuous riot outside the Legislature when the time came to vote, he got them to vote 'Yes'. Once again the PSP had failed. Once again, Bayumi had won through.

So captivated had we all been by this drama that, with the exception of the Sherif, we had barely noticed what was going on in the Yemen and what was going on in the Yemen was, by any standards, exceptional. One week before the Aden Legislature ratified the Agreement, that modern 'BlueBeard', the Imam Ahmed, who survived so many crises, coups and attempts on his life, had died respectably of natural causes. As custom prescribed, the Crown Prince, Mohammed al Badr, succeeded him and, according to the Sherif, the moment had now come for 'our friends' in the Yemen to strike before al Badr picked up the telephone and called in his Egyptian friends. Any moment now, the Sherif assured me, al Badr would be toppled; and, sure enough, on the very day after the vote had been taken in the Aden Legislative Council, the Sherif appeared before me at the crack of dawn to say that all his dreams had come true. There had been a revolution in the Yemen and al Badr had been eliminated. 'Our friends', he declared with great solemnity, had taken over. It was only later in the morning that we heard what had really happened. The Egyptians had stabbed their admirer, al Badr, in the back and got their puppet, Sellal, the Army Commander, to take over. From now on we were to have the Egyptians as our neighbours.

12

CIVIL WAR IN THE YEMEN
TEMPERS THE NASSERITE THREATS

Shortly after the Nasserite coup in the Yemen, I dined at the Hollywood-style palazzo of Aden's multi-millionaire, Peter Besse, and Christianne, his eye- and ear-catching French wife. Peter's father, Antonin—immortalised in Evelyn Waugh's Monsieur Blanc—had been far and away the greatest beneficiary of the peace and good order we had brought to this tip of turbulent South Arabia and he had shown his appreciation, towards the end of his life, by founding and funding St Antony's College at Oxford. Not that he was a sentimentalist. When asked whether his loyalties lay with the Allies or the collaborationist French Government set up at Vichy after the fall of France in 1940, he had replied firmly and without equivocation that he was 'pro-Besse'. He was, in other words, an opportunist and so I imagine was his son when he told me how misguided we were to back an obvious loser in the outdated feudal gang we had put in charge of the Federation. Hadn't we eyes in our head, his wife shrilled. Couldn't we see that the Yemeni Revolution and its Egyptian friends were going to liberate Arabia from the curse of mediaevalism and that there was nothing we could do to stop it? A fellow guest, Abdulqawi Makawee, whose family had been solid, pro-British pillars of the old Aden Association, nodded vigorous agreement.

Les Besses were only echoing what journalists, politicians and Middle East voyeurs almost everywhere were saying. Convinced that revolutionary Arab nationalism of the Nasserite kind was unstoppable, they had written off every 'tinpot' regime in South Arabia, Oman and the Gulf, not to mention the Yemeni Imamate. The PSP were, of course, in ecstasies over the Yemen and their leaders had lost no time in hurrying off there to make contact with the infant Republic's leaders, Abdulla Sallal, the mutinous Army Commander who had become Prime Minister, and his smooth and sophisticated Deputy, the German-educated and Egyptian-bred Dr Abdulrahman Beidhani. Even when news came through that the new Imam, Mohammed al Badr, was not the corpse he had been reported to be but was rallying his supporters to fight back, no one took it too seriously. It was fanciful nonsense, no doubt fed to me by Sherif Hussein, the American Consul said. He could tell me for sure that the Imam was holed up in some cave with barely fifty supporters and he would be a refugee with the Saudis inside the month. Our Foreign Office minder, John Bushell, having said much the same, warned us that we would do best to face facts and not indulge in fantasy.

It was incontestable that Egyptian troops, guns and armour were pouring into the Yemen. If the Imam was on the run, what possible need could there be for them? He would tell me, the Sherif grinned. The tribes were flocking to the Imam and, without Egyptian troops, Sallal's 'half piastre republic' would not last a minute. He was exaggerating, of course—or was he? The Imam might not have the guns and tanks of the Egyptians but, the Sherif pointed out, the Saudis had given him enough money to buy up the Yemen and, as I well knew, that was what won tribal support. Bushell was not impressed. The tribes would no doubt take the cash, he said, but once they knew that they would be up against trained and heavily armed Egyptian troops, they would quickly fade away. This so-called Royalist Counterrevolution was nothing more than Sherifian wishful thinking; and, as the expression on his face made plain, it was only gullible idiots like myself who took it seriously.

The principal source of Bushell's—and the Foreign Office's—information about the Yemen was our Charge d'affaires, Christopher Gandy. He was a gaunt, scholarly recluse whom I remembered as a stubborn opponent of the philistine aspects of the regime at Marlborough and in his demeanour towards us in Aden I had thought I could detect a suspicion that our colonial regime was little better. Always insistent that the Yemenis were far more reasonable and straightforward than we cared to make out, he was once goaded by a sudden furore over the caning of some riotous prisoners in Aden to protest that all his efforts to win Yemeni good will had been ruined by 'this deplorable outburst of Public School spirit'. If we said one thing, it seemed he would have to say the opposite. When we reported that the Royalists dominated Northern and Eastern Yemen, he insisted that they were only to be found in very small numbers on the furthest fringe of the country.

None of this seemed important until Johnston revealed that the Americans, under strong pressure from the Egyptians, were urging us to give the Yemen Arab Republic formal recognition and that the Foreign Office were urging HMG to agree. This could only mean that the Egyptians were in trouble and hoped to deflate Royalist and Saudi morale by getting us and the Americans to recognise and, implicitly, give our blessing to the Republic. If we did so, at this critical moment, it could destroy the Federation. It would be seen everywhere as a sign of capitulation on our part and would be interpreted as an indication that we were contemplating withdrawal. He did not think it would be quite as bad as that, Johnston said, for the Americans did not intend to give recognition without getting something in return. What they were demanding was an Egyptian withdrawal from the Yemen and a Republican declaration that the Republic had no claims on Aden or South Arabia. That was their price for recognition. Payable before or after recognition? 'Well, after,' Johnston said a little uneasily. That meant 'never'. The Americans recognised the Republic but neither the Egyptians nor the Republic ever honoured their undertaking.

Whatever we and our federal friends might think, Johnston said in his best bedside manner, it seemed almost certain that HMG would be recognising the Republic. Quite apart from American pressure, it was a fact that the Republican Government was more or less in control of the country and in recognising a Government that was what mattered, not its complexion. No doubt the Royalists were making a nuisance of themselves, laying an odd ambush here and there, but that was hardly the same thing. Sandys, whom I happened to see on a quick visit to London, knew my views and I knew that I could count on him to argue our case in the corridors of Whitehall. Even so, when it came to the crunch, it seemed hardly likely that our new Prime Minister, Sir Alec Douglas-Home, would support him against the Foreign Office over which he himself had only recently presided. Short of a miracle, I could see nothing but disaster ahead.

And then the miracle happened. Out of the blue, there suddenly appeared a modern edition of John Buchan's Richard Hannay. It was an old friend of mine, Billy (Colonel Neil) McLean, who had fought as a guerilla in Ethiopia with Wingate, with the Albanian resistance and with Heaven knows who in the Far East. He was now an MP and, distrusting the Foreign Office assessment of the situation in the Yemen, he had come out to see what was going on. Could I help? Willingly! I sent him off to Beihan to see the Sherif for what I hoped would be [a] couple of informative days. I should have known Billy better. Once in Beihan he was across the frontier and off on a tour of North and Eastern Yemen under Royalist auspices. On his return, he confirmed that, with the exception of some of the larger towns, the country was entirely in Royalist hands. He reported this directly to the Prime Minister. The decision was taken not to recognise the Republic.

By then everyone knew that the Egyptians must be in difficulties, if only because Egyptian troops and military hardware were still pouring into the Yemen. Nasserite spirits in Aden, so high only a few months before, began to sag and, in desperation, the PSP resorted to its old weapon: strike action. Though Aden had otherwise been self-governing on entering the Federation, HMG had insisted on internal security remaining in our hands which meant, of course, Johnston's hands. What did he intend to do about the situation, Bayumi (who was now Aden's Chief or Prime Minister) wished to know. Was he going to let schoolboys like al Asnaj reduce Aden to anarchy, the Audhali asked in chillingly challenging tones. Poor Johnston, who had been brought up in a Foreign Office tradition which abhorred confrontation, wriggled and writhed looking for ways out of taking tough and, as Foreign Office thinking invariably dubbed it, 'hamfisted' action. There was, in fact, no way out. He had a choice between winning Foreign Office favour by prevaricating or appeasing Bayumi and the federal Rulers by being tough. Prudently, he was tough. Al Asnaj and others were gaoled. Order was promptly restored.

Thwarted in Aden and, with their Egyptian allies bogged down in the Yemen, the PSP switched their efforts to enlisting international help in their struggle. Tailor-made for their purpose was the United Nations' so-called Committee of Twenty Four whose function was to harry the Colonial powers into giving their Colonies independence, the Soviet Union of course excepted. Reports in the newspapers of the Committee's predictable views on the Federation and even more of the appearance before them of the PSP stung Bayumi and the federal Rulers into a state of peevish protest. How was it that a political party without a single representative in Aden's Legislative Council was able to lecture the United Nations when the Federal Government, which was the lawful government of the country, was not? Was it conceivable that any government, which had been insulted and attacked as the Federal Government had been, would remain silent? If we really intended the Federal Government to win any respect, Bayumi fulminated, we should let it behave like a government. We should let it state its case in New York. Rather to my surprise, the Colonial and Foreign Office agreed. The polished and presentable Mohammed Farid was chosen as the Federation's spokesman and I was invited to accompany him.

It could be said that our visit to the Committee of Twenty Four was so much wasted time. Whether any of the Twenty Four ever listened to Mohammed Farid's apologia for the Federation I cannot say but, to judge by their speeches, almost always haltingly delivered read out from wads of typescript, they could not have heard or understood a word of it. Nevertheless, the reports of Mohammed Farid's appearance before this waxwork show gave the federal ministers some gratification. Nor did Mohammed and I go entirely unrewarded. Having listened to Sabhi and Shekan al Habshi, the PSP and South Arabian League representatives, vilify us, the Federation and the federal Rulers in the most extravagant terms to the Committee, we all foregathered later for a most amicable chat over lunch. As we got up to go, Shekan wondered whether they might ask a small favour. The fact of the matter was that sitting around New York was a very expensive business and the allowances the Egyptians were paying them were totally inadequate. Could we lend them some money? Mohammed was a gentleman, and produced the money with a smile.

Farcical the Committee of the Twenty Four might be, but it provided a reminder that we were in fact committed to decolonise and that, if we made no positive move to bring about South Arabian independence, we would find ourselves in a progressively embarrassing position. That was one good reason for getting a move on towards independence. Another, far more cogent, was, as always, the fact that time was not on our side. The Royalists had done surprisingly well but, with 20 to 30,000 Egyptian troops now deployed in the Yemen, they would soon be contained and

Civil War in the Yemen Tempers the Nasserite Threats

when they were, one could be sure that the Egyptians would turn their attention to ourselves. Crawford (later Sir Stewart), the cold, piscine-eyed custodian of Arabian affairs at the Foreign Office, did not agree. With twenty years reconstruction work ahead of them in the Yemen, they would never have the time, he was glad to tell me. I could not believe what I was hearing! Anyone in any coffee shop from Kuwait to Beirut could have told him that Egypt's sole interest in the Yemen was to use it as a springboard to take over the Arabian Peninsula and its oil. We had to get an independent Federation of South Arabia set up before the Egyptians were able to do us too much damage.

I made this point to Sandys when I came home on leave in the Summer of 1963 and got a blank face for an answer. We would have to think about that, he said, adding that he would do some thinking and then come out to Aden and discuss matters in a few weeks' time. In the meantime he had news for me. Johnston wanted to be relieved of his appointment because his wife was ill, so would I take over as Governor? It was unusual for a Governor to come from the Service of the territory to which he was appointed and I could see that, as an old and intimate friend of the federal Rulers, my impartiality as between Aden and the Federation would always be questioned. Nevertheless, I naturally accepted. Here was my chance of finishing the job I had started when I first put pen to paper about federation.

Shortly before returning to Aden I had an audience with the Queen who told me that the one person she was never likely to forget was Ali Abdulkarim of Lahej. Having met him during her visit to Aden, she said, she invited him to call on her when he was next in London. He duly did so and had no sooner set eyes on her than he exclaimed, 'How very fat you have become!' Accustomed though she was to finding a suitable riposte to the remarks made by the thousand and one individuals she [met], she had to confess that on this occasion she was reduced to total tongue-tied silence. Ali, let it be explained, was not trying to insult the Queen. He was merely saying what Arabs say to each other when they wish to say how well they are looking. I was sorry that Ali and I were no longer on speaking terms. He would have enjoyed this little anecdote.

13

FINIS

No one out on the terrace watching the guests wandering about and listening to the band of the Federal Army would have imagined that we were sitting on what Seager would have called a powder keg. The scene was almost Edwardian Colonial pomp and circumstance with Government House in the background. Even Fadhl bin Ali, the Sultan of Lahej who was now Federal Minister of Defence, was sufficiently unconcerned to ask whether the band would play his favourite British tune. It was called 'Bollocks', he said. The band duly obliged by playing 'Colonel Bogey'. We seemed to be ten thousand miles away from trouble yet there it was—right on our door step.

While I had been away on leave, the Nasserite threat from the Yemen had worsened. The Egyptian Army of Occupation had increased to a staggering 30,000. Egyptian Intelligence and 'dirty tricks' units had moved in and were training young South Arabians in terrorist techniques and tactics: Nasser had publicly declared that he was going to throw us out of Arabia and was calling upon all South Arabians to help him do so by rising up in revolt. Egypt and the Yemeni Republicans were in a state of undeclared war with us: which meant that they felt free to hit us as hard and as often as they liked but, if we retaliated, they could squeal 'foul play'. No matter, we could easily hit back with the assurance that, if we did, we had it in our power to knock them for six. This was an Afghan situation and we had only to provide the Royalists with advisers and sophisticated weaponry to have the Egyptians legging it for home before you could say 'Yemen Arab Republic'. Why didn't we?

Because the Foreign Office decided to put their trust in the manifest nonsense that was American policy and were desperately anxious to avoid anything which could be said to upset it. Why, only God could possibly know. Anyone with an ounce of intelligence should have known that, with the Arabian Peninsula as their target, the Egyptians would never willingly withdraw from the Yemen. Having said that they would go if the Americans recognised the Republic, they had predictably found excuses for not doing so. Ah, yes, it was argued, but they would if only the Americans stopped their Saudi proteges from supplying the Royalists with arms and cash. The Americans duly stopped—but not an Egyptian left the country. By then, one really might have thought that the Foreign Office would have realised that no amount of American appeasement would get the Egyptians out and that, if we wanted results, we would have take action. But no! If we did, it was argued, the Russians might intervene in support of the Egyptians. And so, to put it plainly, Foreign Office policy was to let the Egyptians clobber us and do nothing.

Our federal friends voiced querulous incomprehension as the Egyptians took advantage of the withdrawal of Saudi aid from the Royalists to extend their areas of control. Resentful that we had done nothing to preempt the Egyptian take-over which they had been predicting while the Imam Ahmed was still alive, they were more perplexed than indignant at our inactivity. Why didn't we do what any government in the world would do and what they would certainly be doing if they had been independent? Well, it was like this, the Americans... The Americans! It meant nothing to them if the Egyptians took over South Arabia and, in any event, what had they got to do with it? It was with us not the Americans that the Federation had a treaty and we were falling down on our clear duty to protect them. Why? Was it, perhaps, that we were losing interest in South Arabia and preparing to pull out if the going got too rough? Now and again I could see little flashes of suspicion in their eyes. Were we turning into fair-weather friends? That was what they were probably asking themselves. In their place, that is what I would have been doing.

Sandys, I knew, felt as I did but, having had to accept that he would be foolish to take the Foreign Office on again so soon over a subject so clearly within their competence, there was nothing for it but to go full steam ahead for independence. On the constitutional side there was nothing I could do until Sandys came out to talk matters over but there was a great deal we needed to do to give the Federation the look of something real and worthwhile. The Federation? Did I want to know the truth about it, I was asked one day by Hussein Nasser al Buasi, the most candid of our Assistant Political Officers. He would tell me. The Rulers and bigwigs were richer, a few schoolboys had got jobs in the new Federal Ministries and the Federal Army and Federal Guards had received more pay. As for everybody else, the Federation had given them nothing and so it meant nothing to them. That was the naked and disagreeable truth. The need to do something that would capture the public's imagination and respect was as obvious as it was urgent. We needed to make a splash with road projects, agricultural schemes, hospitals, schools and so on. The Federation, that is to say, needed an immediate grant of £15–£20,000,000 on the table. Yes, it was a lot of money but no more than we had been giving Jordan in the past and, anyway, if we wanted to secure our base that was what I believed we would have to pay up to do so. I drafted my proposals and fired them off to the Colonial Office, calling urgently for immediate action.

There was, needless to say, no response. Worse still, Sandys, who had got himself entangled in a multiplicity of colonial crises, kept on postponing his visit to talk matters over. It was difficult to believe but here we were, engaged in a race against time, standing absolutely still. Eventually, after four months of frenetic telexing, I was asked to come to London and see Sandys there. Even so, I was there for more than a week before I was able to get past his office door; and when I did, it was to find a man wan and red-eyed through self-imposed exhaustion. Sandys was a war horse who never spared himself but were those long, torturing hours he inflicted on himself and his unfortunate staff really necessary? Watching him at one, two or three o'clock in the morning with the top mandarins of the Colonial Office slumped around his desk, I could see why so little took so long to be done. Instead of using these highly paid professionals to dig around and serve drafts up to him, he would plod slowly around his office and dictate drafts to them. 'Have you got a pencil, Poynton?' he would ask his Permanent Under Secretary of State. 'Well, take this down.... Now read it back.... H'm, delete the last sentence and...' And so he would go on into the small hours while the other pillars of the Colonial Office sat around wearily twiddling their thumbs. 'C'est magnifique mais...'

Nevertheless, I was grateful to Sandys, for he bulldozed his way steadily past all his officials' objections to our ceding sovreignty in Aden and giving the Federation independence. And so, thanks to him, I was sent back to Aden with all that I could have wished. I was to tell the Aden and federal ministers that we were prepared to give the Federation independence, subject to our negotiating satisfactory arrangements for our military base, and then I was to return to London with them for constitutional discussions. Here, at last, after years of difficulties and setbacks, we were almost at the end of the road. What I and my Political Officers had been working for for so long was at last within reach.

Though ever vociferous in their demands for an end to our colonial regime, the Nasserites immediately flew into fits of outrage and protest once it got out that we were planning to give the Federation independence. I thought he would have been pleased to hear that we had decided to put an end to our colonial presence, I said to al Asnaj when he came waddling in to make his protest. Oh, no, they did not object to independence, he assured me, but they wanted independence in a democratic form: which was to say that they wanted elections throughout the Federation for a new, democratic Federal Government as a preliminary to independence. And who would conduct the elections outside Aden, I asked, having first said that, with nothing more than a staff of a dozen Political Officers who were serving as advisers to the Rulers, it was something that we could not possibly undertake even if the tribal areas had been havens of docility, which they were not. 'A People's Committee' would be responsible, he grinned. And who would appoint the Committee? Why, representatives of popular movements such as the TUC and PSP!

That this chubby, tubby little man was out to sabotage our London talks by raising havoc in Aden was immediately apparent when the Forces Local Employers' Union went on strike for patently trumped-up reasons. What he clearly intended was to provoke us into arresting the strike leaders for acting illegally under the Industrial Relations Ordinance and then set up a monster agitation against us for depriving the People of their democratic rights as a prelude to a General Strike and rampant disorder. If the strikes were not to spread with increasing clamour and commotion, I had to put a stop to them but not as al Asnaj was hoping. Since the strikers were almost all Yemeni immigrants and technically illegal immigrants, I had no difficulty in deciding what to do. I had them

The Deluge

picked up by the Police and dumped by the lorry load over the frontier. We had no more strikes after that.

And so, with Aden serene, the ministers and I were all set to leave for London. Quite why, I cannot say, but just before leaving for the airport I decided to give al Asnaj a ring to say that I was off and hoped to tell him what had happened when I returned. The telephone was answered as usual by his old mother. Abdulla had gone out early that morning, she said, and she had no idea when he would be back. Odd, I thought. He was a notorious sluggard-a-bed who was always tucked up asleep when I telephoned in the earlyish morning. What had got him out of bed so early on this particular day? Maybe I would find him waiting for me at the head of some demonstration when I reached the airport. But no, there was not a sign of him. Waiting there to bid me and the federal ministers farewell was a long line of Arab notables, high officials and others drawn up in front of the airport building. Walking along it shaking hands I was suddenly surprised to hear a hiss and then at my feet was an object exuding smoke. Before I could figure out what this was I was grabbed by George Henderson, one of my Political Officers, and rushed away. An explosion followed but George refused to stop. Bundling me into a taxi outside the airport, he screamed at the driver to get away as fast as he could. We had only been gone a few minutes when George slumped forward, the back of his shirt soaked with blood. He had been hit in the back by a piece of shrapnel which had entered his lung. He died ten days later.

George was one of our stalwarts and his death deprived us of a 'laughing cavalier' who could always be trusted to keep his head and sense of humour when things were at their worst. Of his many memorable exploits, one was an epic. While serving in Aulaqi country he wanted to travel from Said, the Upper Aulaqi sheikh's capital, to Nisab, the seat of the Sultan. Because the road between them was not thought dangerous, he dispensed with the normal escort. News of his intentions, however, had leaked out, and, on approaching the one pass on his route, he was ambushed by a gang of sixteen tribal tearaways. Calculating that there was no long-term future in remaining in the ditch where he and his driver had holed up after their Landrover had overturned, he told his driver to give him covering fire and then raced across the open plain before him and made the dead ground at the foot of the hill where the Enemy were perched. Climbing up, over and behind them, he sent sixteen rattled rascals legging it for their lives a few minutes later. For that he won a George Medal. For saving my life, he was given a Bar, posthumously.

As soon as I had got myself back from the airport, I had to decide what to do. I was, of course, emotionally upset. My wife, who had been with me, would certainly have been killed by the grenade had an unfortunate Indian lady, who later died of wounds, not been standing in front of her. And then, apart from George, there were other friends who had been wounded. Nor was a minor shrapnel wound in my own case calculated to improve my sense of cold-blooded impartiality. But, in a situation of this kind, one cannot afford to be taken for a ride by the emotions. One had to be pragmatic and do what seemed most likely to get the right results. So what were we to do? As I saw it, we could declare a state of emergency and round up the Nasserite Opposition or we could make disapproving noises and bide our time. I called my advisers together and asked what they thought. They all plumped for a state of emergency. In that event, I said there could be no half measures. All bad hats would have to be rounded up. They agreed and, within a couple of days, we had almost all the leaders of the Nasserite opposition behind bars. The Colonial Office let out a wail about not having been consulted before we took this 'controversial step'. Sandys, bless him, sent assurances of his 'fullest support'. 'The Media', you may be sure, took a lofty, disapproving view of what we were doing. It was, they declared, 'short sighted', 'ham fisted', 'counter-productive' and so on. In the event, we only had two further quasi-terrorist incidents in Aden during the next twelve months. Not that the Media ever cared to mention that fact.

It was only when I had dealt with the crisis that I realised the real danger from that grenade. HMG had been thrown into a panic. Independence, giving up sovreignty in Aden—this was not the time, I was told. I could forget about constitutional talks and get down to countering terrorism. And so al Asnaj had got what he wanted after all. He had, in fact, got more than he had probably expected, for that grenade was world news and so were our reactions to it. Orchestrated by the Egyptians and their Third World allies, the United Nations, every conceivable radical and socialist government or body including the inevitable rump of British Labour Parliamentarians and Trades Unionists, passed resolutions and issued declarations demanding an end to our state of emergency, the release of all political prisoners and democratic elections throughout the Federation. At first every body or individual issuing these demands was kind enough to address me directly, usually adding in intimidating tones that I would be held 'personally' responsible for not complying with them. I cannot pretend that all this was easily shrugged off. The sheer volume of their communications alone gave one a sense of chilling isolation and friendlessness which was further deepened by the venom of Cairo's propagandists and, to my dismay, by an increasingly critical and unfriendly British Press.

This adroitly concerted campaign was clearly calculated to breach our Ministers' morale and, by the worst of all possible luck, when we needed that tough and redoubtable leader most, we no longer had Bayumi. Too many cigarettes, too much strain, too much of this and too little of that had had their effect and, still only in his forties, that invaluable little man had passed away. His place had been taken by a face behind huge dark glasses called Seyid Zern Bahroun, a merchant who, in the Besse tradition, was clearly pro-Bahroun. Professing agreement with everything we were doing, he was for ever coming up with objections and criticisms faithfully echoing the Nasserite opposition. He was playing it both ways, and so in time were most of the Aden ministers.

Since Aden was all tranquillity I could see no reason why we could not now go ahead with the constitutional conference which had been interrupted by the grenade incident. I had, I telexed Sandys, repeatedly stated that, to secure the base, we needed money and rapid advance to independence. And yet I had been given no money, nor had there been any advance to independence. My badgering eventually earned me none too enthusiastic an invitation to come to London for talks and since Lord Mountbatten, who was then Chief of Defence Staff, was passing through Aden, I got a lift from him in his personal aeroplane. Since he received copies of all correspondence between myself and Sandys, he knew my views and how I was placed. The difficulty, he explained, was that the Government wanted to be 'firm' and giving the Federation independence did not fit in with their ideas of firmness. He himself agreed with me about independence and suggested that I should try and get the Ministry of Defence involved on my side. I could not see how I could do that. Perhaps he could set the ball rolling by getting me to come to a Chiefs of Staff meeting while I was in London. He was as good as his word. I received the invitation and, on the day before the meeting, an urgent telephone call from him to come over to the Ministry of Defence. He wanted me to agree to the Minutes of the Meeting. What meeting? Why, the Chiefs of Staffs' Meeting to be held the next day! I did as asked and the next day Mountbatten deftly steered the discussions to give him Minutes as he had drafted them the day before. It was an impressive performance.

Whether that helped my cause I cannot say. One brief chat with Sandys, however, was enough to tell me that I needed all the help I could get and I needed it fast. Looking wearier than ever, Sandys grunted despondently as I said my piece. There was no need for me to preach to the converted, he said. He knew my views, he agreed with them but he could not get the Government to agree and that was all there was to it. I spluttered disappointment. 'Very well, then,' he said at last, 'I have failed. See what you can do.' I got my chance at a Meeting of the Cabinet Defence Committee in the Cabinet Room at 10 Downing Street. Since the Committee was busy discussing some other subject at the time of my arrival, I was asked to take a seat in the corridor outside. I did so for some considerable time and eventually entered the Cabinet Room only when the Ministers present were beginning to look at their watches and mumble about arrangements for luncheon. Sir Alec Douglas-Home, the Prime Minister, listened with polite attention but I could see that very few of the others present were taking what I had to say too seriously. Like Sandys, I knew that I had failed to make my point. Nor did I get so much as a glimpse of a green light when I had a drink in private with Sir Alec later that evening.

This was worrying but it was by no means my only problem. One requiring urgent treatment exploded on my return in the form of an uprising in the wild tribal region between Dhala and Lahej known as Radfan. This was nothing new. We had had uprisings there in plenty before but, apart from interfering with traffic on the Aden–Dhala road, they had never done us any serious harm. Though the Egyptians had, on this occasion, sent the Radfanis into battle better armed than before, I could see no reason why we could not deal with them as we had very effectively in the past by using the 'goat technique' which we had first used against Mohammed Bubakr's rebel gangs with such success. I put it to the Commander-in-Chief, General (later Sir Charles) Harrington. 'You want us to shoot up goats from the air?' he asked with courteous incredulity. He clearly thought I was talking nonsense, as did everyone else in the military establishment for there was not one among them who had ever heard about the 'goat technique' before. Those who were with us when we last used it had long since been posted elsewhere.

Having dextrously referred my request to the Ministry of Defence and been told that goat shooting was out, Harrington said we would have to deal with the situation militarily. We could not have these scallywags interfering with our communications to Dhala. Like the Egyptians next door in the Yemen, he clearly had no idea of the hazards and difficulties of using slow-footed regular troops against elusive tribesmen in their own country. A long drawn-out military operation was the last thing I wanted. Set-backs, disasters and casualties were inevitable: success improbable. To mount full-scale military operations against two hundred or so tribal guerillas would convert them into heroes overnight, the Egyptians would lavish even more arms on them and tribesmen from all over the place would then be likely to join in the fun. I could think of nothing more likely to get us critical and damaging publicity when it was least wanted. Fadhli bin Ali, the Minister of Defence, and the Audhali who was Minister of Internal Security, fully agreed but we got nowhere. Even Sandys was unmoved. And so the costly and largely unnecessary Radfan Operations were launched and all our worst fears were subsequently realised.

In the midst of our tribulations, while the Egyptians were pouring arms into Radfan and both Cairo and San'a were exhorting South Arabians to rise up and revolt, a Lady Birdwood descended on me. She was the representative of a pro-Royalist body called 'The Yemen Relief Organisation' and she had flown in from London with a 'plane load of medical supplies for the Yemeni Royalists. What she now wanted was permission to fly on and deposit her cargo at Beihan for removal into the Yemen. To poor Lady Birdwood's clamorous disgust, I had to refuse her permission. I had just received a telex from the Foreign Office saying that she was on no account to be allowed to go on to Beihan. It might look as if we were interfering in the Yemen. A message to say that Egyptian aircraft with Yemeni markings had just attacked a Beihan outpost arrived soon afterwards. What were we supposed to do now? Turn the other cheek?

The Beihan incident was the first of several and, with the Sherif thundering protest and outrage, the Federal Government formally demanded effective protection against Yemeni/Egyptian attack and, by that, they meant retaliation. They were quite right. Short of ringing our frontier posts with anti-aircraft guns and airfields with fighters on the alert, retaliation was the only form of defence available to us. After what I understood to have been a lively debate between the Foreign and Colonial Offices and Ministry of Defence in London, we at last got clearance to hit back at the Yemeni fort at Harib in the event of a further attack. This duly took place and the fort at Harib was destroyed. Judging by the subsequent uproar in New York, London and Heaven knows where, one might have thought we had flattened some open city and massacred thousands of innocents. There was an outcry even in the British Press which began questioning the worth of so-called allies like the Sherif if they were going to let us in for major international headaches. The attack on Harib put an end to any further air attacks but the price we had to pay for it was immeasurable.

All these commotions brought Sandys hurrying out, square-chinned and bulldoggish, to bolster our friends' morale. We needed his support, I said, but we also needed to know where we were going. Had HMG any policy at all? 'Ah, yes!' he said in a rather offhand way, that reminded him. Would I get the Aden and federal ministers ready to come to London for a constitutional conference in July? For reasons unknown, HMG had changed their mind. Was it Mountbatten? Was it Sandys? Or was it, perhaps, even myself that had done the trick? Who cared, it had been done. The Aden ministers were by this time beginning to look decidedly punch drunk. International and particularly Arab vilification of the Federation was beginning to have its effect and the arrival of one critical British Labour MP after another, by courtesy of al Asnaj, had not helped. In the event, two Aden ministers scuttled off, one saying quite openly that it would be mad to stay on and later be sent to the gallows as a traitor to Arabism. Why the rest did not follow suit I could not imagine, until the Sherif opened my eyes. There was nothing these shop-keepers counted more than power, he explained, so while there was still a good chance that the Federation would become independent they did not want to abandon it. At the same time, by criticising it and being uncooperative, they hoped to keep their lines open with the Nasserites. They were a shameless lot, he concluded. They were loyal only to their bellies.

Nothing on this occasion interfered with our departure and I and my team of ministers arrived safe and sound in London where, somewhat to our surprise, we found that al Asnaj had mobilised a few hundred Arabs and left wing Europeans to march through Hyde Park bellowing damnation to the Federation. The Adenis found this a little disturbing but cheered up when red carpets began to be rolled out in our honour. It became apparent that these were to be no ordinary talks. This was to be a constitutional conference and its venue was to be that great prestigious palace overlooking the Mall known as Lancaster House. To set the tone for their visit, a Grade I dinner was laid on for them at Carlton Gardens at which Sandys made a speech which none of the Arabs understood. It included a long drawn-out story about how someone had stuffed a kipper up the exhaust of his car when he had been an undergraduate at Oxford. 'What's a kipper?' Bahroun and others asked me as we rose to go.

Elaborate arrangements had been made for the opening of the Conference. Platoons of reporters had been invited to attend and it had been arranged that Sandys would make a speech welcoming the visitors followed by a suitable reply from the current Chairman of the Federal Supreme Council. On arriving at Lancaster House ten minutes or so before the curtain was due to go up, I was surprised to find the Aden and federal ministers locked in violent argument. Bahroun was insisting that, as the 'head of a Council', he would be making a reply to Sandys in addition to the Chairman of the Federal Supreme Council and, moreover, that he intended to say what he thought of the Federation which was that it had been 'born paralysed'. If he insisted on doing this, the federal ministers declared, they would boycott the meeting. That was up to them, Bahroun said, giving them a leer through his dark glasses. They were still at it when Sandys arrived to open the Conference. I managed to waylay him before he presented himself to the reporters and others in the Conference Hall and explained what had happened. Grim-faced, he looked at his watch and said that he would give me five minutes to get things straight but not a second more. By some miracle, I did.

After such an unpromising start, it was perhaps a little surprising that the Conference should eventually have ended in accord. It was agreed that 'as soon as practicable after the forthcoming elections in Aden, the British Government would convene a meeting of representatives of Aden and the federal states to agree arrangements for the transfer of sovreignty in Aden.' It was also agreed that a date for independence would be fixed by the British and Federal Governments. Agreement on this was not reached easily. The Adenis and federal ministers argued obstinately away at cross purposes while Sandys ground remorselessly on, intent as always on collective exhaustion. All this was predictable. What was not was the behaviour of Ahmed bin Abdulla, the former Naib who had recently become Fadhli Sultan. Whatever was agreed he promptly challenged in wild, extravagant and puerile outbursts. Had he been trying to sabotage the discussions he could not have done more. The thought had no sooner entered my head than I began to wonder. He had been wounded by the grenade at the airport and had clearly been shaken by the experience. Returning afterwards from a holiday in Europe, he had stopped off at Cairo where he had been welcomed by one of Nasser's henchmen, Ali Sabry. This was unusual, to say the least, and though Ahmed had made light of it one could not imagine that Ali Sabry had gone to meet him just for the pleasure of his conversation. All too likely he had been got at and so, to clear the air, I took him out to dinner a couple of days before the Conference ended. It looked to me, I said, as if he was playing the Egyptians' game. If he had decided to go over to them, so be it. That was up to him but, if that was the case, he should come clean and not go on pretending that he was with us. He reacted as I would have expected with laughing denials and assurances of friendship. Later that same night, however, he was off to Cairo and his defection to Nasser became headline news for the next few days.

Sandys agreed that I might take a few weeks' leave after the Conference and so I returned to my hotel when it was all over, agreeably relaxed. I had not been there long when the telephone rang. It was Sandys. He was astounded to find that I was still here. With a crisis in Aden as a result of Ahmed's defection, he would have expected me to be on my way back. I explained that I was in touch with Aden. There had been no reactions to Ahmed's defection amongst the Fadhlis and Robin Young, my most experienced Political Officer, had got everything in hand. No, that was not good enough. He wanted me back in Aden at once. I would leave in a couple of days time, I said. That would not do. He expected me to be off in the morning. That put me in an impossible position. My wife was in hospital and likely to remain there for some time and I was due to collect my three children from their various schools the next morning for their summer holidays. If I was to leave unexpectedly for Aden, I needed a little time to arrange for them to be collected and looked after. My private affairs did not concern him, Sandys snapped. He expected me to be on my way to Aden in the morning. I was landed with a nightmare during which I had some very bitter and hostile thoughts about the inconsiderate and insensitive man who was my master. Later I had second thoughts. Sandys, I knew, was not asking me to do what he would not have done himself in similar circumstances. I felt better after that.

There was one last hurdle to be surmounted. There were to be elections in Aden and if Bahroun who was, of course, committed to the Agreement he had signed in London, failed to win, all our plans for the Federation's independence could come to nothing. Though ostensibly boycotting the 'colonialist' elections, the PSP lined up a number of sympathisers as candidates. Among them I was more than a little surprised to find the man we had every reason to believe had thrown the grenade at the airport. He was a close friend of al Asnaj's called Khalifa and, had the key witness for the Prosecution not been conveniently whisked away to Cairo, he would have been taken to court. As it was, he was a detainee under the Emergency Regulations. And so here was the man who had, in all probability, tried to assassinate me standing for election! As if that was not bizarre enough, I could have found myself having to appoint him Prime Minister after the elections! Mercifully, Bahroun did some wheeling and dealing behind the scenes and managed with some difficulty to get the majority of Legislative Committees to support him and not Khalifa. So now, at last with the Aden elections behind us and Bahroun in the saddle, there was nothing left to stop us freewheeling towards independence.

So I innocently thought. There had, however, been a General Election at home during our little melodrama in Aden and the Labour Party had won with a majority of a mere four seats over the Conservatives. Sandys had gone and his replacement was Anthony Greenwood, a Hampstead Socialist, anti-nuclear pacifist, opponent of blood sports, supporter of colonial freedom and a participant in a dozen or so other fashionable radical causes. It did not seem that he and I would have much in common but I was nevertheless touched to receive a very un-Sandys like telex from him inviting me to come home to attend to my wife and, when I had done that, to brief him about South Arabia. Little knowing it, I was being invited to the chop.

Al Asnaj had hooked the Labour Party long before this and, as very soon became apparent, he had captivated Greenwood within days of his becoming Colonial Secretary. Naturally, someone with my record hardly fitted in with Greenwood's plans for the future and still less with those of al Asnaj who, I later learned, had told Greenwood that he could only agree to cooperate with him if I was removed. And so, in 1965, I was removed. It was a blow but I harboured no hard feelings. Governors are not faceless Civil Servants. They are personally identified with policies and so, if Greenwood and the Labour Party intended, as they did, to change course, it was only reasonable for them to find someone more compatible to represent them. I was only forty-nine at the time and that was the end of Empire for me.

14

SOUTH ARABIAN POSTSCRIPT

THE HISTORY OF ADEN and its hinterland during the quarter century following the conclusion of the preceding narrative has been one of almost continuous violence and bloodshed. By 1965 fighting was taking place in Aden itself as well as in the countryside. In February 1966 the British government announced that it would withdraw from its military base and grant independence in two years. With the start of this withdrawal, National Liberation Front (NLF) forces moved in from the north, ousting the local rulers and seizing their property—just the outcome they had always feared. In Aden itself, the NLF came up against the Egyptian-backed Front for the Liberation of South Yemen (FLOSY) but overcame them too. Thus, on 30th November 1967, the whole territory became independent under the control of the Marxist NLF.

A severe economic crisis followed, compounded in 1972 by war between the two Yemens. The NLF continued to be reft by internal divisions and in 1979 a radical wing allied to the Soviet bloc took control of it. Internal divisions persisted, however, culminating in a two-week-long outbreak of factional fighting in January 1986, in the course of which five thousand persons were killed. More than six thousand foreign nationals, including more than three thousand Soviet citizens, were evacuated, and immense damage was done to property. During the whole of this period there had been active Soviet intervention; in 1979 the USSR signed a twenty-year treaty of friendship and cooperation with the People's Democratic Republic of the Yemen (PDRY), as it was now called, distinguishing it from the North Yemen or Yemen Arab Republic (YAR).

In 1972 and again in 1979 North and South Yemen fought short border wars, but after each of them agreements were reached on eventual union of the two states. In December 1981 a draft constitution for a unified state was agreed and, despite several setbacks, a first session of a joint Yemen Council was held in San'a in 1983 and a second in Aden in 1984. These meetings were interrupted by the bloody events in South Yemen, but were resumed in 1987, when representatives of the armed forces of the two countries met in Taiz. Finally, on 22nd May 1990, the two countries were merged into a single state, the Republic of Yemen. Forces behind this merger were, first, the democratic reforms in eastern Europe which left South Yemen isolated, and second, recent oil discoveries in both countries which raised hopes of economic development and spurred the drive towards unity. Only time will tell whether this has really been achieved.

Index

References to notes are indicated by n.

Abdulla, Fadhl 229–30
Abraha, Dejazmatch 158–9
Abraha, Fitarouri 103–4
Abu al Hum, Sina'an 274
Abyan 209–10, 239
Abyssinia *see* Ethiopia
Abyssinians 60–6, 92, 95
Ad Takleis tribe 76–8
Aden xi, xix–xxiv, xxvi–xviii, 179–84
  and Ali 211–12
  and Asshami 226–8
  and Britain 228–9, 260–2
  and federal plan 212–14, 215–17, 218–22, 278–85, 297–9
  and independence 302–8
  and Lennox-Boyd 266–7
  and Levies 222–6, 229–30, 257–8
  and prosperity 204–6
  and PSP 285–8
  and Rulers 262–6
  and Seager 185–90, 191–3
  and strikes 299–300
  and tribes 206–11
  and Zeidis 177–9
  see also Lahej; Upper Aulaqi Sheikhdom
Agordat 117–20
Aidrus, Mohammed 238–40, 253, 256–7
Ali, Seyid Waris Amir 12–13, 14, 156–8
Ali, Sheikh 76–7, 78
Allen, John 180, 185
Amery, Julian xxiii, xxiv, xxv–xxviii
Amritsar 3, 4
Anglo-Egyptian Agreement 226, 231n2
Antonelli, Count xv–xvi, 58, 60, 86–7, 120
Arab League 219, 220
Arramah, Salem 269, 270, 271
Asmara xiv, xv, xvi, 160–1
al Asnaj, Abdulla 285–6, 293, 299–300, 306, 309
Assab 87, 88–91
Assahm, Mubarak 276

313

Index

Asshami, Muhammed Abdulla 196–7, 219–20, 221, 226–8, 253–5, 271–2
Aussa, Sultan of 89, 90

al Badr, Mohammed 269, 270–1, 288–9
Bahroun, Seyid Zern 302, 308
Baldwin, Oliver 49–51
Bandoeng Conference 232–3, 243n1
Bayumi, Hassan Ali 281–2, 293, 294, 302
Beeley, Sir Harold 255, 259n2
Beidhani, Abdulrahman 291
Beihan 207–9
Beni Amer tribe 117–20, 121–3
Benoy, Brigadier 115–16, 117, 120–1, 126, 127
Besse, Peter 290–1
Bevin, Ernest 114, 151
Bin Abdulla, Ahmed 250–1
Bisa tribe 26–7
Boustead, Colonel Hugh 65–6, 118, 179
Britain *see* Great Britain
al Buasi, Hussein Nasser 298
Bubakr, Mohammed 271–3, 275–6
Bufton, Air Marshal 222, 223, 224, 225
Bushell, John 291
Butler, Sir Montagu 14

Casciani, Filippo 154–6
Chater, Colonel 36, 37
Churchill, Randolph 260–1
Churchill, Winston xii, 13, 14, 15, 42
Clegg-Hill, Major Frederic xiii–xiv, 34, 35, 36–7, 38–40, 42
Cockins, Miss 5–6
Cohen, Andrew 171–2
Communism 11–12
Coptic Christians 63–5, 66
Crawford 100–1, 102, 108, 109, 115, 116
Creech-Jones, Arthur 113, 170
Cumming, Sir Duncan 51, 52–3

Danakil 89–90
Dathina 199–202
Dawson, Geoffrey 21
Djibuti 35, 36, 37–8
Douglas-Home, Sir Alec 303
Drew, Brigadier 133–4, 138, 140–1, 147–8, 161
Dyer, General Reginald xii, 3, 4, 6–7

East Africa 12, 33; *see also* Somaliland
education 83–6, 235–6
Edwards, Robert 286, 287
Egypt xvii, xxii, 81, 179
 and Aden 235–6, 237–8, 285
 and Anglo agreement 226, 231n2
 and Erskine 190–1
 and Jedda Pact 245–6, 247
 and Syria 257
 and Yemen 291, 292, 293, 294–5, 296–7
 see also Nasser, Gamal Abdel

314

Index

Eisenhower, Dwight D. 268
Elizabeth II, Queen 218, 295
Eritrea xi, xiii, xiv–xviii, xxvi, 51–3
  and Britain 112–13
  and education 83–6
  and Ethiopia 68–70, 92, 93–5, 98–9, 100–9
  and industry 81–3
  and partition 113–14, 151–6
  and prisoner of war 43–6
  and religion 60–1
  and Unionist Party 120–2
  and United Nations 160–4
  see also Assab; Hamasien; Keren; Moslems
Erskine, Sir George (Bobbie) 179, 183n1, 190–1, 225, 250
Ethiopia xi, xiii, xv, xvii–xviii, 49–51
  and Eritrea 68–70, 93–9, 100–9, 113–14, 165
  and Italy 91–2
  and Moslems 110–12

Fabian Colonial Bureau 112–13
Fadhl, Sultan 194–6
Farid, Mohammed 294
Feodorov, General 144, 146, 147
al Fiki, Ahmed 71
Fox-Pitt, T. xii–xiii, 22–5, 27–30, 173
France 143, 145–9
Free Yemenis 273–5
Frog, Adam 172–3

Front for the Liberation of South Yemen (FLOSY) 310

Gandhi, Mohandas 3–4, 6, 7, 9, 11
Gandy, Christopher 291–2
Glubb, General 237–8, 243n4
Goode, Sir William 182–3
Gore-Browne, Sir Stewart 28–9
Gorrel-Barnes, Sir William 279–80
Government of India Act (1919) 6, 7n, 9
Grapello, Count di 152
Great Britain xv–xvii, xviii
  and Aden xix–xx, xxii–xxiii, xxiv, 228–9, 285–7
  and Eritrea 111–13
Greater Tigrai 103–9
Greenwood, Anthony xvii, 308–9
Griffiths, James 170–2
Grogan, Colonel 11–12

Habab tribe 74–6
Hadendowa 117, 118–20
Haidera 248–9, 257–8
Haile Selassie, Colonel Negga 137–9
Haile Selassie, Emperor xviii, 50, 68–9, 90, 91, 103
Hamasien 95–8
Harari, Max 58
Harrington, Sir Charles 303–4
Hassan Ali, Dejazmatch 107
Hassano, Omar 119, 120, 128
Hassenebi, Kafel 140–1

Index

Henderson, George 219, 252, 272, 300–1
Hickinbotham, Sir Tom xx–xxii, 182, 187–90, 205
  and Ali 236
  and Dathina 200–1, 202
  and federal plan 215, 216–17, 220, 221–2
  and Jifri 241, 242
  and Lahej 195, 196, 197
  and Levies 223, 225
Hidad, Sheikh 75–6, 78
Hinden, Rita 112–13, 114, 151
Hinit, Saleh 128
Holden, David 260–2, 267n1
Hopkinson, Henry 228–9
Hummed, Shum 85–6
Hussein of Beihan, Sherif 183
Hyatt Khan, Mohammed 44–5
Hyatt Khan, Shaukat 44, 45

Ibrahim Sultan 124–5, 127, 128, 129–32, 135–8, 142, 153–4
India xxii, xix, 8–11, 12–17
  and Aden 180–2
  and independence 135–6
  and Moslems 129
  see also Punjab
Ingrams, Harold 178–9
Iraq xvii, 268
Italy xiii, xiv–xvi, xviii, 33, 37–9
  and Eritrea 139–41
  and Ethiopia 91–2
  and partition 151–6
  and peace treaty 113–14, 132

Jedda Pact 245–7
Jenkins, Sir Evan 15–16
al Jifri, Mohammed Ali 234–5, 237, 238, 240–1, 242, 252–3, 258
Johnston, Sir Charles 280–1, 282, 283–4, 292, 293

Kennedy Cooke, Brigadier 56, 58–9
Keren xvi–xvii, 54–9, 72–80
Kidanemariam, Ras 101–2, 106–7
Kirkbride, Sir Alec 255, 259n3
Klimov, Nikolai 144–5, 149
Kyneston-Snell, Captain 83–5, 86

Lahej 194–7, 209, 232–42, 258
  and conspiracy 244–5, 247–51, 252–4
Last, Major 72, 79, 87
Lea, Officer 54–5, 56–8, 67, 70, 72–3
League of Nations xii
Lee, Basil 103–4
Legentillehomme, Paul 36, 37
Lennox-Boyd, Alan xvii, 262, 266–7
Lloyd, Selwyn 255–6
Longrigg, Brigadier Stephen xvi–xvii, 78–9, 81–2, 87
  and Eritrea 102–3, 104
  and Ethiopia 92, 97–9
Lower Yafa 239–40
Luce, Sir William xxiii, 246, 250, 266, 275, 278–9

Index

Lugman, Mohammed Ali 281
Lynne-Allen, Colonel 34, 35

MacDonald, Ramsay 12
McLean, Colonel Neil (Billy) 293
McLeod, Ian 280, 282, 283–4
Mann, Naunihal Singh 10–11
Marlborough School xii, 13–14
Maudling, Reginald 287
Maybin, Sir John 34
Medawar, Peter 14
Menelik, Emperor 62–3, 101
al Mirghani, Seyid Bubakr 73–4
Montagu, Edwin 6
Moslems 60–1, 65, 66, 69, 70
  and attacks 156–8
  and Beni Amer tribe 117–20, 121–3
  and education 84–5
  and Ethiopia 110–12, 124–5
  and Keren 73–8
  and League 129–32, 134–9, 142–51
  and serfs 116–17
  and Tigrai 107
  and tribes 125–9
Mountbatten, Lord Louis 302–3
Mpika xii–xiii, 21–30
Murray, James 169–70
Musa, Mohammad 55
Mussolini, Benito xiii, xv, 33, 35

Nasser, Gamal Abdel xvii, xxii, 224, 232–4, 268–9

National Liberation Front (NLF) 310
Nauman, Ahmed Muhammed 273–4
Negassi, Chief 63, 64, 83
Newbold, Sir Douglas xvii, 68–70, 79–80, 107, 112, 165–6
Nicholson, John 44–5
Northern Rhodesia xi, xii–xiii, xxv–xxvi, 21–2
  and colour bar 169–70
  and Southern Rhodesia 170–4
  see also Mpika
Northern Rhodesia Regiment 33–42

Oman 233, 243n2

Pankhurst, Sylvia 111, 113, 114, 116
Parker, Stanley 93–4, 97, 99
Passfield, Sidney Webb, Lord 12
People's Democratic Republic of Yemen (PDRY) 310–11
People's Socialist Party (PSP) 285–8, 293–4
Perham, Margery 112
Phillips, Sir Horace 248, 270, 274–5
Pirie-Gordon, Christopher 269–70, 275
police 98–9
Profumo, Jack 257
Punjab xii, 3–7, 44–5

Index

Radas, Mohammad Ali 136–7
Rhodes, Cecil 21
Robinson, Sergeant 84, 85
Rommel, Erwin 81
Royal Air Force (RAF) xix–xx, xxii–xxiii
Roziers, Burin des 145, 147
Russia *see* Soviet Union

Sabry, Ali 307
Sallal, Abdulla 291
San'a, Treaty of 182–3, 190
Sandys, Duncan xvii, xxiii, 253–4, 287–8
  and federal plan 297–9
  and independence 303, 305, 307–8
Saud of Saudi Arabia, King 245, 247, 254, 268, 271–2, 275–6
Seager, Basil xxi, 182–4, 185–90, 191–3, 194–5, 210–11
Seamer, Jake 68
Selby, General 56, 59
serfs 116–17
Seyum, Ras 103
Sforza, Count 151
Sha'aful 248–9
Shafi'is 210–11
Shia Islam xxi
Simon, Sir John 9
Sinha, Lord 11
Somalia 165, 166
Somaliland xiii, xxvi, 35–42, 114
Southern Rhodesia 21, 170–3
Soviet Union 113–14, 143–9, 310–11

Stafford, Frank 141, 142–3, 146–7, 157–9, 163–4
Stranger-Ford, Officer 87, 117
Sudan 67–71, 126–7, 165–6
Suez Canal xix
Sunni Islam xxi

Taiyeh, Mohammad 77, 78
Tamnou, Hagos 154, 155–6
Tedla Bairu 94, 106, 130–1, 142, 146–7, 150–1
Tesemma, Ras 106–7
Thomson, George 286, 287
Trevelyan, Humphrey xvii
Tug Argan, battle of 39
Twoldemedhin, Ishak 84–5

Unionist Party 121–2, 130–1, 134–5, 146–7
United Nations xviii, 151–3, 160–4, 293–4
United States of America (USA) xviii, 113, 143, 268
  and Yemen 292, 297
Upper Aulaqi Sheikhdom 197–203, 251–2

Wavell, Archibald 42, 50
White Nile 67–8
Wilson, Eric 37, 41–2, 43
Wilson, Harold xxiv
Woldemariam, Woldeab 105–6
World War II xiii, xv, 35–42, 49–51

Yahya, Imam 182–3, 186–7, 193n1

Yao, Sultan Mohammed 90–1
Yemen xvii, xxi, xxii
  and Bubakr 275–6
  and civil war 288–9, 290–3, 294–5, 296–7, 304–5
  and coup 230–1
  and division 310–11
  and Jedda Pact 245–6, 247–8, 254–5
  and Nasser 268–71
  and Nauman 273–5

Yemen Arab Republic (YAR) 311
Young, Robin xxiii, 234

Zeidis 177–8, 210